Twelve Years A Slave

by

Sue Lyles Eakin

Eakin Films & Publishing

Fate of
SN
p. 715

Praise for Twelve Years A Slave

"I wish to thank this amazing historian, Sue Eakin, who gave her life's work to preserving Solomon's story"
—*Steve McQueen*

Academy Awards acceptance speech for Best Picture, 2014

"I can never read his account of his days in slavery, of his independence of spirit, of his determination to be free… without believing that it would make a difference in today's world if our contemporaries knew of such a man as Solomon Northup."
—*Dr. John Hope Franklin*

From letter written to his friend and fellow historian Dr. Sue Eakin. Dr. Franklin was Professor Emeritus of History at Duke University, best selling author, past president of American Historical Association and recipient of Presidential Medal of Freedom, the nation's highest civilian honor.

"It's a textured portrait that refuses to deal with the issue in absolutes. The author is articulate and proud, and Louis Gossett, Jr., carries this tone throughout his reading. Northrup writes in a straightforward style, letting facts and details speak more eloquently than emotion. Again, Gossett captures this feeling. But when the author does get emotional, Gossett infuses the words with a quiet, seething power."
—*AudioFile Magazine (2013)*

Review of our audiobook performed by award-winning actor Louis Gossett, Jr., published by the premier source of reviews in the audiobook industry.

5-Stars: Audible.com (Amazon), Downpour.com (BBC), iTunes
Audible.com "Best of 2013" Editor's Pick
Downpour.com Top Editor's Pick

For more reviews, visit the author website:
www.TwelveYearsASlave.org

Our Country is the World, our Countrymen are all Mankind.

BOSTON, FRIDAY, AUGUST 26, 1853.

TWELVE YEARS A SLAVE – ORIGINAL REVIEWS

When originally published, Solomon Northup's autobiography validated the portrayal of slavery depicted in the fictional *Uncle Tom's Cabin* and produced a bombshell in the national political debate over slavery. Here are reviews that appeared in William Lloyd Garrison's famous abolitionist newspaper, *The Liberator*, when the book was released in 1853:

"Next to *Uncle Tom's Cabin*, the extraordinary narrative of Solomon Northup is the most remarkable book that was ever issued from the American press."
-Detroit Tribune

"It is one of the most exciting narratives, full of thrilling incidents... with all the marks of truth. Such a tale is more powerful than any fiction which can be conceived and elaborated."
-Cincinnati Journal

"We hope it will be universally read. If we do not sadly err, it will prove of vast service in the great cause of freedom. If there are those who can peruse it unmoved, we pity them."
-Buffalo Express

"It is a strange history; its truth is far greater than fiction. Think of it. For thirty years a man, with all a man's hopes, fears and aspirations—with a wife and children who call him by the endearing names of husband and father—with a home, humble it may be, but still a home, beneath the shelter of whose roof none had a right to molest or make him afraid. Then for twelve years a thing, a chattel personal, classed with mules and horses, and treated with less consideration than they, torn from his home and family, and the free labor by which he earned their bread, and driven into unremitting, unrequited toil in a cotton field, under a burning Southern sun, by the lash of an inhuman master. It is horrible. It chills the blood to think that such are."
-Frederick Douglass, writer, orator, former slave and abolitionist

"It will be read extensively, both at the North and South. No one can contemplate the scenes which are here so naturally set forth, without a new conviction of the hideousness of the institution from which the subject of the narrative has happily escaped."
-New York Tribune (influential newspaper published by Horace Greeley)

"The narrative will be read with interest by everyone who can sympathize with the human being struggling for freedom."
-Buffalo Courier

"What a tale it tells; what inexpressible reproofs against slavery; what occasion for shame and tears on the part of all! We think the story is affecting as any tale of sorrow could be. We believe its perusal will not only excite an absorbing interest, but minister powerfully to the sound, intelligent anti-slavery sentiment of the country."
-New York Evangelist

HARRIET BEECHER STOWE

"It is a singular coincidence, that Solomon Northup was carried to a plantation in the Red River country—that same region where the scene of Uncle Tom's captivity was laid—and his account of this plantation, and the mode of life there, and some incidents which he describes, form a striking parallel to that history."
-Harriett Beecher Stowe, author of Uncle Tom's Cabin (published in 1852)

Stowe's highly influential work of fiction changed the way many Americans viewed the life of a slave and became the best-selling book of all time in the U.S. (after the Bible). Northup's narrative, published in 1853, closely paralleled aspects of Stowe's novel. It is said that when President Lincoln first met Mrs. Stowe, he shook her hand, smiled and said, "So you're the little woman who wrote the book that started this great war."

Sue Lyles Eakin:
A Lifetime Project

Twelve Years a Slave was lost to history by the early twentieth century when it could not be located by libraries, stores or catalogues nationwide. Then a 12-year-old avid reader in central Louisiana—the future Dr. Sue Eakin— discovered an original copy of the book in a plantation home near the property where Northup was enslaved. It would determine her life's path.

Sue Lyles Eakin

Dr. Eakin went on to write her master's thesis about Solomon Northup's story, and after decades of research, produced the first authenticated edition of the book in 1968. In 2007, at the age of 88, she completed her final definitive edition with over 100 pages of fascinating new information, never-before-published images and unique maps related to the story; this book is the first mass publication of her final edition.

Along the way, Dr. Eakin authored over a dozen acclaimed history books and became an award-winning history professor, Hall of Fame journalist, local civil rights leader and internationally recognized authority on antebellum plantation life. Dr. Eakin's academic career spanned over two decades with intensive historical research supported by grants from the National Endowment for the Humanities, the American Association of University Women, the LSU Foundation and others. She founded and directed the World Plantation Conferences featuring prominent scholars from around the world, served on the boards of many historical foundations, and delivered hundreds of speeches around the country regarding her research and unique perspectives. A popular classroom teacher, her travel courses in Louisiana, Southern and American history developed a large following, and she was recognized as Distinguished Faculty of the LSU System and national Outstanding American History Professor by the Daughters of the American Revolution.

After her passing at age 90 in 2009, her priceless archive was donated by her family to Louisiana State University at Alexandria. The Smithsonian Institute is creating a permanent exhibit featuring a portion of her *Twelve Years a Slave* research materials, and her family carries on her work and spirit with its passionate preservation of Solomon's story and support of civil rights.

Introduction
by Sue Eakin, PhD

The tragic story of Solomon Northup told in *Twelve Years a Slave* stands as an enduring classic in American history. This new edition of the book shows to a fuller extent the tragedy, adding some understanding of the limits to freedom and justice endured by a free man of color in antebellum society.

The tension between North and South forms the background of Solomon Northup's story, which provides unique insights into the escalating conflict over slavery, as the country moved closer to civil war with every passing year. The beginning of the story sheds light on the unpublicized criminal ring that kidnapped people of dark complexion and sold them into slavery in the nation's capital. So cleverly planned were their operations that the criminals were almost never brought to justice, as they shielded themselves with the help of powerful political connections, gained high-level positions in law enforcement and manipulated the rules of the judicial system. Masterminding this Reverse Underground Railroad was James Birch in Washington, D.C., who described his position in subsequent legal documents:

> *I was appointed by the Mayor of Washington D.C. to the Command of the Auxillary Guard Department in June, 1853, which said guard is part of the Police force of the city and District aforesaid and which office I still hold . . .*[1]

When Birch and notorious New Orleans slave trader Theophilus Freeman began as partners as early as 1840, Birch had been in this business for more than a decade.[2] During this time of sharpened feelings between the North and South, further fueled by the Compromise of 1850 and its Fugitive Slave Act, the fiction of Harriet Beecher Stowe's *Uncle Tom's Cabin*, published in 1852, further inflamed the masses for the abolitionist cause.

Uncle Tom's Cabin, though fiction, had such a great impact that it inspired President Lincoln's apochryphal line: "So you are the little woman who wrote the book that started this great war!"

Harriet Beecher Stowe's book sold 10,000 copies within the first week of publication and 300,000 by the end of the first year. There were over a million copies sold in England. Stowe's $10,000 royalty from the first three months of sales was "the largest sum of money ever received by any author, either American or European, from the sale of a single work in so short a time."[3]

Given the record set by Stowe's novel, David Wilson, Solomon Northup's ghost writer of *Twelve Years a Slave*, must have been excited when attorney Henry Northup, along with Solomon, presented him with the proposition to write a book that conceivably could bring fantastic rewards. Wilson had all of the ingredients for a highly successful book. Imagine what could be done with a story built on the factual kidnapping of a free man of color from New York who was shackled in a slave pen in the nation's capital and sold into slavery in New Orleans!

The clincher of the public attraction of Solomon's story was that the Louisiana's Bayou Boeuf area, where he actually served twelve years as Platt the slave, was coincidentally only sixty miles from Stowe's fictional plantation of Simon Legree. Also, the people described by Solomon bore a close resemblance to Stowe's cast of fictional characters.

In 1853, Solomon's autobiography brought immediate reaction from New York newspapers, and his first-hand account was perceived as validation of Stowe's portrayal of Southern slavery. *Twelve Years A Slave* was published less than a year after Stowe's spectacularly successful fiction. About 8,000 copies were sold in the first month, and several subsequent editions appeared until it finally went out of print in 1856. The book remained out of print until I completed the first modern edition in 1968 following decades of research.[4]

Documenting this edition has been the culmination of a lifetime's work. It also represents endless hours of time and tens of thousands of dollars spent in pursuit of the necessary documents to confirm or refute elements of the story. End notes in this edition are expansive and provide the fascinating back story and intrigues of plantation society in the Bayou Boeuf area.

My discovery of Solomon Northup's story began accidentally over seven decades ago when I was twelve years old. On a hot summer day, Mama, my younger siblings, and I were returning to our home on Bayou Boeuf from a ride with Dad, who was driving a long flatbed truck. When we arrived Dad stopped the truck and Mama got out with the younger children to walk down the lane to our home. Dad was driving farther south some miles away to discuss business with Sam Haas, whose family owned a large plantation. As she stepped from the cab with the younger children, Mama asked, "Why don't you take Sue along with you?" That was how I found myself beside Dad in the cab happily riding to Oak Hall Plantation. Once there, the men were momentarily concerned about what I was to do while they talked. Mr. Haas invited me in with plans to give me a book to read while they tended to their business.

O Glory be! Mr. Haas reached up on the bookshelves in the family library and handed me the rare copy of the original edition of Solomon Northup's *Twelve Years A Slave*. The first thing I spied in the flyleaf of the old book was an inscription in the careful handwriting of his father, Dr. W. D. Haas (1868-1940). I began reading the book as rapidly as I could, becoming more and more excited with every passing moment. I recognized place names in Cheneyville, a short distance from our home where our mail was delivered "rural free"; Lecompte, where I attended school; and Bayou Boeuf (English pronunciation: "bef;" French, "buff") all of which delighted me. The names of families well known in the area—the Tanner families, the Fords, the McCoys, and others—kept me making mental notes to inquire later from these people about the Northup story. Never before had I seen a book written by an author actually familiar with our remote plantation country.

I read as fast as I could, but I could not finish it before the men had completed their business and Dad was ready to go home. This meant giving up the book, and the disappointment must have shown in my face. Mrs. Haas, mother of Sam Haas, asked me if I wanted to come back to spend the day with her so I could read the book all day long. I did, and I became involved with *Twelve Years A Slave* from that day forward.

I searched for years for a copy of the old book for my own, but one was nowhere to be found. Then, when I entered Louisiana State

University in 1936, I searched at Otto Claitor's Bookstore, with its storehouse of old books spilling out of his gallery. Suddenly I spied *Twelve Years a Slave* and asked the price with trepidation. "What do you want that for?" asked Mr. Claitor, known as an authority on rare old books. "There ain't nothing to that old book. Pure fiction. You can have it for 25 cents." And that began my life with Solomon Northup.

About the Ghost Writer

David Wilson of Whitehall, New York, was a talented and well-educated man who, at thirty-two years old when he ghostwrote the Northup story, was practicing law. He was writing poetry, editing newspapers, and working on books as a sideline activity.[5]

David Wilson, Ghost Writer

Wilson was born September 21, 1821, in Hebron, New York, to Benjamin and Margaret Flack Wilson.[6] An 1840 graduate of prestigious Union College in Schenectady, New York, he studied law for three years with the Honorable Orville Clark, who submitted one of the affidavits at the end of *Twelve Years a Slave*. The *Whitehall Democrat* wrote of him, ". . . Mr. Wilson is not only one of the most eloquent orators at the bar, but one of the purest and sweetest poets in northern New York. We are sorry he is a Whig."[7]

Clarence E. Holden, writing brief biographies of Whitehall's most prominent citizens in his "Local History Sketches," wrote after Wilson's death in 1870:

David Wilson was a prominent lawyer of the midcentury period in Whitehall. He was something of an author, and a politician as well. Above all, he was a most genial and companionable man, and an all around good fellow. He used to do most of the editing of the local papers, one as well as another, and he could write a Democratic argument with quite as much facility as he could a Whig, altho [sic] he professed himself a member of the latter party . . . He came to Whitehall in early life . . . in that year [1843] he was elected secretary of Torrent Hose company. Apparently he was not much of a fireman . . .[8]

Typographical, Spelling
And Conventions
In This Edition

Published in 1853, the original edition of Solomon Northup's *Twelve Years a Slave* reflects the typography and language conventions used by printers of the time. For instance, in the original there are periods after every title, and there is a rather ornate typeface. We, the editors of the present edition, have elected to preserve the flavor of the work done with the 1853 edition, while changing to a more reader-friendly version if, in our opinion, a particular choice is distracting to the reader. Thus, this edition, though very similar to the original one, is not an exact copy.

Also, the spelling of proper names varies among *Twelve Years a Slave* and other primary sources written at the time. Northup, of course, would not have had the occasion to see most, if any, of these names written, and so he would have used his best guess, or, more likely, David Wilson's best guess. There are many spellings for the same sound, and so it is not surprising that, especially with surnames, a different spelling from the one that the family used was selected. Also, if Solomon Northup mispronounced the name in any way, the mispronunciation is reflected in the spelling; that is the case with Cocodrie Bayou, which Solomon must have heard with a starting "p."

Here is a list of alternative spellings of specific proper names used in the 1853 edition. There may be more than two spellings, because other spellings may appear in documents written in the 1800s that mention these families:

- Burch, Birch
- Buford, Burford
- Carey, Kery, Keary
- Carnal, Carnel, Carnel
- Dunwoodie, Dunwoody
- Eldret, Eldred
- Fogaman, Fogleman
- Pacoudrie in text is actually Cocodrie Bayou
- Pine Woods, Piney woods, pineywoods
- Tibeats, Tibaut
- Windes, Wines

Thank you for purchasing Dr. Eakin's definitive edition of
Twelve Years a Slave.

You may wish to refer back and forth to our website for bonus
content, including additional images, maps, background information,
and audio clips of scenes performed by award-winning actor Louis
Gossett, Jr.

www.TwelveYearsASlave.org

Note: The endnote numbers refer to the Introduction and the
Chapter Notes and Historical Context sections at the back of the
book, which include fascinating details about the people, places and
events, as well as the plantation system that kept so many in bondage.

Digital design by Telemachus Press, LLC: www.TelemachusPress.com

For press kits and interviews, please contact us through our website at
www.TwelveYearsASlave.org. Georgiann Gullett, Publicist.

Version 2014.03.04

Solomon Northep

IN HIS PLANTATION SUIT

FIFTH THOUSAND.

TWELVE YEARS A SLAVE.

NARRATIVE

OF

SOLOMON NORTHUP,

A CITIZEN OF NEW-YORK,

KIDNAPPED IN WASHINGTON CITY IN 1841,

AND

RESCUED IN 1853,

FROM A COTTON PLANTATION NEAR THE RED RIVER,
IN LOUISIANA.

AUBURN:
DERBY AND MILLER.
BUFFALO:
DERBY, ORTON AND MULLIGAN.
LONDON:
SAMPSON LOW, SON & COMPANY, 47 LUDGATE HILL.
1853.

TO
Harriett Beecher Stowe,
WHOSE NAME,
THROUGHOUT THE WORLD, IS IDENTIFIED WITH THE
GREAT REFORM:
THIS NARRATIVE, AFFORDING ANOTHER
Key To Uncle Tom's Cabin,
IS RESPECTFULLY DEDICATED.

—Solomon Northup's dedication to Harriet Beecher Stowe in the second edition of his autobiography

---

"So you are the little woman
who wrote the book
that started this great war."

—President Lincoln's comment to Harriet Beecher Stowe,
author of *Uncle Tom's Cabin*

"Such dupes are men to custom, and so prone
To reverence what is ancient, and can plead
A course of long observance for its use,
That even servitude, the worst of ills,
Because delivered down from sire to son,
Is kept and guarded as a sacred thing.
But is it fit or can it bear the shock
Of rational discussion, that a man
Compounded and made up, like other men,
Of elements tumultuous, in whom lust
And folly in as ample measure meet,
As in the bosom of the slave he rules,
Should be a despot absolute, and boast
Himself the only freeman of his land?"

—Cowper.
Poem from original 1853 publication

Table of Contents

Arthur's Rescue—Theophilus Freeman, the Consignee—Platt—First Night in the New-Orleans Slave Pen,

CHAPTER VI. 40

Freeman's Industry—Cleanliness and Clothes—Exercising in the Show Room—The Dance—Bob, the Fiddler—Arrival of Customers—Slaves Examined—The Old Gentleman of New-Orleans—Sale of David, Caroline, and Lethe—Parting of Randall and Eliza—Small-Pox—The Hospital—Recovery and Return To Freeman's Slave Pen—The Purchaser of Eliza, Harry, and Platt—Eliza's Agony On Parting from Little Emily,

CHAPTER VII. 48

The Steamboat Rodolph—Departure from New-Orleans—William Ford—Arrival at Alexandria, on Red River—Resolutions—The Great Pine Woods—Wild Cattle—Martin's Summer Residence—The Texas Road—Arrival at Master Ford's—Rose—Mistress Ford—Sally and Her Children—John, the Cook—Walter, Sam, and Antony—The Mills on Indian Creek—Sabbath Days—Sam's Conversion—The Profit of Kindness—Rafting—Adam Taydem, the Little White Man—Cascalla and his Tribe—The Indian Ball—John M. Tibeats—The Storm approaching,

CHAPTER VIII. 58

Ford's Embarrassments—The Sale to Tibeats—The Chattel Mortgage—Mistress Ford's Plantation on Bayou Boeuf—Description of the Latter—Ford's Brother-in-Law, Peter Tanner—Meeting with Eliza—She Still Mourns for her Children—Ford's Overseer, Chapin—Tibeats' Abuse—The Keg of Nails—The First Fight with Tibeats —His Discomfiture and Castigation—The Attempt to Hang Me—Chapin's Interference and Speech—Unhappy Reflections—Abrupt Departure of Tibeats, Cook, and Ramsey—Lawson and the Brown Mule—Message to the Pine Woods,

CHAPTER IX. 67

The Hot Sun—Yet Bound—The Cords Sink into My Flesh—Chapin's Uneasiness—Speculation—Rachel, and her Cup of Water—Suffering Increases—The Happiness of Slavery—Arrival of Ford—He Cuts the Cords which Bind Me, and takes the Rope from My Neck—Misery—The Gathering of the Slaves in Eliza's Cabin—Their Kindness—Rachel Repeats the Occurrences of the Day—Lawson Entertains his Companions with an Account of his Ride—Chapin's Apprehensions of Tibeats—Hired to Peter Tanner—Peter Expounds the Scriptures—Description of the Stocks,

CHAPTER X. 75

Return to Tibeats—Impossibility of pleasing him—He attacks me with a Hatchet—The Struggle over the Broad Axe—The Temptation to Murder Him—Escape across the Plantation—Observations from the Fence—Tibeats

Approaches, followed by the Hounds—They take my Track—Their Loud Yells—
They Almost Overtake Me—I Reach the Water—The Hounds Confused—
Moccasin Snakes—Alligators—Night in the "Great Pacoudrie Swamp"—The
Sounds of Life —North-West Course—Emerge into the Pine Woods—Slave and
His Young Master—Arrival at Ford's—Food and Rest,

CHAPTER XI. 84
The Mistress' Garden—The Crimson and Golden Fruit—Orange and
Pomegranate Trees—Return to Bayou Boeuf—Master Ford's Remarks on the
Way—The Meeting with Tibeats—His Account of the Chase—Ford Censures his
Brutality—Arrival at the Plantation—Astonishment of the Slaves on Seeing Me—
The Anticipated Flogging—Kentucky John—Mr. Eldret, the Planter—Eldret's
Sam—Trip to the "Big Cane Brake"—The Tradition of Sutton's Field—Forest
Trees—Gnats and Mosquitoes—The Arrival of Black Women in the Big Cane—
Lumber Women—Sudden Appearance of Tibeats—His Provoking Treatment—
Visit to Bayou Boeuf—The Slave Pass—Southern Hospitality—The Last of
Eliza—Sale to Edwin Epps,

CHAPTER XII. 94
Personal Appearance of Epps—Epps, Drunk and Sober—A Glimpse of his
History—Cotton Growing—The Mode of Ploughing and Preparing Ground—Of
Planting—Of Hoeing, of Picking, of Treating Raw Hands—The Difference in
Cotton Pickers—Patsey a Remarkable One—Tasked According to Ability—Beauty
of a Cotton Field—The Slave's Labors—Fear of Approaching the Gin-House—
Weighing—"Chores"—Cabin Life—The Corn Mill—The Uses of the Gourd—
Fear of Oversleeping—Fear Continually—Mode of Cultivating Corn—Sweet
Potatoes—Fertility of the Soil—Fattening Hogs—Preserving Bacon—Raising
Cattle—Shooting-Matches—Garden Products—Flowers and Verdure,

CHAPTER XIII. 103
The Curious Axe-Helve—Symptoms of Approaching Illness—Continue to
Decline—The Whip Ineffectual—Confined to the Cabin—Visit by Dr. Wines—
Partial Recovery—Failure at Cotton Picking—What May Be Heard on Epps'
Plantation—Lashes Graduated—Epps in a Whipping Mood—Epps in a Dancing
Mood—Description of the Dance—Loss of Rest No Excuse—Epps'
Characteristics—Jim Burns—Removal from Huff Power to Bayou Boeuf—
Description of Uncle Abram; of Wiley; of Aunt Phebe; of Bob, Henry, and
Edward; of Patsey; with a Genealogical Account of Each—Something of their Past
History, and Peculiar Characteristics—Jealousy and Lust—Patsey, the Victim,

CHAPTER XIV. 112
Destruction of the Cotton Crop in 1845—Demand for Laborers in St. Mary's
Parish—Sent Thither in a Drove—The Order of the March—The Grand
Coteau—Hired to Judge Turner on Bayou Salle—Appointed Driver in his Sugar
House—Sunday Services—Slave Furniture; How Obtained—The Party at

Melancholy—Her Idea of God and Eternity—Of Heaven and Freedom—The Effect of Slave-Whipping—Epps' Oldest Son—"The Child is Father to the Man,"

EDITOR'S PREFACE

When the editor commenced the preparation of the following narrative, he did not suppose it would reach the size of this volume. In order, however, to present all the facts which have been communicated to him, it has seemed necessary to extend it to its present length.

Many of the statements contained in the following pages are corroborated by abundant evidence—others rest entirely upon Solomon's assertion. That he has adhered strictly to the truth, the editor, at least, who has had an opportunity of detecting any contradiction or discrepancy in his statements, is well satisfied. He has invariably repeated the same story without deviating in the slightest particular, and has also carefully perused the manuscript, dictating an alteration wherever the most trivial inaccuracy has appeared.

It was Solomon's fortune, during his captivity, to be owned by several masters. The treatment he received while at the "Pine Woods" shows that among slaveholders there are men of humanity as well as of cruelty. Some of them are spoken of with emotions of gratitude—others in a spirit of bitterness. It is believed that the following account of his experience on Bayou Boeuf presents a correct picture of Slavery, in all its lights and shadows, as it now exists in that locality. Unbiased, as he conceives, by any prepossessions or prejudices, the only object of the editor has been to give a faithful history of Solomon Northup's life, as he received it from his lips.

In the accomplishment of that object, he trusts he has succeeded, notwithstanding the numerous faults of style and of expression it may be found to contain.

DAVID WILSON
Whitehall, N.Y., May, 1853

CHAPTER I.

Having been born a freeman, and for more than thirty years enjoyed the blessings of liberty in a free State—and having at the end of that time been kidnapped and sold into Slavery, where I remained, until happily rescued in the month of January, 1853, after a bondage of twelve years—it has been suggested that an account of my life and fortunes would not be uninteresting to the public.[1]   *p. 261 note 1*

Since my return to liberty, I have not failed to perceive the increasing interest throughout the Northern States, in regard to the subject of Slavery. Works of fiction, professing to portray its features in their more pleasing as well as more repugnant aspects, have been circulated to an extent unprecedented, and, as I understand, have   *notes* created a fruitful topic of comment and discussion.[2]   *3, 4*

I can speak of Slavery only so far as it came under my own observation—only so far as I have known and experienced it in my own person.[3] My object is, to give a candid and truthful statement of   *p.* facts: to repeat the story of my life, without exaggeration, leaving it   *263* for others to determine, whether even the pages of fiction present a picture of more cruel wrong or a severer bondage.[4] *Uncle Tom's Cabin*

As far back as I have been able to ascertain, my ancestors on the paternal side were slaves in Rhode Island. They belonged to a family by the name of Northup, one of whom, removing to the State of New-York, settled at Hoosic, in Rensselaer county. He brought with him Mintus Northup, my father.[5] On the death of this gentleman, which must have occurred some fifty years ago, my father became free, having been emancipated by a direction in his will.

Henry B. Northup, Esq., of Sandy Hill, a distinguished counselor at law, and the man to whom, under Providence, I am indebted for my present liberty, and my return to the society of my wife and children, is a relative of the family in which my forefathers were thus held to service, and from which they took the name I bear.[6] To this fact may be attributed the persevering interest he has taken in my behalf.

Sometime after my father's liberation, he removed to the town of Minerva, Essex county, N.Y., where I was born, in the month of July, 1808.[7] How long he remained in the latter place I have not the means of definitely ascertaining. From thence he removed to Granville, Washington county, near a place known as Slyborough, where, for some years, he labored on the farm of Clark Northup[8], also a relative of his old master; from thence he removed to the Alden farm, at Moss Street, a short distance north of the village of Sandy Hill;[9] and from thence to the farm now owned by Russel Pratt, situated on the road leading from Fort Edward to Argyle, where he continued to reside until his death, which took place on the 22d day of November, 1829. He left a widow and two children—myself and Joseph, an elder brother. The latter is still living in the county of Oswego, near the city of that name; my mother died during the period of my captivity.

Though born a slave, and laboring under the disadvantages of which my unfortunate race is subjected, my father was a man respected for his industry and integrity, as many now living, who well remember him, are ready to testify. His whole life was passed in the peaceful pursuits of agriculture, never seeking employment in those more menial positions, which seem to be especially allotted to the children of Africa. Besides giving us an education surpassing that ordinarily bestowed upon children of our condition, he acquired, by his diligence and economy, a sufficient property qualification to entitle him to the right of suffrage.[10] He was accustomed to speak to us of his early life; and although at all times cherishing the warmest emotions of kindness, and even of affection towards the family, in whose house he had been a bondsman, he nevertheless comprehended the system of Slavery, and dwelt with sorrow on the degradation of his race. He endeavored to imbue our minds with sentiments of morality, and to teach us to place our trust and confidence in Him who regards the humblest as well as the highest of his creatures. How often since that time has the recollection of his paternal counsels occurred to me, while lying in a slave hut in the distant and sickly regions of Louisiana,[11] smarting with the undeserved wounds which an inhuman master had inflicted, and longing only for the grave which had covered him, to shield me also from the lash of the oppressor. In the churchyard at Sandy Hill, an humble stone marks the spot where he reposes, after having worthily performed the duties appertaining to the lowly sphere wherein God had appointed him to walk. *n. 11, p. 268*

Up to this period I had been principally engaged with my father in the labors of the farm. The leisure hours allowed me were generally either employed over my books, or playing on the violin— an amusement which was the ruling passion of my youth.[12] It has also been the source of consolation since, affording pleasure to the simple beings with whom my lot was cast, and beguiling my own thoughts, for many hours, from the painful contemplation of my fate.[13]

On Christmas day, 1829, I was married to Anne Hampton, a colored girl then living in the vicinity of our residence. The ceremony was performed at Fort Edward, by Timothy Eddy, Esq., a magistrate of that town, and still a prominent citizen of the place. She had resided a long time at Sandy Hill, with Mr. Baird, proprietor of the Eagle Tavern, and also in the family of Rev. Alexander Proudfit, of Salem. This gentleman for many years had presided over the Presbyterian society at the latter place, and was widely distinguished for his learning and piety. Anne still holds in grateful remembrance the exceeding kindness and the excellent counsels of that good man. She is not able to determine the exact line of her descent, but the blood of three races mingles in her veins. It is difficult to tell whether the red, white, or black predominates. The union of them all, however, in her origin, has given her a singular but pleasing expression, such as is rarely to be seen. Though somewhat resembling, yet she can not properly be styled a quadroon, a class to *mixed* which, I have omitted to mention, my mother belonged. *race*

I had just now passed the period of my minority, having reached the age of twenty-one years in the month of July previous. Deprived of the advice and assistance of my father, with a wife dependent upon me for support, I resolved to enter upon a life of industry; and notwithstanding the obstacle of color, and the consciousness of my lowly state, indulged in pleasant dreams of a good time coming, when the possession of some humble habitation, with a few surrounding acres, should reward my labors, and bring me the means of happiness and comfort.

From the time of my marriage to this day the love I have borne my wife has been sincere and unabated; and only those who have felt the glowing tenderness a father cherishes for his offspring, can appreciate my affection for the beloved children which have since been born to us. This much I deem appropriate and necessary to say, in order that those who read these pages, may comprehend the poignancy of those sufferings I have been doomed to bear.

Immediately upon our marriage we commenced house-keeping, in the old yellow building then standing at the southern extremity of Fort Edward village, and which has since been transformed into a modern mansion, and lately occupied by Captain Lathrop. It is known as the Fort House.[14] In this building the courts were sometime held after the organization of the country. It was also occupied by Burgoyne in 1777, being situated near the old Fort on the left bank of the Hudson.

During the winter I was employed with others repairing the Champlain Canal, on that section over which William Van Nortwick was superintendent. David McEachron had the immediate charge of the men in whose company I labored. By the time the canal opened in the spring, I was enabled, from the savings of my wages, to purchase a pair of horses, and other things necessarily required in the business of navigation.[15]

Having hired several efficient hands to assist me, I entered into contracts for the transportation of large rafts of timber from Lake Champlain to Troy. Dyer Beckwith and a Mr. Bartemy, of Whitehall, accompanied me on several trips. During the season I became perfectly familiar with the art and mysteries of rafting—a knowledge which afterwards enabled me to render profitable service to a worthy master, and to astonish the simple-witted lumbermen on the banks of the Bayou Boeuf.[16]

In one of my voyages down Lake Champlain, I was induced to make a visit to Canada. Repairing to Montreal, I visited the cathedral and other places of interest in that city, from whence I continued my excursion to Kingston and other towns, obtaining a knowledge of localities, which was also of service to me afterwards, as will appear towards the close of this narrative.

Having completed my contracts on the canal satisfactorily to myself and to my employer, and not wishing to remain idle, now that the navigation of the canal was again suspended, I entered into another contract with Medad Gunn, to cut a large quantity of wood. In this business I was engaged during the winter of 1831–32.

With the return of spring, Anne and myself conceived the project of taking a farm in the neighborhood. I had been accustomed from earliest youth to agricultural labors, and it was an occupation congenial to my tastes. I accordingly entered into arrangements for a part of the old Alden farm, on which my father formerly resided. With one cow, one swine, a yoke of fine oxen I had lately purchased of Lewis Brown, in Hartford, and other personal property and effects, we proceeded to our new home in Kingsbury. That year I planted twenty-five acres of corn, sowed large fields of oats, and commenced farming upon as large a scale as my utmost means would permit. Anne was diligent about the house affairs, while I toiled laboriously in the field.

On this place we continued to reside until 1834. In the winter season I had numerous calls to play on the violin. Wherever the young people assembled to dance, I was almost invariably there. Throughout the surrounding villages my fiddle was notorious. Anne, also, during her long residence at the Eagle Tavern, had become somewhat famous as a cook. During court weeks, and on public occasions, she was employed at high wages in the kitchen at Sherrill's Coffee House.

We always returned home from the performance of these services with money in our pockets; so that, with fiddling, cooking, and farming, we soon found ourselves in the possession of abundance, and, in fact, leading a happy and prosperous life. Well, indeed, would it have been for us had we remained on the farm at Kingsbury; but the time came when the next step was to be taken towards the cruel destiny that awaited me.

In March, 1834, we removed to Saratoga Springs.[17] We occupied a house belonging to Daniel O'Brien on the north side of Washington street. At that time Isaac Taylor kept a large boarding house, known as Washington Hall at the north end of Broadway. He employed me to drive a hack, in which capacity I worked for him two years. After this time I was generally employed through the visiting season, as also was Anne, in the United States Hotel, and other public houses of the place.[18] In winter seasons I relied upon my violin, though during the construction of the Troy and Saratoga railroad, I performed many hard days' labor upon it.

I was in the habit, at Saratoga, of purchasing articles necessary for my family at the stores of Mr. Cephas Parker and Mr. William Perry, gentlemen towards whom, for many acts of kindness, I entertained feelings of strong regard. It was for this reason that, twelve years afterwards, I caused to be directed to them the letter, which is hereinafter inserted, and which was the means, in the hands of Mr. Northup, of my fortunate deliverance.

While living at the United States Hotel, I frequently met with slaves, who had accompanied their masters from the South. They were always well dressed and well provided for, leading apparently an easy life, with but few of its ordinary troubles to perplex them. Many times they entered into conversation with me on the subject of Slavery. Almost uniformly I found they cherished a secret desire for liberty. Some of them expressed the most ardent anxiety to escape, and consulted me on the best method of effecting it. The fear of punishment, however, which they knew was certain to attend their re-capture and return, in all cases proved sufficient to deter them from the experiment. Having all my life breathed the free air of the North, and conscious that I possessed the same feelings and affections that find a place in the white man's breast; conscious, moreover, of an intelligence equal to that of some men, at least, with a fairer skin, I was too ignorant, perhaps too independent, to conceive how any one could be content to live in the abject condition of a slave. I could not comprehend the justice of that law, or that religion, which upholds or recognizes the principle of Slavery; and never once, I am proud to say, did I fail to counsel any one who came to me, to watch his opportunity, and strike for freedom.[19]

I continued to reside at Saratoga until the spring of 1841. The flattering anticipations which, seven years before, had seduced us from the quiet farm-house, on the east side of the Hudson, had not been realized. Though always in comfortable circumstances, we had not prospered. The society and associations at that world-renowned watering place, were not calculated to preserve the simple habits of industry and economy to which I had been accustomed, but, on the contrary, to substitute others in their stead, tending to shiftlessness and extravagance.[20]

At this time we were the parents of three children—Elizabeth, Margaret, and Alonzo. Elizabeth, the eldest, was in her tenth year; Margaret was two years younger, and little Alonzo had just passed his fifth birth-day. They filled our house with gladness. Their young voices were music in our ears. Many an airy castle did their mother and myself build for the little innocents. When not at labor I was always walking with them, clad in their best attire, through the streets and groves of Saratoga. Their presence was my delight; and I clasped them to my bosom with as warm and tender love as if their clouded skins had been as white as snow.[21]

Thus far the history of my life presents nothing whatever unusual—nothing but the common hopes, and loves, and labors of an obscure colored man, making his humble progress in the world. But now I had reached a turning point in my existence—reached the threshold of unutterable wrong, and sorrow, and despair. Now had I approached within the shadow of the cloud, into the thick darkness whereof I was soon to disappear, thenceforward to be hidden from the eyes of all my kindred, and shut out from the sweet light of liberty, for many a weary year.

CHAPTER II.

THE TWO STRANGERS—THE CIRCUS COMPANY—DEPARTURE FROM SARATOGA—VENTRILOQUISM AND LEGERDEMAIN—JOURNEY TO NEW-YORK—FREE PAPERS—BROWN AND HAMILTON—THE HASTE TO REACH THE CIRCUS—ARRIVAL IN WASHINGTON—FUNERAL OF HARRISON—THE SUDDEN SICKNESS—THE TORMENT OF THIRST—THE RECEDING LIGHT—INSENSIBILITY—CHAINS AND DARKNESS.

One morning, towards the latter part of the month of March, 1841, having at that time no particular business to engage my attention, I was walking about the village of Saratoga Springs, thinking to myself where I might obtain some present employment, until the busy season should arrive. Anne, as was her usual custom, had gone over to Sandy Hill, a distance of some twenty miles, to take charge of the culinary department at Sherrill's Coffee House, during the session of the court. Elizabeth, I think, had accompanied her. Margaret and Alonzo were with their aunt at Saratoga.

On the corner of Congress street and Broadway, near the tavern, then, and for aught I know to the contrary, still kept by Mr. Moon, I was met by two gentlemen of respectable appearance, both of whom were entirely unknown to me.[22] I have the impression that they were introduced to me by some one of my acquaintances, but who, I have in vain endeavored to recall, with the remark that I was an expert player on the violin. *details, p. 272, n. 22*

At any rate, they immediately entered into conversation on that subject, making numerous inquiries touching my proficiency in that respect. My responses being to all appearances satisfactory, they proposed to engage my services for a short period, stating, at the same time, I was just such a person as their business required. Their names, as they afterwards gave them to me, were Merrill Brown and Abram Hamilton, though whether these were their true appellations I have strong reasons to doubt.[23] The former was a man apparently forty years of age, somewhat short and thick-set, with a countenance indicating shrewdness and intelligence. He wore a black frock coat

aliases

and black hat, and said he resided either at Rochester or at Syracuse. The latter was a young man of fair complexion and light eyes, and, I should judge, had not passed the age of twenty-five. He was tall and slender, dressed in a snuff-colored coat, with glossy hat, and vest of elegant pattern. His whole apparel was in the extreme of fashion. His appearance was somewhat effeminate, but prepossessing, and there was about him an easy air, that showed he had mingled with the world. They were connected, as they informed me, with a circus company, then in the city of Washington; that they were on their way thither to rejoin it, having left it for a short time to make an excursion northward, for the purpose of seeing the country, and were paying their expenses by an occasional exhibition. They also remarked that they had found much difficulty in procuring music for their entertainments, and that if I would accompany them as far as New-York, they would give me one dollar for each day's services, and three dollars in addition for every night I played at their performances, besides sufficient to pay the expenses of my return from New-York to Saratoga.

I at once accepted the tempting offer, both for the reward it promised, and from a desire to visit the metropolis. They were anxious to leave immediately. Thinking my absence would be brief, I did not deem it necessary to write to Anne whither I had gone; in fact supposing that my return, perhaps, would be as soon as hers. So taking a change of linen and my violin, I was ready to depart.[24] The carriage was brought round—a covered one, drawn by a pair of noble bays, altogether forming an elegant establishment. Their baggage, consisting of three large trunks, was fastened on the rack, and mounting to the driver's seat, while they took their places in the rear, I drove away from Saratoga on the road to Albany, elated with my new position, and happy as I had ever been, on any day in all my life.

We passed through Ballston, and striking the ridge road, as it is called, if my memory correctly serves me, followed it direct to Albany. We reached that city before dark, and stopped at a hotel southward from the Museum.

This night I had an opportunity of witnessing one of their performances—the only one, during the whole period I was with them. Hamilton was stationed at the door; I formed the orchestra, while Brown provided the entertainment. It consisted in throwing balls, dancing on the rope, frying pancakes in a hat, causing invisible pigs to squeal, and other like feats of ventriloquism and legerdemain. The audience was extraordinarily sparse, and not of the selectest character at that, and Hamilton's report of the proceeds presented but a "beggarly account of empty boxes."

Early next morning we renewed our journey. The burden of their conversation now was the expression of an anxiety to reach the circus without delay. They hurried forward, without again stopping to exhibit, and in due course of time, we reached New-York, taking lodgings at a house on the west side of the city, in a street running from Broadway to the river. I supposed my journey was at an end, and expected in a day or two at least, to return to my friends and family at Saratoga. Brown and Hamilton, however, began to importune me to continue with them to Washington. They alleged that immediately on their arrival, now that the summer season was approaching, the circus would set out for the north. They promised me a situation and high wages if I would accompany them. Largely did they expatiate on the advantages that would result to me, and such were the flattering representations they made, that I finally concluded to accept the offer.

The next morning they suggested that, inasmuch as we were about entering a slave State, it would be well, before leaving New-York, to procure free papers. The idea struck me as a prudent one, though I think it would scarcely have occurred to me, had they not proposed it. We proceeded at once to what I understood to be the Custom House. They made oath to certain facts showing I was a free man. A paper was drawn up and handed us, with the direction to take it to the clerk's office. We did so, and the clerk having added something to it, for which he was paid six shillings, we returned again to the Custom House. Some further formalities were gone through with before it was completed, when, paying the officer two dollars, I placed the papers in my pocket, and started with my two friends to our hotel. I thought at the time, I must confess, that the papers were scarcely worth the cost of obtaining them—the apprehension of danger to my personal safety never having suggested itself to me in the remotest manner. The clerk, to whom we were directed, I remember, made a memorandum in a large book, which, I presume, is in the office yet. A reference to the entries during the latter part of

March, or first of April, 1841, I have no doubt will satisfy the incredulous, at least so far as this particular transaction is concerned.

With the evidence of freedom in my possession, the next day after our arrival in New-York, we crossed the ferry to Jersey City, and took the road to Philadelphia. Here we remained one night, continuing our journey towards Baltimore early in the morning. In due time, we arrived in the latter city, and stopped at a hotel near the railroad depot, either kept by a Mr. Rathbone, or known as the Rathbone House. All the way from New-York, their anxiety to reach the circus seemed to grow more and more intense. We left the carriage at Baltimore, and entering the cars, proceeded to Washington, at which place we arrived just at nightfall, the evening previous to the funeral of General Harrison, and stopped at Gadsby's Hotel, on Pennsylvania Avenue.[25]

After supper they called me to their apartments, and paid me forty-three dollars, a sum greater than my wages amounted to, which act of generosity was in consequence, they said, of their not having exhibited as often as they had given me to anticipate, during our trip from Saratoga. They moreover informed me that it had been the intention of the circus company to leave Washington the next morning, but that on account of the funeral, they had concluded to remain another day. They were then, as they had been from the time of our first meeting, extremely kind. No opportunity was omitted of addressing me in the language of approbation; while, on the other hand, I was certainly much prepossessed in their favor. I gave them my confidence without reserve, and would freely have trusted them to almost any extent. Their constant conversation and manner towards me—their foresight in suggesting the idea of free papers, and a hundred other little acts, unnecessary to be repeated—all indicated that they were friends indeed, sincerely solicitous for my welfare. I know not but they were. I know not but they were innocent of the great wickedness of which I now believe them guilty. Whether they were accessory to my misfortunes—subtle and inhuman monsters in the shape of men—designedly luring me away from home and family, and liberty, for the sake of gold—those who read these pages will have the same means of determining as myself. If they were innocent, my sudden disappearance must have been unaccountable indeed; but revolving in my mind all the attending circumstances, I never yet could indulge, towards them, so charitable a supposition.

After receiving the money from them, of which they appeared to have an abundance, they advised me not to go into the streets that night, inasmuch as I was unacquainted with the customs of the city. Promising to remember their advice, I left them together, and soon after was shown by a colored servant to a sleeping room in the back part of the hotel, on the ground floor. I laid down to rest, thinking of home and wife, and children, and the long distance that stretched between us, until I fell asleep. But no good angel of pity came to my bedside, bidding me to fly—no voice of mercy forewarned me in my dreams of the trials that were just at hand.

The next day there was a great pageant in Washington. The roar of cannon and the tolling of bells filled the air, while many houses were shrouded with crape, and the streets were black with people. As the day advanced, the procession made its appearance, coming slowly through the Avenue, carriage after carriage, in long succession, while thousands upon thousands followed on foot—all moving to the sound of melancholy music. They were bearing the dead body of Harrison to the grave.

From early in the morning, I was constantly in the company of Hamilton and Brown. They were the only persons I knew in Washington. We stood together as the funeral pomp passed by. I remember distinctly how the window glass would break and rattle to the ground, after each report of the cannon they were firing in the burial ground. We went to the Capitol, and walked a long time about the grounds. In the afternoon, they strolled towards the President's House, all the time keeping me near to them, and pointing out various places of interest. As yet, I had seen nothing of the circus. In fact, I had thought of it but little, if at all, amidst the excitement of the day.

My friends, several times during the afternoon, entered drinking saloons, and called for liquor. They were by no means in the habit, however, so far as I knew them, of indulging to excess. On these occasions, after serving themselves, they would pour out a glass and hand it to me. I did not become intoxicated, as may be inferred from what subsequently occurred. Towards evening, and soon after partaking of one of these potations, I began to experience most unpleasant sensations. I felt extremely ill. My head commenced aching—a dull, heavy pain, inexpressibly disagreeable. At the supper table, I was without appetite; the sight and flavor of food was nauseous. About dark the same servant conducted me to the room I had occupied the previous night. Brown and Hamilton advised me to retire, commiserating me kindly, and expressing hopes that I would be better in the morning. Divesting myself of coat and boots merely, I threw myself upon the bed. It was impossible to sleep. The pain in my head continued to increase, until it became almost unbearable. In a short time I became thirsty. My lips were parched. I could think of nothing but water—of lakes and flowing rivers, of brooks where I had stooped to drink, and of the dripping bucket, rising with its cool and overflowing nectar, from the bottom of the well. Towards midnight, as near as I could judge, I arose, unable longer to bear such intensity of thirst. I was a stranger in the house, and knew nothing of its apartments. There was no one up, as I could observe. Groping about at random, I knew not where, I found the way at last to a kitchen in the basement. Two or three colored servants were moving through it, one of whom, a woman, gave me two glasses of water. It afforded momentary relief, but by the time I had reached my room again, the same burning desire of drink, the same tormenting thirst, had again returned. It was even more torturing than before, as was also the wild pain in my head, if such a thing could be. I was in sore distress—in most excruciating agony! I seemed to stand on the brink of madness! The memory of that night of horrible suffering will follow me to the grave.[26] *drugged*

In the course of an hour or more after my return from the kitchen, I was conscious of some one entering my room. There seemed to be several—a mingling of various voices,—but how many, or who they were, I cannot tell. Whether Brown and Hamilton were among them, is a mere matter of conjecture. I only remember, with any degree of distinctness, that I was told it was necessary to go to a physician and procure medicine, and that pulling on my boots, without coat or hat, I followed them through a long passage-way, or alley, into the open street. It ran out at right angles from Pennsylvania Avenue. On the opposite side there was a light burning in a window. My impression is there were then three persons with me, but it is altogether indefinite and vague, and like the memory of a painful dream. Going towards the light, which I imagined proceeded from a physician's office, and which seemed to recede as I advanced, is the last glimmering recollection I can now recall. From that moment I was insensible. How long I remained in that condition—whether only that night, or many days and nights—I do not know; but when consciousness returned, I found myself alone, in utter darkness, and in chains.

The pain in my head had subsided in a measure, but I was very faint and weak. I was sitting upon a low bench, made of rough boards, and without coat or hat. I was hand-cuffed. Around my ankles also were a pair of heavy fetters. One end of a chain was fastened to a large ring in the floor, the other to the fetters on my ankles. I tried in vain to stand upon my feet. Waking from such a painful trance, it was some time before I could collect my thoughts. Where was I? What was the meaning of these chains? Where were Brown and Hamilton? What had I done to deserve imprisonment in such a dungeon? I could not comprehend. There was a blank of some indefinite period, preceding my awakening in that lonely place, the events of which the utmost stretch of memory was unable to recall. I listened intently for some sign or sound of life, but nothing broke the oppressive silence, save the clinking of my chains, whenever I chanced to move. I spoke aloud, but the sound of my voice startled me. I felt of my pockets, so far as the fetters would allow—far enough, indeed, to ascertain that I had not only been robbed of liberty, but that my money and free papers were also gone! Then did the idea begin to break upon my mind, at first dim and confused, that I had been kidnapped. But that I thought was incredible. There must have been some misapprehension—some unfortunate mistake. It could not be that a free citizen of New-York, who had wronged no man, nor violated any law, should be dealt with thus inhumanly. The more I contemplated my situation, however, the more I became confirmed in my suspicions. It was a desolate thought, indeed. I felt there was no trust or mercy in unfeeling man; and commending myself to the God of the oppressed, bowed my head upon my fettered hands, and wept most bitterly.

CHAPTER III.

PAINFUL MEDITATIONS—JAMES H. BURCH—WILLIAMS' SLAVE PEN IN
WASHINGTON—THE LACKEY, RADBURN—ASSERT MY FREEDOM—
THE ANGER OF THE TRADER—THE PADDLE AND THE CAT-O'-
NINETAILS—THE WHIPPING—NEW ACQUAINTANCES—RAY, WILLIAMS,
AND RANDALL—ARRIVAL OF LITTLE EMILY AND HER MOTHER IN
THE PEN—MATERNAL SORROWS—THE STORY OF ELIZA.

Some three hours elapsed, during which time I remained seated on
the low bench, absorbed in painful meditations. At length I heard the
crowing of a cock, and soon a distant rumbling sound, as of carriages
hurrying through the streets, came to my ears, and I knew that it was
day. No ray of light, however, penetrated my prison. Finally, I heard
footsteps immediately overhead, as of some one walking to and fro.
It occurred to me then that I must be in an underground apartment,
and the damp, mouldy odors of the place confirmed the supposition.
The noise above continued for at least an hour, when, at last, I heard
footsteps approaching from without. A key rattled in the lock—a
strong door swung back upon its hinges, admitting a flood of light,
and two men entered and stood before me. One of them was a large,
powerful man, forty years of age, perhaps, with dark, chestnut-
colored hair, slightly interspersed with gray. His face was full, his
complexion flush, his features grossly coarse, expressive of nothing
but cruelty and cunning. He was about five feet ten inches high, of
full habit, and, without prejudice, I must be allowed to say, was a man
whose whole appearance was sinister and repugnant. His name was
James H. Burch,[27] as I learned afterwards—a well-known slave-dealer
in Washington; and then, or lately, connected in business, as a
partner, with Theophilus Freeman, of New-Orleans.[28] The person
who accompanied him was a simple lackey, named Ebenezer
Radburn, who acted merely in the capacity of turnkey.[29] Both of these
men still live in Washington, or did, at the time of my return through
that city from slavery in January last.

ironic name

The light admitted through the open door enabled me to observe the room in which I was confined. It was about twelve feet square—the walls of solid masonry. The floor was of heavy plank. There was one small window, crossed with great iron bars, with an outside shutter, securely fastened.

An iron-bound door led into an adjoining cell, or vault, wholly destitute of windows, or any means of admitting light. The furniture of the room in which I was, consisted of the wooden bench on which I sat, an old-fashioned, dirty box stove, and besides these, in either cell, there was neither bed, nor blanket, nor any other thing whatever. The door, through which Burch and Radburn entered, led through a small passage, up a flight of steps into a yard, surrounded by a brick wall of ten or twelve feet high, immediately in rear of a building of the same width as itself. The yard extended rearward from the house about thirty feet. In one part of the wall there was a strongly ironed door, opening into a narrow, covered passage, leading along one side of the house into the street. The doom of the colored man, upon whom the door leading out of that narrow passage closed, was sealed. The top of the wall supported one end of a roof, which ascended inwards, forming a kind of open shed. Underneath the roof there was a crazy loft all round, where slaves, if so disposed, might sleep at night, or in inclement weather seek shelter from the storm. It was like a farmer's barnyard in most respects, save it was so constructed that the outside world could never see the human cattle that were herded there.

The building to which the yard was attached, was two stories high, fronting on one of the public streets of Washington. Its outside presented only the appearance of a quiet private residence. A stranger looking at it, would never have dreamed of its execrable uses. Strange as it may seem, within plain sight of this same house looking down from its commanding height upon it, was the Capitol. The voices of patriotic representatives boasting of freedom and equality, and the rattling of the poor slave's chains, almost commingled. A slave pen within the very shadow of the Capitol! *powerful image*

Such is a correct description as it was in 1841, of Williams' slave pen in Washington, in one of the cellars of which I found myself so unaccountably confined.[30]

"Well, my boy, how do you feel now?" said Burch, as he entered through the open door. I replied that I was sick, and inquired the

n. 30 is a description of the slave pen by John Brown. contains "N-word!

cause of my imprisonment. He answered that I was his slave—that he had bought me, and that he was about to send me to New-Orleans. I asserted, aloud and boldly, that I was a free man—a resident of Saratoga, where I had a wife and children, who were also free, and that my name was Northup. I complained bitterly of the strange treatment I had received, and threatened, upon my liberation, to have satisfaction for the wrong. He denied that I was free, and with an emphatic oath, declared that I came from Georgia. Again and again I asserted I was no man's slave, and insisted upon his taking off my chains at once. He endeavored to hush me, as if he feared my voice would be overheard. But I would not be silent, and denounced the authors of my imprisonment, whoever they might be, as unmitigated villains. Finding he could not quiet me, he flew into a towering passion. With blasphemous oaths, he called me a black liar, a runaway from Georgia, and every other profane and vulgar epithet that the most indecent fancy could conceive.

During this time Radburn was standing silently by. His business was, to oversee this human, or rather inhuman stable, receiving slaves, feeding and whipping them, at the rate of two shillings a head per day. Turning to him, Burch ordered the paddle and cat-o'-ninetails to be brought in. He disappeared, and in a few moments returned with these instruments of torture. The paddle, as it is termed in slave-beating parlance, or at least the one with which I first became acquainted, and of which I now speak, was a piece of hard wood board, eighteen or twenty inches long, moulded to the shape of an old-fashioned pudding stick, or ordinary oar. The flattened portion, which was about the size in circumference of two open hands, was bored with a small auger in numerous places. The cat was a large rope of many strands—the strands unraveled, and a knot tied at the extremity of each.

As soon as these formidable whips appeared, I was seized by both of them, and roughly divested of my clothing. My feet, as has been stated, were fastened to the floor. Drawing me over the bench, face downwards, Radburn placed his heavy foot upon the fetters, between my wrists, holding them painfully to the floor. With the paddle, Burch commenced beating me. Blow after blow was inflicted upon my naked body. When his unrelenting arm grew tired, he stopped and asked if I still insisted I was a free man. I did insist upon it, and then the blows were renewed, faster and more energetically, if possible, than before. When again tired, he would repeat the same question, and receiving the same answer, continued his cruel labor. All this time, the incarnate devil was uttering most fiendish oaths. At length the paddle broke, leaving the useless handle in his hand. Still I would not yield. All his brutal blows could not force from my lips the foul lie that I was a slave. Casting madly on the floor the handle of the broken paddle, he seized the rope. This was far more painful than the other. I struggled with all my power, but it was in vain. I prayed for mercy, but my prayer was only answered with imprecations and with stripes. I thought I must die beneath the lashes of the accursed brute. Even now the flesh crawls upon my bones, as I recall the scene. I was all on fire. My sufferings I can compare to nothing else than the burning agonies of hell!

At last I became silent to his repeated questions. I would make no reply. In fact, I was becoming almost unable to speak. Still he plied the lash without stint upon my poor body, until it seemed that the lacerated flesh was stripped from my bones at every stroke.[31] A man with a particle of mercy in his soul would not have beaten even a dog so cruelly. At length Radburn said that it was useless to whip me any more—that I would be sore enough. Thereupon, Burch desisted, saying, with an admonitory shake of his fist in my face, and hissing the words through his firm-set teeth, that if ever I dared to utter again that I was entitled to my freedom, that I had been kidnapped, or any thing whatever of the kind, the castigation I had just received was nothing in comparison with what would follow. He swore that he would either conquer or kill me. With these consolatory words, the fetters were taken from my wrists, my feet still remaining fastened to the ring; the shutter of the little barred window, which had been opened, was again closed, and going out, locking the great door behind them, I was left in darkness as before.

In an hour, perhaps two, my heart leaped to my throat, as the key rattled in the door again. I, who had been so lonely, and who had longed so ardently to see some one, I cared not who, now shuddered at the thought of man's approach. A human face was fearful to me, especially a white one. Radburn entered, bringing with him, on a tin plate, a piece of shriveled fried pork, a slice of bread and a cup of water. He asked me how I felt, and remarked that I had received a pretty severe flogging. He remonstrated with me against the propriety of asserting my freedom. In rather a patronizing and confidential

101

n. 31 scars could be bad for sales

manner, he gave it to me as his advice, that the less I said on that subject the better it would be for me. The man evidently endeavored to appear kind—whether touched at the sight of my sad condition, or with the view of silencing, on my part, any further expression of my rights, it is not necessary now to conjecture. He unlocked the fetters from my ankles, opened the shutters of the little window, and departed, leaving me again alone. *Good cop, bad cop?*

By this time I had become stiff and sore; my body was covered with blisters, and it was with great pain and difficulty that I could move. From the window I could observe nothing but the roof resting on the adjacent wall. At night I laid down upon the damp, hard floor, without any pillow or covering whatever. Punctually, twice a day, Radburn came in, with his pork, and bread, and water. I had but little appetite, though I was tormented with continual thirst. My wounds would not permit me to remain but a few minutes in any one position; so, sitting, or standing, or moving slowly round, I passed the days and nights. I was heart sick and discouraged. Thoughts of my family, of my wife and children, continually occupied my mind. When sleep overpowered me I dreamed of them—dreamed I was again in Saratoga—that I could see their faces, and hear their voices calling me. Awakening from the pleasant phantasms of sleep to the bitter realities around me, I could but groan and weep. Still my spirit was not broken. I indulged the anticipation of escape, and that speedily. It was impossible, I reasoned, that men could be so unjust as to detain me as a slave, when the truth of my case was known. Burch, ascertaining I was no runaway from Georgia, would certainly let me go. Though suspicions of Brown and Hamilton were not unfrequent, I could not reconcile myself to the idea that they were instrumental to my imprisonment. Surely they would seek me out— they would deliver me from thralldom. Alas! I had not then learned the measure of "man's inhumanity to man," nor to what limitless extent of wickedness he will go for the love of gain. *discuss*

In the course of several days the outer door was thrown open, allowing me the liberty of the yard. There I found three slaves—one of them a lad of ten years, the others young men of about twenty and twenty-five. I was not long in forming an acquaintance, and learning their names and the particulars of their history.

The eldest was a colored man named Clemens Ray.[32] He had lived in Washington; had driven a hack, and worked in a livery stable

^.32 pres. Clem Woodard #56 see manifest

there for a long time. He was very intelligent, and fully comprehended his situation. The thought of going south overwhelmed him
with grief. Burch had purchased him a few days before, and had
placed him there until such time as he was ready to send him to the
New-Orleans market. From him I learned for the first time that I was
in William's Slave Pen, a place I had never heard of previously. He
described to me the uses for which it was designed. I repeated to him
the particulars of my unhappy story, but he could only give me the
consolation of his sympathy. He also advised me to be silent henceforth on the subject of my freedom; for, knowing the character of
Burch, he assured me that it would only be attended with renewed
whipping. The next eldest was named John Williams.[33] He was raised
in Virginia, not far from Washington. Burch had taken him in payment of a debt, and he constantly entertained the hope that his master would redeem him—a hope that was subsequently realized. The
lad was a sprightly child, that answered to the name of Randall.[34]
Most of the time he was playing about the yard, but occasionally
would cry, calling for his mother, and wondering when she would
come. His mother's absence seemed to be the great and only grief in
his little heart. He was too young to realize his condition, and when
the memory of his mother was not in his mind, he amused us with
his pleasant pranks.

At night, Ray, Williams, and the boy, slept in the loft of the shed,
while I was locked in the cell. Finally we were each provided with
blankets, such as are used upon horses—the only bedding I was
allowed to have for twelve years afterwards. Ray and Williams asked
me many questions about New-York—how colored people were
treated there; how they could have homes and families of their own,
with none to disturb and oppress them; and Ray, especially, sighed
continually for freedom. Such conversations, however, were not in
the hearing of Burch, or the keeper Radburn. Aspirations such as
these would have brought down the lash upon our backs.

It is necessary in this narrative, in order to present a full and
truthful statement of all the principal events in the history of my
life, and to portray the institution of Slavery as I have seen and
known it, to speak of well-known places, and of many persons who
are yet living. I am, and always was, an entire stranger in
Washington and its vicinity—aside from Burch and Radburn,
knowing no man there, except as I have heard of them through my

n. 34 Rudal Ames_ child, 4-7" #35
on manifest

enslaved companions. What I am about to say, if false, can be easily contradicted.

I remained in Williams' slave pen about two weeks. The night previous to my departure a woman was brought in, weeping bitterly, and leading by the hand a little child. They were Randall's mother and half-sister. On meeting them he was overjoyed, clinging to her dress, kissing the child, and exhibiting every demonstration of delight. The mother also clasped him in her arms, embraced him tenderly, and gazed at him fondly through her tears, calling him by many an endearing name.

Emily, the child, was seven or eight years old, of light complexion, and with a face of admirable beauty.[35] Her hair fell in curls around her neck, while the style and richness of her dress, and the neatness of her whole appearance indicated she had been brought up in the midst of wealth. She was a sweet child indeed. The woman also was arrayed in silk, with rings upon her fingers, and golden ornaments suspended from her ears. Her air and manners, the correctness and propriety of her language—all showed, evidently, that she had sometime stood above the common level of a slave. She seemed to be amazed at finding herself in such a place as that. It was plainly a sudden and unexpected turn of fortune that had brought her there. Filling the air with her complainings, she was hustled, with the children and myself, into the cell. Language can convey but an inadequate impression of the lamentations to which she gave incessant utterance. Throwing herself upon the floor, and encircling the children in her arms, she poured forth such touching words as only maternal love and kindness can suggest. They nestled closely to her, as if *there* only was there any safety or protection. At last they slept, their heads resting upon her lap. While they slumbered, she smoothed the hair back from their little foreheads, and talked to them all night long. She called them her darlings—her sweet babes— poor innocent things, that knew not the misery they were destined to endure. Soon they would have no mother to comfort them—they would be taken from her. What would become of them? Oh! she could not live away from her little Emmy and her dear boy. They had always been good children, and had such loving ways. It would break her heart, God knew, she said, if they were taken from her; and yet she knew they meant to sell them, and may be, they would be separated, and could never see each other any more. It was enough to melt a heart of stone to listen to the pitiful expressions of that desolate and distracted mother. Her name was Eliza; and this was the story of her life, as she afterwards related it:[36]

She was the slave of Elisha Berry, a rich man, living in the neighborhood of Washington.[37] She was born, I think she said, on his plantation. Years before, he had fallen into dissipated habits, and quarreled with his wife. In fact, soon after the birth of Randall, they separated. Leaving his wife and daughter in the house they had always occupied, he erected a new one near by, on the estate. Into this house he brought Eliza; and, on condition of her living with him, she and her children were to be emancipated. She resided with him there nine years, with servants to attend upon her, and provided with every comfort and luxury of life. Emily was his child! Finally, her young mistress, who had always remained with her mother at the homestead, married a Mr. Jacob Brooks.[38] At length, for some cause, (as I gathered from her relation,) beyond Berry's control, a division of his property was made. She and her children fell to the share of Mr. Brooks. During the nine years she had lived with Berry, in consequence of the position she was compelled to occupy, she and Emily had become the object of Mrs. Berry and her daughter's hatred and dislike. Berry himself she represented as a man of naturally a kind heart, who always promised her that she would have her freedom, and who, she had no doubt, would grant it to her then, if it were only in his power. As soon as they thus came into the possession and control of the daughter, it became very manifest they would not live long together. The sight of Eliza seemed to be odious to Mrs. Brooks; neither could she bear to look upon the child, half-sister, and beautiful as she was!

The day she was led into the pen, Brooks had brought her from the estate into the city, under pretence that the time had come when her free papers were to be executed, in fulfillment of her master's promise. Elated at the prospect of immediate liberty, she decked herself and little Emmy in their best apparel, and accompanied him with a joyful heart. On their arrival in the city, instead of being baptized into the family of freemen, she was delivered to the trader Burch. The paper that was executed was a bill of sale. The hope of years was blasted in a moment. From the height of most exulting happiness to the utmost depths of wretchedness, she had that day

n. 36 - Eliza Cooper, 27
#38 on manifest

descended. No wonder that she wept, and filled the pen with wailings and expressions of heart-rending woe.

Eliza is now dead. Far up the Red River, where it pours its waters sluggishly through the unhealthy low lands of Louisiana,[39] she rests in the grave at last—the only resting place of the poor slave! How all her fears were realized—how she mourned day and night, and never would be comforted—how, as she predicted, her heart did indeed break, with the burden of maternal sorrow, will be seen as the narrative proceeds.

Scene in the slave pen at Washington

CHAPTER IV.

ELIZA'S SORROWS—PREPARATION TO EMBARK—DRIVEN THROUGH
THE STREETS OF WASHINGTON—HAIL, COLUMBIA—THE TOMB OF
WASHINGTON—CLEM RAY—THE BREAKFAST ON THE STEAMER—
THE HAPPY BIRDS—AQUIA CREEK—FREDERICKSBURGH—ARRIVAL
IN RICHMOND—GOODIN AND HIS SLAVE PEN—ROBERT, OF
CINCINNATI—DAVID AND HIS WIFE—MARY AND LETHE—CLEM'S
RETURN—HIS SUBSEQUENT ESCAPE TO CANADA—THE BRIG
ORLEANS—JAMES H. BURCH.

At intervals during the first night of Eliza's incarceration in the pen, she complained bitterly of Jacob Brooks, her young mistress' husband.[40] She declared that had she been aware of the deception he intended to practice upon her, he never would have brought her there alive. They had chosen the opportunity of getting her away when Master Berry was absent from the plantation.[41] He had always been kind to her. She wished that she could see him; but she knew that even he was unable now to rescue her. Then would she commence weeping again—kissing the sleeping children—talking first to one, then to the other, as they lay in their unconscious slumbers, with their heads upon her lap. So wore the long night away; and when the morning dawned, and night had come again, still she kept mourning on, and would not be consoled.

About midnight following, the cell door opened, and Burch and Radburn entered, with lanterns in their hands. Burch, with an oath, ordered us to roll up our blankets without delay, and get ready to go on board the boat. He swore we would be left unless we hurried fast. He aroused the children from their slumbers with a rough shake, and said they were d——d sleepy, it appeared. Going out into the yard, he called Clem Ray, ordering him to leave the loft and come into the cell, and bring his blanket with him. When Clem appeared, he placed us side by side, and fastened us together with hand-cuffs—my left hand to his right. John Williams had been taken out a day or two before, his master having redeemed him, greatly to his delight. Clem

details

and I were ordered to march, Eliza and the children following. We were conducted into the yard, from thence into the covered passage, and up a flight of steps through a side door into the upper room, where I had heard the walking to and fro. Its furniture was a stove, a few old chairs, and a long table, covered with papers. It was a white-washed room, without any carpet on the floor, and seemed a sort of office. By one of the windows, I remember, hung a rusty sword, which attracted my attention. Burch's trunk was there. In obedience to his orders, I took hold of one of its handles with my unfettered hand, while he taking hold of the other, we proceeded out of the front door into the street in the same order as we had left the cell.

help carry Burch's trunk

It was a dark night. All was quiet. I could see lights, or the reflection of them, over towards Pennsylvania Avenue, but there was no one, not even a straggler, to be seen. I was almost resolved to attempt to break away. Had I not been hand-cuffed the attempt would certainly have been made, whatever consequence might have followed. Radburn was in the rear, carrying a large stick, and hurrying up the children as fast as the little ones could walk. So we passed, hand-cuffed and in silence, through the streets of Washington— through the Capital of a nation, whose theory of government, we were told, rests on the foundation of man's inalienable right to life, LIBERTY, and the pursuit of happiness! Hail! Columbia, happy land, indeed! *Sarcasm*

Reaching the steamboat, we were quickly hustled into the hold, among barrels and boxes of freight. A colored servant brought a light, the bell rung, and soon the vessel started down the Potomac, carrying us we knew not where. The bell tolled as we passed the tomb of Washington! Burch, no doubt, with uncovered head, bowed reverently before the sacred ashes of the man who devoted his illustrious life to the liberty of his country. *significance?*

None of us slept that night but Randall and little Emmy. For the first time Clem Ray was wholly overcome. To him the idea of going south was terrible in the extreme. He was leaving the friends and associations of his youth—every thing that was dear and precious to his heart—in all probability never to return. He and Eliza mingled their tears together, bemoaning their cruel fate. For my own part, difficult as it was, I endeavored to keep up my spirits. I revolved in my mind a hundred plans of escape, and fully determined to make the attempt the first desperate chance that offered. I had by this time become satisfied, however, that my true policy was to say nothing further on the subject of my having been born a freeman. It would but expose me to mal-treatment, and diminish the chances of liberation.

After sunrise in the morning we were called up on deck to breakfast. Burch took our hand-cuffs off, and we sat down to table. He asked Eliza if she would take a dram. She declined, thanking him politely. During the meal we were all silent—not a word passed between us. A mulatto woman who served at table seemed to take an interest in our behalf—told us to cheer up, and not to be so cast down. Breakfast over, the hand-cuffs were restored, and Burch ordered us out on the stern deck. We sat down together on some boxes, still saying nothing in Burch's presence. Occasionally a passenger would walk out to where we were, look at us for a while, then silently return.

It was a very pleasant morning. The fields along the river were covered with verdure, far in advance of what I had been accustomed to see at that season of the year. The sun shone out warmly; the birds were singing in the trees. The happy birds—I envied them. I wished for wings like them, that I might cleave the air to where my birdlings waited vainly for their father's coming, in the cooler region of the North. *imagery*

In the forenoon the steamer reached Aquia Creek. There the passengers took stages—Burch and his five slaves occupying one exclusively. He laughed with the children, and at one stopping place went so far as to purchase them a piece of gingerbread. He told me to hold up my head and look smart. That I might, perhaps, get a good master if I behaved myself. I made him no reply. His face was hateful to me, and I could not bear to look upon it. I sat in the corner, cherishing in my heart the hope, not yet extinct, of some day meeting the tyrant on the soil of my native State. *why?*

At Fredericksburgh we were transferred from the stage coach to a car, and before dark arrived in Richmond, the chief city of Virginia .At this city we were taken from the cars, and driven through the street to a slave pen, between the railroad depot and the river, kept by a Mr. Goodin. This pen is similar to Williams' in Washington, except it is somewhat larger; and besides, there were two small houses standing at opposite corners within the yard. These houses are usually found within slave yards, being used as rooms for the examination of human chattels by purchasers before concluding a bargain. Unsoundness in a slave, as well as in a horse, detracts materially from his value. If no warranty is given, a close examination is a matter of particular importance to the negro jockey.

We were met at the door of Goodin's yard by that gentleman himself—a short, fat man, with a round, plump face, black hair and whiskers, and a complexion almost as dark as some of his own negroes. He had a hard, stern look, and was perhaps about fifty years of age. Burch and he met with great cordiality.[42] They were evidently old friends. Shaking each other warmly by the hand, Burch remarked he had brought some company, inquired at what time the brig would leave, and was answered that it would probably leave the next day at such an hour. Goodin then turned to me, took hold of my arm, turned me partly round, looked at me sharply with the air of one who considered himself a good judge of property, and as if estimating in his own mind about how much I was worth. _1st use of dialogue_

"Well, boy, where did you come from?"

Forgetting myself, for a moment, I answered, "From New-York."

"New-York! H—l! what have you been doing up there?" was his astonished interrogatory.

Observing Burch at this moment looking at me with an angry expression that conveyed a meaning it was not difficult to understand, I immediately said, "0, I have only been up that way a piece," in a manner intended to imply that although I might have been as far as New-York, yet I wished it distinctly understood that I did not belong to that free State, nor to any other. _?_

Goodin then turned to Clem, and then to Eliza and the children, examining them severally, and asking various questions. He was pleased with Emily, as was every one who saw the child's sweet countenance. She was not as tidy as when I first beheld her; her hair was now somewhat disheveled; but through its unkempt and soft profusion there still beamed a little face of most surpassing loveliness. "Altogether we were a fair lot—a devilish good lot," he said, enforcing that opinion with more than one emphatic adjective not found in the Christian vocabulary. Thereupon we passed into the yard. Quite a number of slaves, as many as thirty I should say, were moving about, or sitting on benches under the shed. They were all

1. wz on auctions

cleanly dressed—the men with hats, the women with handkerchiefs tied about their heads.

Burch and Goodin, after separating from us, walked up the steps at the back part of the main building, and sat down upon the door sill. They entered into conversation, but the subject of it I could not hear. Presently Burch came down into the yard, unfettered me, and led me into one of the small houses.

"You told that man you came from New-York," said he.

I replied, "I told him I had been up as far as New-York, to be sure, but did not tell him I belonged there, nor that I was a freeman. I meant no harm at all, Master Burch. I would not have said it had I thought."

He looked at me a moment as if he was ready to devour me, then turning round went out. In a few minutes he returned. "If ever I hear you say a word about New-York, or about your freedom, I will be the death of you—I will kill you; you may rely on that," he ejaculated fiercely.

I doubt not he understood then better than I did, the danger and the penalty of selling a free man into slavery. He felt the necessity of closing my mouth against the crime he knew he was committing. Of course, my life would not have weighed a feather, in any emergency requiring such a sacrifice. Undoubtedly, he meant precisely what he said.

Under the shed on one side of the yard, there was constructed a rough table, while overhead were sleeping lofts—the same as in the pen at Washington. After partaking at this table of our supper of pork and bread, I was hand-cuffed to a large yellow man, quite stout and fleshy, with a countenance expressive of the utmost melancholy. He was a man of intelligence and information. Chained together, it was not long before we became acquainted with each other's history. His name was Robert. Like myself, he had been born free, and had a wife and two children in Cincinnati. He said he had come south with two men, who had hired him in the city of his residence. Without free papers, he had been seized at Fredricksburgh, placed in confinement, and beaten until he had learned, as I had, the necessity and the policy of silence.[43] He had been in Goodin's pen about three weeks. To this man I became much attached. We could sympathize with, and understand each other. It was with tears and a heavy heart, not many days subsequently, that I saw him die, and looked for the last time upon his lifeless form!

Robert and myself, with Clem, Eliza and her children, slept that night upon our blankets, in one of the small houses in the yard. There were four others, all from the same plantation, who had been sold, and were now on their way south, who also occupied it with us. David and his wife, Caroline, both mulattoes, were exceedingly affected.[44] They dreaded the thought of being put into the cane and cotton fields; but their greatest source of anxiety was the apprehension of being separated. Mary, a tall, lithe girl, of a most jetty black, was listless and apparently indifferent.[45] Like many of the class, she scarcely knew there was such a word as freedom. Brought up in the ignorance of a brute, she possessed but little more than a brute's intelligence. She was one of those, and there are very many, who fear nothing but their master's lash, and know no further duty than to obey his voice. The other was Lethe.[46] She was of an entirely different character. She had long, straight hair, and bore more the appearance of an Indian than a negro woman. She had sharp and spiteful eyes, and continually gave utterance to the language of hatred and revenge. Her husband had been sold. She knew not where she was. An exchange of masters, she was sure, could not be for the worse. She cared not whither they might carry her. Pointing to the scars upon her face, the desperate creature wished that she might see the day when she could wipe them off in some man's blood!

While we were thus learning the history of each other's wretchedness, Eliza was seated in a corner by herself, singing hymns and praying for her children. Wearied from the loss of so much sleep, I could no longer bear up against the advances of that "sweet restorer," and laying down by the side of Robert, on the floor, soon forgot my troubles, and slept until the dawn of day.

In the morning, having swept the yard, and washed ourselves, under Goodin's superintendence, we were ordered to roll up our blankets, and make ready for the continuance of our journey. Clem Ray was informed that he would go no further, Burch, for some cause, having concluded to carry him back to Washington. He was much rejoiced. Shaking hands, we parted in the slave pen at Richmond, and I have not seen him since. But, much to my surprise, since my return, I learned that he had escaped from bondage, and on his way to the free soil of Canada, lodged one night at the house of

separation of families

my brother-in-law in Saratoga, informing my family of the place and the condition in which he left me.

In the afternoon we were drawn up, two abreast, Robert and myself in advance, and in this order, driven by Burch and Goodin from the yard, through the streets of Richmond to the brig Orleans.[47] She was a vessel of respectable size, full rigged, and freighted principally with tobacco. We were all on board by five o'clock. Burch brought us each a tin cup and a spoon. There were forty of us in the brig, being all, except Clem, that were in the pen.

With a small pocket knife that had not been taken from me, I began cutting the initials of my name upon the tin cup. The others immediately flocked round me, requesting me to mark theirs in a similar manner. In time, I gratified them all, of which they did not appear to be forgetful.

We were all stowed away in the hold at night, and the hatch barred down. We laid on boxes, or wherever there was room enough to stretch our blankets on the floor.

Burch accompanied us no farther than Richmond, returning from that point to the capital with Clem. Not until the lapse of almost twelve years, to wit, in January last, in the Washington police office, did I set my eyes upon his face again.

James H. Burch was a slave-trader—buying men, women and children at low prices, and selling them at an advance. He was a speculator in human flesh—a disreputable calling—and so considered at the South. For the present he disappears from the scenes recorded in this narrative, but he will appear again before its close, not in the character of a man-whipping tyrant, but as an arrested, cringing criminal in a court of law, that failed to do him justice.

CHAPTER V.

ARRIVAL AT NORFOLK—FREDERICK AND MARIA—ARTHUR, THE
FREEMAN—APPOINTED STEWARD—JIM, CUFFEE, AND JENNY—
THE STORM—BAHAMA BANKS—THE CALM—THE CONSPIRACY—
THE LONG BOAT—THE SMALL-POX—DEATH OF ROBERT—
MANNING, THE SAILOR—THE MEETING IN THE FORECASTLE—THE
LETTER—ARRIVAL AT NEW-ORLEANS—ARTHUR'S RESCUE—
THEOPHILUS FREEMAN, THE CONSIGNEE—PLATT—FIRST NIGHT
IN THE NEW-ORLEANS SLAVE PEN.

After we were all on board, the brig Orleans proceeded down James
River.[48] Passing into Chesapeake Bay, we arrived next day opposite
the city of Norfolk. While lying at anchor, a lighter approached us
from the town, bringing four more slaves. Frederick, a boy of
eighteen, had been born a slave, as also had Henry, who was some
years older.[49] They had both been house servants in the city. Maria
was a rather genteel looking colored girl, with a faultless form, but
ignorant and extremely vain.[50] The idea of going to New-Orleans was
pleasing to her. She entertained an extravagantly high opinion of her
own attractions. Assuming a haughty mien, she declared to her
companions, that immediately on our arrival in New Orleans, she had
no doubt, some wealthy single gentleman of good taste would
purchase her at once!

But the most prominent of the four, was a man named Arthur.[51]
As the lighter approached, he struggled stoutly with his keepers. It
was with main force that he was dragged aboard the brig. He
protested, in a loud voice, against the treatment he was receiving, and
demanded to be released. His face was swollen, and covered with
wounds and bruises, and, indeed, one side of it was a complete raw
sore. He was forced, with all haste, down the hatchway into the hold.
I caught an outline of his story as he was borne struggling along, of
which he afterwards gave me a more full relation, and it was as
follows: He had long resided in the city of Norfolk, and was a free
man. He had a family living there, and was a mason by trade. Having
been unusually detained, he was returning late one night to his house

in the suburbs of the city, when he was attacked by a gang of persons in an unfrequented street. He fought until his strength failed him. Overpowered at last, he was gagged and bound with ropes, and beaten, until he became insensible. For several days they secreted him in the slave pen at Norfolk—a very common establishment, it appears, in the cities of the South. The night before, he had been taken out and put on board the lighter, which, pushing out from shore, had awaited our arrival. For some time he continued his protestations, and was altogether irreconcilable. At length, however, he became silent. He sank into a gloomy and thoughtful mood, and appeared to be counseling with himself. There was in the man's determined face, something that suggested the thought of desperation.

After leaving Norfolk the hand-cuffs were taken off, and during the day we were allowed to remain on deck. The captain selected Robert as his waiter, and I was appointed to superintend the cooking department, and the distribution of food and water. I had three assistants, Jim, Cuffee, and Jenny.[52] Jenny's business was to prepare the coffee, which consisted of corn meal scorched in a kettle, boiled and sweetened with molasses. Jim and Cuffee baked the hoe-cake and boiled the bacon.

Standing by a table, formed of a wide board resting on the heads of the barrels, I cut and handed to each a slice of meat and a "dodger" of the bread, and from Jenny's kettle also dipped out for each a cup of the coffee. The use of plates was dispensed with, and their sable fingers took the place of knives and forks. Jim and Cuffee were very demure and attentive to business, somewhat inflated with their situations as second cooks, and without doubt feeling that there was a great responsibility resting on them. I was called steward—a name given me by the captain.

The slaves were fed twice a day, at ten and five o'clock—always receiving the same kind and quantity of fare, and in the same manner as above described. At night we were driven into the hold, and securely fastened down.

Scarcely were we out of sight of land before we were overtaken by a violent storm. The brig rolled and plunged, until we feared she would go down. Some were sea-sick, others on their knees praying, while some were fast holding to each other, paralyzed with fear. The sea-sickness rendered the place of our confinement loathsome and

Effective ?

disgusting. It would have been a happy thing for most of us—it would have saved the agony of many hundred lashes, and miserable deaths at last—had the compassionate sea snatched us that day from the clutches of remorseless men. The thought of Randall and little Emmy sinking down among the monsters of the deep, is a more pleasant contemplation than to think of them as they are now, perhaps, dragging out lives of unrequited toil.

When in sight of the Bahama Banks, at a place called Old Point Compass, or the Hole in the Wall, we were becalmed three days. There was scarcely a breath of air. The waters of the gulf presented a singularly white appearance, like lime water.

In the order of events, I come now to the relation of an occurrence, which I never call to mind but with sensations of regret. I thank God, who has since permitted me to escape from the thralldom of slavery, that through his merciful interposition I was prevented from imbruing my hands in the blood of his creatures. Let not those who have never been placed in like circumstances, judge me harshly. Until they have been chained and beaten—until they find themselves in the situation I was, borne away from home and family towards a land of bondage—let them refrain from saying what they would not do for liberty. How far I should have been justified in the sight of God and man, it is unnecessary now to speculate upon. It is enough to say that I am able to congratulate myself upon the harmless termination of an affair which threatened, for a time, to be attended with serious results.

Towards evening, on the first day of the calm, Arthur and myself were in the bow of the vessel, seated on the windlass. We were conversing together of the probable destiny that awaited us, and mourning together over our misfortunes. Arthur said, and I agreed with him, that death was far less terrible than the living prospect that was before us. For a long time we talked of our children, our past lives, and of the probabilities of escape. Obtaining possession of the brig was suggested by one of us. We discussed the possibility of our being able, in such an event, to make our way to the harbor of New-York. I knew little of the compass; but the idea of risking the experiment was eagerly entertained. The chances, for and against us, in an encounter with the crew, was canvassed. Who could be relied upon, and who could not, the proper time and manner of the attack, were all talked over and over again. From the moment the plot suggested itself I began to hope. I revolved it constantly in my mind. As difficulty after difficulty arose, some ready conceit was at hand, demonstrating how it could be overcome. While others slept, Arthur and I were maturing our plans. At length, with much caution, Robert was gradually made acquainted with our intentions. He approved of them at once, and entered into the conspiracy with a zealous spirit. There was not another slave we dared to trust. Brought up in fear and ignorance as they are, it can scarcely be conceived how servilely they will cringe before a white man's look. It was not safe to deposit so bold a secret with any of them, and finally we three resolved to take upon ourselves alone the fearful responsibility of the attempt.

At night, as has been said, we were driven into the hold, and the hatch barred down. How to reach the deck was the first difficulty that presented itself. On the bow of the brig, however, I had observed the small boat lying bottom upwards. It occurred to me that by secreting ourselves underneath it, we would not be missed from the crowd, as they were hurried down into the hold at night. I was selected to make the experiment, in order to satisfy ourselves of its feasibility. The next evening, accordingly, after supper, watching my opportunity, I hastily concealed myself beneath it. Lying close upon the deck, I could see what was going on around me, while wholly unperceived myself. In the morning, as they came up, I slipped from my hiding place without being observed. The result was entirely satisfactory.

The captain and mate slept in the cabin of the former. From Robert, who had frequent occasion, in his capacity of waiter, to make observations in that quarter, we ascertained the exact position of their respective berths. He further informed us that there were always two pistols and a cutlass lying on the table. The crew's cook slept in the cook galley on deck, a sort of vehicle on wheels, that could be moved about as convenience required, while the sailors, numbering only six, either slept in the forecastle, or in hammocks swung among the rigging.

Finally our arrangements were all completed. Arthur and I were to steal silently to the captain's cabin, seize the pistols and cutlass, and as quickly as possible dispatch him and the mate. Robert, with a club, was to stand by the door leading from the deck down into the cabin, and, in case of necessity, beat back the sailors, until we could hurry to his assistance. We were to proceed then as circumstances

Escape attempt

might require. Should the attack be so sudden and successful as to prevent resistance, the hatch was to remain barred down; otherwise the slaves were to be called up, and in the crowd, and hurry, and confusion of the time, we resolved to regain our liberty or lose our lives. I was then to assume the unaccustomed place of pilot, and, steering northward, we trusted that some lucky wind might bear us to the soil of freedom.

The mate's name was Biddee, the captain's I cannot now recall, though I rarely ever forget a name once heard. The captain was a small, genteel man, erect and prompt, with a proud bearing, and looked the personification of courage. If he is still living, and these pages should chance to meet his eye, he will learn a fact connected with the voyage of the brig, from Richmond to New-Orleans, in 1841, not entered on his logbook.

We were all prepared, and impatiently waiting an opportunity of putting our designs into execution, when they were frustrated by a sad and unforeseen event. Robert was taken ill. It was soon announced that he had the small-pox. He continued to grow worse, and four days previous to our arrival in New-Orleans he died. One of the sailors sewed him in his blanket, with a large stone from the ballast at his feet, and then laying him on a hatchway, and elevating it with tackles above the railing, the inanimate body of poor Robert was consigned to the white waters of the gulf.[53]

We were all panic-stricken by the appearance of the small-pox. The captain ordered lime to be scattered through the hold, and other prudent precautions to be taken. The death of Robert, however, and the presence of the malady, oppressed me sadly, and I gazed out over the great waste of waters with a spirit that was indeed disconsolate.

An evening or two after Robert's burial, I was leaning on the hatchway near the forecastle, full of desponding thoughts, when a sailor in a kind voice asked me why I was so down-hearted. The tone and manner of the man assured me, and I answered, because I was a freeman, and had been kidnapped. He remarked that it was enough to make any one down-hearted, and continued to interrogate me until he learned the particulars of my whole history. He was evidently much interested in my behalf, and, in the blunt speech of a sailor, swore he would aid me all he could, if it "split his timbers." I requested him to furnish me pen, ink and paper, in order that I might write to some of my friends. He promised to obtain them—but how

n. 53 re Robert's death

I could use them undiscovered was a difficulty. If I could only get into the forecastle while his watch was off, and the other sailors asleep, the thing could be accomplished. The small boat instantly occurred to me. He thought we were not far from the Balize, at the mouth of the Mississippi, and it was necessary that the letter be written soon, or the opportunity would be lost. Accordingly, by arrangement, I managed the next night to secret myself again under the long-boat. His watch was off at twelve. I saw him pass into the forecastle, and in about an hour followed him. He was nodding over a table, half asleep, on which a sickly light was flickering, and on which also was a pen and sheet of paper. As I entered he aroused, beckoned me to a seat beside him, and pointed to the paper. I directed the letter to Henry B. Northup, of Sandy Hill—stating that I had been kidnapped, was then on board the brig Orleans, bound for New-Orleans; that it was then impossible for me to conjecture my ultimate destination, and requesting he would take measures to rescue me. The letter was sealed and directed, and Manning, having read it, promised to deposit it in the New-Orleans post office. I hastened back to my place under the long-boat, and in the morning, as the slaves came up and were walking round, crept out unnoticed and mingled with them.

My good friend, whose name was John Manning, was an Englishman by birth, and a noble-hearted, generous sailor as ever walked a deck. He had lived in Boston—was a tall, well-built man, about twenty-four years old, with a face somewhat pock-marked, but full of benevolent expression.

Nothing to vary the monotony of our daily life occurred, until we reached New-Orleans. On coming to the levee, and before the vessel was made fast, I saw Manning leap on shore and hurry away into the city. As he started off he looked back over his shoulder significantly, giving me to understand the object of his errand.[54] Presently he returned, and passing close by me, hunched me with his elbow, with a peculiar wink, as much as to say, "it is all right."

The letter, as I have since learned, reached Sandy Hill. Mr. Northup visited Albany and laid it before Governor Seward, but inasmuch as it gave no definite information as to my probable locality, it was not, at that time, deemed advisable to institute measures for my liberation. It was concluded to delay, trusting that a knowledge of where I was might eventually be obtained.

n. 54 confirms letter was mailed + rec'd

A happy and touching scene was witnessed immediately upon our reaching the levee. Just as Manning left the brig, on the way to the post-office, two men came up and called aloud for Arthur. The latter, as he recognized them, was almost crazy with delight. He could hardly be restrained from leaping over the brig's side; and when they met soon after, he grasped them by the hand, and clung to them a long, long time. They were men from Norfolk, who had come on to New-Orleans to rescue him. His kidnappers, they informed him, had been arrested, and were then confined in the Norfolk prison. They conversed a few moments with the captain, and then departed with the rejoicing Arthur. *Arthur is rescued.*

But in all the crowd that thronged the wharf, there was no one who knew or cared for me. Not one. No familiar voice greeted my ears, nor was there a single face that I had ever seen. Soon Arthur would rejoin his family, and have the satisfaction of seeing his wrongs avenged: my family alas, should I ever see them more? There was a feeling of utter desolation in my heart, filling it with a despairing and regretful sense, that I had not gone down with Robert to the bottom of the sea. *Emotion*

Very soon traders and consignees came on board. One, a tall, thin-faced man, with light complexion and a little bent, made his appearance, with a paper in his hand. Burch's gang, consisting of myself, Eliza and her children,[55] Harry, Lethe, and some others, who had joined us at Richmond, were consigned to him. This gentleman was Mr. Theophilus Freeman. Reading from his paper, he called, "Platt." No one answered. The name was called again and again, but still there was no reply. Then Lethe was called, then Eliza, then Harry, until the list was finished, each one stepping forward as his or her name was called.[56]

"Captain, where's Platt?" demanded Theophilus Freeman.

The captain was unable to inform him, no one being on board answering to that name.

"Who shipped *that* nigger?" he again inquired of the captain, pointing to me.

"Burch," replied the captain.

"Your name is Platt—you answer my description. Why don't you come forward?" he demanded of me, in an angry tone.

I informed him that was not my name; that I had never been called by it, but that I had no objection to it as I knew of.

"Well, I will learn you your name," said he; "and so you won't forget it either, by—," he added.

Mr. Theophilus Freeman, by the way, was not a whit behind his partner, Burch, in the matter of blasphemy. On the vessel I had gone by the name of "Steward," and this was the first time I had ever been designated as Platt—the name forwarded by Burch to his consignee. From the vessel I observed the chain-gang at work on the levee. We passed near them as we were driven to Freeman's slave pen. This pen is very similar to Goodin's in Richmond, except the yard was enclosed by plank, standing upright, with ends sharpened, instead of brick walls.

Including us, there were now at least fifty in this pen. Depositing our blankets in one of the small buildings in the yard, and having been called up and fed, we were allowed to saunter about the enclosure until night, when we wrapped our blankets round us and laid down under the shed, or in the loft, or in the open yard, just as each one preferred.

It was but a short time I closed my eyes that night. Thought was busy in my brain. Could it be possible that I was thousands of miles from home—that I had been driven through the streets like a dumb beast—that I had been chained and beaten without any mercy—that I was even herded with a drove of slaves, a slave myself? Were the events of the last few weeks realities indeed?—or was I passing only through the dismal phases of a long, protracted dream? It was no illusion. My cup of sorrow was full to overflowing. Then I lifted up my hands to God, and in the still watches of the night, surrounded by the sleeping forms of my companions, begged for mercy on the poor, forsaken captive. To the Almighty Father of us all—the freeman and the slave—I poured forth the supplications of a broken spirit, imploring strength from on high to bear up against the burden of my troubles, until the morning light aroused the slumberers, ushering in another day of bondage.

Prayer
sub human

CHAPTER VI.

FREEMAN'S INDUSTRY—CLEANLINESS AND CLOTHES—EXERCISING
IN THE SHOW ROOM—THE DANCE—BOB, THE FIDDLER—ARRIVAL
OF CUSTOMERS—SLAVES EXAMINED—THE OLD GENTLEMAN OF
NEW-ORLEANS—SALE OF DAVID, CAROLINE AND LETHE—PARTING
OF RANDALL AND ELIZA—SMALL POX—THE HOSPITAL—RECOVERY
AND RETURN TO FREEMAN'S SLAVE PEN—THE PURCHASER OF
ELIZA, HARRY AND PLATT—ELIZA'S AGONY ON PARTING FROM
LITTLE EMILY.

The very amiable, pious-hearted Mr. Theophilus Freeman, a partner
or consignee of James H. Burch, and keeper of the slave pen in New-
Orleans, was out among his animals early in the morning.[57] With an
occasional kick of the older men and women, and many a sharp crack
of the whip about the ears of the younger slaves, it was not long
before they were all astir, and wide awake. Mr. Theophilus Freeman
bustled about in a very industrious manner, getting his property ready
for the sales-room, intending, no doubt, to do that day a rousing
business.
    In the first place we were required to wash thoroughly, and
those with beards, to shave. We were then furnished with a new suit
each, cheap, but clean. The men had hat, coat, shirt, pants and shoes;
the women frocks of calico, and handkerchiefs to bind about their
heads. We were now conducted into a large room in the front part of
the building to which the yard was attached, in order to be properly
trained, before the admission of customers. The men were arranged
on one side of the room, the women on the other. The tallest was
placed at the head of the row, then the next tallest, and so on in the
order of their respective heights. Emily was at the foot of the line of
women. Freeman charged us to remember our places; exhorted us to
appear smart and lively,—sometimes threatening, and again, holding
out various inducements. During the day he exercised us in the art of
"looking smart," and of moving to our places with exact precision.
    After being fed, in the afternoon, we were again paraded and
made to dance. Bob, a colored boy, who had some time belonged to

Freeman, played on the violin. Standing near him, I made bold to inquire if he could play the "Virginia Reel." He answered he could not, and asked me if I could play. Replying in the affirmative, he handed me the violin. I struck up a tune, and finished it. Freeman ordered me to continue playing, and seemed well pleased, telling Bob that I far excelled him—a remark that seemed to grieve my musical companion very much.

Next day many customers called to examine Freeman's "new lot." The latter gentleman was very loquacious, dwelling at much length upon our several good points and qualities. He would make us hold up our heads, walk briskly back and forth, while customers would feel of our hands and arms and bodies, turn us about, ask us what we could do, make us open our mouths and show our teeth, precisely as a jockey examines a horse which he is about to barter for or purchase. Sometimes a man or woman was taken back to the small house in the yard, stripped, and inspected more minutely. Scars upon a slave's back were considered evidence of a rebellious or unruly spirit, and hurt his sale.[58]

One old gentleman, who said he wanted a coachman, appeared to take a fancy to me. From his conversation with Burch, I learned he was a resident in the city. I very much desired that he would buy me, because I conceived it would not be difficult to make my escape from New-Orleans on some northern vessel. Freeman asked him fifteen hundred dollars for me. The old gentleman insisted it was too much, as times were very hard. Freeman, however, declared that I was sound and healthy, of good constitution, and intelligent. He made it a point to enlarge upon my musical attainments. The old gentleman argued quite adroitly that there was nothing extraordinary about the nigger, and finally, to my regret, went out, saying he would call again. During the day, however, a number of sales were made. David and Caroline were purchased together by a Natchez planter. They left us, grinning broadly, and in the most happy state of mind, caused by the fact of their not being separated. Lethe was sold to a planter of Baton Rouge, her eyes flashing with anger as she was led away.

The same man also purchased Randall. The little fellow was made to jump, and run across the floor, and perform many other feats, exhibiting his activity and condition. All the time the trade was going on, Eliza was crying aloud, and wringing her hands. She besought the man not to buy him, unless he also bought herself and

slaves were expensive

Emily. She promised, in that case, to be the most faithful slave that ever lived. The man answered that he could not afford it, and then Eliza burst into a paroxysm of grief, weeping plaintively. Freeman turned round to her, savagely, with his whip in his uplifted hand, ordering her to stop her noise, or he would flog her. He would not have such work—such snivelling; and unless she ceased that minute, he would take her to the yard and give her a hundred lashes. Yes, he would take the nonsense out of her pretty quick—if he didn't, might he be d—d. *damned* Eliza shrunk before him, and tried to wipe away her tears, but it was all in vain. She wanted to be with her children, she said, the little time she had to live. All the frowns and threats of Freeman, could not wholly silence the afflicted mother. She kept on begging and beseeching them, most piteously, not to separate the three. Over and over again she told them how she loved her boy. A great many times she repeated her former promises—how very faithful and obedient she would be; how hard she would labor day and night, to the last moment of her life, if he would only buy them all together. But it was of no avail; the man could not afford it. The bargain was agreed upon, and Randall must go alone. Then Eliza ran to him; embraced him passionately; kissed him again and again; told him to remember her— all the while her tears falling in the boy's face like rain.

Freeman damned her, calling her a blubbering, bawling wench, and ordered her to go to her place, and behave herself, and be somebody. He swore he wouldn't stand such stuff but a little longer. He would soon give her something to cry about, if she was not mighty careful, and *that* she might depend upon.

The planter from Baton Rouge, with his new purchases, was ready to depart.

"Don't cry, mama. I will be a good boy. Don't cry," said Randall, looking back, as they passed out of the door.

What has become of the lad, God knows. It was a mournful scene indeed. I would have cried myself if I had dared.

That night, nearly all who came in on the brig Orleans, were taken ill. They complained of violent pain in the head and back. Little Emily—a thing unusual with her—cried constantly. In the morning a physician was called in, but was unable to determine the nature of our complaint. While examining me, and asking questions touching my symptoms, I gave it as my opinion that it was an attack of small-pox—mentioning the fact of Robert's death as the reason of my belief. It might be so indeed, he thought, and he would send for the head physician of the hospital. Shortly, the head physician came—a small, light-haired man, whom they called Dr. Carr.[59] He pronounced it small-pox, whereupon there was much alarm throughout the yard. Soon after Dr. Carr left, Eliza, Emmy, Harry and myself were put into a hack and driven to the hospital—a large white marble building, standing on the outskirts of the city.[60] Harry and I were placed in a room in one of the upper stories. I became very sick. For three days I was entirely blind. While lying in this state one day, Bob came in, saying to Dr. Carr that Freeman had sent him over to inquire how we were getting on. Tell him, said the doctor, that Platt is very bad, but that if he survives until nine o'clock, he may recover.[61]

I expected to die. Though there was little in the prospect before me worth living for, the near approach of death appalled me. I thought I could have been resigned to yield up my life in the bosom of my family, but to expire in the midst of strangers, under such circumstances, was a bitter reflection.

There were a great number in the hospital, of both sexes, and of all ages. In the rear of the building coffins were manufactured. When one died, the bell tolled—a signal to the undertaker to come and bear away the body to the potter's field. Many times, each day and night, the tolling bell sent forth its melancholy voice, announcing another death. But my time had not yet come. The crisis having passed, I began to revive, and at the end of two weeks and two days, returned with Harry to the pen, bearing upon my face the effects of the malady, which to this day continues to disfigure it. Eliza and Emily were also brought back next day in a hack,[62] and again were we paraded in the sales-room, for the inspection and examination of purchasers. I still indulged the hope that the old gentleman in search of a coachman would call again, as he had promised, and purchase me. In that event I felt an abiding confidence that I would soon regain my liberty. Customer after customer entered, but the old gentleman never made his appearance.

At length, one day, while we were in the yard, Freeman came out and ordered us to our places, in the great room. A gentleman was waiting for us as we entered, and inasmuch as he will be often mentioned in the progress of this narrative, a description of his personal appearance, and my estimation of his character, at first sight, may not be out of place.

He was a man above the ordinary height, somewhat bent and stooping forward. He was a good-looking man, and appeared to have reached about the middle age of life. There was nothing repulsive in his presence; but on the other hand, there was something cheerful and attractive in his face, and in his tone of voice. The finer elements were all kindly mingled in his breast, as any one could see. He moved about among us, asking many questions, as to what we could do, and what labor we had been accustomed to; if we thought we would like to live with him, and would be good boys if he would buy us, and other interrogatories of like character.

After some further inspection, and conversation touching prices, he finally offered Freeman one thousand dollars for me, nine hundred for Harry, and seven hundred for Eliza. Whether the small-pox had depreciated our value, or from what cause Freeman had concluded to fall five hundred dollars from the price I was before held at, I cannot say. At any rate, after a little shrewd reflection, he announced his acceptance of the offer.[63]

As soon as Eliza heard it, she was in an agony again. By this time she had become haggard and hollow-eyed with sickness and with sorrow. It would be a relief if I could consistently pass over in silence the scene that now ensued. It recalls memories more mournful and affecting than any language can portray. I have seen mothers kissing for the last time the faces of their dead offspring; I have seen them looking down into the grave, as the earth fell with a dull sound upon their coffins, hiding them from their eyes forever; but never have I seen such an exhibition of intense, unmeasured, and unbounded grief, as when Eliza was parted from her child. She broke from her place in the line of women, and rushing down where Emily was standing, caught her in her arms. The child, sensible of some impending danger, instinctively fastened her hands around her mother's neck, and nestled her little head upon her bosom. Freeman sternly ordered her to be quiet, but she did not heed him. He caught her by the arm and pulled her rudely, but she only clung closer to the child. Then, with a volley of great oaths, he struck her such a heartless blow, that she staggered backward, and was like to fall. Oh! how piteously then did she beseech and beg and pray that they might not be separated. Why could they not be purchased together? Why not let her have one of her dear children? "Mercy, mercy, master!" she cried, falling on her knees. "Please, master, buy Emily. I can never work any if she is taken from me: I will die."

Freeman interfered again, but, disregarding him, she still pled most earnestly, telling how Randall had been taken from her—how she never would see him again, and now it was too bad—oh, God! it was too bad, too cruel, to take her away from Emily—her pride—her only darling, that could not live, it was so young, without its mother!

Finally, after much more supplication, the purchaser of Eliza stepped forward, evidently affected, and said to Freeman he would buy Emily, and asked him what her price was.

"What is her *price? Buy* her?" was the responsive interrogatory of Theophilus Freeman. And instantly answering his own inquiry, he added, "I won't sell her. She's not for sale."[64]

The man remarked he was not in need of one so young—that it would be of no profit to him, but since the mother was so fond of her, rather than see them separated, he would pay a reasonable price. But to this humane proposal Freeman was entirely deaf. He would not sell her then on any account whatever. There were heaps and piles of money to be made of her, he said, when she was a few years older. There were men enough in New-Orleans who would give five thousand dollars for such an extra, handsome, fancy piece as Emily would be, rather than not get her. No, no, he would not sell her then. She was a beauty—a picture—a doll—one of the regular bloods—none of your thick-lipped, bullet-headed, cotton-picking niggers—if she was might he be d—d.

When Eliza heard Freeman's determination not to part with Emily, she became absolutely frantic.

"I will *not* go without her. They shall *not* take her from me," she fairly shrieked, her shrieks commingling with the loud and angry voice of Freeman, commanding her to be silent.

Meantime Harry and myself had been to the yard and returned with our blankets, and were at the front door ready to leave. Our purchaser stood near us, gazing at Eliza with an expression indicative of regret at having bought her at the expense of so much sorrow. We waited some time, when, finally, Freeman, out of patience, tore Emily from her mother by main force, the two clinging to each other with all their might.

"Don't leave me, mama—don't leave me," screamed the child, as its mother was pushed harshly forward. "Don't leave me—come back, mama," she still cried, stretching forth her little arms imploringly.[65] But she cried in vain. Out of the door and into the street we were quickly hurried. Still we could hear her calling to her mother, "Come back—don't leave me—come back, mama," until her infant voice grew faint and still more faint, and gradually died away, as distance intervened, and finally was wholly lost. *A 65 re writing style*

Eliza never after saw or heard of Emily or Randall. Day nor night, however, were they ever absent from her memory. In the cotton field, in the cabin, always and everywhere, she was talking of them—often *to* them, as if they were actually present. Only when absorbed in that illusion, or asleep, did she ever have a moment's comfort afterwards.

She was no common slave, as has been said. To a large share of natural intelligence which she possessed, was added a general knowledge and information on most subjects. She had enjoyed opportunities such as are afforded to very few of her oppressed class. She had been lifted up into the regions of a higher life. Freedom— freedom for herself and for her offspring, for many years had been her cloud by day, her pillar of fire by night. In her pilgrimage through the wilderness of bondage, with eyes fixed upon that hope-inspiring beacon, she had at length ascended to "the top of Pisgah," and beheld "the land of promise." In an unexpected moment she was ut- terly overwhelmed with disappointment and despair. The glorious vision of liberty faded from her sight as they led her away into captivity. Now "she weepeth sore in the night, and tears are on her cheeks: all her friends have dealt treacherously with her: they have become her enemies."

Separation of Eliza and her last child

CHAPTER VII.

THE STEAMBOAT RODOLPH—DEPARTURE FROM NEW-ORLEANS—
WILLIAM FORD—ARRIVAL AT ALEXANDRIA, ON RED RIVER—
RESOLUTIONS—THE GREAT PINE WOODS—WILD CATTLE—MARTIN'S
SUMMER RESIDENCE—THE TEXAS ROAD—ARRIVAL AT MASTER
FORD'S—ROSE—MISTRESS FORD—SALLY, AND HER CHILDREN—
JOHN, THE COOK—WALTER, SAM, AND ANTONY—THE MILLS ON
INDIAN CREEK—SABBATH DAYS—SAM'S CONVERSION—THE PROFIT
OF KINDNESS—RAFTING—ADAM TAYDEM, THE LITTLE WHITE
MAN—CASCALLA AND HIS TRIBE—THE INDIAN BALL—JOHN M.
TIBEATS—THE STORM APPROACHING.

On leaving the New-Orleans slave pen, Harry and I followed our new master through the streets, while Eliza, crying and turning back, was forced along by Freeman and his minions, until we found ourselves on board the steamboat Rodolph, then lying at the levee.[66] In the course of half an hour we were moving briskly up the Mississippi, bound for some point on Red River. There were quite a number of slaves on board beside ourselves, just purchased in the New-Orleans market. I remember a Mr. Kelsow, who was said to be a well known and extensive planter, had in charge a gang of women.[67]

Our master's name was William Ford.[68] He resided then in the "Great Pine Woods," in the parish of Avoyelles, situated on the right bank of Red River, in the heart of Louisiana.[69] He is now a Baptist preacher. Throughout the whole parish of Avoyelles, and especially along both shores of Bayou Boeuf, where he is more intimately known, he is accounted by his fellow-citizens as a worthy minister of God. In many northern minds, perhaps, the idea of a man holding his brother man in servitude, and the traffic in human flesh, may seem altogether incompatible with their conceptions of a moral or religious life. From descriptions of such men as Burch and Freeman, and others hereinafter mentioned, they are led to despise and execrate the whole class of slaveholders, indiscriminately. But I was sometime his slave, and had an opportunity of learning well his character and disposition, and it is but simple justice to him when I say, in my

discuss.

opinion, there never was a more kind, noble, candid, Christian man than William Ford. The influences and associations that had always surrounded him, blinded him to the inherent wrong at the bottom of the system of Slavery. He never doubted the moral right of one man holding another in subjection. Looking through the same medium with his fathers before him, he saw things in the same light. Brought up under other circumstances and other influences, his notions would undoubtedly have been different. Nevertheless, he was a model master, walking uprightly, according to the light of his understanding, and fortunate was the slave who came to his possession. Were all men such as he, Slavery would be deprived of more than half its bitterness. *discuss. why would SN feel this way?*

We were two days and three nights on board the steamboat Rodolph, during which time nothing of particular interest occurred. I was now known as Platt, the name given me by Burch, and by which I was designated through the whole period of my servitude. Eliza was sold by the name of "Dradey." She was so distinguished in the conveyance to Ford, now on record in the recorder's office in New-Orleans.

On our passage I was constantly reflecting on my situation, and consulting with myself on the best course to pursue in order to effect my ultimate escape. Sometimes, not only then, but afterwards, I was almost on the point of disclosing fully to Ford the facts of my history. I am inclined now to the opinion it would have resulted in my benefit. This course was often considered, but through fear of its miscarriage, never put into execution, until eventually my transfer and his pecuniary embarrassments rendered it evidently unsafe. Afterwards, under other masters, unlike William Ford, I knew well enough the slightest knowledge of my real character would consign me at once to the remoter depths of Slavery. I was too costly a chattel to be lost, and was well aware that I would be taken farther on, into some by-place, over the Texan border, perhaps, and sold; that I would be disposed of as the thief disposes of his stolen horse, if my right to freedom was even whispered. So I resolved to lock the secret closely in my heart—never to utter one word or syllable as to who or what I was—trusting in Providence and my own shrewdness for deliverance. *reasons for not disclosing his free status*

At length we left the steamboat Rodolph at a place called Alexandria, several hundred miles from New-Orleans.[70] It is a small

town on the southern shore of Red River. Having remained there
over night, we entered the morning train of cars, and were soon at
Bayou Lamourie, a still smaller place, distant eighteen miles from
Alexandria.[71] At that time it was the termination of the railroad.[72]
Ford's plantation was situated on the Texas road, twelve miles from
Lamourie, in the Great Pine Woods.[73] This distance, it was
announced to us, must be traveled on foot, there being public
conveyances no farther. Accordingly we all set out in the company of
Ford. It was an excessively hot day. Harry, Eliza, and myself were yet
weak, and the bottoms of our feet were very tender from the effects
of the small-pox. We proceeded slowly, Ford telling us to take our
time and sit down and rest whenever we desired—a privilege that was
taken advantage of quite frequently. After leaving Lamourie and
crossing two plantations, one belonging to Mr. Carnell, the other to a
Mr. Flint,[74] we reached the Pine Woods, a wilderness that stretches to
the Sabine River.

The whole country about Red River is low and marshy.[75] The
Pine Woods, as they are called, is comparatively upland, with
frequent small intervals, however, running through them. This upland
is covered with numerous trees—the white oak, the chincopin,
resembling chestnut, but principally the yellow pine. They are of great
size, running up sixty feet, and perfectly straight. The woods were full
of cattle, very shy and wild, dashing away in herds, with a loud snuff,
at our approach. Some of them were marked or branded, the rest
appeared to be in their wild and untamed state. They are much
smaller than northern breeds, and the peculiarity about them that
most attracted my attention was their horns. They stand out from the
sides of the head precisely straight, like two iron spikes.[76]

At noon we reached a cleared piece of ground, containing three
or four acres. Upon it was a small, unpainted, wooden house, a corn
crib, or, as we would say, a barn, and a log kitchen, standing about a
rod from the house. It was the summer residence of Mr. Martin.[77]
Rich planters, having large establishments on Bayou Boeuf, are
accustomed to spend the warmer season in these woods. Here they
find clear water and delightful shades. In fact, these retreats are to the
planters of that section of the country what Newport and Saratoga
are to the wealthier inhabitants of northern cities.

We were sent around into the kitchen, and supplied with sweet
potatoes, corn-bread, and bacon, while Master Ford dined with

Martin in the house. There were several slaves about the premises. Martin came out and took a look at us, asking Ford the price of each, if we were green hands, and so forth, and making inquiries in relation to the slave market generally.

After a long rest we set forth again, following the Texas road, which had the appearance of being very rarely traveled. For five miles we passed through continuous woods without observing a single habitation. At length, just as the sun was sinking in the west, we entered another opening, containing some twelve or fifteen acres.

In this opening stood a house much larger than Mr. Martin's. It was two stories high, with a piazza in front. In the rear of it was also a log kitchen, poultry house, corncribs, and several negro cabins. Near the house was a peach orchard, and gardens of orange and pomegranate trees. The space was entirely surrounded by woods, and covered with a carpet of rich, rank verdure. It was a quiet, lonely, pleasant place—literally a green spot in the wilderness. It was the residence of my master, William Ford.

As we approached, a yellow girl—her name was Rose—was standing on the piazza. Going to the door, she called her mistress, who presently came running out to meet her lord. She kissed him, and laughingly demanded if he had bought "those niggers." Ford said he had, and told us to go round to Sally's cabin and rest ourselves. Turning the corner of the house, we discovered Sally washing—her two baby children near her, rolling on the grass. They jumped up and toddled towards us, looked at us a moment like a brace of rabbits, then ran back to their mother as if afraid of us.

Sally conducted us into the cabin, told us to lay down our bundles and be seated, for she was sure that we were tired. Just then John, the cook, a boy some sixteen years of age and blacker than any crow, came running in, looked steadily in our faces, then turning round, without saying as much as "how d'ye do," ran back to the kitchen, laughing loudly, as if our coming was a great joke indeed.

Much wearied with our walk, as soon as it was dark, Harry and I wrapped our blankets round us, and laid down upon the cabin floor. My thoughts, as usual, wandered back to my wife and children. The consciousness of my real situation; the hopelessness of any effort to escape through the wide forests of Avoyelles, pressed heavily upon me, yet my heart was at home in Saratoga.

I was awakened early in the morning by the voice of Master Ford, calling Rose. She hastened into the house to dress the children, Sally to the field to milk the cows, while John was busy in the kitchen preparing breakfast. In the meantime Harry and I were strolling about the yard, looking at our new quarters. Just after breakfast a colored man, driving three yoke of oxen, attached to a wagon load of lumber, drove into the opening. He was a slave of Ford's, named Walton, the husband of Rose. By the way, Rose was a native of Washington, and had been brought from thence five years before. She had never seen Eliza, but she had heard of Berry, and they knew the same streets, and the same people, either personally, or by reputation. They became fast friends immediately, and talked a great deal together of old times, and of friends they had left behind.

Ford was at that time a wealthy man. Besides his seat in the Pine Woods, he owned a large lumbering establishment on Indian Creek, four miles distant, and also, in his wife's right, an extensive plantation and many slaves on Bayou Boeuf.[78]

Walton had come with his load of lumber from the mills on Indian Creek. Ford directed us to return with him, saying he would follow us as soon as possible. Before leaving, Mistress Ford called me into the storeroom, and handed me, as it is there termed, a tin bucket of molasses for Harry and myself.

Eliza was still wringing her hands and deploring the loss of her children. Ford tried as much as possible to console her—told her she need not work very hard; that she might remain with Rose, and assist the madam in the house affairs.

Riding with Walton in the wagon, Harry and I became quite well acquainted with him long before reaching Indian Creek. He was a "born thrall" of Ford's, and spoke kindly and affectionately of him, as a child would speak of his own father. In answer to his inquiries from whence I came, I told him from Washington. Of that city, he had heard much from his wife, Rose, and all the way plied me with many extravagant and absurd questions.

On reaching the mills at Indian Creek, we found two more of Ford's slaves, Sam and Antony. Sam, also, was a Washingtonian, having been brought out in the same gang with Rose. He had worked on a farm near Georgetown. Antony was a blacksmith, from Kentucky, who had been in his present master's service about ten years. Sam knew Burch, and when informed that he was the trader who had sent me on from Washington, it was remarkable how well we agreed upon the subject of his superlative rascality. He had forwarded Sam, also.

On Ford's arrival at the mills, we were employed in piling lumber, and chopping logs, which occupation we continued during the remainder of the summer.

We usually spent our Sabbaths at the opening, on which days our master would gather all his slaves about him, and read and expound the Scriptures. He sought to inculcate in our minds feelings of kindness towards each other, of dependence upon God—setting forth the rewards promised unto those who lead an upright and prayerful life. Seated in the doorway of his house, surrounded by his man-servants and his maid-servants, who looked earnestly into the good man's face, he spoke of the loving kindness of the Creator, and of the life that is to come. Often did the voice of prayer ascend from his lips to heaven, the only sound that broke the solitude of the place.

In the course of the summer Sam became deeply convicted, his mind dwelling intensely on the subject of religion. His mistress gave him a Bible, which he carried with him to his work. Whatever leisure time was allowed him, he spent in perusing it, though it was only with great difficulty that he could master any part of it.[79] I often read to him, a favor which he well repaid me by many expressions of gratitude. Sam's piety was frequently observed by white men who came to the mill, and the remark it most generally provoked was, that a man like Ford, who allowed his slaves to have Bibles, was "not fit to own a nigger." *n. 79 on blacks/slaves as church members*

He, however, lost nothing by his kindness. It is a fact I have more than once observed, that those who treated their slaves most leniently, were rewarded by the greatest amount of labor. I know it from my own experience. It was a source of pleasure to surprise Master Ford with a greater day's work than was required, while, under subsequent masters, there was no prompter to extra effort but the overseer's lash.

It was the desire of Ford's approving voice that suggested to me an idea that resulted to his profit. The lumber we were manufacturing was contracted to be delivered at Lamourie. It had hitherto been transported by land, and was an important item of expense. Indian Creek, upon which the mills were situated, was a narrow but deep stream emptying into Bayou Boeuf. In some places it was not more than twelve feet wide,_and much obstructed with trunks of trees. Bayou Boeuf was connected with Bayou Lamourie. I ascertained the distance from the mills to the point on the latter bayou, where our lumber was to be delivered, was but a few miles less by land than by water. Provided the creek could be made navigable for rafts, it occurred to me that the expense of transportation would be materially diminished.

Adam Taydem, a little white man, who had been a soldier in Florida, and had strolled into that distant region, was foreman and superintendent of the mills.[80] He scouted the idea; but Ford, when I laid it before him, received it favorably, and permitted me to try the experiment.

Having removed the obstructions, I made up a narrow raft, consisting of twelve cribs. At this business I think I was quite skillful, not having forgotten my experience years before on the Champlain canal. I labored hard, being extremely anxious to succeed, both from a desire to please my master, and to show Adam Taydem that my scheme was not such a visionary one as he incessantly pronounced it. One hand could manage three cribs. I took charge of the forward three, and commenced poling down the creek. In due time we entered the first bayou, and finally reached our destination in a shorter period of time than I had anticipated.

The arrival of the raft at Lamourie created a sensation, while Mr. Ford loaded me with commendations.[81] On all sides I heard Ford's Platt pronounced the "smartest nigger in the Pine Woods"—in fact I was the Fulton of Indian Creek. I was not insensible to the praise bestowed upon me, and enjoyed, especially, my triumph over Taydem, whose half-malicious ridicule had stung my pride. From this time the entire control of bringing the lumber to Lamourie was placed in my hands until the contract was fulfilled.

Indian Creek, in its whole length, flows through a magnificent forest. There dwells on its shore a tribe of Indians, a remnant of the Chickasaws or Chickopees, if I remember rightly.[82] They live in simple huts, ten or twelve feet square, constructed of pine poles and covered with bark. They subsist principally on the flesh of the deer, the coon, and opossum, all of which are plenty in these woods. Sometimes they exchange venison for a little corn and whisky with the planters on the bayous. Their usual dress is buckskin breeches and calico hunting shirts of fantastic colors, buttoned from belt to

SN's idea : rafting logs to save $

chin. They wear brass rings on their wrists, and in their ears and noses. The dress of the squaws is very similar. They are fond of dogs and horses—owning many of the latter, of a small, tough breed—and are skillful riders. Their bridles, girths and saddles were made of raw skins of animals; their stirrups of a certain kind of wood. Mounted astride their ponies, men and women, I have seen them dash out into the woods at the utmost of their speed, following narrow winding paths, and dodging trees, in a manner that eclipsed the most miraculous feats of civilized equestrianism. Circling away in various directions, the forest echoing and re-echoing with their whoops, they would presently return at the same dashing, headlong speed with which they started. Their village was on Indian Creek, known as Indian Castle, but their range extended to the Sabine River. Occasionally a tribe from Texas would come over on a visit, and then there was indeed a carnival in the "Great Pine Woods." Chief of the tribe was Cascalla; second in rank, John Baltese, his son-in-law; with both of whom, as with many others of the tribe, I became acquainted during my frequent voyages down the creek with rafts. Sam and myself would often visit them when the day's task was done. They were obedient to the chief; the word of Cascalla was their law. They were a rude but harmless people, and enjoyed their wild mode of life. They had little fancy for the open country, the cleared lands on the shores of the bayous, but preferred to hide themselves within the shadows of the forest. They worshiped the Great Spirit, loved whiskey, and were happy.

On one occasion I was present at a dance, when a roving herd from Texas had encamped in their village. The entire carcass of a deer was roasting before a large fire, which threw its light a long distance among the trees under which they were assembled. When they had formed in a ring, men and squaws alternately, a sort of Indian fiddle set up an indescribable tune. It was a continuous, melancholy kind of wavy sound, with the slightest possible variation. At the first note, if indeed there was more than one note in the whole tune, they circled around, trotting after each other, and giving utterance to a guttural, sing-song noise, equally as nondescript as the music of the fiddle. At the end of the third circuit, they would stop suddenly, whoop as if their lungs would crack, then break from the ring, forming in couples, man and squaw, each jumping backwards as far as possible from the other, then forwards—which graceful feat having been twice or thrice accomplished, they would form in a ring, and go trotting round again. The best dancer appeared to be considered the one who could whoop the loudest, jump the farthest, and utter the most excruciating noise. At intervals, one or more would leave the dancing circle, and going to the fire, cut from the roasting carcass a slice of venison.

In a hole, shaped like a mortar, cut in the trunk of a fallen tree, they pounded corn with a wooden pestle, and of the meal made cake. Alternately they danced and ate. Thus were the visitors from Texas entertained by the dusky sons and daughters of the Chicopees, and such is a description, as I saw it, of an Indian ball in the Pine Woods of Avoyelles.[83]

In the autumn, I left the mills, and was employed at the opening. One day the mistress was urging Ford to procure a loom, in order that Sally might commence weaving cloth for the winter garments of the slaves. He could not imagine where one was to be found, when I suggested that the easiest way to get one would be to make it, informing him at the same time, that I was a sort of "Jack at all trades," and would attempt it, with his permission. It was granted very readily, and I was allowed to go to a neighboring planter's to inspect one before commencing the undertaking. At length it was finished and pronounced by Sally to be perfect. She could easily weave her task of fourteen yards, milk the cows, and have leisure time besides each day. It worked so well, I was continued in the employment of making looms, which were taken down to the plantation on the bayou.

At this time one John M. Tibeats, a carpenter, came to the opening to do some work on master's house. I was directed to quit the looms and assist him. For two weeks I was in his company, planing and matching boards for ceiling, a plastered room being a rare thing in the parish of Avoyelles.

John M. Tibeats was the opposite of Ford in all respects. He was a small, crabbed, quick-tempered, spiteful man.[84] He had no fixed residence that I ever heard of, but passed from one plantation to another, wherever he could find employment. He was without standing in the community, not esteemed by white men, nor even respected by slaves. He was ignorant, withal, and of a revengeful disposition. He left the parish long before I did, and I know not whether he is at present alive or dead. Certain it is, it was a most unlucky day for me that brought us together. During my residence with Master Ford I had seen only the bright side of slavery. His was no heavy hand crushing us to the earth. *He* pointed upwards, and with benign and cheering words addressed us as his fellow-mortals, accountable, like himself, to the Maker of us all. I think of him with affection, and had my family been with me, could have borne his gentle servitude, without murmuring, all my days. But clouds were gathering in the horizon—forerunners of a pitiless storm that was soon to break over me. I was doomed to endure such bitter trials as the poor slave only knows, and to lead no more the comparatively happy life which I had led in the "Great Pine Woods."

closing of the chapters nicely lead into what follows. always well-written. a "tag."

CHAPTER VIII.

FORD'S EMBARRASSMENTS—THE SALE TO TIBEATS—THE CHATTEL
MORTGAGE—MISTRESS FORD'S PLANTATION ON BAYOU BOEUF—
DESCRIPTION OF THE LATTER—FORD'S BROTHER-IN-LAW, PETER
TANNER—MEETING WITH ELIZA—SHE STILL MOURNS FOR HER
CHILDREN—FORD'S OVERSEER, CHAPIN—TIBEAT'S ABUSE—THE KEG
OF NAILS—THE FIRST FIGHT WITH TIBEATS—HIS DISCOMFITURE
AND CASTIGATION—THE ATTEMPT TO HANG ME—CHAPIN'S
INTERFERENCE AND SPEECH—UNHAPPY REFLECTIONS—ABRUPT
DEPARTURE OF TIBEATS, COOK AND RAMSEY—LAWSON AND THE
BROWN MULE—MESSAGE TO THE PINE WOODS.

William Ford unfortunately became embarrassed in his pecuniary
affairs. A heavy judgment was rendered against him in consequence
of his having become security for his brother, Franklin Ford, residing
on Red River, above Alexandria, and who had failed to meet his
liabilities.[85] He was also indebted to John M. Tibeats to a considerable
amount in consideration of his services in building the mills on
Indian Creek, and also a weaving-house, corn-mill and other erec-
tions on the plantation at Bayou Boeuf, not yet completed. It was
therefore necessary, in order to meet these demands, to dispose of
eighteen slaves, myself among the number. Seventeen of them,
including Sam and Harry, were purchased by Peter Compton, a
planter also residing on Red River.[86]

I was sold to Tibeats, in consequence, undoubtedly, of my slight
skill as a carpenter. This was in the winter of 1842. The deed of
myself from Freeman to Ford, as I ascertained from the public
records in New-Orleans on my return, was dated June 23d 1841. At
the time of my sale to Tibeats, the price agreed to be given for me
being more than the debt, Ford took a chattel mortgage of four
hundred dollars.[87] I am indebted for my life, as will hereafter be seen,
to that mortgage.

I bade farewell to my good friends at the opening, and departed
with my new master Tibeats. We went down to the plantation on
Bayou Boeuf, distant twenty-seven miles from the Pine Woods, to

complete the unfinished contract. Bayou Boeuf is a sluggish, winding stream—one of those stagnant bodies of water common in that region, setting back from Red River.[88] It stretches from a point not far from Alexandria, in a south-easterly direction, and following its tortuous course, is more than fifty miles in length. Large cotton and sugar plantations line each shore, extending back to the borders of interminable swamps. It is alive with alligators, rendering it unsafe for swine, or unthinking slave children to stroll along its banks. Upon a bend in this bayou, a short distance from Cheneyville, was situated the plantation of Madam Ford—her brother, Peter Tanner, a great landholder, living on the opposite side.[89]

On my arrival at Bayou Boeuf, I had the pleasure of meeting Eliza, whom I had not seen for several months. She had not pleased Mrs. Ford, being more occupied in brooding over her sorrows than in attending to her business, and had, in consequence, been sent down to work in the field on the plantation. She had grown feeble and emaciated, and was still mourning for her children. She asked me if I had forgotten them, and a great many times inquired if I still remembered how handsome little Emily was—how much Randall loved her—and wondered if they were living still, and where the darlings could then be. She had sunk beneath the weight of an excessive grief. Her drooping form and hollow cheeks too plainly indicated that she had well nigh reached the end of her weary road.

Ford's overseer on this plantation, and who had the exclusive charge of it, was a Mr. Chapin, a kindly-disposed man, and a native of Pennsylvania.[90] In common with others, he held Tibeats in light estimation, which fact, in connection with the four hundred dollar mortgage, was fortunate for me.

I was now compelled to labor very hard. From earliest dawn until late at night, I was not allowed to be a moment idle. Notwithstanding which, Tibeats was never satisfied. He was continually cursing and complaining. He never spoke to me a kind word. I was his faithful slave, and earned him large wages every day, and yet I went to my cabin nightly, loaded with abuse and stinging epithets.

We had completed the corn mill, the kitchen, and so forth, and were at work upon the weaving-house, when I was guilty of an act, in that State punishable with death. It was my first fight with Tibeats. The weaving-house we were erecting stood in the orchard a few rods from the residence of Chapin, or the "great house," as it was called.[91] One night, having worked until it was too dark to see, I was ordered by Tibeats to rise very early in the morning, procure a keg of nails from Chapin, and commence putting on the clapboards. I retired to the cabin extremely tired, and having cooked a supper of bacon and corn cake, and conversed a while with Eliza, who occupied the same cabin, as also did Lawson and his wife Mary, and a slave named Bristol, laid down upon the ground floor, little dreaming of the sufferings that awaited me on the morrow. Before daylight I was on the piazza of the "great house," awaiting the appearance of overseer Chapin.[92] To have aroused him from his slumbers and stated my errand, would have been an unpardonable boldness. At length he came out. Taking off my hat, I informed him Master Tibeats had directed me to call upon him for a keg of nails. Going into the store-room, he rolled it out, at the same time saying, if Tibeats preferred a different size, he would endeavor to furnish them, but that I might use those until further directed. Then mounting his horse, which stood saddled and bridled at the door, he rode away into the field, whither the slaves had preceded him, while I took the keg on my shoulder, and proceeding to the weaving-house, broke in the head, and commenced nailing on the clapboards.

As the day began to open, Tibeats came out of the house to where I was, hard at work. He seemed to be that morning even more morose and disagreeable than usual. He was my master, entitled by law to my flesh and blood, and to exercise over me such tyrannical control as his mean nature prompted; but there was no law that could prevent my looking upon him with intense contempt. I despised both his disposition and his intellect. I had just come round to the keg for a further supply of nails, as he reached the weaving-house.

"I thought I told you to commence putting on weather-boards this morning," he remarked.

"Yes, master, and I am about it," I replied.

"Where?" he demanded.

"On the other side," was my answer.

He walked round to the other side, examined my work for a while, muttering to himself in a fault-finding tone.

"Didn't I tell you last night to get a keg of nails of Chapin?" he broke forth again.

"Yes, master, and so I did; and overseer said he would get another size for you, if you wanted them, when he came back from the field."

Tibeats walked to the keg, looked a moment at the contents, then kicked it violently. Coming towards me in a great passion, he exclaimed,

"G—d d—n you! I thought you *knowed* something."

I made answer: "I tried to do as you told me, master. I didn't mean anything wrong. Overseer said—" But he interrupted me with such a flood of curses that I was unable to finish the sentence. At length he ran towards the house, and going to the piazza, took down one of the overseer's whips. The whip had a short wooden stock, braided over with leather, and was loaded at the butt. The lash was three feet long, or thereabouts, and made of raw-hide strands.

At first I was somewhat frightened, and my impulse was to run. There was no one about except Rachel, the cook, and Chapin's wife, and neither of them were to be seen. The rest were in the field. I knew he intended to whip me, and it was the first time any one had attempted it since my arrival at Avoyelles. I felt, moreover, that I had been faithful—that I was guilty of no wrong whatever, and deserved commendation rather than punishment. My fear changed to anger, and before he reached me I had made up my mind fully not to be whipped, let the result be life or death.

Winding the lash around his hand, and taking hold of the small end of the stock, he walked up to me, and with a malignant look, ordered me to strip.

"Master Tibeats," said I, looking him boldly in the face, "I will *not*." I was about to say something further in justification, but with concentrated vengeance, he sprang upon me, seizing me by the throat with one hand, raising the whip with the other, in the act of striking. Before the blow descended, however, I had caught him by the collar of the coat, and drawn him closely to me. Reaching down, I seized him by the ankle, and pushing him back with the other hand, he fell over on the ground. Putting one arm around his leg, and holding it to my breast, so that his head and shoulders only touched the ground, I placed my foot upon his neck. He was completely in my power. My blood was up. It seemed to course through my veins like fire. In the frenzy of my madness I snatched the whip from his hand. He struggled with all his power; swore that I should not live to see

another day; and that he would tear out my heart. But his struggles and his threats were alike in vain. I cannot tell how many times I struck him. Blow after blow fell fast and heavy upon his wriggling form. At length he screamed—cried murder—and at last the blasphemous tyrant called on God for mercy. But he who had never shown mercy did not receive it. The stiff stock of the whip warped round his cringing body until my right arm ached.

Until this time I had been too busy to look about me. Desisting for a moment, I saw Mrs. Chapin looking from the window, and Rachel standing in the kitchen door. Their attitudes expressed the utmost excitement and alarm. His screams had been heard in the field. Chapin was coming as fast as he could ride. I struck him a blow or two more, then pushed him from me with such a well-directed kick that he went rolling over on the ground.

Rising to his feet, and brushing the dirt from his hair, he stood looking at me, pale with rage. We gazed at each other in silence. Not a word was uttered until Chapin galloped up to us.

"What is the matter?" he cried out.

"Master Tibeats wants to whip me for using the nails you gave me," I replied.

"What is the matter with the nails?" he inquired, turning to Tibeats.

Tibeats answered to the effect that they were too large, paying little heed, however, to Chapin's question, but still keeping his snakish eyes fastened maliciously on me.

"I am overseer here," Chapin began. "I told Platt to take them and use them, and if they were not of the proper size I would get others on returning from the field. It is not his fault. Besides, I shall furnish such nails as I please. I hope you will understand *that*, Mr. Tibeats."

Tibeats made no reply, but, grinding his teeth and shaking his fist, swore he would have satisfaction, and that it was not half over yet. Thereupon he walked away, followed by the overseer, and entered the house, the latter talking to him all the while in a suppressed tone, and with earnest gestures.

I remained where I was, doubting whether it was better to fly or abide the result, whatever it might be. Presently Tibeats came out of the house, and, saddling his horse, the only property he possessed besides myself, departed on the road to Cheneyville.

He owns a horse & a man?

When he was gone, Chapin came out, visibly excited, telling me not to stir, not to attempt to leave the plantation on any account whatever. He then went to the kitchen, and calling Rachel out, conversed with her some time. Coming back, he again charged me with great earnestness not to run, saying my master was a rascal; that he had left on no good errand, and that there might be trouble before night. But at all events, he insisted upon it, I must not stir.

As I stood there, feelings of unutterable agony overwhelmed me. I was conscious that I had subjected myself to unimaginable punishment. The reaction that followed my extreme ebullition of anger produced the most painful sensations of regret. An unfriended, helpless slave—what could I *do*, what could I *say*, to justify, in the remotest manner, the heinous act I had committed, of resenting a *white* man's contumely and abuse.[93] I tried to pray—I tried to beseech my Heavenly Father to sustain me in my sore extremity, but emotion choked my utterance, and I could only bow my head upon my hands and weep. For at least an hour I remained in this situation, finding relief only in tears, when, looking up, I beheld Tibeats, accompanied by two horsemen, coming down the bayou. They rode into the yard, jumped from their horses, and approached me with large whips, one of them also carrying a coil of rope.

"Cross your hands," commanded Tibeats, with the addition of such a shuddering expression of blasphemy as is not decorous to repeat.

"You need not bind me, Master Tibeats, I am ready to go with you anywhere," said I.

One of his companions then stepped forward, swearing if I made the least resistance he would break my head—he would tear me limb from limb—he would cut my black throat—and giving wide scope to other similar expressions. Perceiving any importunity altogether vain, I crossed my hands, submitting humbly to whatever disposition they might please to make of me. Thereupon Tibeats tied my wrists, drawing the rope around them with his utmost strength. Then he bound my ankles in the same manner. In the meantime the other two had slipped a cord within my elbows, running it across my back, and tying it firmly. It was utterly impossible to move hand or foot. With a remaining piece of rope Tibeats made an awkward noose, and placed it about my neck.

read

"Now, then," inquired one of Tibeats' companions, "where shall we hang the nigger?" *oopsie*

One proposed such a limb, extending from the body of a peach tree, near the spot where we were standing. His comrade objected to it, alleging it would break, and proposed another. Finally they fixed upon the latter.

During this conversation, and all the time they were binding me, I uttered not a word. Overseer Chapin, during the progress of the scene, was walking hastily back and forth on the piazza. Rachel was crying by the kitchen door, and Mrs. Chapin was still looking from the window. Hope died within my heart. Surely my time had come. I should never behold the light of another day—never behold the faces of my children—the sweet anticipation I had cherished with such fondness. I should that hour struggle through the fearful agonies of death! None would mourn for me—none revenge me. Soon my form would be mouldering in that distant soil, or, perhaps, be cast to the slimy reptiles that filled the stagnant waters of the bayou! Tears flowed down my cheeks, but they only afforded a subject of insulting comment for my executioners. *explain*

At length, as they were dragging me towards the tree, Chapin, who had momentarily disappeared from the piazza, came out of the house and walked towards us. He had a pistol in each hand, and as near as I can now recall to mind, spoke in a firm, determined manner, as follows:

"Gentlemen, I have a few words to say. You had better listen to them. Whoever moves that slave another foot from where he stands is a dead man. In the first place, he does not deserve this treatment. It is a shame to murder him in this manner. I never knew a more faithful boy than Platt. You, Tibeats, are in the fault yourself. You are pretty much of a scoundrel, and I know it, and you richly deserve the flogging you have received. In the next place, I have been overseer of this plantation seven years, and, in the absence of William Ford, am master here. My duty is to protect his interests, and that duty I shall perform. You are not responsible—you are a worthless fellow. Ford holds a mortgage on Platt of four hundred dollars. If you hang him, he loses his debt. Until that is canceled you have no right to take his life. You have no right to take it any way. There is a law for the slave as well as for the white man. You are no better than a murderer.

discuss

Chapin saves him

"As for you," addressing Cook and Ramsay, a couple of overseers from neighboring plantations, "as for you—begone! If you have any regard for your own safety, I say, begone."[94]

Cook and Ramsay, without a further word, mounted their horses and rode away. Tibeats, in a few minutes, evidently in fear, and overawed by the decided tone of Chapin, sneaked off like a coward, as he was, and mounting his horse, followed his companions.

I remained standing where I was, still bound, with the rope around my neck. As soon as they were gone, Chapin called Rachel, ordering her to run to the field, and tell Lawson to hurry to the house without delay, and bring the brown mule with him, an animal much prized for its unusual fleetness. Presently the boy appeared.

"Lawson," said Chapin, "you must go to the Pine Woods. Tell your Master Ford to come here at once—that he must not delay a single moment. Tell him they are trying to murder Platt. Now hurry, boy. Be at the Pine Woods by noon if you kill the mule."

Chapin stepped into the house and wrote a pass. When he returned, Lawson was at the door, mounted on his mule. Receiving the pass, he plied the whip right smartly to the beast, dashed out of the yard, and turning up the bayou on a hard gallop, in less time than it has taken me to describe the scene, was out of sight.[95]

Chapin rescues Solomon from hanging

CHAPTER IX.

THE HOT SUN—YET BOUND—THE CORDS SINK INTO MY FLESH—
CHAPIN'S UNEASINESS—SPECULATION—RACHEL, AND HER CUP OF
WATER—SUFFERING INCREASES—THE HAPPINESS OF SLAVERY—
ARRIVAL OF FORD—HE CUTS THE CORDS WHICH BIND ME, AND
TAKES THE ROPE FROM MY NECK—MISERY—THE GATHERING OF
THE SLAVES IN ELIZA'S CABIN—THEIR KINDNESS—RACHEL REPEATS
THE OCCURRENCES OF THE DAY—LAWSON ENTERTAINS HIS
COMPANIONS WITH AN ACCOUNT OF HIS RIDE—CHAPIN'S
APPREHENSIONS OF TIBEATS—HIRED TO PETER TANNER—PETER
EXPOUNDS THE SCRIPTURES—DESCRIPTION OF THE STOCKS.

As the sun approached the meridian that day it became insufferably warm. Its hot rays scorched the ground. The earth almost blistered the foot that stood upon it. I was without coat or hat, standing bareheaded, exposed to its burning blaze. Great drops of perspiration rolled down my face, drenching the scanty apparel wherewith I was clothed. Over the fence, a very little way off, the peach trees cast their cool, delicious shadows on the grass. I would gladly have given a long year of service to have been enabled to exchange the heated oven, as it were, wherein I stood, for a seat beneath their branches. But I was yet bound, the rope still dangling from my neck, and standing in the same tracks where Tibeats and his comrades left me. I could not move an inch, so firmly had I been bound. To have been enabled to lean against the weaving house would have been a luxury indeed. But it was far beyond my reach, though distant less than twenty feet. I wanted to lie down, but knew I could not rise again. The ground was so parched and boiling hot I was aware it would but add to the discomfort of my situation. If I could have only moved my position, however slightly, it would have been relief unspeakable. But the hot rays of a southern sun, beating all the long summer day on my bare head, produced not half the suffering I experienced from my aching limbs. My wrists and ankles, and the cords of my legs and arms began to swell, burying the rope that bound them into the swollen flesh.

All day Chapin walked back and forth upon the stoop, but not once approached me. He appeared to be in a state of great uneasiness, looking first towards me, and then up the road, as if expecting some arrival every moment. He did not go to the field, as was his custom. It was evident from his manner that he supposed Tibeats would return with more and better armed assistance, perhaps, to renew the quarrel, and it was equally evident he had prepared his mind to defend my life at whatever hazard. Why he did not relieve me—why he suffered me to remain in agony the whole weary day, I never knew. It was not for want of sympathy, I am certain. Perhaps he wished Ford to see the rope about my neck, and the brutal manner in which I had been bound; perhaps his interference with another's property in which he had no legal interest might have been a trespass, which would have subjected him to the penalty of the law. Why Tibeats was all day absent was another mystery I never could divine. He knew well enough that Chapin would not harm him unless he persisted in his design against me. Lawson told me afterwards, that, as he passed the plantation of John David Cheney,[96] he saw the three, and that they turned and looked after him as he flew by. I think his supposition was, that Lawson had been sent out by Overseer Chapin to arouse the neighboring planters, and to call on them to come to his assistance. He, therefore, undoubtedly, acted on that principle, that "discretion is the better part of valor," and kept away.

But whatever motive may have governed the cowardly and malignant tyrant, it is of no importance. There I still stood in the noon-tide sun, groaning with pain. From long before daylight I had not eaten a morsel. I was growing faint with pain, and thirst, and hunger. Once only, in the very hottest portion of the day, Rachel, half fearful she was acting contrary to the overseer's wishes, ventured to me, and held a cup of water to my lips. The humble creature never knew, nor could she comprehend if she had heard them, the blessings I invoked upon her, for that balmy draught. She could only say, "Oh, Platt, how I do pity you," and then hastened back to her labors in the kitchen.

Never did the sun move so slowly through the heavens—never did it shower down such fervent and fiery rays, as it did that day. At least, so it appeared to me. What my meditations were—the innumerable thoughts that thronged through my distracted brain—I will not attempt to give expression to. Suffice it to say, during the whole long day I came not to the conclusion, even once, that the southern slave, fed, clothed, whipped and protected by his master, is happier than the free colored citizen of the North. To that conclusion I have never since arrived. There are many, however, even in the Northern States, benevolent and well-disposed men, who will pronounce my opinion erroneous, and gravely proceed to substantiate the assertion with an argument. Alas! they have never drunk, as I have, from the bitter cup of slavery. Just at sunset my heart leaped with unbounded joy, as Ford came riding into the yard, his horse covered with foam. Chapin met him at the door, and after conversing a short time, he walked directly to me.

"Poor Platt, you are in a bad state," was the only expression that escaped his lips.

"Thank God!" said I, "thank God, Master Ford, that you have come at last."

Drawing a knife from his pocket, he indignantly cut the cord from my wrists, arms, and ankles, and slipped the noose from my neck. I attempted to walk, but staggered like a drunken man, and fell partially to the ground.

Ford returned immediately to the house, leaving me alone again. As he reached the piazza, Tibeats and his two friends rode up. A long dialogue followed. I could hear the sound of their voices, the mild tones of Ford mingling with the angry accents of Tibeats, but was unable to distinguish what was said. Finally, the three departed again, apparently not well pleased.

I endeavored to raise the hammer, thinking to show Ford how willing I was to work, by proceeding with my labors on the weaving house, but it fell from my nerveless hand. At dark I crawled into the cabin, and laid down. I was in great misery—all sore and swollen—the slightest movement producing excruciating suffering. Soon the hands came in from the field. Rachel, when she went after Lawson, had told them what had happened. Eliza and Mary broiled me a piece of bacon, but my appetite was gone. Then they scorched some corn meal and made coffee. It was all that I could take. Eliza consoled me and was very kind. It was not long before the cabin was full of slaves. They gathered round me, asking many questions about the difficulty with Tibeats in the morning—and the particulars of all the occurrences of the day. Then Rachel came in, and in her simple language, repeated it over again—dwelling emphatically on the kick that sent Tibeats rolling over on the ground—whereupon there was a general titter throughout the crowd. Then she described how Chapin walked out with his pistols and rescued me, and how Master Ford cut the ropes with his knife, just as if he was mad.

By this time Lawson had returned. He had to regale them with an account of his trip to the Pine Woods—how the brown mule bore him faster than a "streak o'lightnin"—how he astonished everybody as he flew along—how Master Ford started right away—how he said Platt was a good nigger, and they shouldn't kill him, concluding with pretty strong intimations that there was not another human being in the wide world, who could have created such a universal sensation on the road, or performed such a marvelous John Gilpin feat, as he had done that day on the brown mule.[97]

The kind creatures loaded me with the expression of their sympathy—saying, Tibeats was a hard, cruel man, and hoping "Massa Ford" would get me back again. In this manner they passed the time, discussing, chatting, talking over and over again the exciting affair, until suddenly Chapin presented himself at the cabin door and called me.

"Platt," said he, "you will sleep on the floor in the great house to-night; bring your blanket with you."

I arose as quickly as I was able, took my blanket in my hand, and followed him. On the way he informed me that he should not wonder if Tibeats was back again before morning—that he intended to kill me—and that he did not mean he should do it without witnesses. Had he stabbed me to the heart in the presence of a hundred slaves, not one of them, by the laws of Louisiana, could have given evidence against him.[98] I laid down on the floor in the "great house"—the first and the last time such a sumptuous resting place was granted me during my twelve years of bondage—and tried to sleep. Near midnight the dog began to bark. Chapin arose, looked from the window, but could discover nothing. At length the dog was quiet. As he returned to his room, he said, "I believe, Platt, that scoundrel is skulking about the premises somewhere. If the dog barks again, and I am sleeping, wake me."

I promised to do so. After the lapse of an hour or more, the dog re-commenced his clamor, running towards the gate, then back again, all the while barking furiously.

Chapin was out of bed without waiting to be called. On this occasion, he stepped forth upon the piazza, and remained standing there a considerable length of time. Nothing, however, was to be seen, and the dog returned to his kennel. We were not disturbed again during the night. The excessive pain that I suffered, and the dread of some impending danger, prevented any rest whatever. Whether or not Tibeats did actually return to the plantation that night, seeking an opportunity to wreak his vengeance upon me, is a secret known only to himself, perhaps. I thought then, however, and have the strong impression still, that he was there. At all events, he had the disposition of an assassin—cowering before a brave man's words, but ready to strike his helpless or unsuspecting victim in the back, as I had reason afterwards to know. *foreshadowing narrative technique*

At daylight in the morning, I arose, sore and weary, having rested little. Nevertheless, after partaking breakfast, which Mary and Eliza had prepared for me in the cabin, I proceeded to the weaving house and commenced the labors of another day. It was Chapin's practice, as it is the practice of overseers generally, immediately on arising, to bestride his horse, always saddled and bridled and ready for him—the particular business of some slave—and ride into the *info* field. This morning, on the contrary, he came to the weaving house, asking if I had seen anything of Tibeats yet. Replying in the negative, he remarked there was something not right about the fellow—there was bad blood in him—that I must keep a sharp watch of him, or he would do me wrong some day when I least expected it.

While he was yet speaking, Tibeats rode in, hitched his horse, and entered the house. I had little fear of him while Ford and Chapin were at hand, but they could not be near me always.

Oh! how heavily the weight of slavery pressed upon me then. I must toil day after day, endure abuse and taunts and scoffs, sleep on the hard ground, live on the coarsest fare, and not only this, but live the slave of a blood-seeking wretch, of whom I must stand henceforth in continued fear and dread. Why had I not died in my young years—before God had given me children to love and live for? *family* What unhappiness and suffering and sorrow it would have prevented. I sighed for liberty; but the bondman's chain was round me, and could not be shaken off. I could only gaze wistfully towards the North, and think of the thousands of miles that stretched between me and the soil of freedom, over which a *black* freeman may not pass.

Tibeats, in the course of half an hour, walked over to the weaving-house, looked at me sharply, then returned without saying

yearning for freedom

anything. Most of the fore-noon he sat on the piazza, reading a newspaper and conversing with Ford. After dinner, the latter left for the Pine Woods, and it was indeed with regret that I beheld him depart from the plantation.

Once more during the day Tibeats came to me, gave me some order, and returned.

During the week the weaving-house was completed—Tibeats in the meantime making no allusion whatever to the difficulty—when I was informed he had hired me to Peter Tanner, to work under another carpenter by the name of Myers.[99] This announcement was received with gratification, as any place was desirable that would relieve me of his hateful presence.

Peter Tanner, as the reader has already been informed, lived on the opposite shore, and was the brother of Mistress Ford.[100] He is one of the most extensive planters on Bayou Boeuf, and owns a large number of slaves. *P-793 A.100 important*

Over I went to Tanner's, joyfully enough. He had heard of my late difficulties—in fact, I ascertained the flogging of Tibeats was soon blazoned far and wide. This affair, together with my rafting experiment, had rendered me somewhat notorious. More than once I heard it said that Platt Ford, now Platt Tibeats—a slave's name changes with his change of master—was "a devil of a nigger." But I was destined to make a still further noise, as will presently be seen, throughout the little world of Bayou Boeuf.

Peter Tanner endeavored to impress upon me the idea that he was quite severe, though I could perceive there was a vein of good humor in the old fellow, after all.

"You're the nigger," he said to me on my arrival—"You're the nigger that flogged your master, eh? You're the nigger that kicks, and holds carpenter Tibeats by the leg, and wallops him, are ye? I'd like to see you hold me by the leg—I should. You're a 'portant character— you're a great nigger—very remarkable nigger, ain't ye? *I'd* lash you— *I'd* take the tantrums out of ye. Jest take hold of my leg, if you please. None of your pranks here, my boy, remember *that*. Now go to work, you *kickin'* rascal," concluded Peter Tanner, unable to suppress a half-comical grin at his own wit and sarcasm.

After listening to this salutation, I was taken charge of by Myers, and labored under his direction for a month, to his and my own satisfaction.

AVOID

Like William Ford, his brother-in-law, Tanner was in the habit of reading the Bible to his slaves on the Sabbath, but in a somewhat different spirit. He was an impressive commentator on the New Testament. The first Sunday after my coming to the plantation, he called them together, and began to read the twelfth chapter of Luke. When he came to the 47th verse, he looked deliberately around him, and continued—"And that servant which knew his lord's *will*"—here he paused, looking around more deliberately than before, and again proceeded—"which knew his lord's *will*, and *prepared* not himself"— here was another pause—"*prepared* not himself, neither did *according* to his will, shall be beaten with many *stripes*."

"D'ye hear that?" demanded Peter, emphatically. "*Stripes*," he repeated, slowly and distinctly, taking off his spectacles, preparatory to making a few remarks.

"That nigger that don't take care—that don't obey his lord— that's his master—d'ye see?—that 'ere nigger shall be beaten with many stripes. Now, 'many' signifies a *great* many—forty, a hundred, a hundred and fifty lashes. *That's* Scripter!" and so Peter continued to elucidate the subject for a great length of time, much to the edification of his sable audience.

At the conclusion of the exercises, calling up three of his slaves, Warner, Will and Major, he cried out to me—

"Here, Platt, you held Tibeats by the legs; now I'll see if you can hold these rascals in the same way, till I get back from meetin'."

Thereupon he ordered them to the stocks—a common thing on plantations in the Red River country.[101] The stocks are formed of two planks, the lower one made fast at the ends to two short posts, driven firmly into the ground. At regular distances half circles are cut in the upper edge. The other plank is fastened to one of the posts by a hinge, so that it can be opened or shut down, in the same manner as the blade of a pocket-knife is shut or opened. In the lower edge of the upper plank corresponding half circles are also cut, so that when they close, a row of holes is formed large enough to admit a negro's leg above the ankle, but not large enough to enable him to draw out his foot. The other end of the upper plank, opposite the hinge, is fastened to its post by lock and key. The slave is made to sit upon the ground, when the uppermost plank is elevated, his legs, just above the ankles, placed in the sub-half circles, and shutting it down again, and locking it, he is held secure and fast. Very often the neck instead of the ankle is enclosed. In this manner they are held during the operation of whipping.

Warner, Will and Major, according to Tanner's account of them, were melon-stealing, Sabbath-breaking niggers, and not approving of such wickedness, he felt it his duty to put them in the stocks. Handing me the key, himself, Myers, Mistress Tanner, and the children entered the carriage and drove away to church at Cheneyville.[102] When they were gone, the boys begged me to let them out. I felt sorry to see them sitting on the hot ground, and remembered my own sufferings in the sun. Upon their promise to return to the stocks at any moment they were required to do so, I consented to release them. Grateful for the lenity shown them, and in order in some measure to repay it, they could do no less, of course, than pilot me to the melon-patch. Shortly before Tanner's return, they were in the stocks again. Finally he drove up, and looking at the boys, said, with a chuckle,—

"Aha! ye haven't been strolling about much to-day, any way. *I'll* teach you what's what. *I'll* tire ye of eating water-melons on the Lord's day, ye Sabbath-breaking niggers."

Peter Tanner prided himself upon his strict religious observances; he was a deacon in the church.[103]

But I have now reached a point in the progress of my narrative, when it becomes necessary to turn away from these light descriptions, to the more grave and weighty matter of the second battle with Master Tibeats, and the flight through the great Pacoudrie Swamp.

CHAPTER X.

RETURN TO TIBEATS—IMPOSSIBILITY OF PLEASING HIM—HE
ATTACKS ME WITH A HATCHET—THE STRUGGLE OVER THE BROAD
AXE—THE TEMPTATION TO MURDER HIM—ESCAPE ACROSS THE
PLANTATION—OBSERVATIONS FROM THE FENCE—TIBEATS
APPROACHES, FOLLOWED BY THE HOUNDS—THEY TAKE MY
TRACK—THEIR LOUD YELLS—THEY ALMOST OVERTAKE ME—I
REACH THE WATER—THE HOUNDS CONFUSED—MOCCASIN SNAKES
ALLIGATORS—NIGHT IN THE "GREAT PACOUDRIE SWAMP"—THE
SOUNDS OF LIFE—NORTH-WEST COURSE—EMERGE INTO THE PINE
WOODS—THE SLAVE AND HIS YOUNG MASTER—ARRIVAL AT
FORD'S—FOOD AND REST.

At the end of a month, my services being no longer required at
Tanner's I was sent over the bayou again to my master, whom I
found engaged in building the cotton press. This was situated at some
distance from the great house, in a rather retired place.[104] I
commenced working once more in company with Tibeats, being
entirely alone with him most part of the time. I remembered the
words of Chapin, his precautions, his advice to beware, lest in some
unsuspecting moment he might injure me. They were always in my
mind, so that I lived in a most uneasy state of apprehension and fear.
One eye was on my work, the other on my master. I determined to
give him no cause of offence, to work still more diligently, if possible,
than I had done, to bear whatever abuse he might heap upon me,
save bodily injury, humbly and patiently, hoping thereby to soften in
some degree his manner towards me, until the blessed time might
come when I should be delivered from his clutches.

The third morning after my return, Chapin left the plantation for
Cheneyville, to be absent until night. Tibeats, on that morning, was
attacked with one of those periodical fits of spleen and ill-humor to
which he was frequently subject, rendering him still more
disagreeable and venomous than usual.

It was about nine o'clock in the forenoon, when I was busily
employed with the jack-plane on one of the sweeps. Tibeats was

standing by the work-bench, fitting a handle into the chisel, with which he had been engaged previously in cutting the thread of the screw.

"You are not planing that down enough," said he.

"It is just even with the line," I replied.

"You're a d—d liar," he exclaimed passionately.

"Oh, well, master," I said, mildly, "I will plane it down more if you say so," at the same time proceeding to do as I supposed he desired. Before one shaving had been removed, however, he cried out, saying I had now planed it too deep—it was too small—I had spoiled the sweep entirely. Then followed curses and imprecations. I had endeavored to do exactly as he directed, but nothing would satisfy the unreasonable man. In silence and in dread I stood by the sweep, holding the jack-plane in my hand, not knowing what to do, and not daring to be idle. His anger grew more and more violent, until, finally, with an oath, such a bitter, frightful oath as only Tibeats could utter, he seized a hatchet from the work-bench and darted towards me, swearing he would cut my head open.

It was a moment of life or death. The sharp, bright blade of the hatchet glittered in the sun. In another instant it would be buried in my brain, and yet in that instant—so quick will a man's thoughts come to him in such a fearful strait—I reasoned with myself. If I stood still, my doom was certain; if I fled, ten chances to one the hatchet, flying from his hand with a too-deadly and unerring aim, would strike me in the back. There was but one course to take. Springing towards him with all my power, and meeting him full half-way, before he could bring down the blow, with one hand I caught his uplifted arm, with the other seized him by the throat. We stood looking each other in the eyes. In his I could see murder. I felt as if I had a serpent by the neck, watching the slightest relaxation of my grip, to coil itself round my body, crushing and stinging it to death. I thought to scream aloud, trusting that some ear might catch the sound—but Chapin was away; the hands were in the field; there was no living soul in sight or hearing.

The good genius, which thus far through life has saved me from the hands of violence, at that moment suggested a lucky thought. With a vigorous and sudden kick, that brought him on one knee, with a groan, I released my hold upon his throat, snatched the hatchet, and cast it beyond reach.

Frantic with rage, maddened beyond control, he seized a white oak stick, five feet long, perhaps, and as large in circumference as his hand could grasp, which was lying on the ground. Again he rushed towards me, and again I met him, seized him about the waist, and being the stronger of the two, bore him to the earth. While in that position, I obtained possession of the stick, and rising, cast it from me, also.

He likewise arose and ran for the broad-axe, on the workbench. Fortunately, there was a heavy plank lying upon its broad blade, in such a manner that he could not extricate it, before I had sprung upon his back. Pressing him down closely and heavily on the plank, so that the axe was held more firmly to its place, I endeavored, but in vain, to break his grasp upon the handle. In that position we remained some minutes.

There have been hours in my unhappy life, many of them, when the contemplation of death as the end of earthly sorrow—of the grave as a resting place for the tired and worn out body—has been pleasant to dwell upon. But such contemplations vanish in the hour of peril. No man, in his full strength, can stand undismayed, in the presence of the "king of terrors." Life is dear to every living thing; the worm that crawls upon the ground will struggle for it. At that moment it was dear to me, enslaved and treated as I was.

Not able to unloose his hand, once more I seized him by the throat, and this time, with a vice-like grip that soon relaxed his hold. He became pliant and unstrung. His face, that had been white with passion, was now black from suffocation. Those small serpent eyes that spat such venom, were now full of horror—two great white orbs starting from their sockets!

There was "a lurking devil" in my heart that prompted me to kill the human blood-hound on the spot—to retain the grip on his accursed throat till the breath of life was gone! I dared not murder him, and I dared not let him live. If I killed him, my life must pay the forfeit—if he lived, my life only would satisfy his vengeance. A voice within whispered me to fly. To be a wanderer among the swamps, a fugitive and a vagabond on the face of the earth, was preferable to the life that I was leading.

My resolution was soon formed, and swinging him from the work-bench to the ground, I leaped a fence near by, and hurried

across the plantation, passing the slaves at work in the cotton field.
At the end of a quarter of a mile I reached the wood-pasture, and it
was a short time indeed that I had been running it. Climbing on to a
high fence, I could see the cotton press, the great house, and the
space between. It was a conspicuous position, from whence the
whole plantation was in view. I saw Tibeats cross the field towards
the house, and enter it—then he came out, carrying his saddle, and
presently mounted his horse and galloped away.

I was desolate, but thankful. Thankful that my life was spared,—
desolate and discouraged with the prospect before me. What would
become of me? Who would befriend me? Whither should I fly? Oh,
God! Thou who gavest me life, and implanted in my bosom the love
of life—who filled it with emotions such as other men, thy creatures,
have, do not forsake me. Have pity on the poor slave—let me not
perish. If thou dost not protect me, I am lost—lost! Such supplications, silently and unuttered, ascended from my inmost heart to
Heaven. But there was no answering voice—no sweet, low tone,
coming down from on high, whispering to my soul, "It is I, be not
afraid." I was the forsaken of God, it seemed—the despised and
hated of men! *prayer mention Anne Frank*

In about three-fourths of an hour several of the slaves shouted
and made signs for me to run. Presently, looking up the bayou, I saw
Tibeats and two others on horse-back, coming at a fast gait, followed
by a troop of dogs. There were as many as eight or ten. Distant as I
was, I knew them. They belonged on the adjoining plantation. The
dogs used on Bayou Boeuf for hunting slaves are a kind of blood-
hound, but a far more savage breed than is found in the Northern
States. They will attack a negro, at their master's bidding, and cling to
him as the common bull-dog will cling to a four footed animal.
Frequently their loud bay is heard in the swamps, and then there is
speculation as to what point the runaway will be overhauled—the
same as a New-York hunter stops to listen to the hounds coursing
along the hillsides, and suggests to his companion that the fox will be
taken at such a place. I never knew a slave escaping with his life from
Bayou Boeuf. One reason is, they are not allowed to learn the art of
swimming, and are incapable of crossing the most inconsiderable
stream.[105] In their flight they can go in no direction but a little way
without coming to a bayou, when the inevitable alternative is
presented, of being drowned or overtaken by the dogs. In youth I

had practiced in the clear streams that flow through my native district, until I had become an expert swimmer, and felt at home in the watery element.

I stood upon the fence until the dogs had reached the cotton press. In an instant more, their long, savage yells announced they were on my track. Leaping down from my position, I ran toward the swamp. Fear gave me strength, and I exerted it to the utmost. Every few moments I could hear the yelpings of the dogs. They were gaining upon me. Every howl was nearer and nearer. Each moment I expected they would spring upon my back—expected to feel their long teeth sinking into my flesh. There were so many of them, I knew they would tear me to pieces, that they would worry me, at once, to death. I gasped for breath—gasped forth a half-uttered, choking prayer to the Almighty to save me—to give me strength to reach some wide, deep bayou where I could throw them off the track, or sink into its waters. Presently I reached a thick palmetto bottom. As I fled through them they made a loud rustling noise, not loud enough, however, to drown the voices of the dogs.

Continuing my course due south, as nearly as I can judge, I came at length to water just over shoe. The hounds at that moment could not have been five rods behind me. I could hear them crashing and plunging through the palmettoes, their loud, eager yells making the whole swamp clamorous with the sound. Hope revived a little as I reached the water. If it were only deeper, they might lose the scent, and thus disconcerted, afford me the opportunity of evading them. Luckily, it grew deeper the farther I proceeded—now over my ankles—now half-way to my knees—now sinking a moment to my waist, and then emerging presently into more shallow places. The dogs had not gained upon me since I struck the water. Evidently they were confused. Now their savage intonations grew more and more distant, assuring me that I was leaving them. Finally I stopped to listen, but the long howl came booming on the air again, telling me I was not yet safe. From bog to bog, where I had stepped, they could still keep upon the track, though impeded by the water. At length, to my great joy, I came to a wide bayou, and plunging in, had soon stemmed its sluggish current to the other side. There, certainly, the dogs would be confounded—the current carrying down the stream all traces of that slight, mysterious scent, which enables the quick-smelling hound to follow in the track of the fugitive.

After crossing this bayou the water became so deep I could not run. I was now in what I afterwards learned was the "Great Pacoudrie Swamp."[106] It was filled with immense trees—the sycamore, the gum, the cotton wood and cypress, and extends, I am informed, to the shore of the Calcasieu river. For thirty or forty miles it is without habitants, save wild beasts—the bear, the wild-cat, the tiger, and great slimy reptiles, that are crawling through it everywhere.[107] Long before I reached the bayou, in fact, from the time I struck the water until I emerged from the swamp on my return, these reptiles surrounded me. I saw hundreds of moccasin snakes. Every log and bog—every trunk of a fallen tree, over which I was compelled to step or climb, was alive with them. They crawled away at my approach, but sometimes in my haste, I almost placed my hand or foot upon them. They are poisonous serpents—their bite more fatal than the rattlesnake's. Besides, I had lost one shoe, the sole having come entirely off, leaving the upper only dangling to my ankle.

I saw also many alligators, great and small, lying in the water, or on pieces of floodwood. The noise I made usually startled them, when they moved off and plunged into the deepest places. Sometimes, however, I would come directly upon a monster before observing it. In such cases, I would start back, run a short way round, and in that manner shun them. Straight forward, they will run a short distance rapidly, but do not possess the power of turning. In a crooked race, there is no difficulty in evading them.

About two o'clock in the afternoon, I heard the last of the hounds. Probably they did not cross the bayou. Wet and weary, but relieved from the sense of instant peril, I continued on, more cautious and afraid, however, of the snakes and alligators than I had been in the earlier portion of my flight. Now, before stepping into a muddy pool, I would strike the water with a stick. If the waters moved, I would go around it, if not, would venture through.

At length the sun went down, and gradually night's trailing mantle shrouded the great swamp in darkness. Still I staggered on, fearing every instant I should feel the dreadful sting of the moccasin, or be crushed within the jaws of some disturbed alligator. The dread of them now almost equaled the fear of the pursuing hounds. The moon arose after a time, its mild light creeping through the overspreading branches, loaded with long, pendent moss. I kept traveling forwards until after midnight, hoping all the while that I would soon emerge into some less desolate and dangerous region. But the water grew deeper and the walking more difficult than ever. I perceived it would be impossible to proceed much farther, and knew not, moreover, what hands I might fall into, should I succeed in reaching a human habitation. Not provided with a pass, any white man would be at liberty to arrest me, and place me in prison until such time as my master should "prove property, pay charges, and take me away." I was an estray, and if so unfortunate as to meet a law-abiding citizen of Louisiana, he would deem it his duty to his neighbor, perhaps, to put me forthwith in the pound. Really, it was difficult to determine which I had most reason to fear—dogs, alligators or men! *snakes?*

After midnight, however, I came to a halt. Imagination cannot picture the dreariness of the scene. The swamp was resonant with the quacking of innumerable ducks! Since the foundation of the earth, in all probability, a human footstep had never before so far penetrated the recesses of the swamp. It was not silent now—silent to a degree that rendered it oppressive,—as it was when the sun was shining in the heavens. My midnight intrusion had awakened the feathered tribes, which seemed to throng the morass in hundreds of thousands, and their garrulous throats poured forth such multitudinous sounds—there was such a fluttering of wings—such sullen plunges in the water all around me—that I was affrighted and appalled. All the fowls of the air, and all the creeping things of the earth appeared to have assembled together in that particular place, for the purpose of filling it with clamor and confusion. Not by human dwellings—not in crowded cities alone, are the sights and sounds of life. The wildest places of the earth are full of them. Even in the heart of that dismal swamp, God had provided a refuge and a dwelling place for millions of living things.

The moon had now risen above the trees, when I resolved upon a new project. Thus far I had endeavored to travel as nearly south as possible. Turning about I proceeded in a north-west direction, my object being to strike the Pine Woods in the vicinity of Master Ford's. Once within the shadow of his protection, I felt I would be comparatively safe.

My clothes were in tatters, my hands, face, and body covered with scratches, received from the sharp knots of fallen trees, and in

Yuck!

climbing over piles of brush and flood wood. My bare foot was full of thorns. I was besmeared with muck and mud, and the green slime that had collected on the surface of the dead water, in which I had been immersed to the neck many times during the day and night. Hour after hour, and tiresome indeed had they become, I continued to plod along on my north-west course. The water began to grow less deep, and the ground more firm under my feet. At last I reached the Pacoudrie, the same wide bayou I had swam while "outward bound." I swam it again, and shortly after, thought I heard a cock crow, but the sound was faint, and it might have been a mockery of the ear. The water receded from my advancing footsteps—now I had left the bogs behind me—now I was on dry land that gradually ascended to the plain, and I knew I was somewhere in the "Great Pine Woods."

Just at day-break I came to an opening—a sort of small plantation—but one I had never seen before. In the edge of the woods I came upon two men, a slave and his young master, engaged in catching wild hogs. The white man I knew would demand my pass, and not able to give him one, would take me into possession. I was too wearied to run again, and too desperate to be taken, and therefore adopted a ruse that proved entirely successful. Assuming a fierce expression, I walked directly towards him, looking him steadily in the face. As I approached, he moved backwards with an air of alarm. It was plain he was much affrighted—that he looked upon me as some infernal goblin, just arisen from the bowels of the swamp!

"Where does William Ford live?" I demanded, in no gentle tone.

"He lives seven miles from here," was the reply.

"Which is the way to his place?" I again demanded, trying to look more fiercely than ever.   *Why?*

"Do you see those pine trees yonder?" he asked, pointing to two, a mile distant, that rose far above their fellows, like a couple of tall sentinels, overlooking the broad expanse of forest.

"I see them," was the answer.

"At the feet of those pine trees," he continued, "runs the Texas road. Turn to the left, and it will lead you to William Ford's."[108]

Without further parley, I hastened forward, happy as he was, no doubt, to place the widest possible distance between us. Striking the Texas road, I turned to the left hand, as directed, and soon passed a great fire, where a pile of logs were burning. I went to it, thinking I would dry my clothes; but the gray light of the morning was fast breaking away,—some passing white man might observe me; besides, the heat overpowered me with the desire of sleep; so, lingering no longer, I continued my travels, and finally, about eight o'clock, reached the house of Master Ford.

The slaves were all absent from the quarters, at their work. Stepping on to the piazza, I knocked at the door, which was soon opened by Mistress Ford. My appearance was so changed—I was in such a wobegone and forlorn condition, she did not know me. Inquiring if Master Ford was at home, that good man made his appearance, before the question could be answered. I told him of my flight, and all the particulars connected with it. He listened attentively, and when I had concluded, spoke to me kindly and sympathetically, and taking me to the kitchen, called John, and ordered him to prepare me food. I had tasted nothing since daylight the previous morning.

When John had set the meal before me, the madam came out with a bowl of milk, and many little delicious dainties, such as rarely please the palate of a slave. I was hungry, and I was weary, but neither food nor rest afforded half the pleasure as did the blessed voices speaking kindness and consolation. It was the oil and wine which the Good Samaritan in the "Great Pine Woods" was ready to pour into the wounded spirit of the slave, who came to him, stripped of his raiment and half-dead.

They left me in the cabin, that I might rest. Blessed be sleep! It visiteth all alike, descending as the dews of heaven on the bond and free. Soon it nestled to my bosom, driving away the troubles that oppressed it, and bearing me to that shadowy region, where I saw again the faces, and listened to the voices of my children, who, alas, for aught I knew in my waking hours, had fallen into the arms of that _other_ sleep, from which they _never_ would arouse.

CHAPTER XI.

THE MISTRESS' GARDEN—THE CRIMSON AND GOLDEN FRUIT—
ORANGE AND POMEGRANATE TREES—RETURN TO BAYOU BOEUF—
MASTER FORD'S REMARKS ON THE WAY—THE MEETING WITH
TIBEATS—HIS ACCOUNT OF THE CHASE—FORD CENSURES HIS
BRUTALITY—ARRIVAL AT THE PLANTATION—ASTONISHMENT OF
THE SLAVES ON SEEING ME—THE ANTICIPATED FLOGGING—
KENTUCKY JOHN—MR. ELDRET, THE PLANTER—ELDRET'S SAM—
TRIP TO THE "BIG CANE BRAKE"—THE TRADITION OF "SUTTON'S
FIELD"—FOREST TREES—GNATS AND MOSQUITOES—THE ARRIVAL
OF BLACK WOMEN IN THE BIG CANE—LUMBER WOMEN—SUDDEN
APPEARANCE OF TIBEATS—HIS PROVOKING TREATMENT—VISIT TO
BAYOU BOEUF—THE SLAVE PASS—SOUTHERN HOSPITALITY—THE
LAST OF ELIZA—SALE TO EDWIN EPPS.

After a long sleep, sometime in the afternoon I awoke, refreshed, but
very sore and stiff. Sally came in and talked with me, while John
cooked me some dinner. Sally was in great trouble, as well as myself,
one of her children being ill, and she feared it could not survive.
Dinner over, after walking about the quarters for a while, visiting
Sally's cabin and looking at the sick child, I strolled into the madam's
garden. Though it was a season of the year when the voices of the
birds are silent, and the trees are stripped of their summer glories in
more frigid climes, yet the whole variety of roses were then blooming
there, and the long, luxuriant vines creeping over the frames. The
crimson and golden fruit hung half hidden amidst the younger and
older blossoms of the peach, the orange, the plum, and the
pomegranate; for, in that region of almost perpetual warmth, the
leaves are falling and the buds bursting into bloom the whole year
long.

I indulged the most grateful feelings towards Master and
Mistress Ford, and wishing in some manner to repay their kindness,
commenced trimming the vines, and afterwards weeding out the
grass from among the orange and pomegranate trees. The latter
grows eight or ten feet high, and its fruit, though larger, is similar in
appearance to the jelly-flower. It has the luscious flavor of the

strawberry. Oranges, peaches, plums, and most other fruits are indigenous to the rich, warm soil of Avoyelles; but the apple, the most common of them all in colder latitudes, is rarely to be seen.[109]

Mistress Ford came out presently, saying it was praise-worthy in me, but I was not in a condition to labor, and might rest myself at the quarters until master should go down to Bayou Boeuf, which would not be that day, and it might not be the next. I said to her—to be sure, I felt bad, and was stiff, and that my foot pained me, the stubs and thorns having so torn it; but thought such exercise would not hurt me, and that it was a great pleasure to work for so good a mistress. Thereupon she returned to the great house, and for three days I was diligent in the garden, cleaning the walks, weeding the flower beds, and pulling up the rank grass beneath the jessamine vines, which the gentle and generous hand of my protectress had taught to clamber along the walls.

The fourth morning, having become recruited and refreshed, Master Ford ordered me to make ready to accompany him to the bayou. There was but one saddle horse at the opening, all the others with the mules having been sent down to the plantation. I said I could walk, and bidding Sally and John good-bye, left the opening, trotting along by the horse's side.

That little paradise in the Great Pine Woods was the oasis in the desert, towards which my heart turned lovingly, during many years of bondage. I went forth from it now with regret and sorrow, not so overwhelming, however, as if it had then been given me to know that I should never return to it again.

Master Ford urged me to take his place occasionally on the horse, to rest me; but I said no, I was not tired, and it was better for me to walk than him. He said many kind and cheering things to me on the way, riding slowly, in order that I might keep pace with him. The goodness of God was manifest, he declared, in my miraculous escape from the swamp. As Daniel came forth unharmed from the den of lions, and as Jonah had been preserved in the whale's belly, even so I had been delivered from evil by the Almighty. He interrogated me in regard to the various fears and emotions I had experienced during the day and night, and if I had felt, at any time, a desire to pray. I felt forsaken of the whole world, I answered him, and was praying mentally all the while. At such times, said he, the heart of man turns instinctively towards his Maker. In prosperity, and when there is nothing to injure or make him afraid, he remembers Him not, and is ready to defy Him; but place him in the midst of dangers, cut him off from human aid, let the grave open before him—then it is, in the time of his tribulation, that the scoffer and unbelieving man turns to God for help, feeling there is no other hope, or refuge, or safety, save in His protecting arm.

So did that benignant man speak to me of this life and of the life hereafter; of the goodness and power of God, and of the vanity of earthly things, as we journeyed along the solitary road towards Bayou Boeuf.

 When within some five miles of the plantation, we discovered a horseman at a distance, galloping towards us. As he came near I saw that it was Tibeats! He looked at me a moment, but did not address me, and turning about, rode along side by side with Ford. I trotted silently at their horses' heels, listing to their conversation. Ford informed him of my arrival in the Pine Woods three days before, of the sad plight I was in, and of the difficulties and dangers I had encountered.

"Well," exclaimed Tibeats, omitting his usual oaths in the presence of Ford, "I never saw such running before. I'll bet him against a hundred dollars, he'll beat any nigger in Louisiana. I offered John David Cheney[110] twenty-five dollars to catch him, dead or alive, but he outran his dogs in a fair race. Them Cheney dogs ain't much, after all. Dunwoodie's hounds[111] would have had him down before he touched the palmettoes. Somehow the dogs got off the track, and we had to give up the hunt. We rode the horses as far as we could, and then kept on foot till the water was three feet deep. The boys said he was drowned, sure. I allow I wanted a shot at him mightily. Ever since, I have been riding up and down the bayou, but hadn't much hope of catching him—thought he was dead, *sartin*. Oh, he's a cuss to run—that nigger is!"

In this way Tibeats ran on, describing his search in the swamp, the wonderful speed with which I had fled before the hounds, and when he had finished, Master Ford responded by saying, I had always been a willing and faithful boy with him; that he was sorry we had such trouble; that, according to Platt's story, he had been inhumanly treated, and that he, Tibeats, was himself at fault. Using hatchets and broad-axes upon slaves was shameful, and should not be allowed, he remarked. "This is no way of dealing with them, when first brought into the country. It will have a pernicious influence, and set them all running away. The swamps will be full of them. A little kindness would be far more effectual in restraining them, and rendering them obedient, than the use of such deadly weapons. Every planter on the bayou should frown upon such inhumanity. It is for the interest of all to do so. It is evident enough, Mr. Tibeats, that you and Platt cannot live together. You dislike him, and would not hesitate to kill him, and knowing it, he will run from you again through fear of his life. Now, Tibeats, you must sell him, or hire him out, at least. Unless you do so, I shall take measures to get him out of your possession."[112]

In this spirit Ford addressed him the remainder of the distance. I opened not my mouth. On reaching the plantation they entered the great house, while I repaired to Eliza's cabin. The slaves were astonished to find me there, on returning from the field, supposing I was drowned. That night, again, they gathered about the cabin to listen to the story of my adventure. They took it for granted I would be whipped, and that it would be severe, the well-known penalty of running away being five hundred lashes.

"Poor fellow," said Eliza, taking me by the hand, "it would have been better for you if you had drowned. You have a cruel master, and he will kill you yet, I am afraid."

Lawson suggested that it might be, overseer Chapin would be appointed to inflict the punishment, in which case it would not be severe, whereupon Mary, Rachel, Bristol, and others hoped it would be Master Ford, and then it would be no whipping at all. They all pitied me and tried to console me, and were sad in view of the castigation that awaited me, except Kentucky John. There were no bounds to his laughter; he filled the cabin with cachinnations, holding his sides to prevent an explosion, and the cause of his noisy mirth was the idea of my outstripping the hounds. Somehow, he looked at the subject in a comical light. "I *know'd* dey wouldn't cotch him, when he run cross de plantation. O, de lor', didn't Platt pick his feet right up, tho', hey? When dem dogs got whar he was, he wasn't *dar*—haw, haw, haw! O, de lor' a' mity!"—and then Kentucky John relapsed into another of his boisterous fits.

Early the next morning, Tibeats left the plantation. In the course of the forenoon, while sauntering about the gin-house, a tall, good-looking man came to me, and inquired if I was Tibeats' boy, that youthful appellation being applied indiscriminately to slaves even though they may have passed the number of three score years and ten. I took off my hat, and answered that I was.

"How would you like to work for me?" he inquired.

"Oh, I would like to, very much," said I, inspired with a sudden hope of getting away from Tibeats.

"You worked under Myers at Peter Tanner's, didn't you?"

I replied I had, adding some complimentary remarks that Myers had made concerning me.

"Well, boy," said he, "I have hired you of your master to work for me in the 'Big Cane Brake,' thirty-eight miles from here, down on Red River."[113]

This man was Mr. Eldret, who lived below Ford's, on the same side of the bayou.[114] I accompanied him to his plantation, and in the morning started with his slave Sam, and a wagon-load of provisions, drawn by four mules, for the Big Cane, Eldret and Myers having preceded us on horseback. This Sam was a native of Charleston, where he had a mother, brother and sisters. He "allowed"—a common word among both black and white—that Tibeats was a mean man, and hoped, as I most earnestly did also, that his master would buy me.

We proceeded down the south shore of the bayou, crossing it at Carey's plantation;[115] from thence to Huff Power, passing which, we came upon the Bayou Rouge road, which runs towards Red River. After passing through Bayou Rouge Swamp, and just at sunset, turning from the highway, we struck off into the "Big Cane Brake." We followed an unbeaten track, scarcely wide enough to admit the wagon. The cane, such as are used for fishing-rods, were as thick as they could stand. A person could not be seen through them the distance of a rod. The paths of wild beasts run through them in various directions—the bear and the American tiger abounding in these brakes, and wherever there is a basin of stagnant water, it is full of alligators.[116]

We kept on our lonely course through the "Big Cane" several miles, when we entered a clearing, known as "Sutton's Field." Many years before, a man by the name of Sutton had penetrated the wilderness of cane to this solitary place. Tradition has it, that he fled thither, a fugitive, not from service, but from justice. Here he lived alone—recluse and hermit of the swamp—with his own hands planting the seed and gathering in the harvest. One day a band of

Indians stole upon his solitude, and after a bloody battle, over-powered and massacred him. For miles the country round, in the slaves' quarters, and on the piazzas of "great houses," where white children listen to superstitious tales, the story goes, that that spot, in the heart of the "Big Cane," is a haunted place. For more than a quarter of a century, human voices had rarely, if ever, disturbed the silence of the clearing. Rank and noxious weeds have overspread the once cultivated field—serpents sunned themselves on the doorway of the crumbling cabin. It was indeed a dreary picture of desolation.

Passing "Sutton's Field," we followed a new-cut road two miles farther, which brought us to its termination. We had now reached the wild lands of Mr. Eldret, where he contemplated clearing up an extensive plantation. We went to work next morning with our cane-knives, and cleared a sufficient space to allow the erection of two cabins—one for Myers and Eldret, the other for Sam, myself, and the slaves that were to join us. We were now in the midst of trees of enormous growth, whose wide-spreading branches almost shut out the light of the sun, while the space between the trunks was an impervious mass of cane, with here and there an occasional palmetto.

The bay and the sycamore, the oak and the cypress, reach a growth unparalleled, in those fertile lowlands bordering the Red River. From every tree, moreover, hang long, large masses of moss, presenting to the eye unaccustomed to them, a striking and singular appearance. This moss, in large quantities, is sent north, and there used for manufacturing purposes.

We cut down oaks, split them into rails, and with these erected temporary cabins. We covered the roofs with the broad palmetto leaf, an excellent substitute for shingles, as long as they last.

The greatest annoyance I met with here were small flies, gnats and mosquitoes. They swarmed the air. They penetrated the porches of the ear, the nose, the eyes, the mouth. They sucked themselves beneath the skin. It was impossible to brush or beat them off. It seemed, indeed, as if they would devour us—carry us away piecemeal, in their small tormenting mouths.

A lonelier spot, or one more disagreeable, than the centre of the "Big Cane Brake," it would be difficult to conceive; yet to me it was a paradise, in comparison with any other place in the company of Master Tibeats. I labored hard, and oft-times was weary and fatigued,

yet I could lie down at night in peace, and arise in the morning
without fear.

In the course of a fortnight, four black girls came down from
Eldret's plantation—Charlotte, Fanny, Cresia and Nelly. They were
all large and stout. Axes were put into their hands, and they were sent
out with Sam and myself to cut trees. They were excellent choppers,
the largest oak or sycamore standing but a brief season before their
heavy and well-directed blows. At piling logs, they were equal to any
man. There are lumberwomen as well as lumbermen in the forests of
the South. In fact, in the region of the Bayou Boeuf they perform
their share of all the labor required on the plantation. They plough,
drag, drive team, clear wild lands, work on the highway, and so forth.
Some planters, owning large cotton and sugar plantations, have none
other than the labor of slave women. Such an one is Jim Burns,[117]
who lives on the north shore of the bayou, opposite the plantation of
John Fogaman.[118]

On our arrival in the brake, Eldret promised me, if I worked
well, I might go up to visit my friends at Ford's in four weeks. On
Saturday night of the fifth week, I reminded him of his promise,
when he told me I had done so well, that I might go. I had set my
heart upon it, and Eldret's announcement thrilled me with pleasure. I
was to return in time to commence the labors of the day on Tuesday
morning.

While indulging the pleasant anticipation of so soon meeting my
old friends again, suddenly the hateful form of Tibeats appeared
among us. He inquired how Myers and Platt got along together, and
was told, very well, and that Platt was going up to Ford's plantation
in the morning on a visit.

"Poh, poh!" sneered Tibeats; "it isn't worth while—the nigger
will get unsteady. He can't go."

But Eldret insisted I had worked faithfully—that he had given
me his promise, and that, under the circumstances, I ought not to be
disappointed. They then, it being about dark, entered one cabin and I
the other. I could not give up the idea of going; it was a sore
disappointment. Before morning I resolved, if Eldret made no
objection, to leave at all hazards. At daylight I was at his door, with
my blanket rolled up into a bundle, and hanging on a stick over my
shoulder, waiting for a pass. Tibeats came out presently in one of his
disagreeable moods, washed his face, and going to a stump near by,

sat down upon it, apparently busily thinking with himself. After standing there a long time, impelled by a sudden impulse of impatience, I started off.

"Are you going without a pass?" he cried out to me.

"Yes, master, I thought I would," I answered.

"How do you think you'll get there?" demanded he.

"Don't know," was all the reply I made him.

"You'd be taken and sent to jail, where you ought to be, before you got half-way there," he added, passing into the cabin as he said it. He came out soon with the pass in his hand, and calling me a "d—d nigger that deserved a hundred lashes," threw it on the ground. I picked it up, and hurried away right speedily.

A slave caught off his master's plantation without a pass, may be seized and whipped by any white man whom he meets. The one I now received was dated, and read as follows:

"Platt has permission to go to Ford's plantation, on Bayou Boeuf, and return by Tuesday morning.
JOHN M. TIBEATS."

This is the usual form. On the way, a great many demanded it, read it, and passed on. Those having the air and appearance of gentlemen, whose dress indicated the possession of wealth, frequently took no notice of me whatever; but a shabby fellow, an unmistakable loafer, never failed to hail me, and to scrutinize and examine me in the most thorough manner. Catching runaways is sometimes a money-making business. If, after advertising, no owner appears, they may be sold to the highest bidder; and certain fees are allowed the finder for his services, at all events, even if reclaimed. "A mean white," therefore,—a name applied to the species loafer—considers it a god-send to meet an unknown negro without a pass.

There are no inns along the highways in that portion of the State where I sojourned. I was wholly destitute of money, neither did I carry any provisions, on my journey from the Big Cane to Bayou Boeuf; nevertheless, with his pass in his hand, a slave need never suffer from hunger or from thirst. It is only necessary to present it to the master or overseer of a plantation, and state his wants, when he will be sent round to the kitchen and provided with food or shelter, as the case may require. The traveler stops at any house and calls for a meal with as much freedom as if it was a public tavern. It is the general custom of the country. Whatever their faults may be, it is certain the inhabitants along Red River, and around the bayous in the interior of Louisiana are not wanting in hospitality.

I arrived at Ford's plantation towards the close of the afternoon, passing the evening in Eliza's cabin, with Lawson, Rachel, and others of my acquaintance. When we left Washington Eliza's form was round and plump. She stood erect, and in her silks and jewels, presented a picture of graceful strength and elegance. Now she was but a thin shadow of her former self. Her face had become ghastly haggard, and the once straight and active form was bowed down, as if bearing the weight of a hundred years. Crouching on her cabin floor, and clad in the coarse garments of a slave, old Elisha Berry would not have recognized the mother of his child. I never saw her afterwards. Having become useless in the cotton-field, she was bartered for a trifle, to some man residing in the vicinity of Peter Compton's.[119] Grief had gnawed remorselessly at her heart, until her strength was gone; and for that, her last master, it is said, lashed and abused her most unmercifully. But he could not whip back the departed vigor of her youth, nor straighten up that bended body to its full height, such as it was when her children were around her, and the light of freedom was shining on her path.

I learned the particulars relative to her departure from this world, from some of Compton's slaves, who had come over Red River to the bayou, to assist young Madam Tanner during the "busy season."[120] She became at length, they said, utterly helpless, for several weeks lying on the ground floor in a dilapidated cabin, dependent upon the mercy of her fellow thralls for an occasional drop of water, and a morsel of food. Her master did not "knock her on the head," as is sometimes done to put a suffering animal out of misery, but left her unprovided for, and unprotected, to linger through a life of pain and wretchedness to its natural close. When the hands returned from the field one night they found her dead! During the day the Angel of the Lord, who moveth invisibly over all the earth, gathering in his harvest of departing souls, had silently entered the cabin of the dying woman, and taken her from thence. She was *free* at last!

Next day, rolling up my blanket, I started on my return to the Big Cane. After traveling five miles, at a place called Huff Power, the ever-present Tibeats met me in the road.[121] He inquired why I was going back so soon, and when informed I was anxious to return by the time I was directed, he said I need go no farther than the next plantation, as he had that day sold me to Edwin Epps.[122] We walked down into the yard, where we met the latter gentleman, who examined me, and asked me the usual questions propounded by purchasers. Having been duly delivered over, I was ordered to the quarters, and at the same time directed to make a hoe and axe handle for myself.

I was now no longer the property of Tibeats—his dog, his brute, dreading his wrath and cruelty day and night; and whoever or whatever my new master might prove to be, I could not, certainly, regret the change. So it was good news when the sale was announced, and with a sigh of relief I sat down for the first time in my new abode.

Tibeats soon after disappeared from that section of the country. Once afterwards, and only once, I caught a glimpse of him. It was many miles from Bayou Boeuf. He was seated in the doorway of a low groggery. I was passing, in a drove of slaves, through St. Mary's parish.

CHAPTER XII.

PERSONAL APPEARANCE OF EPPS—EPPS, DRUNK AND SOBER—A GLIMPSE OF HIS HISTORY—COTTON GROWING—THE MODE OF PLOUGHING AND PREPARING GROUND—OF PLANTING—OF HOEING, OF PICKING, OF TREATING RAW HANDS—THE DIFFERENCE IN COTTON PICKERS—PATSEY A REMARKABLE ONE—TASKED ACCORDING TO ABILITY—BEAUTY OF A COTTON FIELD—THE SLAVE'S LABORS—FEAR ON APPROACHING THE GIN-HOUSE—WEIGHING—"CHORES"—CABIN LIFE—THE CORN MILL—THE USES OF THE GOURD—FEAR OF OVERSLEEPING—FEAR CONTINUALLY—MODE OF CULTIVATING CORN—SWEET POTATOES—FERTILITY OF THE SOIL—FATTENING HOGS—PRESERVING BACON—RAISING CATTLE—SHOOTING-MATCHES—GARDEN PRODUCTS—FLOWERS AND VERDURE.

Edwin Epps, of whom much will be said during the remainder of this history, is a large, portly, heavy-bodied man with light hair, high cheek bones, and a Roman nose of extraordinary dimensions. He has blue eyes, a fair complexion, and is, as I should say, full six feet high. He has the sharp, inquisitive expression of a jockey. His manners are repulsive and coarse, and his language gives speedy and unequivocal evidence that he has never enjoyed the advantages of an education. He has the faculty of saying most provoking things, in that respect even excelling old Peter Tanner. At the time I came into his possession, Edwin Epps was fond of the bottle, his "sprees" sometimes extending over the space of two whole weeks. Latterly, however, he had reformed his habits, and when I left him, was as strict a specimen of temperance as could be found on Bayou Boeuf. When "in his cups," Master Epps was a roistering, blustering, noisy fellow, whose chief delight was in dancing with his "niggers," or lashing them about the yard with his long whip, just for the pleasure of hearing them screech and scream, as the great welts were planted on their backs. When sober, he was silent, reserved and cunning, not beating us indiscriminately, as in his drunken moments, but sending the end of his rawhide to some tender spot of a lagging slave, with a sly dexterity peculiar to himself.

He had been a driver and overseer in his younger years, but at this time was in possession of a plantation on Bayou Huff Power, two and a half miles from Holmesville, eighteen from Marksville, and twelve from Cheneyville. It belonged to Joseph B. Roberts, his wife's uncle, and was leased by Epps.[123] His principal business was raising cotton, and in as much as some may read this book who have never seen a cotton field, a description of the manner of its culture may not be out of place.[124]

The ground is prepared by throwing up beds or ridges, with the plough—back-furrowing, it is called. Oxen and mules, the latter almost exclusively, are used in ploughing. The women as frequently as the men perform this labor, feeding, currying, and taking care of their teams, and in all respects doing the field and stable work, precisely as do the ploughboys of the North.

The beds, or ridges, are six feet wide, that is, from water furrow to water furrow. A plough drawn by one mule is then run along the top of the ridge or center of the bed, making the drill, into which a girl usually drops the seed, which she carries in a bag hung round her neck. Behind her comes a mule and harrow, covering up the seed, so that two mules, three slaves, a plough and harrow, are employed in planting a row of cotton. This is done in the months of March and April. Corn is planted in February. When there are no cold rains, the cotton usually makes its appearance in a week. In the course of eight or ten days afterwards the first hoeing is commenced. This is performed in part, also, by the aid of the plough and mule. The plough passes as near as possible to the cotton on both sides, throwing the furrow from it. Slaves follow with their hoes, cutting up the grass and cotton, leaving hills two feet and a half apart. This is called scraping cotton. In two weeks more commences the second hoeing. This time the furrow is thrown towards the cotton. Only one stalk, the largest, is now left standing in each hill. In another fortnight it is hoed the third time, throwing the furrow towards the cotton in the same manner as before, and killing all the grass between the rows. About the first of July, when it is a foot high or thereabouts, it is hoed the fourth and last time. Now the whole space between the rows is ploughed, leaving a deep water furrow in the center. During all these hoeings the overseer or driver follows the slaves on horseback with a whip, such as has been described. The fastest hoer takes the lead row. He is usually about a rod in advance of his

n-175 on violence READ † *n.176*

companions. If one of them passes him, he is whipped.[125] If one falls behind or is a moment idle, he is whipped. In fact, the lash is flying from morning until night, the whole day long. The hoeing season thus continues from April until July, a field having no sooner been finished once, than it is commenced again.

In the latter part of August begins the cotton picking season. At this time each slave is presented with a sack. A strap is fastened to it, which goes over the neck, holding the mouth of the sack breast high, while the bottom reaches nearly to the ground. Each one is also presented with a large basket that will hold about two barrels. This is to put the cotton in when the sack is filled. The baskets are carried to the field and placed at the beginning of the rows.

When a new hand, one unaccustomed to the business, is sent for the first time into the field, he is whipped up smartly, and made for that day to pick as fast as he can possibly.[126] At night it is weighed, so that his capability in cotton picking is known. He must bring in the same weight each night following. If it falls short, it is considered evidence that he has been laggard, and a greater or less number of lashes is the penalty. *Explain* *of cotton is light!*

An ordinary day's work is two hundred pounds. A slave who is accustomed to picking, is punished, if he or she brings in a less quantity than that. There is a great difference among them as regards this kind of labor. Some of them seem to have a natural knack, or quickness, which enables them to pick with great celerity, and with both hands, while others, with whatever practice or industry, are utterly unable to come up to the ordinary standard. Such hands are taken from the cotton field and employed in other business. Patsey, of whom I shall have more to say, was known as the most remarkable cotton picker on Bayou Boeuf. She picked with both hands and with such surprising rapidity, that five hundred pounds a day was not unusual for her.[127] *n.177 on picking READ*

Each one is tasked, therefore, according to his picking abilities, none, however, to come short of two hundred weight. I, being unskillful always in that business, would have satisfied my master by bringing in the latter quantity, while on the other hand, Patsey would surely have been beaten if she failed to produce twice as much.

The cotton grows from five to seven feet high, each stalk having a great many branches, shooting out in all directions, and lapping each other above the water furrow.

There are few sights more pleasant to the eye, than a wide cotton field when it is in the bloom. It presents an appearance of purity, like an immaculate expanse of light, new-fallen snow.

Sometimes the slave picks down one side of a row, and back upon the other, but more usually, there is one on either side, gathering all that has blossomed, leaving the unopened bolls for a succeeding picking. When the sack is filled, it is emptied into the basket and trodden down. It is necessary to be extremely careful the first time going through the field, in order not to break the branches off the stalks. The cotton will not bloom upon a broken branch. Epps never failed to inflict the severest chastisement on the unlucky servant who, either carelessly or unavoidably, was guilty in the least degree in this respect.

The hands are required to be in the cotton field as soon as it is light in the morning, and, with the exception of ten or fifteen minutes, which is given them at noon to swallow their allowance of cold bacon, they are not permitted to be a moment idle until it is too dark to see, and when the moon is full, they often times labor till the middle of the night.[128] They do not dare to stop even at dinner time, nor return to the quarters, however late it be, until the order to halt is given by the driver.

The day's work over in the field, the baskets are "toted," or in other words, carried to the gin-house, where the cotton is weighed. No matter how fatigued and weary he may be—no matter how much he longs for sleep and rest—a slave never approaches the gin-house with his basket of cotton but with fear. If it falls short in weight—if he has not performed the full task appointed him, he knows that he must suffer. And if he has exceeded it by ten or twenty pounds, in all probability his master will measure the next day's task accordingly. So, whether he has too little or too much, his approach to the gin-house is always with fear and trembling. Most frequently they have too little, and therefore it is they are not anxious to leave the field. After weighing, follow the whippings; and then the baskets are carried to the cotton house, and their contents stored away like hay, all hands being sent in to tramp it down. If the cotton is not dry, instead of taking it to the gin-house at once, it is laid upon platforms, two feet high, and some three times as wide, covered with boards or plank, with narrow walks running between them.

This done, the labor of the day is not yet ended, by any means. Each one must then attend to his respective chores. One feeds the mules, another the swine—another cuts the wood, and so forth; besides, the packing is all done by candle light. Finally, at a late hour, they reach the quarters, sleepy and overcome with the long day's toil. Then a fire must be kindled in the cabin, the corn ground in the small hand-mill, and supper, and dinner for the next day in the field, prepared. All that is allowed them is corn and bacon, which is given out at the corncrib and smoke-house every Sunday morning.[129] Each one receives, as his weekly allowance, three and a half pounds of bacon, and corn enough to make a peck of meal. That is all—no tea, coffee, sugar, and with the exception of a very scanty sprinkling now and then, no salt. I can say, from a ten years' residence with Master Epps, that no slave of his is ever likely to suffer from the gout, superinduced by excessive high living. Master Epps' hogs were fed on *shelled* corn—it was thrown out to his "niggers" in the ear. The former, he thought, would fatten faster by shelling, and soaking it in the water—the latter, perhaps, if treated in the same manner, might grow too fat to labor. Master Epps was a shrewd calculator, and knew how to manage his own animals, drunk or sober.

The corn mill stands in the yard beneath a shelter. It is like a common coffee mill, the hopper holding about six quarts. There was one privilege which Master Epps granted freely to every slave he had. They might grind their corn nightly, in such small quantities as their daily wants required, or they might grind the whole week's allowance at one time, on Sundays, just as they preferred. A very generous man was Master Epps!

I kept my corn in a small wooden box, the meal in a gourd; and, by the way, the gourd is one of the most convenient and necessary utensils on a plantation. Besides supplying the place of all kinds of crockery in a slave cabin, it is used for carrying water to the fields. Another, also, contains the dinner. It dispenses with the necessity of pails, dippers, basins, and such tin and wooden superfluities altogether.

When the corn is ground, and fire is made, the bacon is taken down from the nail on which it hangs, a slice cut off and thrown upon the coals to broil. The majority of slaves have no knife, much less a fork. They cut their bacon with the axe at the woodpile. The corn meal is mixed with a little water, placed in the fire, and baked.

When it is "done brown," the ashes are scraped off, and being placed upon a chip, which answers for a table, the tenant of the slave hut is ready to sit down upon the ground to supper. By this time it is usually midnight. The same fear of punishment with which they approach the gin-house, possesses them again on lying down to get a snatch of rest. It is the fear of oversleeping in the morning. Such an offence would certainly be attended with not less than twenty lashes. With a prayer that he may be on his feet and wide awake at the first sound of the horn, he sinks to his slumbers nightly.

The softest couches in the world are not to be found in the log mansion of the slave. The one whereon I reclined year after year, was a plank twelve inches wide and ten feet long. My pillow was a stick of wood. The bedding was a coarse blanket, and not a rag or shred beside. Moss might be used, were it not that it directly breeds a swarm of fleas.[130]

The cabin is constructed of logs, without floor or window. The latter is altogether unnecessary, the crevices between the logs admitting sufficient light. In stormy weather the rain drives through them, rendering it comfortless and extremely disagreeable. The rude door hangs on great wooden hinges. In one end is constructed an awkward fire-place.[131]

An hour before day light the horn is blown. Then the slaves arouse, prepare their breakfast, fill a gourd with water, in another deposit their dinner of cold bacon and corn cake, and hurry to the field again. It is an offence invariably followed by a flogging, to be found at the quarters after daybreak. Then the fears and labors of another day begin; and until its close there is no such thing as rest. He fears he will be caught lagging through the day; he fears to approach the gin-house with his basket-load of cotton at night; he fears, when he lies down, that he will oversleep himself in the morning. Such is a true, faithful, unexaggerated picture and description of the slave's daily life, during the time of cotton-picking, on the shores of Bayou Boeuf.

In the month of January, generally, the fourth and last picking is completed. Then commences the harvesting of corn. This is considered a secondary crop, and receives far less attention than the cotton. It is planted, as already mentioned, in February. Corn is grown in that region for the purpose of fattening hogs and feeding slaves; very little, if any, being sent to market. It is the white variety, the ear of great size, and the stalk growing to the height of eight, and often times ten feet. In August the leaves are stripped off, dried in the sun, bound in small bundles, and stored away as provender for the mules and oxen. After this the slaves go through the field, turning down the ear, for the purpose of keeping the rains from penetrating to the grain. It is left in this condition until after cotton-picking is over, whether earlier or later. Then the ears are separated from the stalks, and deposited in the corncrib with the husks on; otherwise, stripped of the husks, the weevil would destroy it. The stalks are left standing in the field.

The Carolina, or sweet potato, is also grown in that region to some extent.[132] They are not fed, however, to hogs or cattle, and are considered but of small importance. They are preserved by placing them upon the surface of the ground, with a slight covering of earth or cornstalks. There is not a cellar on Bayou Boeuf.[133] The ground is so low it would fill with water. Potatoes are worth from two to three "bits," or shillings a barrel; corn, except when there is an unusual scarcity, can be purchased at the same rate.

As soon as the cotton and corn crops are secured, the stalks are pulled up, thrown into piles and burned. The ploughs are started at the same time, throwing up the beds again, preparatory to another planting. The soil, in the parishes of Rapides and Avoyelles, and throughout the whole country, so far as my observation extended, is of exceeding richness and fertility. It is a kind of marl, of a brown or reddish color. It does not require those invigorating composts necessary to more barren lands, and on the same field the same crop is grown for many successive years.

Ploughing, planting, picking cotton, gathering the corn, and pulling and burning stalks, occupies the whole of the four seasons of the year. Drawing and cutting wood, pressing cotton, fattening and killing hogs, are but incidental labors.

In the month of September or October, the hogs are run out of the swamps by dogs, and confined in pens. On a cold morning, generally about New Year's day, they are slaughtered. Each carcass is cut into six parts, and piled one above the other in salt, upon large tables in the smoke-house. In this condition it remains a fortnight, when it is hung up, and a fire built, and continued more than half the time during the remainder of the year. This thorough smoking is necessary to prevent the bacon from becoming infested with worms.

In so warm a climate it is difficult to preserve it, and very many times myself and my companions have received our weekly allowance of three pounds and a half, when it was full of these disgusting vermin.[134] *n. 134 unintentional?*

Although the swamps are overrun with cattle, they are never made the source of profit, to any considerable extent. The planter cuts his mark upon the ear, or brands his initials upon the side, and turns them into the swamps, to roam unrestricted within their almost limitless confines. They are the Spanish breed, small and spike-horned. I have known of droves being taken from Bayou Boeuf, but it is of very rare occurrence. The value of the best cows is about five dollars each. Two quarts at one milking, would be considered an unusual large quantity. They furnish little tallow, and that of a soft, inferior quality.[135] Notwithstanding the great number of cows that throng the swamps, the planters are indebted to the North for their cheese and butter, which is purchased in the New-Orleans market. Salted beef is not an article of food either in the great house, or in the cabin.

Master Epps was accustomed to attend shooting matches for the purpose of obtaining what fresh beef he required. These sports occurred weekly at the neighboring village of Holmesville. Fat beeves are driven thither and shot at, a stipulated price being demanded for the privilege. The lucky marksman divides the flesh among his fellows, and in this manner the attending planters are supplied.

The great number of tame and untamed cattle which swarm the woods and swamps of Bayou Boeuf, most probably suggested that appellation to the French, inasmuch as the term, translated, signifies the creek or river of the wild ox.

Garden products, such as cabbages, turnips and the like, are cultivated for the use of the master and his family. They have greens and vegetables at all times and seasons of the year. "The grass withereth and the flower fadeth" before the desolating winds of autumn in the chill northern latitudes, but perpetual verdure overspreads the hot lowlands, and flowers bloom in the heart of winter, in the region of Bayou Boeuf.[136]

There are no meadows appropriated to the cultivation of the grasses. The leaves of the corn supply a sufficiency of food for the laboring cattle, while the rest provide for themselves all the year in the ever growing pasture.

There are many other peculiarities of climate, habit, custom, and of the manner of living and laboring at the South, but the foregoing, it is supposed, will give the reader an insight and general idea of life on a cotton plantation in Louisiana. The mode of cultivating cane, and the process of sugar manufacturing, will be mentioned in another place.

CHAPTER XIII.

THE CURIOUS AXE-HELVE—SYMPTOMS OF APPROACHING ILLNESS—
CONTINUE TO DECLINE—THE WHIP INEFFECTUAL—CONFINED
TO THE CABIN—VISIT BY DR. WINES—PARTIAL RECOVERY—
FAILURE AT COTTON PICKING—WHAT MAY BE HEARD ON EPPS'
PLANTATION—LASHES GRADUATED—EPPS IN A WHIPPING MOOD—
EPPS IN A DANCING MOOD—DESCRIPTION OF THE DANCE—LOSS
OF REST NO EXCUSE—EPPS' CHARACTERISTICS—JIM BURNS—
REMOVAL FROM HUFF POWER TO BAYOU BOUEF—DESCRIPTION
OF UNCLE ABRAM; OF WILEY; OF AUNT PHEBE; OF BOB, HENRY,
AND EDWARD; OF PATSEY; WITH A GENEALOGICAL ACCOUNT OF
EACH—SOMETHING OF THEIR PAST HISTORY, AND PECULIAR
CHARACTERISTICS—JEALOUSY AND LUST—PATSEY, THE VICTIM.

On my arrival at Master Epps', in obedience to his order, the first
business upon which I entered was the making of an axe-helve. The
handles in use there are simply a round, straight stick. I made a
crooked one, shaped like those to which I had been accustomed in
the North. When finished, and presented to Epps, he looked at it
with astonishment, unable to determine exactly what it was. He had
never before seen such a handle, and when I explained its
conveniences, he was forcibly struck with the novelty of the idea. He
kept it in the house a long time, and when his friends called, was
wont to exhibit it as a curiosity.

It was now the season of hoeing. I was first sent into the cornfield, and afterwards set to scraping cotton.[137] In this employment I
remained until hoeing time was nearly passed, when I began to
experience the symptoms of approaching illness. I was attacked with
chills, which were succeeded by a burning fever. I became weak and
emaciated, and frequently so dizzy it caused me to reel and stagger
like a drunken man. Nevertheless, I was compelled to keep up my
row. When in health I found little difficulty in keeping pace with my
fellow-laborers, but now it seemed to be an utter impossibility. Often
I fell behind, when the driver's lash was sure to greet my back,
infusing into my sick and drooping body a little temporary energy.[138] I

continued to decline until at length the whip became entirely ineffectual. The sharpest sting of the rawhide could not arouse me. Finally, in September, when the busy season of cotton picking was at hand, I was unable to leave my cabin. Up to this time I had received no medicine, nor any attention from my master or mistress. The old cook visited me occasionally, preparing me corn-coffee, and sometimes boiling a bit of bacon, when I had grown too feeble to accomplish it myself. *Corn-coffee again*

When it was said that I would die, Master Epps, unwilling to bear the loss, which the death of an animal worth a thousand dollars would bring upon him, concluded to incur the expense of sending to Holmesville for Dr. Wines.[139] He announced to Epps that it was the effect of the climate, and there was a probability of his losing me. He directed me to eat no meat, and to partake of no more food than was absolutely necessary to sustain life. Several weeks elapsed, during which time, under the scanty diet to which I was subjected, I had partially recovered. One morning, long before I was in a proper condition to labor, Epps appeared at the cabin door, and, presenting me a sack, ordered me to the cotton field. At this time I had had no experience whatever in cotton picking. It was an awkward business indeed. While others used both hands, snatching the cotton and depositing it in the mouth of the sack, with a precision and dexterity that was incomprehensible to me, I had to seize the boll with one hand, and deliberately draw out the white, gushing blossom with the other. *He is picking cotton.*

Depositing the cotton in the sack, moreover, was a difficulty that demanded the exercise of both hands and eyes. I was compelled to pick it from the ground where it would fall, nearly as often as from the stalk where it had grown. I made havoc also with the branches, loaded with the yet unbroken bolls, the long, cumbersome sack swinging from side to side in a manner not allowable in the cotton field. After a most laborious day I arrived in the gin-house with my load. When the scale determined its weight to be only ninety-five pounds, not half the quantity required of the poorest picker, Epps threatened the severest flogging, but in consideration of my being a "raw hand," concluded to pardon me on that occasion.[140] The following day, and many days succeeding, I returned at night with no better success—I was evidently not designed for that kind of labor. I had not the gift—the dexterous fingers and quick motion of Patsey, who could fly along one side of a row of cotton, stripping it of its undefiled and fleecy whiteness miraculously fast. Practice and whipping were alike unavailing, and Epps, satisfied of it at last, swore I was a disgrace—that I was not fit to associate with a cotton-picking "nigger"—that I could not pick enough in a day to pay the trouble of weighing it, and that I should go into the cotton field no more. I was now employed in cutting and hauling wood, drawing cotton from the field to the gin-house, and performed whatever other service was required. Suffice to say, I was never permitted to be idle.

It was rarely that a day passed by without one or more whippings. This occurred at the time the cotton was weighed. The delinquent, whose weight had fallen short, was taken out, stripped, made to lie upon the ground, face downwards, when he received a punishment proportioned to his offence. It is the literal, unvarnished truth, that the crack of the lash, and the shrieking of the slaves, can be heard from dark till bed time, on Epps' plantation, any day almost during the entire period of the cotton-picking season. [141]

The number of lashes is graduated according to the nature of the case. Twenty-five are deemed a mere brush, inflicted, for instance, when a dry leaf or piece of boll is found in the cotton, or when a branch is broken in the field; fifty is the ordinary penalty following all delinquencies of the next higher grade; one hundred is called severe: it is the punishment inflicted for the serious offence of standing idle in the field; from one hundred and fifty to two hundred is bestowed upon him who quarrels with his cabin-mates, and five hundred, well laid on, besides the mangling of the dogs, perhaps, is certain to consign the poor, unpitied runaway to weeks of pain and agony.

During the two years Epps remained on the plantation at Bayou Huff Power, he was in the habit, as often as once in a fortnight at least, of coming home intoxicated from Holmesville. The shooting-matches almost invariably concluded with a debauch. At such times he was boisterous and half-crazy. Often he would break the dishes, chairs, and whatever furniture he could lay his hands on. When satisfied with his amusement in the house, he would seize the whip and walk forth into the yard. Then it behooved the slaves to be watchful and exceeding wary. The first one who came within reach felt the smart of his lash. Sometimes for hours he would keep them running in all directions, dodging around the corners of the cabins. Occasionally he would come upon one unawares, and if he succeeded in inflicting a fair, round blow, it was a feat that much delighted him. The younger children, and the aged, who had become inactive, suffered then. In the midst of the confusion he would slyly take his stand behind a cabin, waiting with raised whip, to dash it into the first black face that peeped cautiously around the corner.

At other times he would come home in a less brutal humor. Then there must be a merry-making. Then all must move to the measure of a tune. Then Master Epps must needs regale his melodious ears with the music of a fiddle. Then did he become buoyant, elastic, gaily "tripping the light fantastic toe" around the piazza and all through the house. *He likes music.*

Tibeats, at the time of my sale, had informed him I could play the violin. He had received this information from Ford. Through the importunities of Mistress Epps, her husband had been induced to purchase me one during a visit to New-Orleans. Frequently I was called into the house to play before the family, mistress being passionately fond of music.

All of us would be assembled in the large room of the great house, whenever Epps came home in one of his dancing moods. No matter how worn out and tired we were, there must be a general dance. When properly stationed on the floor, I would strike up a tune.

"Dance you d——d niggers, dance," Epps would shout.

Then there must be no halting or delay, no slow or languid movements; all must be brisk, and lively, and alert. "Up and down, heel and toe, and away we go," was the order of the hour. Epps' portly form mingled with those of his dusky slaves, moving rapidly through all the mazes of the dance.

Usually his whip was in his hand, ready to fall about the ears of the presumptuous thrall, who dared to rest a moment, or even stop to catch his breath. When he was himself exhausted, there would be a brief cessation, but it would be very brief. With a slash, and crack, and flourish of the whip, he would shout again, "Dance, niggers dance," and away they would go once more, pell-mell, while I, spurred by an occasional sharp touch of the lash, sat in a corner, extracting from my violin a marvelous quick-stepping tune. The mistress often upbraided him, declaring she would return to her father's house at Cheneyville; nevertheless, there were times she could not restrain a burst of laughter, on witnessing his uproarious pranks. Frequently, we were thus detained until almost morning. Bent with excessive toil—actually suffering for a little refreshing rest, and feeling rather as if we could cast ourselves upon the earth and weep, many a night in the house of Edwin Epps have his unhappy slaves been made to dance and laugh.

Notwithstanding these deprivations in order to gratify the whim of an unreasonable master, we had to be in the field as soon as it was light, and during the day perform the ordinary and accustomed task. Such deprivations could not be urged at the scales in extenuation of any lack of weight, or in the cornfield for not hoeing with the usual rapidity. The whippings were just as severe as if we had gone forth in the morning, strengthened and invigorated by a night's repose. Indeed, after such frantic revels, he was always more sour and savage than before, punishing for slighter causes, and using the whip with increased and more vindictive energy.

Ten years I toiled for that man without reward. Ten years of my incessant labor has contributed to increase the bulk of his possessions. Ten years I was compelled to address him with down-cast eyes and uncovered head—in the attitude and language of a slave. I am indebted to him for nothing, save undeserved abuse and stripes. *How would you feel?*

Beyond the reach of his inhuman thong, and standing on the soil of the free State where I was born, thanks be to Heaven, I can raise my head once more among men. I can speak of the wrongs I have suffered, and of those who inflicted them, with upraised eyes. But I have no desire to speak of him or any other one otherwise than truthfully. Yet to speak truthfully of Edwin Epps would be to say— he is a man in whose heart the quality of kindness or of justice is not found. A rough, rude energy, united with an uncultivated mind and an avaricious spirit, are his prominent characteristics. He is known as a "nigger breaker," distinguished for his faculty of subduing the spirit of the slave, and priding himself upon his reputation in this respect, as a jockey boasts of his skill in managing a refractory horse. He looked upon a colored man, not as a human being, responsible to his Creator for the small talent entrusted to him, but as a "chattel personal," as mere live property, no better, except in value, than his mule or dog. When the evidence, clear and indisputable, was laid before him that I was a free man, and as much entitled to my liberty as he—when, on the day I left, he was informed that I had a wife and children, as dear to me as his own babes to him, he only raved and swore, denouncing the law that tore me from him, and declaring he would find out the man who forwarded the letter that disclosed the place of my captivity, if there was any virtue or power in money, and would take his life. He thought of nothing but his loss, and cursed me for having been born free. He could have stood unmoved and seen the tongues of his poor slaves torn out by the roots—he could have seen them burned to ashes over a slow fire, or gnawed to death by dogs, if it only brought him profit. Such a hard, cruel, unjust man is Edwin Epps.

There was but one greater savage on Bayou Boeuf than he. Jim Burns' plantation was cultivated, as already mentioned, exclusively by women. That barbarian kept their backs so sore and raw, that they could not perform the customary labor demanded daily of the slave. He boasted of his cruelty, and through all the country round was accounted a more thorough-going, energetic man than even Epps. A brute himself, Jim Burns had not a particle of mercy for his subject brutes, and like a fool, whipped and scourged away the very strength upon which depended his amount of gain. *explain ?*

Epps remained on Huff Power two years, when, having accumulated a considerable sum of money, he expended it in the purchase of the plantation on the east bank of Bayou Boeuf, where he still continues to reside.[142] He took possession of it in 1845, after the holidays were passed. He carried thither with him nine slaves, all of whom, except myself, and Susan, who has since died, remain there yet. He made no addition to this force, and for eight years the following were my companions in his quarter, viz: Abram, Wiley, Phebe, Bob, Henry, Edward, and Patsey. All these, except Edward, born since, were purchased out of a drove by Epps during the time he was overseer for Archy B. Williams, whose plantation is situated on the shore of Red River, not far from Alexandria.[143]

Abram was tall, standing a full head above any common man. He is sixty years of age, and was born in Tennessee. Twenty years ago, he was purchased by a trader, carried into South Carolina, and sold to James Buford, of Williamsburgh county, in that State. In his youth he was renowned for his great strength, but age and unremitting toil have somewhat shattered his powerful frame and enfeebled his mental faculties.

Wiley is forty-eight. He was born on the estate of William Tassle, and for many years took charge of that gentlemen's ferry over the Big Black River, in South Carolina.

Phebe was a slave of Buford, Tassle's neighbor, and having married Wiley, he bought the latter, at her instigation. Buford was a kind master, sheriff of the county, and in those days a man of wealth.

Bob and Henry are Phebe's children, by a former husband, their father having been abandoned to give place to Wiley. That seductive youth had insinuated himself into Phebe's affections, and therefore the faithless spouse had gently kicked her first husband out of her cabin door. Edward had been born to them on Bayou Huff Power.

Patsey is twenty-three—also from Buford's plantation. She is in no wise connected with the others, but glories in the fact that she is the offspring of a "Guinea nigger," brought over to Cuba in a slave ship, and in the course of trade transferred to Buford, who was her mother's owner.

This, as I learned from them, is a genealogical account of my master's slaves. For years they had been together. Often they recalled the memories of other days, and sighed to retrace their steps to the old home in Carolina. Troubles came upon their Master Buford, which brought far greater troubles upon them. He became involved in debt, and unable to bear up against his failing fortunes, was compelled to sell these, and others of his slaves.[144] In a chain gang they had been driven from beyond the Mississippi to the plantation of Archy B. Williams.[145] Edwin Epps, who, for a long while had been his driver and overseer, was about establishing himself in business on his own account, at the time of their arrival, and accepted them in payment of his wages.

Old Abram was a kind-hearted being—a sort of patriarch among us, fond of entertaining his younger brethren with grave and serious discourse. He was deeply versed in such philosophy as is taught in the cabin of the slave; but the great absorbing hobby of Uncle Abram was General Jackson, whom his younger master in Tennessee had followed to the wars. He loved to wander back, in imagination, to the place where he was born, and to recount the scenes of his youth during those stirring times when the nation was in arms. He had been athletic, and more keen and powerful than the generality of his race, but now his eye had become dim, and his natural force abated. Very often, indeed, while discussing the best method of baking the hoe-cake, or expatiating at large upon the glory of Jackson, he would forget where he left his hat, or his hoe, or his basket; and then would the old man be laughed at, if Epps was absent, and whipped if he was present. So was he perplexed continually, and sighed to think that he was growing aged and going to decay. Philosophy and Jackson and forgetfulness had played the mischief with him, and it was evident that all of them combined were fast bringing down the gray hairs of Uncle Abram to the grave.

Aunt Phebe had been an excellent field hand, but latterly was put into the kitchen, where she remained, except occasionally, in a time of uncommon hurry. She was a sly old creature, and when not in the presence of her mistress or her master, was garrulous in the extreme.

Wiley, on the contrary, was silent. He performed his task without murmur or complaint, seldom indulging in the luxury of speech, except to utter a wish that he was away from Epps, back once more in South Carolina.

Bob and Henry had reached the ages of twenty and twenty-three, and were distinguished for nothing extraordinary or unusual, while Edward, a lad of thirteen, not able to maintain his row in the corn or the cotton field, was kept in the great house, to wait on the little Eppses.

Patsey was slim and straight. She stood erect as the human form is capable of standing. There was an air of loftiness in her movement, that neither labor, nor weariness, nor punishment could destroy. Truly, Patsey was a splendid animal, and were it not that bondage had enshrouded her intellect in utter and everlasting darkness, would have been chief among ten thousand of her people. She could leap the highest fences, and a fleet hound it was indeed, that could outstrip her in a race. No horse could fling her from his back. She was a skillful teamster. She turned as true a furrow as the best, and at splitting rails there were none that could excel her. When the order to halt was heard at night, she would have her mules at the crib, unharnessed, fed and curried, before uncle Abram had found his hat. Not, however, for all or any of these, was she chiefly famous. Such lightning-like motion was in her fingers as no other fingers ever possessed, and therefore it was, that in cotton picking time, Patsey was queen of the field.

She had a genial and pleasant temper, and was faithful and obedient. Naturally, she was a joyous creature, a laughing, light-hearted girl, rejoicing in the mere sense of existence. Yet Patsey wept oftener, and suffered more, than any of her companions. She had been literally excoriated. Her back bore the scars of a thousand stripes; not because she was backward in her work, nor because she was of an unmindful and rebellious spirit, but because it had fallen to her lot to be the slave of a licentious master and a jealous mistress. She shrank before the lustful eye of the one, and was in danger even of her life at the hands of the other, and between the two, she was indeed accursed. In the great house, for days together, there were high and angry words, poutings and estrangement, whereof she was the innocent cause. Nothing delighted the mistress so much as to see her suffer, and more than once, when Epps had refused to sell her, has she tempted me with bribes to put her secretly to death, and bury her body in some lonely place in the margin of the swamp. Gladly would Patsey have appeased this unforgiving spirit, if it had been in her power, but not like Joseph, dared she escape from Master Epps, leaving her garment in his hand. Patsey walked under a cloud. If she uttered a word in opposition to her master's will, the lash was resorted to at once, to bring her to subjection; if she was not watchful when about her cabin, or when walking in the yard, a billet of wood, or a broken bottle perhaps, hurled from her mistress' hand, would smite her unexpectedly in the face. The enslaved victim of lust and hate, Patsey had no comfort of her life.

These were my companions and fellow-slaves, with whom I was accustomed to be driven to the field, and with whom it had been my lot to dwell for ten years in the log cabins of Edwin Epps. They, if living, are yet toiling on the banks of Bayou Boeuf, never destined to breathe, as I now do, the blessed air of liberty, nor to shake off the heavy shackles that enthrall them, until they shall lie down forever in the dust.

CHAPTER XIV.

DESTRUCTION OF THE COTTON CROP IN 1845—DEMAND FOR
LABORERS IN ST. MARY'S PARISH—SENT THITHER IN A DROVE—THE
ORDER OF THE MARCH—THE GRAND COTEAU—HIRED TO JUDGE
TURNER OF BAYOU SALLE—APPOINTED DRIVER IN HIS SUGAR
HOUSE—SUNDAY SERVICES—SLAVE FURNITURE, HOW OBTAINED—
THE PARTY AT YARNEY'S IN CENTREVILLE—GOOD FORTUNE—THE
CAPTAIN OF THE STEAMER—HIS REFUSAL TO SECRETE ME—
RETURN TO BAYOU BOEUF—SIGHT OF TIBEATS—PATSEY'S
SORROWS—TUMULT AND CONTENTION—HUNTING THE COON
AND OPOSSUM—THE CUNNING OF THE LATTER—THE LEAN
CONDITION OF THE SLAVE—DESCRIPTION OF THE FISH TRAP—THE
MURDER OF THE MAN FROM NATCHEZ—EPPS CHALLENGED BY
MARSHALL—THE INFLUENCE OF SLAVERY—THE LOVE OF
FREEDOM.

The first year of Epps' residence on the bayou, 1845, the caterpillars almost totally destroyed the cotton crop throughout that region.[146] There was little to be done, so that the slaves were necessarily idle half the time. However, there came a rumor to Bayou Boeuf that wages were high, and laborers in great demand on the sugar plantations in St. Mary's parish.[147] This parish is situated on the coast of the Gulf of Mexico, about one hundred and forty miles from Avoyelles. The Rio Teche, a considerable stream, flows through St. Mary's to the gulf.[148]

It was determined by the planters, on the receipt of this intelligence, to make up a drove of slaves to be sent down to Tuckapaw in St. Mary's, for the purpose of hiring them out in the cane fields. Accordingly, in the month of September, there were one hundred and forty-seven collected at Holmesville, Abram, Bob and myself among the number. Of these about one-half were women. Epps, Alonson Pierce, Henry Toler, and Addison Roberts, were the white men, selected to accompany, and take charge of the drove.[149] They had a two-horse carriage and two saddle horses for their use. A large wagon, drawn by four horses, and driven by John, a boy belonging to Mr. Roberts, carried the blankets and provisions.

About 2 o'clock in the afternoon, having been fed, preparations were made to depart. The duty assigned to me was, to take charge of the blankets and provisions, and see that none were lost by the way. The carriage proceeded in advance, the wagon following; behind this the slaves were arranged, while the two horsemen brought up the rear, and in this order the procession moved out of Holmesville.

That night we reached a Mr. McCrow's plantation, a distance of ten or fifteen miles, when we were ordered to halt. Large fires were built, and each one spreading his blanket on the ground, laid down upon it. The white men lodged in the great house. An hour before day we were aroused by the drivers coming among us, cracking their whips and ordering us to arise. Then the blankets were rolled up, and being severally delivered to me and deposited in the wagon, the procession set forth again.

The following night it rained violently. We were all drenched, our clothes saturated with mud and water. Reaching an open shed, formerly a gin-house, we found beneath it such shelter as it afforded. There was not room for all of us to lay down. There we remained, huddled together, through the night, continuing our march, as usual, in the morning. During the journey we were fed twice a day, boiling our bacon and baking our corn-cake at the fires in the same manner as in our huts. We passed through Lafayetteville, Mountsville, New-Town, to Centreville, where Bob and Uncle Abram were hired.[150] Our number decreased as we advanced—nearly every sugar plantation requiring the services of one or more.

On our route we passed the Grand Coteau or prairie, a vast space of level, monotonous country, without a tree, except an occasional one which had been transplanted near some dilapidated dwelling.[151] It was once thickly populated, and under cultivation, but for some cause had been abandoned. The business of the scattered inhabitants that now dwell upon it is principally raising cattle. Immense herds were feeding upon it as we passed. In the centre of the Grand Coteau one feels as if he were on the ocean, out of sight of land. As far as the eye can see, in all directions, it is but a ruined and deserted waste.

I was hired to Judge Turner,[152] a distinguished man and extensive planter, whose large estate is situated on Bayou Salle,

within a few miles of the gulf. Bayou Salle is a small stream flowing
into the bay of Atchafalaya. For some days I was employed at
Turner's in repairing his sugar house, when a cane knife was put
into my hand, and with thirty or forty others, I was sent into the
field. I found no such difficulty in learning the art of cutting cane
that I had in picking cotton. It came to me naturally and intuitively,
and in a short time I was able to keep up with the fastest knife.
Before the cutting was over, however, Judge Tanner [Turner]
transferred me from the field to the sugar house, to act there in the
capacity of driver. From the time of the commencement of sugar
making to the close, the grinding and boiling does not cease day or
night. The whip was given me with directions to use it upon any
one who was caught standing idle. If I failed to obey them to the
letter, there was another one for my own back. In addition to this
my duty was to call on and off the different gangs at the proper
time. I had no regular periods of rest, and could never snatch but a
few moments of sleep at a time.

It is the custom in Louisiana, as I presume it is in other slave
States, to allow the slave to retain whatever compensation he may
obtain for services performed on Sundays.[153] In this way, only, are
they able to provide themselves with any luxury or convenience
whatever. When a slave, purchased, or kidnapped in the North, is
transported to a cabin on Bayou Boeuf, he is furnished with neither
knife, nor fork, nor dish, nor kettle, nor any other thing in the shape
of crockery, or furniture of any nature or description. He is furnished
with a blanket before he reaches there, and wrapping that around
him, he can either stand up, or lie down upon the ground, or on a
board, if his master has no use for it. He is at liberty to find a gourd
in which to keep his meal, or he can eat his corn from the cob, just as
he pleases. To ask the master for a knife, or skillet, or any small
convenience of the kind, would be answered with a kick, or laughed
at as a joke. Whatever necessary article of this nature is found in a
cabin has been purchased with Sunday money. However injurious to

the morals, it is certainly a blessing to the physical condition of the
slave, to be permitted to break the Sabbath. Otherwise, there would
be no way to provide himself with any utensils, which seem to be
indispensable to him who is compelled to be his own cook.

On cane plantations in sugar time, there is no distinction as to
the days of the week. It is well understood that all hands must labor

on the Sabbath, and it is equally well understood that those especially who are hired, as I was to Judge Turner, and others in succeeding years, shall receive remuneration for it. It is usual, also, in the most hurrying time of cotton-picking, to require the same extra service. From this source, slaves generally are afforded an opportunity of earning sufficient to purchase a knife, a kettle, tobacco and so forth. The females, discarding the latter luxury, are apt to expend their little revenue in the purchase of gaudy ribbons, wherewithal to deck their hair in the merry season of the holidays.

I remained in St. Mary's until the first of January, during which time my Sunday money amounted to ten dollars. I met with other good fortune, for which I was indebted to my violin, my constant companion, the source of profit, and soother of my sorrows during years of servitude. There was a grand party of whites assembled at Mr. Yarney's, in Centreville, a hamlet in the vicinity of Turner's plantation.[154] I was employed to play for them, and so well pleased were the merry-makers with my performance, that a contribution was taken for my benefit, which amounted to seventeen dollars.

With this sum in possession, I was looked upon by my fellows as a millionaire. It afforded me great pleasure to look at it—to count it over and over again, day after day. Visions of cabin furniture, of water pails, of pocket knives, new shoes and coats and hats, floated through my fancy, and up through all rose the triumphant contemplation, that I was the wealthiest "nigger" on Bayou Boeuf.

Vessels run up the Rio Teche to Centreville. While there, I was bold enough one day to present myself before the captain of a steamer, and beg permission to hide myself among the freight. I was emboldened to risk the hazard of such a step, from overhearing a conversation, in the course of which I ascertained he was a native of the North. I did not relate to him the particulars of my history, but only expressed an ardent desire to escape from slavery to a free State. He pitied me, but said it would be impossible to avoid the vigilant custom house officers in New-Orleans, and that detection would subject him to punishment, and his vessel to confiscation. My earnest entreaties evidently excited his sympathies, and doubtless he would have yielded to them, could he have done so with any kind of safety. I was compelled to smother the sudden flame that lighted up my bosom with sweet hope of liberation, and turn my steps once more towards the increasing darkness of despair.

Immediately after this event the drove assembled at Centreville, and several of the owners having arrived and collected the monies due for our services, we were driven back to Bayou Boeuf. It was on our return, while passing through a small village, that I caught sight of Tibeats, seated in the door of a dirty grocery, looking somewhat seedy and out of repair. Passion and poor whiskey, I doubt not, have ere this laid him on the shelf.

bad whiskey

During our absence, I learned from Aunt Phebe and Patsey, that the latter had been getting deeper and deeper into trouble. The poor girl was truly an object of pity. "Old Hogjaw," the name by which Epps was called, when the slaves were by themselves, had beaten her more severely and frequently than ever. As surely as he came from Holmesville, elated with liquor—and it was often in those days—he would whip her, merely to gratify the mistress; would punish her to an extent almost beyond endurance, for an offence of which he himself was the sole and irresistible cause. In his sober moments he could not always be prevailed upon to indulge his wife's insatiable thirst for vengeance.

To be rid of Patsey—to place her beyond sight or reach, by sale, or death, or in any other manner, of late years, seemed to be the ruling thought and passion of my mistress. Patsey had been a favorite when a child, even in the great house. She had been petted and admired for her uncommon sprightliness and pleasant disposition. She had been fed many a time, so Uncle Abram said, even on biscuit and milk, when the madam, in her younger days, was wont to call her to the piazza, and fondle her as she would a playful kitten. But a sad change had come over the spirit of the woman. Now, only black and angry fiends ministered in the temple of her heart, until she could look on Patsey but with concentrated venom.

Mistress Epps was not naturally such an evil woman, after all. She was possessed of the devil, jealousy, it is true, but aside from that, there was much in her character to admire. Her father, Mr. Roberts, resided in Cheneyville, an influential and honorable man, and as much respected throughout the parish as any other citizen.[155] She had been well educated at some institution this side the Mississippi; was beautiful, accomplished and usually good-humored. She was kind to all of us but Patsey—frequently, in the absence of her husband, sending out to us some little dainty from her own table. In other situations—in a different society from that which exists on the shores of Bayou

n. 155 on education

Boeuf, she would have been pronounced an elegant and fascinating woman. An ill wind it was that blew her into the arms of Epps. *explain*

He respected and loved his wife as much as a coarse nature like his is capable of loving, but supreme selfishness always overmastered conjugal affection.

> "He loved as well as baser natures can,
> But a mean heart and soul were in that man."

He was ready to gratify any whim—to grant any request she made, provided it did not cost too much. Patsey was equal to any two of his slaves in the cotton field. He could not replace her with the same money she would bring. The idea of disposing of her, therefore, could not be entertained. The mistress did not regard her at all in that light. The pride of the haughty woman was aroused; the blood of the fiery southern boiled at the sight of Patsey, and nothing less than trampling out the life of the helpless bondwoman would satisfy her.

Sometimes the current of her wrath turned upon him whom she had just cause to hate. But the storm of angry words would pass over at length, and there would be a season of calm again. At such times Patsey trembled with fear, and cried as if her heart would break, for she knew from painful experience, that if mistress should work herself to the red-hot pitch of rage, Epps would quiet her at last with a promise that Patsey should be flogged—a promise he was sure to keep. Thus did pride, jealousy, and vengeance war with avarice and brute-passion in the mansion of my master, filling it with daily tumult and contention. Thus, upon the head of Patsey—the simple-minded slave, in whose heart God had implanted the seeds of virtue—the force of all these domestic tempests spent itself at last.

During the summer succeeding my return from St. Mary's parish, I conceived a plan of providing myself with food, which, though simple, succeeded beyond expectation. It has been followed by many others in my condition, up and down the bayou, and of such benefit has it become that I am almost persuaded to look upon myself as a benefactor. That summer the worms got into the bacon. *Eew!* Nothing but ravenous hunger could induce us to swallow it. The weekly allowance of meal scarcely sufficed to satisfy us. It was customary with us, as it is with all in that region, where the allowance is exhausted before Saturday night, or is in such a state as to render it nauseous and disgusting, to hunt in the swamps for coon and opossum. This, however, must be done at night, after the day's work is accomplished. There are planters whose slaves, for months at a time, have no other meat than such as is obtained in this manner. No objections are made to hunting, inasmuch as it dispenses with drafts upon the smoke-house, and because every marauding coon that is killed is so much saved from the standing corn. They are hunted with dogs and clubs, slaves not being allowed the use of fire-arms.[156]

The flesh of the coon is palatable, but verily there is nothing in all butcherdom so delicious as a roasted 'possum. They are a round, rather long-bodied, little animal, of a whitish color, with nose like a pig, and caudal extremity like a rat. They burrow among the roots and in the hollows of the gum tree, and are clumsy and slow of motion. They are deceitful and cunning creatures. On receiving the slightest tap of a stick, they will roll over on the ground and feign death. If the hunter leaves him, in pursuit of another, without first taking particular pains to break his neck, the chances are, on his return, he is not to be found. The little animal has out witted the enemy—has "played 'possum"—and is off. But after a long and hard day's work, the weary slave feels little like going to the swamp for his supper, and half the time prefers throwing himself on the cabin floor without it. It is for the interest of the master that the servant should not suffer in health from starvation, and it is also for his interest that he should not become gross from over-feeding. In the estimation of the owner, a slave is most serviceable when in rather a lean and lank condition, such a condition as the race-horse is in, when fitted for the course, and in that condition they are generally to be found on the sugar and cotton plantations along Red River.

My cabin was within a few rods of the bayou bank, and necessity being indeed the mother of invention, I resolved upon a mode of obtaining the requisite amount of food, without the trouble of resorting nightly to the woods. This was to construct a fish trap.[157] Having, in my mind, conceived the manner in which it could be done, the next Sunday I set about putting it into practical execution. It may be impossible for me to convey to the reader a full and correct idea of its construction, but the following will serve as a general description:

A frame between two and three feet square is made, and of a greater or less height, according to the depth of water. Boards or slats are nailed on three sides of this frame, not so closely, however, as to prevent the water circulating freely through it. A door is fitted into the fourth side, in such manner that it will slide easily up and down in the grooves cut in the two posts. A movable bottom is then so fitted that it can be raised to the top of the frame without difficulty. In the centre of the movable bottom an auger hole is bored, and into this one end of a handle or round stick is fastened on the under side so loosely that it will turn. The handle ascends from the centre of the movable bottom to the top of the frame, or as much higher as is desirable. Up and down this handle, in a great many places, are gimlet holes, through which small sticks are inserted, extending to opposite sides of the frame. So many of these small sticks are running out from the handle in all directions, that a fish of any considerable dimensions cannot pass through without hitting one of them. The frame is then placed in the water and made stationary.

The trap is "set" by sliding or drawing up the door, and kept in that position by another stick, one end of which rests in a notch on the inner side, the other end in a notch made in the handle, running up from the centre of the movable bottom. The trap is baited by rolling a handful of wet meal and cotton together until it becomes hard, and depositing it in the back part of the frame. A fish swimming through the upraised door towards the bait, necessarily strikes one of the small sticks turning the handle, which displacing the stick supporting the door, the latter falls, securing the fish within the frame. Taking hold of the top of the handle, the movable bottom is then drawn up to the surface of the water, and the fish taken out. There may have been other such traps in use before mine was constructed, but if there were I had never happened to see one. Bayou Boeuf abounds in fish of large size and excellent quality, and after this time I was very rarely in want of one for myself, or for my comrades. Thus a mine was opened—a new resource was developed, hitherto unthought of by the enslaved children of Africa, who toil and hunger along the shores of that sluggish, but prolific stream.

About the time of which I am now writing, an event occurred in our immediate neighborhood, which made a deep impression upon me, and which shows the state of society existing there, and the manner in which affronts are oftentimes avenged. Directly opposite our quarters, on the other side of the bayou, was situated the plantation of Mr. Marshall.[158] He belonged to a family among the most wealthy and aristocratic in the country. A gentleman from the vicinity of Natchez had been negotiating with him for the purchase of the estate. One day a messenger came in great haste to our plantation, saying that a bloody and fearful battle was going on at Marshall's—that blood had been spilled—and unless the combatants were forthwith separated, the result would be disastrous.

On repairing to Marshall's house, a scene presented itself that beggars description. On the floor of one of the rooms lay the ghastly corpse of the man from Natchez, while Marshall, enraged and covered with wounds and blood, was stalking back and forth, "breathing out threatenings and slaughter."[159] A difficulty had arisen in the course of their negotiation, high words ensued, when drawing their weapons, the deadly strife began that ended so unfortunately. Marshall was never placed in confinement. A sort of trial or investigation was had at Marksville, when he was acquitted, and returned to his plantation, rather more respected, as I thought, than ever, from the fact that the blood of a fellow being was on his soul.

Epps interested himself in his behalf, accompanying him to Marksville, and on all occasions loudly justifying him, but his services in the respect did not afterwards deter a kinsman of this same Marshall from seeking his life also. A brawl occurred between them over a gambling-table, which terminated in a deadly feud. Riding up on horseback in front of the house one day, armed with pistols and bowie knife, Marshall challenged him to come forth and make a final settlement of the quarrel, or he would brand him as a coward, and shoot him like a dog the first opportunity. Not through cowardice, nor from any conscientious scruples, in my opinion, but through the influence of his wife, he was restrained from accepting the challenge of his enemy. A reconciliation, however, was effected afterward, since which time they have been on terms of the closest intimacy.

Such occurrences, which would bring upon the parties concerned in them merited and condign punishment in the Northern States, are frequent on the bayou, and pass without notice, and almost without comment. Every man carries his bowie knife, and when two fall out, they set to work hacking and thrusting at each other, more like savages than civilized and enlightened beings.

The existence of Slavery in its most cruel form among them, has a tendency to brutalize the humane and finer feelings of their nature.

Daily witnesses of human suffering—listening to the agonizing screeches of the slave—beholding him writhing beneath the merciless lash—bitten and torn by dogs—dying without attention, and buried without shroud or coffin—it cannot otherwise be expected, than that they should become brutified and reckless of human life. It is true there are many kind-hearted and good men in the parish of Avoyelles—such men as William Ford—who can look with pity upon the sufferings of a slave, just as there are, over all the world, sensitive and sympathetic spirits, who cannot look with indifference upon the sufferings of any creature which the Almighty has endowed with life. It is not the fault of the slaveholder that he is cruel, so much as it is the fault of the system under which he lives. He cannot withstand the influence of habit and associations that surround him. Taught from earliest childhood, by all that he sees and hears, that the rod is for the slave's back, he will not be apt to change his opinions in maturer years.

There may be humane masters, as there certainly are inhuman ones—there may be slaves well-clothed, well-fed, and happy, as there are surely those half-clad, half-starved and miserable; nevertheless, the institution that tolerates such wrong and inhumanity as I have witnessed, is a cruel, unjust and barbarous one. Men may write fictions portraying lowly life as it is, or as it is not—may expatiate with owlish gravity upon the bliss of ignorance—discourse flippantly from arm chairs of the pleasures of slave life; but let them toil with him in the field—sleep with him in the cabin—feed with him on husks; let them behold him scourged, hunted, trampled on, and they will come back with another story in their mouths. Let them know the *heart* of the poor slave—learn his secret thoughts—thoughts he dare not utter in the hearing of the white man; let them sit by him in the silent watches of the night—converse with him in trustful confidence, of "life, liberty, and the pursuit of happiness," and they will find that ninety-nine out of every hundred are intelligent enough to understand their situation, and to cherish in their bosoms the love of freedom, as passionately as themselves.

On pity + empathy

CHAPTER XV.

LABORS ON SUGAR PLANTATIONS—THE MODE OF PLANTING CANE—OF HOEING CANE—CANE RICKS—CUTTING CANE—DESCRIPTION OF THE CANE KNIFE—WINROWING—PREPARING FOR SUCCEEDING CROPS—DESCRIPTION OF HAWKINS' SUGAR MILL ON BAYOU BOEUF—THE CHRISTMAS HOLIDAYS—THE CARNIVAL SEASON OF THE CHILDREN OF BONDAGE—THE CHRISTMAS SUPPER—RED, THE FAVORITE COLOR—THE VIOLIN, AND THE CONSOLATION IT AFFORDED—THE CHRISTMAS DANCE—LIVELY, THE COQUETTE—SAM ROBERTS, AND HIS RIVALS—SLAVE SONGS—SOUTHERN LIFE AS IT IS—THREE DAYS IN THE YEAR—THE SYSTEM OF MARRIAGE—UNCLE ABRAM'S CONTEMPT OF MATRIMONY.

In consequence of my inability in cotton-picking, Epps was in the habit of hiring me out on sugar plantations during the season of cane-cutting and sugar-making. He received for my services a dollar a day, with the money supplying my place on his cotton plantation. Cutting cane was an employment that suited me, and for three successive years I held the lead row at Hawkins', leading a gang of from fifty to an hundred hands![160]

In a previous chapter the mode of cultivating cotton is described. This may be the proper place to speak of the manner of cultivating cane.[161]

The ground is prepared in beds, the same as it is prepared for the reception of the cotton seed, except it is ploughed deeper. Drills are made in the same manner. Planting commences in January, and continues until April. It is necessary to plant a sugar field only once in three years. Three crops are taken before the seed or plant is exhausted.

Three gangs are employed in the operation. One draws the cane from the rick, or stack, cutting the top and flags from the stalk, leaving only that part which is sound and healthy. Each joint of the cane has an eye, like the eye of a potato, which sends forth a sprout when buried in the soil. Another gang lays the cane in the drill, placing two stalks side by side in such manner that joints will occur once in four or six inches. The third gang follows with hoes, drawing earth upon the stalks, and covering them to the depth of three inches.

In four weeks, at the farthest, the sprouts appear above the ground, and from this time forward grow with great rapidity. A sugar field is hoed three times, the same as cotton, save that a greater quantity of earth is drawn to the roots. By the first of August hoeing is usually over. About the middle of September, whatever is required for seed is cut and stacked in ricks, as they are termed. In October it is ready for the mill or sugar-house, and then the general cutting begins. The blade of a cane-knife is fifteen inches long, three inches wide in the middle, and tapering towards the point and handle. The blade is thin, and in order to be at all serviceable must be kept very sharp. Every third hand takes the lead of two others, one of whom is on each side of him. The lead hand, in the first place, with a blow of his knife shears the flags from the stalk. He next cuts off the top down as far as it is green. He must be careful to sever all the green from the ripe part, inasmuch as the juice of the former sours the molasses, and renders it unsalable. Then he severs the stalk at the root, and lays it directly behind him. His right and left hand companions lay their stalks, when cut in the same manner, upon his. To every three hands there is a cart, which follows, and the stalks are thrown into it by the younger slaves, when it is drawn to the sugar-house and ground.

If the planter apprehends a frost, the cane is winrowed. Winrowing is the cutting the stalks at an early period and throwing them lengthwise in the water furrow in such a manner that the tops will cover the butts of the stalks.[162] They will remain in this condition three weeks or a month without souring, and secure from frost. When the proper time arrives, they are taken up, trimmed and carted to the sugar-house.

In the month of January the slaves enter the field again to prepare for another crop. The ground is now strewn with the tops, and flags cut from the past year's cane. On a dry day fire is set to this combustible refuse, which sweeps over the field, leaving it bare and clean, and ready for the hoes. The earth is loosened about the roots of the old stubble, and in process of time another crop springs up from the last year's seed. It is the same the year following; but the third year the seed has exhausted its strength, and the field must be ploughed and planted again. The second year the cane is sweeter and yields more than the first, and the third year more than the second.

During the three seasons I labored on Hawkins' plantation, I was employed a considerable portion of the time in the sugar-house. He is celebrated as the producer of the finest variety of white sugar. The following is a general description of his sugar-house and the process of manufacture:[163]

The mill is an immense brick building, standing on the shore of the bayou. Running out from the building is an open shed, at least an hundred feet in length and forty or fifty feet in width. The boiler in which the steam is generated is situated outside the main building; the machinery and engine rest on a brick pier, fifteen feet above the floor, within the body of the building. The machinery turns two great iron rollers, between two and three feet in diameter and six or eight feet in length. They are elevated above the brick pier, and roll in towards each other. An endless carrier, made of chain and wood, like leathern belts used in small mills, extends from the iron rollers out of the main building and through the entire length of the open shed. The carts in which the cane is brought from the field as fast as it is cut, are unloaded at the sides of the shed. All along the endless carrier are ranged slave children, whose business it is to place the cane upon it, when it is conveyed through the shed into the main building, where it falls between the rollers, is crushed, and drops upon another carrier that conveys it out of the main building in an opposite direction, depositing it in the top of a chimney upon a fire beneath, which consumes it. It is necessary to burn it in this manner, because otherwise it would soon fill the building, and more especially because it would soon sour and engender disease. The juice of the cane falls into a conductor underneath the iron rollers, and is carried into a reservoir. Pipes convey it from thence into five filterers, holding several hogsheads each. These filterers are filled with bone-black, a substance resembling pulverized charcoal. It is made of bones calcined in close vessels, and is used for the purpose of decolorizing, by filtration, the cane juice before boiling. Through these five filterers it passes in succession, and then runs into a large reservoir underneath the ground floor, from whence it is carried up, by means of a steam pump, into a clarifier made of sheet iron, where it is heated by steam until it boils. From the first clarifier it is carried in pipes to a second and a third, and thence into close iron pans, through which tubes pass, filled with steam. While in a boiling state it flows through three pans in succession, and is then carried in other pipes down to the coolers on the ground floor. Coolers are wooden boxes with sieve bottoms made of the finest wire. As soon as the syrup passes into the coolers, and is met by the air, it grains, and the molasses at once escapes through the sieves into a cistern below. It is then white or loaf sugar of the finest kind—clear, clean, and as white as snow. When cool, it is taken out, packed in hogsheads, and is ready for market. The molasses is then carried from the cistern into the upper story again, and by another process converted into brown sugar.

There are larger mills, and those constructed differently from the one thus imperfectly described, but none, perhaps, more celebrated than this anywhere on Bayou Boeuf. Lambert, of New-Orleans, is a partner of Hawkins. He is a man of vast wealth, holding, as I have been told, an interest in over forty different sugar plantations in Louisiana.[164]

* * * * *

The only respite from constant labor the slave has through the whole year, is during the Christmas holidays. Epps allowed us three—others allow four, five and six days, according to the measure of their generosity. It is the only time to which they look forward with any interest or pleasure. They are glad when night comes, not only because it brings them a few hours repose, but because it brings them one day nearer Christmas. It is hailed with equal delight by the old and the young; even Uncle Abram ceases to glorify Andrew Jackson, and Patsey forgets her many sorrows, amid the general hilarity of the holidays. It is the time of feasting, and frolicking, and fiddling—the carnival season with the children of bondage. They are the only days when they are allowed a little restricted liberty, and heartily indeed do they enjoy it.[165]

It is the custom for one planter to give a "Christmas supper," inviting the slaves from neighboring plantations to join his own on the occasion; for instance, one year it is given by Epps, the next by Marshall, the next by Hawkins, and so on. Usually from three to five hundred are assembled,[166] coming together on foot, in carts, on horseback, on mules, riding double and triple, sometimes a boy and

n. 166 on entertainment

girl, at others a girl and two boys, and at others again a boy, a girl and an old woman. Uncle Abram astride a mule, with Aunt Phebe and Patsey behind him, trotting towards a Christmas supper, would be no uncommon sight on Bayou Boeuf.

Then, too, "of all days i' the year," they array themselves in their best attire. The cotton coat has been washed clean, the stump of a tallow candle has been applied to the shoes, and if so fortunate as to possess a rimless or a crownless hat, it is placed jauntily on the head. They are welcomed with equal cordiality, however, if they come bare-headed and bare-footed to the feast. As a general thing, the women wear handkerchiefs tied about their heads, but if chance has thrown in their way a fiery red ribbon, or a cast-off bonnet of their mistress' grandmother, it is sure to be worn on such occasions. Red—the deep blood red—is decidedly the favorite color among the enslaved damsels of my acquaintance. If a red ribbon does not encircle the neck, you will be certain to find all the hair of their woolly heads tied up with red strings of one sort or another.

The table is spread in the open air, and loaded with varieties of meat and piles of vegetables. Bacon and corn meal at such times are dispensed with. Sometimes the cooking is performed in the kitchen on the plantation, at others in the shade of wide branching trees. In the latter case, a ditch is dug in the ground, and wood laid in and burned until it is filled with glowing coals, over which chickens, ducks, turkeys, pigs, and not unfrequently the entire body of a wild ox, are roasted. They are furnished also with flour, of which biscuits are made, and often with peach and other preserves, with tarts, and every manner and description of pies, except the mince, that being an article of pastry as yet unknown among them. Only the slave who has lived all the years on his scanty allowance of meal and bacon, can appreciate such suppers.[167] White people in great numbers assemble to witness the gastronomical enjoyments. They seat themselves at the rustic table—the males on one side, the females on the other. The two between whom there may have been an exchange of tenderness, invariably manage to sit opposite; for the omnipresent Cupid disdains not to hurl his arrows into the simple hearts of slaves. Unalloyed and exulting happiness lights up the dark faces of them all. The ivory teeth, contrasting with their black complexions, exhibit two long, white streaks the whole extent of the table. All round the bountiful board a multitude of eyes roll in ecstacy. Giggling and laughter and the clattering of cutlery and crockery succeed. Cuffee's elbow hunches his neighbor's side, impelled by an involuntary impulse of delight; Nelly shakes her finger at Sambo and laughs, she knows not why, and so the fun and merriment flow on.

When the viands have disappeared, and the hungry maws of the children of toil are satisfied, then, next in the order of amusement, is the Christmas dance. My business on these gala days always was to play on the violin. The African race is a music-loving one, proverbially; and many there were among my fellow-bondsmen whose organs of tune were strikingly developed, and who could thumb the banjo with dexterity; but at the expense of appearing egotistical, I must, nevertheless, declare, that I was considered the Ole Bull of Bayou Boeuf. My master often received letters, sometimes from a distance of ten miles, requesting him to send me to play at a ball or festival of the whites. He received his compensation, and usually I also returned with many picayunes jingling in my pockets—the extra contributions of those to whose delight I had administered. In this manner I became more acquainted than I otherwise would, up and down the bayou. The young men and maidens of Holmesville always knew there was to be a jollification somewhere, whenever Platt Epps was seen passing through the town with his fiddle in his hand. "Where are you going now, Platt?" and "What is coming off tonight, Platt?" would be interrogatories issuing from every door and window, and many a time when there was no special hurry, yielding to pressing importunities, Platt would draw his bow, and sitting astride his mule, perhaps, discourse musically to a crowd of delighted children, gathered around him in the street.

Alas! had it not been for my beloved violin, I scarcely can conceive how I could have endured the long years of bondage. It introduced me to great houses—relieved me of many days' labor in the field—supplied me with conveniences for my cabin—with pipes and tobacco, and extra pair of shoes, and oftentimes led me away from the presence of a hard master, to witness scenes of jollity and mirth. It was my companion—the friend of my bosom—triumphing loudly when I was joyful, and uttering its soft, melodious consolations when I was sad. Often, at midnight, when sleep had fled affrighted from the cabin, and my soul was disturbed and troubled with the contemplation of my fate, it would sing me a song of peace. On holy Sabbath days, when an hour or two of leisure was allowed, it would accompany me to some quiet place on the bayou bank, and, lifting up its voice, discourse kindly and pleasantly indeed. It heralded my name round the country—made me friends, who, otherwise would not have noticed me—gave me an honored seat at the yearly feasts, and secured the loudest and heartiest welcome of them all at the Christmas dance. The Christmas dance! Oh, ye pleasure-seeking sons and daughters of idleness, who move with measured step, listless and snail-like, through the slow-winding cotillon, if ye wish to look upon the celerity, if not the "poetry of motion"—upon genuine happiness, rampant and unrestrained—go down to Louisiana, and see the slaves dancing in the starlight of a Christmas night.

On that particular Christmas I have now in my mind, a description whereof will serve as a description of the day generally, Miss Lively and Mr. Sam the first belonging to Stewart, the latter to Roberts, started the ball. It was well known that Sam cherished an ardent passion for Lively, as also did one of Marshall's and another of Carey's boys; for Lively was *lively* indeed, and a heart-breaking coquette withal. It was a victory for Sam Roberts, when, rising from the repast, she gave him her hand for the first "figure" in preference to either of his rivals. They were somewhat crest-fallen, and, shaking their heads angrily, rather intimated they would like to pitch into Mr. Sam and hurt him badly. But not an emotion of wrath ruffled the placid bosom of Samuel as his legs flew like drum-sticks down the outside and up the middle, by the side of his bewitching partner. The whole company cheered them vociferously, and, excited with the applause, they continued "tearing down" after all the others had become exhausted and halted a moment to recover breath. But Sam's superhuman exertions overcame him finally, leaving Lively alone, yet whirling like a top. Thereupon one of Sam's rivals, Pete Marshall, dashed in, and, with might and main, leaped and shuffled and threw himself into every conceivable shape, as if determined to show Miss Lively and all the world that Sam Roberts was of no account.

Pete's affection, however, was greater than his discretion. Such violent exercise took the breath out of him directly, and he dropped like an empty bag. Then was the time for Harry Carey to try his hand; but Lively also soon out-winded him, amidst hurrahs and shouts, fully sustaining her well-earned reputation of being the "fastest gal" on the bayou.

One "set" off, another takes its place, he or she remaining longest on the floor receiving the most uproarious commendation, and so the dancing continues until broad daylight. It does not cease with the sound of the fiddle, but in that case they set up a music peculiar to themselves. This is called "patting," accompanied with one of those unmeaning songs, composed rather for its adaptation to a certain tune or measure, than for the purpose of expressing any distinct idea. The patting is performed by striking the hands on the knees, then striking the hands together, then striking the right shoulder with one hand, the left with the other—all the while keeping time with the feet, and singing, perhaps, this song:[168]

> "Harper's creek and roarin' ribber,
> Thar, my dear, we'll live forebber;
> Den we'll go to de Ingin Nation,
> All I want in dis creation,
> Is pretty little wife and big plantation.

> *Chorus.* Up dat oak and down dat ribber,
> Two overseers and one little nigger"

Or, if these words are not adapted to the tune called for, it may be that "Old Hog Eye" *is*—a rather solemn and startling specimen of versification, not, however, to be appreciated unless heard at the South. It runneth as follows:

> "Who's been here since I've been gone?
> Pretty little gal wid a josey on.
> Hog eye!
> Old Hog Eye.
> And Hosey too !

> Never see de like since I was born,
> Here comes a little gal wid a josey on
> Hog Eye!
> Old Hog Eye!
> And Hosey too!"

Or, may be the following, perhaps, equally nonsensical, but full of melody, nevertheless, as it flows from the negro's mouth:

"Ebo Dick and Jurdan's Jo,
Them two niggers stole my yo'.

Chorus. Hop Jim along,
Walk Jim along,
Talk Jim along, &c.

Old black Dan, as black as tar,
He dam glad he was not dar.

Hop Jim along," &c.

During the remaining holidays succeeding Christmas, they are provided with passes, and permitted to go where they please within a limited distance, or they may remain and labor on the plantation, in which case they are paid for it. It is very rarely, however, that the latter alternative is accepted. They may be seen at these times hurrying in all directions, as happy looking mortals as can be found on the face of the earth. They are different beings from what they are in the field; the temporary relaxation, the brief deliverance from fear, and from the lash, producing an entire metamorphosis in their appearance and demeanor. In visiting, riding, renewing old friendships, or, perchance, reviving some old attachment, or pursuing whatever pleasure may suggest itself, the time is occupied. Such is "southern life as it is," *three days in the year*, as I found it—the other three hundred and sixty-two being days of weariness, and fear, and suffering, and unremitting labor.

Marriage is frequently contracted during the holidays, if such an institution may be said to exist among them.[169] The only ceremony required before entering into that "holy estate," is to obtain the consent of the respective owners. It is usually encouraged by the masters of female slaves. Either party can have as many husbands or wives as the owner will permit, and either is at liberty to discard the other at pleasure. The law in relation to divorce, or to bigamy, and so forth, is not applicable to property, of course. If the wife does not belong on the same plantation with the husband, the latter is permitted to visit her on Saturday nights, if the distance is not too far. Uncle Abram's wife lived seven miles from Epps', on Bayou Huff Power. He had permission to visit her once a fortnight, but he was growing old, as has been said, and truth to say, had latterly well nigh forgotten her. Uncle Abram had no time to spare from his meditations on General Jackson—connubial dalliance being well enough for the young and thoughtless, but unbecoming a grave and solemn philosopher like himself.

Law against blacks + whites marrying n. 169

CHAPTER XVI.

OVERSEERS—HOW THEY ARE ARMED AND ACCOMPANIED—THE
HOMICIDE—HIS EXECUTION AT MARKSVILLE—SLAVE-DRIVERS—
APPOINTED DRIVER ON REMOVING TO BAYOU BOEUF—PRACTICE
MAKES PERFECT—EPPS' ATTEMPT TO CUT PLATT'S THROAT—THE
ESCAPE FROM HIM—PROTECTED BY THE MISTRESS—FORBIDS
READING AND WRITING—OBTAIN A SHEET OF PAPER AFTER NINE
YEARS' EFFORT—THE LETTER—ARMSBY, THE MEAN WHITE—
PARTIALLY CONFIDE IN HIM—HIS TREACHERY—EPPS' SUSPICIONS—
HOW THEY WERE QUIETED—BURNING THE LETTER—ARMSBY
LEAVES THE BAYOU—DISAPPOINTMENT AND DESPAIR.

With the exception of my trip to St. Mary's Parish, and my absence
during the cane-cutting seasons, I was constantly employed on the
plantation of Master Epps. He was considered but a small planter,
not having a sufficient number of hands to require the services of an
overseer, acting in the latter capacity himself. Not able to increase his
force, it was his custom to hire during the hurry of cotton-picking.

On larger estates, employing fifty or a hundred, or perhaps two
hundred hands, an overseer is deemed indispensible. These
gentlemen ride into the field on horseback, without an exception, to
my knowledge, armed with pistols, bowie knife, whip, and
accompanied by several dogs.[170] They follow, equipped in this
fashion, in rear of the slaves, keeping a sharp lookout upon them all.
The requisite qualifications in an overseer are utter heartlessness,
brutality and cruelty. It is his business to produce large crops, and if
that is accomplished, no matter what amount of suffering it may have
cost.[171] The presence of the dogs are necessary to overhaul a fugitive
who may take to his heels, as is sometimes the case, when faint or
sick, he is unable to maintain his row, and unable, also, to endure the
whip. The pistols are reserved for any dangerous emergency, there
having been instances when such weapons were necessary. Goaded
into uncontrollable madness, even the slave will sometimes turn upon
his oppressor. The gallows were standing at Marksville last January,
upon which one was executed a year ago for killing his overseer. It

n. 171 on excessive cruelty

occurred not many miles from Epps' plantation on Red River. The slave was given his task at splitting rails. In the course of the day the overseer sent him on an errand, which occupied so much time that it was not possible for him to perform the task. The next day he was called to an account, but the loss of time occasioned by the errand was no excuse, and he was ordered to kneel and bare his back for the reception of the lash. They were in the woods alone—beyond the reach of sight or hearing. The boy submitted until maddened at such injustice, and insane with pain, he sprang to his feet, and seizing an axe, literally chopped the overseer in pieces. He made no attempt whatever at concealment, but hastening to his master, related the whole affair, and declared himself ready to expiate the wrong by the sacrifice of his life. He was led to the scaffold, and while the rope was around his neck, maintained an undismayed and fearless bearing, and with his last words justified the act.

Besides the overseer, there are drivers under him, the number being in proportion to the number of hands in the field. The drivers are black, who, in addition to the performance of their equal share of work, are compelled to do the whipping of their several gangs. Whips hang around their necks, and if they fail to use them thoroughly, are whipped themselves. They have a few privileges, however; for example, in cane-cutting the hands are not allowed to sit down long enough to eat their dinners.[172] Carts filled with corn cake, cooked at the kitchen, are driven into the fields at noon. The cake is distributed by the drivers, and must be eaten with the least possible delay.

When the slave ceases to perspire, as he often does when taxed beyond his strength, he falls to the ground and becomes entirely helpless. It is then the duty of the driver to drag him into the shade of the standing cotton or cane, or of a neighboring tree, where he dashes buckets of water upon him, and uses other means of bringing out perspiration again, when he is ordered to his place, and compelled to continue his labor.

At Huff Power, when I first came to Epps', Tom, one of Roberts' negroes, was driver. He was a burly fellow, and severe in the extreme. After Epps' removal to Bayou Boeuf, that distinguished honor was conferred upon myself. Up to the time of my departure I had to wear a whip about my neck in the field. If Epps was present, I dared not show any lenity, not having the Christian fortitude of a certain well-known Uncle Tom sufficiently to brave his wrath, by refusing to perform the office. In that way, only, I escaped the immediate martyrdom he suffered, and, withal, saved my companions much suffering, as it proved in the end. Epps, I soon found, whether actually in the field or not, had his eyes pretty generally upon us. From the piazza, from behind some adjacent tree, or other concealed point of observation, he was perpetually on the watch. If one of us had been backward or idle through the day, we were apt to be told all about it on returning to the quarters, and as it was a matter of principle with him to reprove every offence of that kind that came within his knowledge, the offender not only was certain of receiving a castigation for his tardiness, but I likewise was punished for permitting it.

If, on the other hand, he had seen me use the lash freely, the man was satisfied. "Practice makes perfect," truly; and during my eight years' experience as a driver I learned to handle my whip with marvelous dexterity and precision, throwing the lash within a hair's breadth of the back, the ear, the nose, without, however, touching either of them. If Epps was observed at a distance, or we had reason to apprehend he was sneaking somewhere in the vicinity, I would commence plying the lash vigorously, when, according to arrangement, they would squirm and screech as if in agony, although not one of them had in fact been even grazed. Patsey would take occasion, if he made his appearance presently, to mumble in his hearing some complaints that Platt was lashing them the whole time, and Uncle Abram, with an appearance of honesty peculiar to himself, would declare roundly I had just whipped them worse than General Jackson whipped the enemy at New-Orleans. If Epps was not drunk, and in one of his beastly humors, this was, in general, satisfactory. If he was, some one or more of us must suffer, as a matter of course. Sometimes his violence assumed a dangerous form, placing the lives of his human stock in jeopardy. On one occasion the drunken madman thought to amuse himself by cutting my throat.

He had been absent at Holmesville, in attendance at a shooting-match, and none of us were aware of his return. While hoeing by the side of Patsey, she exclaimed in a low voice, suddenly, "Platt, d'ye see old Hog-Jaw beckoning me to come to him?"

Glancing sideways, I discovered him in the edge of the field, motioning and grimacing, as was his habit when half-intoxicated. Aware of his lewd intentions, Patsey began to cry. I whispered her not to look up, and to continue at her work, as if she had not observed him. Suspecting the truth of the matter, however, he soon staggered up to me in a great rage.

"What did you say to Pats?" he demanded, with an oath. I made him some evasive answer, which only had the effect of increasing his violence.

"How long have you owned this plantation, *say*, you d—d nigger?" he inquired, with a malicious sneer, at the same time taking hold of my shirt collar with one hand, and thrusting the other into his pocket. "Now I'll cut your black throat; that's what I'll do," drawing his knife from his pocket as he said it. But with one hand he was unable to open it, until finally seizing the blade in his teeth, I saw he was about to succeed, and felt the necessity of escaping from him, for in his present reckless state, it was evident he was not joking, by any means. My shirt was open in front, and as I turned round quickly and sprang from him, while he still retained his grip, it was stripped entirely from my back. There was no difficulty now in eluding him. He would chase me until out of breath, then stop until it was recovered, swear, and renew the chase again. Now he would command me to come to him, now endeavor to coax me, but I was careful to keep at a respectful distance. In this manner we made the circuit of the field several times, he making desperate plunges, and I always dodging them, more amused than frightened, well knowing that when his sober senses returned, he would laugh at his own drunken folly. At length I observed the mistress standing by the yard fence, watching our half-serious, half-comical maneuvers. Shooting past him, I ran directly to her. Epps, on discovering her, did not follow. He remained about the field an hour or more, during which time I stood by the mistress, having related the particulars of what had taken place. Now, *she* was aroused again, denouncing her husband and Patsey about equally. Finally, Epps came towards the house, by this time nearly sober, walking demurely, with his hands behind his back, and attempting to look as innocent as a child.

As he approached, nevertheless, Mistress Epps began to berate him roundly, heaping upon him many rather disrespectful epithets, and demanding for what reason he had attempted to cut my throat. Epps made wondrous strange of it all, and to my surprise, swore by all the saints in the calendar he had not spoken to me that day.

"Platt, you lying nigger, *have* I?" was his brazen appeal to me.

It is not safe to contradict a master, even by the assertion of a truth. So I was silent, and when he entered the house I returned to the field, and the affair was never after alluded to.

Shortly after this time a circumstance occurred that came nigh divulging the secret of my real name and history, which I had so long and carefully concealed, and upon which I was convinced depended my final escape. Soon after he purchased me, Epps asked me if I could write and read, and on being informed that I had received some instruction in those branches of education, he assured me, with emphasis, if he ever caught me with a book, or with pen and ink, he would give me a hundred lashes. He said he wanted me to understand that he bought "niggers" to work and not to educate. He never inquired a word of my past life, or from whence I came. The mistress, however, cross-examined me frequently about Washington, which she supposed was my native city, and more than once remarked that I did not talk nor act like the other "niggers," and she was sure I had seen more of the world than I admitted.

My great object always was to invent means of getting a letter secretly into the post-office, directed to some of my friends or family at the North. The difficulty of such an achievement cannot be comprehended by one unacquainted with the severe restrictions imposed upon me. In the first place, I was deprived of pen, ink, and paper. In the second place, a slave cannot leave his plantation without a pass, nor will a post-master mail a letter for one without written instructions from his owner. I was in slavery nine years, and always watchful and on the alert, before I met with the good fortune of obtaining a sheet of paper. While Epps was in New-Orleans, one winter, disposing of his cotton, the mistress sent me to Holmesville, with an order for several articles, and among the rest a quantity of foolscap. I appropriated a sheet, concealing it in the cabin, under the board on which I slept.[173] *paper was scarce*

After various experiments I succeeded in making ink, by boiling white maple bark, and with a feather plucked from the wing of a duck, manufactured a pen. When all were asleep in the cabin, by the light of the coals, lying upon my plank couch, I managed to complete a somewhat lengthy epistle. It was directed to an old acquaintance at Sandy Hill, stating my condition, and urging him to take measures to restore me to liberty. This letter I kept a long time, contriving measures by which it could safely be deposited in the post-office. At length, a low fellow, by the name of Armsby, hitherto a stranger, came into the neighborhood, seeking a situation as overseer. He applied to Epps, and was about the plantation for several days. He next went over to Shaw's, near by, and remained with him several weeks. Shaw was generally surrounded by such worthless characters, being himself noted as a gambler and unprincipled man. He had made a wife of his slave Charlotte, and a brood of young mulattoes were growing up in his house.[174] Armsby became so much reduced at last, that he was compelled to labor with the slaves. A white man working in the field is a rare and unusual spectacle on Bayou Boeuf. I improved every opportunity of cultivating his acquaintance privately, desiring to obtain his confidence so far as to be willing to intrust the letter to his keeping. He visited Marksville repeatedly, he informed me, a town some twenty miles distant, and there, I proposed to myself, the letter should be mailed.

Carefully deliberating on the most proper manner of approaching him on the subject, I concluded finally to ask him simply if he would deposit a letter for me in the Marksville post-office the next time he visited that place, without disclosing to him that the letter was written, or any of the particulars it contained; for I had fears that he might betray me, and knew that some inducement must be held out to him of a pecuniary nature, before it would be safe to confide in him. As late as one o'clock one night I stole noiselessly from my cabin, and, crossing the field to Shaw's, found him sleeping on the piazza. I had but a few picayunes—the proceeds of my fiddling performances, but all I had in the world I promised him if he would do me the favor required. I begged him not to expose me if he could not grant the request. He assured me, upon his honor, he would deposit it in the Marksville post-office, and that he would keep it an inviolable secret forever. Though the letter was in my pocket at the time, I dared not then deliver it to him, but stating I would have it written in a day or two, bade him good night, and returned to my cabin. It was impossible for me to expel the suspicions I entertained, and all night I lay awake, revolving in my mind the safest course to pursue. I was willing to risk a great deal to accomplish my purpose, but should the letter by any means fall into the hands of Epps, it would be a death-blow to my aspirations. I was "perplexed in the extreme."

My suspicions were well-founded, as the sequel demonstrated. The next day but one, while scraping cotton in the field, Epps seated himself on the line fence between Shaw's plantation and his own, in such a position as to overlook the scene of our labors. Presently Armsby made his appearance, and, mounting the fence, took a seat beside him. They remained two or three hours, all of which time I was in an agony of apprehension.

That night, while broiling my bacon, Epps entered the cabin with his rawhide in his hand.

"Well, boy," said he, "I understand I've got a larned nigger, that writes letters, and tries to get white fellows to mail 'em. Wonder if you know who he is?"

My worst fears were realized, and although it may not be considered entirely creditable, even under the circumstances, yet a resort to duplicity and downright falsehood was the only refuge that presented itself.

"Don't know nothing about it, Master Epps," I answered him, assuming an air of ignorance and surprise; "Don't know nothing at all about it, sir."

"Wan't you over to Shaw's night before last?" he inquired.

"No, master," was the reply.

"Hav'nt you asked that fellow, Armsby, to mail a letter for you at Marksville?"

"Why, Lord, master, I never spoke three words to him in all my life. I don't know what you mean."

"Well," he continued, "Armsby told me to-day the devil was among my niggers; that I had one that needed close watching or he would run away; and when I axed him why, he said you come over to Shaw's, and waked him up in the night, and wanted him to carry a letter to Marksville. What have you got to say to that, ha?"

"All I've got to say, master," I replied, "is, there is no truth in it. How could I write a letter without any ink or paper? There is nobody I want to write to, 'cause I haint got no friends living as I know of. That Armsby is a lying, drunken fellow, they say, and nobody believes him anyway. You know I always tell the truth, and that I never go off the plantation without a pass. Now, master, I can see what that Armsby is after, plain enough. Didn't he want you to hire him for an overseer?"

"Yes, he wanted me to hire him," answered Epps.

"That's it," said I, "he wants to make you believe we're all going to run away, and then he thinks you'll hire an overseer to watch us.

He just made that story out of whole cloth, 'cause he wants to get a situation. It's all a lie, master, you may depend on't."

Epps mused awhile, evidently impressed with the plausibility of my theory, and exclaimed, "I'm d—d, Platt, if I don't believe you tell the truth. He must take me for a soft, to think he can come it over me with them kind of yarns, mustn't he? Maybe he thinks he can fool me; maybe he thinks I don't know nothing—can't take care of my own niggers, eh! Soft soap old Epps, eh! Ha, ha, ha! D—n Armsby! Set the dogs on him, Platt," and with many other comments descriptive of Armsby's general character, and his capability of taking care of his own business, and attending to his own "niggers," Master Epps left the cabin. As soon as he was gone I threw the letter in the fire, and, with a desponding and despairing heart, beheld the epistle which had cost me so much anxiety and thought, and which I fondly hoped would have been my forerunner to the land of freedom, writhe and shrivel on its bed of coals, and dissolve into smoke and ashes. Armsby, the treacherous wretch, was driven from Shaw's plantation not long subsequently, much to my relief, for I feared he might renew his conversation, and perhaps induce Epps to credit him.

I knew not now whither to look for deliverance. Hopes sprang up in my heart only to be crushed and blighted. The summer of my life was passing away; I felt I was growing prematurely old; that a few years more, and toil, and grief, and the poisonous miasmas of the swamps would accomplish their work upon me—would consign me to the grave's embrace, to moulder and be forgotten.[175] Repelled, betrayed, cut off from the hope of succor, I could only prostrate myself upon the earth and groan in unutterable anguish. The hope of rescue was the only light that cast a ray of comfort on my heart. That was now flickering, faint and low; another breath of disappointment would extinguish it altogether, leaving me to grope in midnight darkness to the end of life.

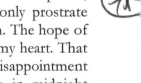

loss of hope

CHAPTER XVII.

Resistance

WILEY DISREGARDS THE COUNSELS OF AUNT PHEBE AND UNCLE
ABRAM, AND IS CAUGHT BY THE PATROLLERS—THE ORGANIZATION
AND DUTIES OF THE LATTER—WILEY RUNS AWAY—SPECULATION IN
REGARD TO HIM—HIS UNEXPECTED RETURN—HIS CAPTURE ON
RED RIVER, AND CONFINEMENT IN ALEXANDRIA JAIL—
DISCOVERED BY JOSEPH B. ROBERTS—SUBDUING DOGS IN
ANTICIPATION OF ESCAPE—THE FUGITIVES IN THE GREAT PINE
WOODS—CAPTURED BY ADAM TAYDEM AND THE INDIANS—
AUGUSTUS KILLED BY DOGS—NELLY, ELDRET'S SLAVE WOMAN—
THE STORY OF CELESTE—THE CONCERTED MOVEMENT—LEW
CHENEY, THE TRAITOR—THE IDEA OF INSURRECTION.

The year 1850, down to which time I have now arrived, omitting
many occurrences uninteresting to the reader, was an unlucky year
for my companion Wiley, the husband of Phebe, whose taciturn and
retiring nature has thus far kept him in the background.
Notwithstanding Wiley seldom opened his mouth, and revolved in
his obscure and unpretending orbit without a grumble, nevertheless
the warm elements of sociality were strong in the bosom of that
silent "nigger." In the exuberance of his self-reliance, disregarding the
philosophy of Uncle Abram, and setting the counsels of Aunt Phebe
utterly at naught, he had the fool-hardiness to essay a nocturnal visit
to a neighboring cabin without a pass.

So attractive was the society in which he found himself, that Wiley
took little note of the passing hours, and the light began to break in the
east before he was aware. Speeding homeward as fast as he could run,
he hoped to reach the quarters before the horn would sound; but,
unhappily, he was spied on the way by a company of patrollers.

How it is in other dark places of slavery, I do not know, but on
Bayou Boeuf there is an organization of patrollers, as they are styled,
whose business it is to seize and whip any slave they may find
wandering from the plantation.[176] They ride on horseback, headed by
a captain, armed, and accompanied by dogs. They have the right,
either by law, or by general consent, to inflict discretionary

n. 176 on patrils

chastisement upon a black man caught beyond the boundaries of his master's estate without a pass, and even to shoot him, if he attempts to escape. Each company has a certain distance to ride up and down the bayou. They are compensated by the planters, who contribute in proportion to the number of slaves they own. The clatter of their horses' hoofs dashing by can be heard at all hours of the night, and frequently they may be seen driving a slave before them, or leading him by a rope fastened around his neck, to his owner's plantation.

Wiley fled before one of these companies, thinking he could reach his cabin before they could overtake him; but one of their dogs, a great ravenous hound, gripped him by the leg and held him fast. The patrollers whipped him severely, and brought him, a prisoner, to Epps. From him he received another flagellation still more severe, so that the cuts of the lash and the bites of the dog rendered him sore, stiff and miserable, insomuch he was scarcely able to move. It was impossible in such a state to keep up his row and consequently there was not an hour in the day but Wiley felt the sting of his master's rawhide on his raw and bleeding back. His sufferings became intolerable, and finally he resolved to run away. Without disclosing his intentions to run away even to his wife Phebe, he proceeded to make arrangements for carrying his plan into execution. Having cooked his whole week's allowance, he cautiously left the cabin on a Sunday night, after the inmates of the quarters were asleep. When the horn sounded in the morning, Wiley did not make his appearance. Search was made for him in the cabins, in the corn-crib, in the cotton-house, and in every nook and corner of the premises. Each of us was examined, touching any knowledge we might have that could throw light upon his sudden disappearance or present whereabouts. Epps raved and stormed, and mounting his horse, galloped to neighboring plantations, making inquiries in all directions. The search was fruitless. Nothing whatever was elicited, going to show what had become of the missing man. The dogs were led to the swamp, but were unable to strike his trail. They would circle away through the forest, their noses to the ground, but invariably returned in a short time to the spot from whence they started.

Wiley had escaped, and so secretly and cautiously as to elude and baffle all pursuit. Days and even weeks passed away, and nothing could be heard of him. Epps did nothing but curse and swear. It was the only topic of conversation among us when alone. We indulged in

a great deal of speculation in regard to him, one suggesting he might
have been drowned in some bayou, inasmuch as he was a poor swimmer; another, that perhaps he might have been devoured by
alligators, or stung by the venomous moccasin, whose bite is certain
and sudden death. The warm and hearty sympathies of us all,
however, were with poor Wiley, wherever he might be. Many an
earnest prayer ascended from the lips of Uncle Abram, beseeching
safety for the wanderer.

In about three weeks, when all hope of ever seeing him again
was dismissed, to our surprise, he one day appeared among us. On
leaving the plantation, he informed us, it was his intention to make
his way back to South Carolina—to the old quarters of Master
Buford. During the day he remained secreted, sometimes in the
branches of a tree, and at night pressed forward through the swamps.
Finally, one morning, just at dawn, he reached the shore of Red
River. While standing on the bank, considering how he could cross it,
a white man accosted him and demanded a pass. Without one, and
evidently a runaway, he was taken to Alexandria, the shire town of
the parish of Rapides, and confined in prison. It happened several
days after that Joseph B. Roberts, uncle of Mistress Epps, was in
Alexandria, and going into the jail, recognized him. Wiley had worked
on his plantation, when Epps resided at Huff Power. Paying the jail
fee, and writing him a pass, underneath which was a note to Epps,
requesting him not to whip him on his return, Wiley was sent back to
Bayou Boeuf. It was the hope that hung upon this request, and which
Roberts assured him would be respected by his master, that sustained
him as he approached the house. The request, however, as may be
readily supposed, was entirely disregarded. After being kept in
suspense three days, Wiley was stripped, and compelled to endure
one of those inhuman floggings to which the poor slave is so often
subjected. It was the first and last attempt of Wiley to run away. The
long scars upon his back, which he will carry with him to the grave,
perpetually remind him of the dangers of such a step.

There was not a day throughout the ten years I belonged to
Epps that I did not consult with myself upon the prospect of escape.
I laid many plans, which at the time I considered excellent ones, but
one after the other they were all abandoned. No man who has never
been placed in such a situation, can comprehend the thousand
obstacles thrown in the way of the flying slave. Every white man's

hand is raised against him—the patrollers are watching for him—the hounds are ready to follow on his track, and the nature of the country is such as renders it impossible to pass through it with any safety.[177] I thought, however, that the time might come, perhaps, when I should be running through the swamps again. I concluded, in that case, to be prepared for Epps' dogs, should they pursue me. He possessed several, one of which was a notorious slave-hunter, and the most fierce and savage of his breed. While out hunting the coon or the opossum, I never allowed an opportunity to escape, when alone, of whipping them severely. In this manner I succeeded at length in subduing them completely. They feared me, obeying my voice at once when others had no control over them whatever. Had they followed and overtaken me, I doubt not they would have shrank from attacking me.

Notwithstanding the certainty of being captured, the woods and swamps are, nevertheless, continually filled with runaways. Many of them, when sick, or so worn out as to be unable to perform their tasks, escape into the swamps, willing to suffer the punishment inflicted for such offences, in order to obtain a day or two of rest.

While I belonged to Ford, I was unwittingly the means of disclosing the hiding-place of six or eight, who had taken up their residence in the "Great Pine Woods." Adam Taydem frequently sent me from the mills over to the opening after provisions. The whole distance was then a thick pine forest. About ten o'clock of a beautiful moonlight night, while walking along the Texas road, returning to the mills, carrying a dressed pig in a bag swung over my shoulder, I heard footsteps behind me, and turning round, beheld two black men in the dress of slaves approaching at a rapid pace. When within a short distance, one of them raised a club, as if intending to strike me; the other snatched at the bag. I managed to dodge them both, and seizing a pine knot, hurled it with such force against the head of one of them that he was prostrated apparently senseless to the ground. Just then two more made their appearance from one side of the road. Before they could grapple me, however, I succeeded in passing them, and taking to my heels, fled, much affrighted, towards the mills. When Adam was informed of the adventure, he hastened straightway to the Indian village, and arousing Cascalla and several of his tribe, started in pursuit of the highwaymen. I accompanied them to the scene of attack, when we discovered a puddle of blood in the road, where the man whom I had smitten with the pine knot had fallen. After searching carefully through the woods a long time, one of Cascalla's men discovered a smoke curling up through the branches of several prostrate pines, whose tops had fallen together. The rendezvous was cautiously surrounded, and all of them taken prisoners. They had escaped from a plantation in the vicinity of Lamourie, and had been secreted there three weeks. They had no evil design upon me, except to frighten me out of my pig. Having observed me passing towards Ford's just at night-fall, and suspecting the nature of my errand, they had followed me, seen me butcher and dress the porker, and start on my return. They had been pinched for food, and were driven to this extremity by necessity. Adam conveyed them to the parish jail, and was liberally rewarded.

Not unfrequently the runaway loses his life in the attempt to escape. Epps' premises were bounded on one side by Carey's, a very extensive sugar plantation.[178] He cultivates annually at least fifteen hundred acres of cane, manufacturing twenty-two or twenty-three hundred hogsheads of sugar; an hogshead and a half being the usual yield of an acre. Besides this he also cultivates five or six hundred acres of corn and cotton. He owned last year one hundred and fifty-three field hands, besides nearly as many children, and yearly hires a drove during the busy season from this side of the Mississippi.

One of his negro drivers, a pleasant, intelligent boy, was named Augustus. During the holidays, and occasionally while at work in adjoining fields, I had an opportunity of making his acquaintance, which eventually ripened into a warm and mutual attachment. Summer before last he was so unfortunate as to incur the displeasure of the overseer, a coarse, heartless brute, who whipped him most cruelly. Augustus ran away. Reaching a cane rick on Hawkins' plantation, he secreted himself in the top of it. All Carey's dogs were put upon his track—some fifteen of them—and soon scented his footsteps to the hiding place. They surrounded the rick, baying and scratching, but could not reach him. Presently, guided by the clamor of the hounds, the pursuers rode up, when the overseer, mounting on the rick, drew him forth. As he rolled to the ground the whole pack plunged upon him, and before they could be beaten off, had gnawed and mutilated his body in the most shocking manner, their teeth having penetrated to the bone in an hundred places. He was taken up, tied upon a mule and carried home. But this was Augustus' last

dead for
desire for freedom

trouble. He lingered until the next day, when death sought the unhappy boy, and kindly relieved him from his agony.

It was not unusual for slave women as well as slave men to endeavor to escape. Nelly, Eldret's girl, with whom I lumbered for a time in the "Big Cane Brake," lay concealed in Epps' corn crib three days. At night, when his family were asleep, she would steal into the quarters for food, and return to the crib again. We concluded it would no longer be safe for us to allow her to remain, and accordingly she retraced her steps to her own cabin.

But the most remarkable instance of a successful evasion of dogs and hunters was the following: Among Carey's girls was one by the name of Celeste. She was nineteen or twenty, and far whiter than her owner, or any of his offspring. It required a close inspection to distinguish in her features the slightest trace of African blood. A stranger would never have dreamed that she was the descendant of slaves. I was sitting in my cabin late at night, playing a low air on my violin, when the door opened carefully, and Celeste stood before me. She was pale and haggard. Had an apparition arisen from the earth, I could not have been more startled.

"Who are you?" I demanded, after gazing at her a moment.

"I'm hungry; give me some bacon," was her reply.

My first impression was that she was some deranged young mistress, who, escaping from home, was wandering, she knew not whither, and had been attracted to my cabin by the sound of the violin. The coarse cotton slave dress she wore, however, soon dispelled such a supposition.

"What is your name?" I again interrogated.

"My name is Celeste," she answered. "I belong to Carey, and have been two days among the palmettoes. I am sick and can't work, and would rather die in the swamp than be whipped to death by the overseer. Carey's dogs won't follow me. They have tried to set them on. There's a secret between them and Celeste, and they won't mind the devilish orders of the overseer. Give me some meat—I'm starving."

I divided my scanty allowance with her, and while partaking of it, she related how she managed to escape, and described the place of her concealment. In the edge of the swamp, not half a mile from Epps' house, was a large space, thousands of acres in extent, thickly covered with palmetto. Tall trees, whose long arms interlocked each other, formed a canopy above them, so dense as to exclude the beams of the sun. It was like twilight always, even in the middle of the brightest day. In the centre of this great space, which nothing but serpents very often explore—a sombre and solitary spot—Celeste had erected a rude hut of dead branches that had fallen to the ground, and covered it with the leaves of the palmetto. This was the abode she had selected. She had no fear of Carey's dogs, any more than I had of Epps'. It is a fact, which I have never been able to explain, that there are those whose tracks the hounds will absolutely refuse to follow. Celeste was one of them.

For several nights she came to my cabin for food. On one occasion our dogs barked as she approached, which aroused Epps, and induced him to reconnoiter the premises. He did not discover her, but after that it was not deemed prudent for her to come to the yard. When all was silent I carried provisions to a certain spot agreed upon, where she could find them.

In this manner Celeste passed the greater part of the summer. She regained her health, and became strong and hearty. At all seasons of the year the howlings of wild animals can be heard at night along the borders of the swamps. Several times they had made her a midnight call, awakening her from slumber with a growl. Terrified by such unpleasant salutations, she finally concluded to abandon her lonely dwelling; and, accordingly, returning to her master, was scourged, her neck meanwhile being fastened in the stocks, and sent into the field again.[179]

The year before my arrival in the country there was a concerted movement among a number of slaves on Bayou Boeuf, that terminated tragically indeed. It was, I presume, a matter of newspaper notoriety at the time, but all the knowledge I have of it, has been derived from the relation of those living at that period in the immediate vicinity of the excitement. It has become a subject of general and unfailing interest in every slave-hut on the bayou, and will doubtless go down to succeeding generations as their chief tradition. Lew Cheney, with whom I became acquainted—a shrewd, cunning negro, more intelligent than the generality of his race, but unscrupulous and full of treachery—conceived the project of organizing a company sufficiently strong to fight their way against all opposition, to the neighboring territory of Mexico.[180]

A remote spot, far within the depths of the swamp, back of Hawkins' plantation, was selected as the rallying point. Lew flitted from one plantation to another, in the dead of night, preaching a crusade to Mexico, and, like Peter the Hermit, creating a furor of excitement wherever he appeared. At length a large number of runaways were assembled; stolen mules, and corn gathered from the fields, and bacon filched from smoke-houses, had been conveyed into the woods. The expedition was about ready to proceed, when their hiding place was discovered. Lew Cheney, becoming convinced of the ultimate failure of his project, in order to curry favor with his master, and avoid the consequences which he foresaw would follow, deliberately determined to sacrifice all his companions. Departing secretly from the encampment, he proclaimed among the planters the number collected in the swamp, and, instead of stating truly the object they had in view, asserted their intention was to emerge from their seclusion the first favorable opportunity, and murder every white person along the bayou.

Such an announcement, exaggerated as it passed from mouth to mouth, filled the whole country with terror. The fugitives were surrounded and taken prisoners, carried in chains to Alexandria, and hung by the populace. Not only those, but many who were suspected, though entirely innocent, were taken from the field and from the cabin, and without the shadow of process or form of trial, hurried to the scaffold. The planters on Bayou Boeuf finally rebelled against such reckless destruction of property, but it was not until a regiment of soldiers had arrived from some fort on the Texas frontier, demolished the gallows, and opened the doors of the Alexandria prison, that the indiscriminate slaughter was stayed. Lew Cheney escaped, and was even rewarded for his treachery.[181] He is still living, but his name is despised and execrated by all his race throughout the parishes of Rapides and Avoyelles.

Such an idea as insurrection, however, is not new among the enslaved population of Bayou Boeuf. More than once I have joined in serious consultation, when the subject has been discussed, and there have been times when a word from me would have placed hundreds of my fellow-bondsmen in an attitude of defiance. Without arms or ammunition, or even with them, I saw such a step would result in certain defeat, disaster and death, and always raised my voice against it.

During the Mexican war I well remember the extravagant hopes that were excited. The news of victory filled the great house with rejoicing, but produced only sorrow and disappointment in the cabin. In my opinion—and I have had the opportunity to know something of the feeling of which I speak—there are not fifty slaves on the shores of Bayou Boeuf, but would hail with unmeasured delight the approach of an invading army. They are deceived who flatter themselves that the ignorant and debased slave has no conception of the magnitude of his wrongs. They are deceived who imagine that he arises from his knees, with back lacerated and bleeding, cherishing only a spirit of meekness and forgiveness. A day may come—it will come, if his prayer is heard—a terrible day of vengeance, when the master in his turn will cry in vain for mercy.

n. 182 is a
6 page note!
Slaves not prepared
for freedom.

CHAPTER XVIII.

O'NIEL, THE TANNER—CONVERSATION WITH AUNT PHEBE
OVERHEARD—EPPS IN THE TANNING BUSINESS—STABBING OF
UNCLE ABRAM—THE UGLY WOUND—EPPS IS JEALOUS—PATSEY IS
MISSING—HER RETURN FROM SHAW'S—HARRIET, SHAW'S BLACK
WIFE—EPPS ENRAGED—PATSEY DENIES HIS CHARGES—SHE IS
TIED DOWN NAKED TO FOUR STAKES—THE INHUMAN
FLOGGING—FLAYING OF PATSEY—THE BEAUTY OF THE DAY—
THE BUCKET OF SALT WATER—THE DRESS STIFF WITH BLOOD—
PATSEY GROWS MELANCHOLY—HER IDEA OF GOD AND
ETERNITY—OF HEAVEN AND FREEDOM—THE EFFECT OF SLAVE-
WHIPPING—EPPS' OLDEST SON—"THE CHILD IS FATHER TO THE
MAN."

Wiley suffered severely at the hands of Master Epps, as has been
related in the preceding chapter, but in this respect he fared no worse
than his unfortunate companions. "Spare the rod," was an idea
scouted by our master. He was constitutionally subject to periods of
ill-humor, and at such times, however little provocation there might
be, a certain amount of punishment was inflicted. The circumstances
attending the last flogging but one that I received, will show how
trivial a cause was sufficient with him for resorting to the whip.

A Mr. O'Niel, residing in the vicinity of the Big Pine Woods,
called upon Epps for the purpose of purchasing me.[183] He was a
tanner and currier by occupation, transacting an extensive business,
and intended to place me at service in some department of his
establishment, provided he bought me. Aunt Phebe, while preparing
the dinner-table in the great house, overheard their conversation. On
returning to the yard at night, the old woman ran to meet me,
designing, of course, to overwhelm me with the news. She entered
into a minute repetition of all she had heard, and Aunt Phebe was
one whose ears never failed to drink in every word of conversation
uttered in her hearing. She enlarged upon the fact that "Massa Epps
was g'wine to sell me to a tanner ober in de Pine Woods," so long
and loudly as to attract the attention of the mistress, who, standing

unobserved on the piazza at the time, was listening to our conversation.

"Well, Aunt Phebe," said I, "I'm glad of it. I'm tired of scraping cotton, and would rather be a tanner. I hope he'll buy me."

O'Niel did not effect a purchase, however, the parties differing as to price, and the morning following his arrival, departed homewards. He had been gone but a short time, when Epps made his appearance in the field. Now nothing will more violently enrage a master, especially Epps, than the intimation of one of his servants that he would like to leave him. Mistress Epps had repeated to him my expressions to Aunt Phebe the evening previous, as I learned from the latter afterwards, the mistress having mentioned to her that she had overheard us. On entering the field, Epps walked directly to me.

"So, Platt, you're tired of scraping cotton, are you? You would like to change your master, eh? You're fond of moving round— traveler—ain't ye? Ah, yes—like to travel for your health, may be? Feel above cotton-scraping, I 'spose. So you're going into the tanning business? Good business—devilish fine business. Enterprising nigger! B'lieve I'll go into that business myself. Down on your knees, and strip that rag off your back! I'll try my hand at tanning."

I begged earnestly, and endeavored to soften him with excuses, but in vain. There was no other alternative; so kneeling down, I presented my bare back for the application of the lash.

"How do you like *tanning*?" he exclaimed, as the rawhide descended upon my flesh. "How do you like *tanning*?" he repeated at every blow. In this manner he gave me twenty or thirty lashes, incessantly giving utterance to the word "tanning," in one form of expression or another. When sufficiently "tanned," he allowed me to arise, and with a half-malicious laugh assured me, if I still fancied the business, he would give me further instruction in it whenever I desired. This time, he remarked, he had only given me a short lesson in "*tanning*"—the next time he would "curry me down."

Uncle Abram, also, was frequently treated with great brutality, although he was one of the kindest and most faithful creatures in the world.[184] He was my cabin-mate for years. There was a benevolent expression in the old man's face, pleasant to behold. He regarded us with a kind of parental feeling, always counseling us with remarkable gravity and deliberation.

^. 184 states he might be based on HBS's Uncle Tom.

Returning from Marshall's plantation one afternoon, whither I had been sent on some errand of the mistress, I found him lying on the cabin floor, his clothes saturated with blood. He informed me that he had been stabbed! While spreading cotton on the scaffold, Epps came home intoxicated from Holmesville. He found fault with every thing, giving many orders so directly contrary that it was impossible to execute any of them. Uncle Abram, whose faculties were growing dull, became confused, and committed some blunder of no particular consequence. Epps was so enraged thereat, that, with drunken recklessness, he flew upon the old man, and stabbed him in the back. It was a long, ugly wound, but did not happen to penetrate far enough to result fatally. It was sewed up by the mistress, who censured her husband with extreme severity, not only denouncing his inhumanity, but declaring that she expected nothing else than that he would bring the family to poverty—that he would kill all the slaves on the plantation in some of his drunken fits.

It was no uncommon thing with him to prostrate Aunt Phebe with a chair or stick of wood; but the most cruel whipping that ever I was doomed to witness—one I can never recall with any other emotion than that of horror—was inflicted on the unfortunate Patsey.

It has been seen that the jealousy and hatred of Mistress Epps made the daily life of her young and agile slave completely miserable. I am happy in the belief that on numerous occasions I was the means of averting punishment from the inoffensive girl. In Epps' absence the mistress often ordered me to whip her without the remotest provocation. I would refuse, saying that I feared my master's displeasure, and several times ventured to remonstrate with her against the treatment Patsey received. I endeavored to impress her with the truth that the latter was not responsible for the acts of which she complained, but that she being a slave, and subject entirely to her master's will, he alone was answerable.

At length "the green-eyed monster" crept into the soul of Epps also, and then it was that he joined with his wrathful wife in an infernal jubilee over the girl's miseries.

On a Sabbath day in hoeing time, not long ago, we were on the bayou bank, washing our clothes, as was our usual custom. Presently Patsey was missing. Epps called aloud, but there was no answer. No one had observed her leaving the yard, and it was a wonder with us whither she had gone. In the course of a couple of hours she was seen

A. 185: prev. called her Charlotte

approaching from the direction of Shaw's. This man, as has been
intimated, was a notorious profligate, and withal not on the most
friendly terms with Epps. Harriet, his black wife, knowing Patsey's
troubles, was kind to her, in consequence of which the latter was in
the habit of going over to see her every opportunity.[185] Her visits were
prompted by friendship merely, but the suspicion gradually entered
the brain of Epps, that another and a baser passion led her thither—
that it was not Harriet she desired to meet, but rather the unblushing
libertine, his neighbor. Patsey found her master in a fearful rage on
her return. His violence so alarmed her that at first she attempted to
evade direct answers to his questions, which only served to increase
his suspicions. She finally, however, drew herself up proudly, and in a
spirit of indignation boldly denied his charges.

"Missus don't give me soap to wash with, as she does the rest,"
said Patsey, "and you know why. I went over to Harriet's to get a
piece," and saying this, she drew it forth from a pocket in her dress
and exhibited it to him. "That's what I went to Shaw's for, Massa
Epps," continued she; "the Lord knows that was all."

"You lie, you black wench!" Epps shouted.

"I *don't* lie, massa. If you kill me, I'll stick to that."

"Oh, I'll fetch you down. I'll learn you to go to Shaw's. I'll take
the starch out of ye," he muttered fiercely through his shut teeth.

Then, turning to me, he ordered four stakes to be driven into the
ground, pointing with the toe of his boot to the places where he
wanted them. When the stakes were driven down, he ordered her to
be stripped of every article of dress. Ropes were then brought, and
the naked girl was laid upon her face, her wrists and feet each tied
firmly to a stake. Stepping to the piazza, he took a heavy whip, and
placing it in my hands, commanded me to lash her. Unpleasant as it
was, I was compelled to obey him. Nowhere that day, on the whole
face of the earth, I venture to say, was such a demoniac exhibition
witnessed as then ensued.

Mistress Epps stood on the piazza among her children, gazing
on the scene with an air of heartless satisfaction. The slaves were
huddled together at a little distance, their countenances indicating the
sorrow of their hearts. Poor Patsey prayed piteously for mercy, but
her prayers were in vain. Epps ground his teeth, and stamped upon
the ground, screaming at me, like a mad fiend, to strike harder.

"Strike harder, or *your* turn comes next, you scoundrel," he yelled.

"Oh, mercy, massa!—Oh, have mercy, *do*. Oh, God! pity me," Patsey exclaimed continually, struggling fruitlessly, and the flesh quivering at every stroke.

When I had struck her as many as thirty times, I stopped and turned round towards Epps, hoping he was satisfied; but with bitter oaths and threats, he ordered me to continue. I inflicted ten or fifteen blows more. By this time her back was covered with long welts, intersecting each other like net work. Epps was yet furious and savage as ever; demanding if she would like to go to Shaw's again, and swearing he would flog her until she wished she were in h—l. Throwing down the whip, I declared I could punish her no more. He ordered me to go on, threatening me with a severer flogging than she had received, in case of refusal. My heart revolted at the inhuman scene, and risking the consequences, I absolutely refused to raise the whip. He then seized it himself, and applied it with ten-fold greater force than I had. The painful cries and shrieks of the tortured Patsey, mingling with the loud and angry curses of Epps, loaded the air. She was terribly lacerated—I may say, without exaggeration, literally flayed. The lash was wet with blood, which flowed down her sides and dropped upon the ground. At length she ceased struggling. Her head sank listlessly on the ground. Her screams and supplications gradually decreased and died away into a low moan. She no longer writhed and shrank beneath the lash when it bit out small pieces of her flesh. I thought that she was dying!

It was the Sabbath of the Lord. The fields smiled in the warm sunlight—the birds chirped merrily amidst the foliage of the trees—peace and happiness seemed to reign everywhere, save in the bosoms of Epps and his panting victim and the silent witnesses around him. The tempestuous emotions that were raging there were little in harmony with the calm and quiet beauty of the day. I could look on Epps only with unutterable loathing and abhorrence, and thought within myself—"Thou devil, sooner or later, somewhere in the course of eternal justice, thou shalt answer for this sin!"

Finally, he ceased whipping from mere exhaustion, and ordered Phebe to bring a bucket of salt and water. After washing her thoroughly with this, I was told to take her to her cabin. Untying the rope, I raised her in my arms. She was unable to stand, and as her head rested on my shoulder, she repeated many times, in a faint voice scarcely perceptible, "Oh, Platt—oh, Platt!" but nothing further. Her dress was replaced, but it clung to her back, and was soon stiff with blood. We laid her on some boards in the hut, where she remained a long time, with eyes closed and groaning in agony. At night Phebe applied melted tallow to her wounds, and so far as we were able, all endeavored to assist and console her. Day after day she lay in her cabin upon her face, the sores preventing her resting in any other position.

A blessed thing it would have been for her—days and weeks and months of misery it would have saved her—had she never lifted her head in life again.[186] Indeed, from that time forward she was not what she had been. The burden of a deep melancholy weighed heavily on her spirits. She no longer moved with that buoyant and elastic step— there was not that mirthful sparkle in her eyes that formerly distinguished her. The bounding vigor—the sprightly, laughter-loving spirit of her youth, were gone. She fell into a mournful and desponding mood, and often-times would start up in her sleep, and with raised hands, plead for mercy. She became more silent than she was, toiling all day in our midst, not uttering a word. A care-worn, pitiful expression settled on her face, and it was her humor now to weep, rather than rejoice. If ever there was a broken heart—one crushed and blighted by the rude grasp of suffering and misfortune— it was Patsey's.

She had been reared no better than her master's beast—looked upon merely as a valuable and handsome animal—and consequently possessed but a limited amount of knowledge. And yet a faint light cast its rays over her intellect, so that it was not wholly dark. She had a dim perception of God and of eternity, and a still more dim perception of a Saviour who had died even for such as her. She entertained but confused notions of a future life—not comprehending the distinction between the corporeal and spiritual existence. Happiness, in her mind, was exemption from stripes— from labor—from the cruelty of masters and overseers. Her idea of the joy of heaven was simply *rest*, and is fully expressed in these lines of a melancholy bard:

> "I ask no paradise on high,
> With cares on earth oppressed,
> The only heaven for which I sigh,
> Is rest, eternal rest."

It is a mistaken opinion that prevails in some quarters, that the slave does not understand the term—does not comprehend the idea of freedom. Even on Bayou Boeuf, where I conceive slavery exists in its most abject and cruel form—where it exhibits features altogether unknown in more northern States—the most ignorant of them generally know full well its meaning.[187] They understand the privileges and exemptions that belong to it—that it would bestow upon them the fruits of their own labors, and that it would secure to them the enjoyment of domestic happiness. They do not fail to observe the difference between their own condition and the meanest white man's, and to realize the injustice of the laws which place it in his power not only to appropriate the profits of their industry, but to subject them to unmerited and unprovoked punishment, without remedy, or the right to resist, or to remonstrate.

Patsey's life, especially after her whipping, was one long dream of liberty. Far away, to her fancy an immeasurable distance, she knew there was a land of freedom. A thousand times she had heard that somewhere in the distant North there were no slaves—no masters. In her imagination it was an enchanted region, the Paradise of the earth.[188] To dwell where the black man may work for himself—live in his own cabin—till his own soil, was a blissful dream of Patsey's—a dream, alas! the fulfillment of which she can never realize.

The effect of these exhibitions of brutality on the household of the slave-holder, is apparent. Epps' oldest son is an intelligent lad of ten or twelve years of age. It is pitiable, sometimes, to see him chastising, for instance, the venerable Uncle Abram. He will call the old man to account, and if in his childish judgment it is necessary, sentence him to a certain number of lashes, which he proceeds to inflict with much gravity and deliberation. Mounted on his pony, he often rides into the field with his whip, playing the overseer, greatly to his father's delight. Without discrimination, at such times, he applies the rawhide, urging the slaves forward with shouts, and occasional expressions of profanity, while the old man laughs, and commends him as a thorough-going boy.

"The child is father to the man," and with such training, whatever may be his natural disposition, it cannot well be otherwise than that, on arriving at maturity, the sufferings and miseries of the slave will be looked upon with entire indifference. The influence of the iniquitous system necessarily fosters an unfeeling and cruel spirit, even in the bosoms of those who, among their equals, are regarded as humane and generous.

Young Master Epps possessed some noble qualities, yet no process of reasoning could lead him to comprehend, that in the eye of the Almighty there is no distinction of color. He looked upon the black man simply as an animal, differing in no respect from any other animal, save in the gift of speech and the possession of somewhat higher instincts, and, therefore, the more valuable. To work like his father's mules—to be whipped and kicked and scourged through life—to address the white man with hat in hand, and eyes bent servilely on the earth, in his mind, was the natural and proper destiny of the slave. Brought up with such ideas in the notion that we stand without the pale of humanity—no wonder the oppressors of my people are a pitiless and unrelenting race.

The staking out and the flogging of the girl Patsey

CHAPTER XIX.

AVERY, OF BAYOU ROUGE—PECULIARITY OF DWELLINGS—EPPS
BUILDS A NEW HOUSE—BASS, THE CARPENTER—HIS NOBLE
QUALITIES—HIS PERSONAL APPEARANCE AND ECCENTRICITIES—
BASS AND EPPS DISCUSS THE QUESTION OF SLAVERY—EPPS'
OPINION OF BASS—I MAKE MYSELF KNOWN TO HIM—OUR
CONVERSATION—HIS SURPRISE—THE MIDNIGHT MEETING ON THE
BAYOU BANK—BASS' ASSURANCES—DECLARES WAR AGAINST
SLAVERY—WHY I DID NOT DISCLOSE MY HISTORY—BASS WRITES
LETTERS—COPY OF HIS LETTER TO MESSRS. PARKER AND PERRY—
THE FEVER OF SUSPENSE—DISAPPOINTMENTS—BASS ENDEAVORS
TO CHEER ME—MY FAITH IN HIM.

In the month of June, 1852, in pursuance of a previous contract, Mr.
Avery, a carpenter of Bayou Rouge, commenced the erection of a
house for Master Epps.[189] It has previously been stated that there are
no cellars on Bayou Boeuf; on the other hand, such is the low and
swampy nature of the ground, the great houses are usually built upon
spiles. Another peculiarity is, the rooms are not plastered, but the
ceiling and sides are covered with matched cypress boards, painted
such color as most pleases the owner's taste. Generally the plank and
boards are sawed by slaves with whip-saws, there being no water-
power upon which mills might be built within many miles. When the
planter erects for himself a dwelling, therefore, there is plenty of extra
work for his slaves. Having had some experience under Tibeats as a
carpenter, I was taken from the field altogether, on the arrival of
Avery and his hands.

Among them was one to whom I owe an immeasurable debt of
gratitude. Only for him, in all probability, I should have ended my
days in slavery. He was my deliverer—a man whose true heart
overflowed with noble and generous emotions. To the last moment
of my existence I shall remember him with feelings of thankfulness.
His name was Bass, and at that time he resided in Marksville.[190] It will
be difficult to convey a correct impression of his appearance or
character. He was a large man, between forty and fifty years old, of

Mr Bass

light complexion, and light hair. He was very cool and self-possessed, fond of argument, but always speaking with extreme deliberation. He was that kind of person whose peculiarity of manner was such that nothing he uttered ever gave offence. What would be intolerable, coming from the lips of another, could be said by him with impunity. There was not a man on Red River, perhaps, that agreed with him on the subject of politics or religion, and not a man, I venture to say, who discussed either of those subjects half as much. It seemed to be taken for granted that he would espouse the unpopular side of every local question, and it always created amusement rather than displeasure among his auditors, to listen to the ingenious and original manner in which he maintained the controversy. He was a bachelor—an "old bachelor," according to the true acceptation of the term—having no kindred living, as he knew of, in the world. Neither had he any permanent abiding place—wandering from one State to another, as his fancy dictated. He had lived in Marksville three or four years, and in the prosecution of his business as a carpenter; and in consequence, likewise, of his peculiarities, was quite extensively known throughout the parish of Avoyelles. He was liberal to a fault; and his many acts of kindness and transparent goodness of heart rendered him popular in the community, the sentiment of which he unceasingly combated.

He was a native of Canada, from whence he had wandered in early life, and after visiting all the principal localities in the northern and western States, in the course of his peregrinations, arrived in the unhealthy region of the Red River.[191] His last removal was from Illinois. Whither he has now gone, I regret to be obliged to say, is unknown to me. He gathered up his effects and departed quietly from Marksville the day before I did, the suspicions of his instrumentality in procuring my liberation rendering such a step necessary. For the commission of a just and righteous act he would undoubtedly have suffered death, had he remained within reach of the slave-whipping tribe on Bayou Boeuf.

One day, while working on the new house, Bass and Epps became engaged in a controversy, to which, as will be readily supposed, I listened with absorbing interest. They were discussing the subject of Slavery.

"I tell you what it is Epps," said Bass, "it's all wrong—all wrong, sir—there's no justice nor righteousness in it. I wouldn't own a slave if I was rich as Croesus, which I am not, as is perfectly well understood, more particularly among my creditors. *There's* another humbug—the credit system—humbug, sir; no credit—no debt. Credit leads a man into temptation. Cash down is the only thing that will deliver him from evil. But this question of *Slavery*; what *right* have you to your niggers when you come down to the point?"

"What right!" said Epps, laughing; "why, I bought 'em, and paid for 'em."

"Of *course* you did; the law says you have the right to hold a nigger, but begging the law's pardon, it *lies*. Yes, Epps, when the law says that it's a *liar,* and the truth is not in it. Is every thing right because the law allows it? Suppose they'd pass a law taking away your liberty and making you a slave?" *Connect to White Rose !*

"Oh, that ain't a supposable case," said Epps, still laughing; "hope you don't compare me to a nigger, Bass."

"Well," Bass answered gravely, "no, not exactly. But I have seen niggers before now as good as I am, and I have no acquaintance with any white man in these parts that I consider a whit better than myself. Now, in the sight of God, what is the difference, Epps, between a white man and a black one?"

"All the difference in the world," replied Epps. "You might as well ask what the difference is between a white man and a baboon. Now, I've seen one of them critters in Orleans that knowed just as much as any nigger I've got. You'd call them feller citizens, I s'pose?"—and Epps indulged in a loud laugh at his own wit.

"Look here, Epps," continued his companion; "you can't laugh me down in that way. Some men are witty, and some ain't so witty as they think they are. Now let me ask you a question. Are all men created free and equal as the Declaration of Independence holds they are?"

"Yes," responded Epps, "but all men, niggers, and monkeys *ain't;*" and hereupon he broke forth into a more boisterous laugh than before.

"There are monkeys among white people as well as black, when you come to that," coolly remarked Bass. "I know some white men that use arguments no sensible monkey would. But let that pass. These niggers are human beings. If they don't know as much as their masters, whose fault is it? They are not *allowed* to know anything. You have books and papers, and can go where you please, and gather intelligence in a thousand ways. But your slaves have no privileges.

You'd whip one of them if caught reading a book. They are held in bondage, generation after generation, deprived of mental improvement, and who can expect them to possess much knowledge? If they are not brought down to a level with the brute creation, you slaveholders will never be blamed for it. If they are baboons, or stand no higher in the scale of intelligence than such animals, you and men like you will have to answer for it. There's a sin, a fearful sin, resting on this nation, that will not go unpunished forever. There will be a reckoning yet—yes, Epps, there's a day coming that will burn as an oven. It may be sooner or it may be later, but it's a coming as sure as the Lord is just."

"If you lived up among the Yankees in New-England," said Epps, "I expect you'd be one of them cursed fanatics that know more than the constitution, and go about peddling clocks and coaxing niggers to run away."

"If I was in New-England," returned Bass, "I would be just what I am here. I would say that Slavery was an iniquity, and ought to be abolished. I would say there was no reason nor justice in the law, or the constitution that allows one man to hold another man in bondage. It would be hard for you to lose your property, to be sure, but it wouldn't be half as hard as it would be to lose your liberty. You have no more right to your freedom, in exact justice, than Uncle Abram yonder. Talk about black skin, and black blood; why, how many slaves are there on this bayou as white as either of us? And what difference is there in the color of the soul? Pshaw! the whole system is as absurd as it is cruel. You may own niggers and be hanged, but I wouldn't own one for the best plantation in Louisiana."

"You like to hear yourself talk, Bass, better than any man I know of. You would argue that black was white, or white black, if any body would contradict you. Nothing suits you in this world, and I don't believe you will be satisfied with the next, if you should have your choice of them."

Conversations substantially like the foregoing were not unusual between the two after this; Epps drawing him out more for the purpose of creating a laugh at his expense, than with a view of fairly discussing the merits of the question. He looked upon Bass, as a man ready to say anything merely for the pleasure of hearing his own voice; as somewhat self-conceited, perhaps, contending against his faith and judgment, in order, simply, to exhibit his dexterity in argumentation.

He remained at Epps' through the summer, visiting Marksville generally once a fortnight. The more I saw of him, the more I became convinced he was a man in whom I could confide. Nevertheless, my previous ill-fortune had taught me to be extremely cautious. It was not my place to speak to a white man except when spoken to, but I omitted no opportunity of throwing myself in his way, and endeavored constantly in every possible manner to attract his attention. In the early part of August he and myself were at work alone in the house, the other carpenters having left, and Epps being absent in the field.[192] Now was the time, if ever, to broach the subject, and I resolved to do it, and submit to whatever consequences might ensue. We were busily at work in the afternoon, when I stopped suddenly and said—

"Master Bass, I want to ask you what part of the country you came from?"

"Why, Platt, what put that into your head?" he answered. "You wouldn't know if I should tell you." After a moment or two he added—"I was born in Canada; now guess where that is."

"Oh, I know where Canada is," said I, "I have been there myself."

"Yes, I expect you are well acquainted all through that country," he remarked, laughing incredulously.

"As sure as I live, Master Bass," I replied, "I have been there. I have been in Montreal and Kingston, and Queenston, and a great many places in Canada, and I have been in New York State too—in Buffalo, and Rochester, and Albany, and can tell you the names of the villages on the Erie canal and the Champlain canal."

Bass turned round and gazed at me a long time without uttering a syllable.

"How came you here?" he inquired, at length. "Master Bass," I answered, "if justice had been done, I never would have been here."

"Well, how's this?" said he. "Who are you? You have been in Canada sure enough; I know all the places you mention. How did you happen to get here? Come, tell me all about it."

"I have no friends here," was my reply, "that I can put confidence in. I am afraid to tell you, though I don't believe you would tell Master Epps if I should."

He assured me earnestly he would keep every word I might speak to him a profound secret, and his curiosity was evidently strongly excited. It was a long story, I informed him, and would take some time to relate it. Master Epps would be back soon, but if he would see me that night after all were asleep, I would repeat it to him. He consented readily to the arrangement, and directed me to come into the building where we were then at work, and I would find him there. About midnight, when all was still and quiet, I crept cautiously from my cabin, and silently entering the unfinished building, found him awaiting me.

After further assurances on his part that I should not be betrayed, I began a relation of the history of my life and misfortunes. He was deeply interested, asking numerous questions in reference to localities and events. Having ended my story I besought him to write to some of my friends at the North, acquainting them with my situation, and begging them to forward free papers, or take such steps as they might consider proper to secure my release. He promised to do so, but dwelt upon the danger of such an act in case of detection, and now impressed upon me the great necessity of strict silence and secrecy. Before we parted our plan of operation was arranged.

We agreed to meet the next night at a specified place among the high weeds on the bank of the bayou, some distance from master's dwelling. There he was to write down on paper the names and address of several persons, old friends in the North, to whom he would direct letters during his next visit to Marksville. It was not deemed prudent to meet in the new house, inasmuch as the light it would be necessary to use might possibly be discovered. In the course of the day I managed to obtain a few matches and a piece of candle, unperceived, from the kitchen, during a temporary absence of Aunt Phebe. Bass had pencil and paper in his tool chest.

At the appointed hour we met on the bayou bank, and creeping among the high weeds, I lighted the candle, while he drew forth pencil and paper and prepared for business. I gave him the names of William Perry, Cephas Parker and Judge Marvin, all of Saratoga Springs, Saratoga county, New-York.[193] I had been employed by the latter in the United States Hotel, and had transacted business with the former to a considerable extent, and trusted that at least one of them would be still living at that place. He carefully wrote the names, and then remarked, thoughtfully—"It is so many years since you left Saratoga, all these men may be dead, or may have removed. You say you obtained papers at the custom house in New-York. Probably there is a record of them there, and I think it would be well to write and ascertain."

I agreed with him, and again repeated the circumstances related heretofore, connected with my visit to the custom house with Brown and Hamilton. We lingered on the bank of the Bayou an hour or more, conversing upon the subject which now engrossed our thoughts. I could no longer doubt his fidelity, and freely spoke to him of the many sorrows I had borne in silence, and so long. I spoke of my wife and children, mentioning their names and ages, and dwelling upon the unspeakable happiness it would be to clasp them to my heart once more before I died. I caught him by the hand, and with tears and passionate entreaties implored him to befriend me—to restore me to my kindred and to liberty—promising I would weary Heaven the remainder of my life with prayers that it would bless and prosper him. In the enjoyment of freedom—surrounded by the associations of youth, and restored to the bosom of my family—that promise is not yet forgotten, nor shall it ever be so long as I have strength to raise my imploring eyes on high.

> "Oh, blessings on his kindly voice and on his silver hair,
> And blessings on his whole life long, until he meet me there."

He overwhelmed me with assurances of friendship and faithfulness, saying he had never before taken so deep an interest in the fate of anyone. He spoke of himself in a somewhat mournful tone, as a lonely man, a wanderer about the world—that he was growing old, and must soon reach the end of his earthly journey, and lie down to his final rest without kith or kin to mourn for him, or to remember him—that his life was of little value to himself, and henceforth should be devoted to the accomplishment of my liberty, and to an unceasing warfare against the accursed shame of Slavery.

After this time we seldom spoke to, or recognized each other. He was, moreover, less free in his conversation with Epps on the subject of Slavery. The remotest suspicion that there was any unusual intimacy—any secret understanding between us—never once entered the mind of Epps, or any other person, white or black, on the plantation.

I am often asked, with an air of incredulity, how I succeeded so many years in keeping from my daily and constant companions the knowledge of my true name and history. The terrible lesson Burch taught me, impressed indelibly upon my mind the danger and uselessness of asserting I was a freeman. There was no possibility of any slave being able to assist me, while, on the other hand, there *was* a possibility of his exposing me. When it is recollected the whole current of my thoughts, for twelve years, turned to the contemplation of escape, it will not be wondered at, that I was always cautious and on my guard. It would have been an act of folly to have proclaimed my *right* to freedom; it would only have subjected me to severer scrutiny—probably have consigned me to some more distant and inaccessible region than even Bayou Boeuf. Edwin Epps was a person utterly regardless of a black man's rights or wrongs—utterly destitute of any natural sense of justice, as I well knew. It was important, therefore, not only as regarded my hope of deliverance, but also as regarded the few personal privileges I was permitted to enjoy, to keep from him the history of my life.

The Saturday night subsequent to our interview at the water's edge, Bass went home to Marksville. The next day, being Sunday, he employed himself in his own room writing letters. One he directed to the Collector of Customs at New-York, another to Judge Marvin, and another to Messrs. Parker and Perry jointly. The latter was the one which led to my recovery. He subscribed my true name, but in the postscript intimated I was not the writer. The letter itself shows that he considered himself engaged in a dangerous undertaking—no less than running "the risk of his life, if detected." I did not see the letter before it was mailed, but have since obtained a copy, which is here inserted:

Bayou Boeuf, August 15,1852.[194]

"Mr. William Perry or Mr. Cephas Parker

"Gentlemen—It having been a long time since I have seen or heard from you, and not knowing that you are living, it is with uncertainty that I write to you, but the necessity of the case must be my excuse.

"Having been born free, just across the river from you, I am certain you must know me, and I am here now a slave. I wish you to obtain free papers for me, and forward them to me at Marksville, Louisiana, Parish of Avoyelles, and oblige

"Yours, SOLOMON NORTHUP.

"The way I came to be a slave, I was taken sick in Washington City, and was insensible for some time. When I recovered my reason, I was robbed of my free-papers, and in irons on my way to this State, and have never been able to get anyone to write for me until now; and he that is writing for me runs the risk of his life if detected."

The allusion to myself in the work recently issued, entitled "A Key to Uncle Tom's Cabin," contains the first part of this letter, omitting the postscript. Neither are the full names of the gentlemen to whom it is directed correctly stated, there being a slight discrepancy, probably a typographical error. To the postscript more than to the body of the communication am I indebted for my liberation, as will presently be seen.

When Bass returned from Marksville he informed me of what he had done. We continued our midnight consultations, never speaking to each other through the day, excepting as it was necessary about the work. As nearly as he was able to ascertain, it would require two weeks for the letter to reach Saratoga in due course of mail, and the same length of time for an answer to return. Within six weeks, at the farthest, we concluded, an answer would arrive, if it arrived at all. A great many suggestions were now made, and a great deal of conversation took place between us, as to the most safe and proper course to pursue on receipt of the free papers. They would stand between him and harm, in case we were over-taken and arrested leaving the country altogether. It would be no infringement of law, however much it might provoke individual hostility, to assist a freeman to regain his freedom.

At the end of four weeks he was again at Marksville, but no answer had arrived. I was sorely disappointed, but still reconciled myself with the reflection that sufficient length of time had not yet elapsed—that there might have been delays—and that I could not reasonably expect one so soon. Six, seven, eight, and ten weeks passed by, however, and nothing came. I was in a fever of suspense whenever Bass visited Marksville, and could scarcely close my eyes until his return. Finally my master's house was finished, and the time came when Bass must leave me. The night before his departure I was wholly given up to despair. I had clung to him as a drowning man clings to the floating spar, knowing if it slips from his grasp he must forever sink beneath the waves. The all-glorious hope, upon which I had laid such eager hold, was crumbling to ashes in my hands. I felt as if sinking down, down, amidst the bitter waters of Slavery, from the unfathomable depths of which I should never rise again.

The generous heart of my friend and benefactor was touched with pity at the sight of my distress. He endeavored to cheer me up, promising to return the day before Christmas, and if no intelligence was received in the meantime, some further step would be undertaken to effect our design. He exhorted me to keep up my spirits—to rely upon his continued efforts in my behalf, assuring me, in most earnest and impressive language, that my liberation should, from thenceforth, be the chief object of his thoughts.

In his absence the time passed slowly indeed. I looked forward to Christmas with intense anxiety and impatience. I had about given up expectation of receiving any answer to the letters. They might have miscarried, or might have been misdirected. Perhaps those at Saratoga, to whom they had been addressed, were all dead; perhaps, engaged in their pursuits, they did not consider the fate of an obscure, unhappy black man of sufficient importance to be noticed. My whole reliance was in Bass. The faith I had in him was continually re-assuring me, and enabled me to stand up against the tide of disappointment that had overwhelmed me.

So wholly was I absorbed in reflecting upon my situation and prospects, that the hands with whom I labored in the field often observed it. Patsey would ask me if I was sick, and Uncle Abram, and Bob, and Wiley frequently expressed a curiosity to know what I could be thinking about so steadily. But I evaded their inquiries with some light remark, and kept my thoughts locked closely in my breast.

CHAPTER XX.

BASS FAITHFUL TO HIS WORD—HIS ARRIVAL ON CHRISTMAS EVE—
THE DIFFICULTY OF OBTAINING AN INTERVIEW—THE MEETING IN
THE CABIN—NON-ARRIVAL OF THE LETTER—BASS ANNOUNCES HIS
INTENTION TO PROCEED NORTH—CHRISTMAS—CONVERSATION
BETWEEN EPPS AND BASS—YOUNG MISTRESS M'COY, THE BEAUTY
OF BAYOU BOEUF—THE "NE PLUS ULTRA" OF DINNERS—MUSIC AND
DANCING—PRESENCE OF THE MISTRESS—HER EXCEEDING BEAUTY—
THE LAST SLAVE DANCE—WILLIAM PIERCE—OVERSLEEP MYSELF—
THE LAST WHIPPING—DESPONDENCY—THE COLD MORNING—EPPS'
THREATS—THE PASSING CARRIAGE—STRANGERS APPROACHING
THROUGH THE COTTON-FIELD—LAST HOUR ON BAYOU BOEUF.

Faithful to his word on the night before Christmas, Bass came riding
into the yard.

"How are you," said Epps, shaking him by the hand, "glad to see
you."

He would not have been *very* glad had he known the object of his
errand.

"Quite well, quite well," answered Bass. "Had some business out
on the bayou, and concluded to call and see you, and stay over
night."

Epps ordered one of the slaves to take charge of his horse, and
with much talk and laughter they passed into the house together; not,
however, until Bass had looked at me significantly, as much as to say,
"Keep dark, we understand each other." It was ten o'clock at night
before the labors of the day were performed, when I entered the
cabin. At that time Uncle Abram and Bob occupied it with me. I laid
down upon my board and feigned I was asleep. When my
companions had fallen into a profound slumber, I moved stealthily
out of the door, and watched, and listened attentively for some sign
or sound from Bass. There I stood until long after midnight, but
nothing could be seen or heard. As I suspected, he dared not leave
the house, through fear of exciting the suspicion of some of the
family. I judged, correctly, he would rise earlier than was his custom,

and take the opportunity of seeing me before Epps was up. Accordingly I aroused Uncle Abram an hour sooner than usual, and sent him into the house to build a fire, which, at that season of the year, is a part of Uncle Abram's duties.

I also gave Bob a violent shake, and asked him if he intended to sleep until noon, saying master would be up before the mules were fed. He knew right well the consequence that would follow such an event, and, jumping to his feet, was at the horse-pasture in a twinkling.

Presently when both were gone, Bass slipped into the cabin.

"No letter yet, Platt," said he. The announcement fell upon my heart like lead.

"Oh, *do* write again, Master Bass," I cried; "I will give you the names of a great many I know. Surely they are not all dead. Surely some one will pity me."

"No use," Bass replied, "no use. I have made up my mind to that. I fear the Marksville post-master will mistrust something, I had inquired so often at his office. Too uncertain—too dangerous."[195]

"Then it is all over," I exclaimed. "Oh, my God, how can I end my days here!"

"You're not going to end them here," he said, "unless you die very soon. I've thought this matter all over, and have come to a determination. There are more ways than one to manage this business, and a better and surer way than writing letters. I have a job or two on hand which can be completed by March or April. By that time I shall have a considerable sum of money, and then, Platt, I am going to Saratoga myself."

I could scarcely credit my own senses as the words fell from his lips. But he assured me, in a manner that left no doubt of the sincerity of his intention, that if his life was spared until spring, he should certainly undertake the journey.

"I have lived in this region long enough," he continued; "I may as well be in one place as another. For a long time I have been thinking of going back once more to the place where I was born. I'm tired of Slavery as well as you. If I can succeed in getting you away from here, it will be a good act that I shall like to think of all of my life. And I *shall* succeed, Platt; I'm *bound* to do it. Now let me tell you what I want. Epps will be up soon, and it won't do to be caught here. Think of a great many men at Saratoga and Sandy Hill, and in that neighborhood, who once knew you. I shall make excuse to come here again in the course of the winter, when I will write down their names. I will then know who to call on when I go north. Think of all you can. Cheer up! Don't be discouraged. I'm with you, life or death. Good-bye. God bless you," and saying that he left the cabin quickly and entered the great house.

It was Christmas morning—the happiest day in the whole year for the slave. That morning he need not hurry to the field, with his gourd and cotton-bag. Happiness sparkled in the eyes and overspread the countenances of all. The time of feasting and dancing had come. The cane and cotton fields were deserted. That day the clean dress was to be donned—the red ribbon displayed; there were to be re-unions, and joy and laughter, and hurrying to and fro. It was to be a day of *liberty* among the children of Slavery. Wherefore they were happy, and rejoiced.

After breakfast Epps and Bass sauntered about the yard, conversing upon the price of cotton, and various other topics.

"Where do your niggers hold Christmas?" Bass inquired.

"Platt is going to Tanners to-day. His fiddle is in great demand. They want him at Marshall's Monday, and Miss Mary McCoy, on the old Norwood plantation, writes me a note that she wants him to play for her niggers Tuesday."[196]

"He is rather a smart boy, ain't he?" said Bass. "Come here, Platt," he added, looking at me as I walked up to them, as if he had never thought before to take any special notice of me.

"Yes," replied Epps, taking hold of my arm and feeling it, "there isn't a bad joint in him. There ain't a boy on the bayou worth more than he is—perfectly sound, and no bad tricks. D—n him, he isn't like other niggers; doesn't look like 'em—don't act like 'em. I was offered seventeen hundred dollars for him last week."

"And didn't take it?" Bass inquired, with an air of surprise.

"Take it—no; devilish clear of it. Why, he's a reg'lar genius; can make a plough beam, wagon tongue—anything, as well as you can. Marshall wanted to put up one of his niggers agin him and raffle for them, but I told him I would see the devil have him first."

"I don't see anything remarkable about him," Bass observed.

"Why, just feel of him, now," Epps rejoined. "You don't see a boy very often put together any closer than he is. He's a thin-skin'd cuss, and won't bear as much whipping as some; but he's got the muscle in him, and no mistake."

Bass felt of me, turned me round, and made a thorough examination, Epps all the while dwelling on my good points. But his visitor seemed to take but little interest finally in the subject, and consequently it was dropped. Bass soon departed, giving me another sly look of recognition and significance, as he trotted out of the yard.

When he was gone I obtained a pass, and started for Tanner's—not Peter Tanner's, of whom mention has previously been made, but a relative of his. I played during the day and most of the night, and spending the next day, Sunday, in my cabin. Monday I crossed the bayou to Douglas Marshall's,[197] all Epps' slaves accompanying me, and on Tuesday went to the old Norwood place, which is the third plantation above Marshall's, on the same side of the water.

This estate is now owned by Miss Mary McCoy, a lovely girl, some twenty years of age. She is the beauty and the glory of Bayou Boeuf. She owns about a hundred working hands, besides a great many house servants, yard boys, and young children. Her brother-in-law, who resides on the adjoining estate, is her general agent. She is beloved by all her slaves, and good reason indeed have they to be thankful that they have fallen into such gentle hands. Nowhere on the bayou are there such feasts, such merrymaking, as at young Madam McCoy's. Thither, more than to any other place, do the old and the young for miles around love to repair in the time of the Christmas holidays; for nowhere else can they find such delicious repasts; nowhere else can they hear a voice speaking to them so pleasantly. No one is so well beloved—no one fills so large a space in the hearts of a thousand slaves, as young Madam McCoy, the orphan mistress of the old Norwood estate.

On my arrival at her place, I found two or three hundred had assembled. The table was prepared in a long building, which she had erected expressly for her slaves to dance in. It was covered with every variety of food the country afforded, and was pronounced by general acclamation to be the rarest of dinners. Roast turkey, pig, chicken, duck, and all kinds of meat, baked, boiled, and broiled, formed a line the whole length of the extended table, while the vacant spaces were filled with tarts, jellies, and frosted cake, and pastry of many kinds. The young mistress walked around the table, smiling and saying a kind word to each one, and seemed to enjoy the scene exceedingly.

When the dinner was over the tables were removed to make room for the dancers. I tuned my violin and struck up a lively air; while some joined in a nimble reel, others patted and sang their simple but melodious songs, filling the great room with music mingled with the sound of human voices and the clatter of many feet.

In the evening the mistress returned, and stood in the door a long time, looking at us. She was magnificently arrayed. Her dark hair and eyes contrasted strongly with her clear and delicate complexion. Her form was slender but commanding, and her movement was a combination of unaffected dignity and grace. As she stood there, clad in her rich apparel, her face animated with pleasure, I thought I had never looked upon a human being half so beautiful. I dwell with delight upon the description of this fair and gentle lady, not only because she inspired me with emotions of gratitude and admiration, but because I would have the reader understand that all slave-owners on Bayou Boeuf are not like Epps, or Tibeats, or Jim Burns. Occasionally can be found, rarely it may be, indeed, a good man like William Ford, or an angel of kindness like young Mistress McCoy.

Tuesday concluded the three holidays Epps yearly allowed us. On my way home, Wednesday morning, while passing the plantation of William Pierce, that gentleman hailed me, saying he had received a line from Epps, brought down by William Varnell, permitting him to detain me for the purpose of playing for his slaves that night.[198] It was the last time I was destined to witness a slave dance on the shores of Bayou Boeuf. The party at Pierce's continued their jollification until broad daylight, when I returned to my master's house; somewhat wearied with the loss of rest, but rejoicing with the possession of numerous bits and picayunes, which the whites, who were pleased with my musical performances, had contributed. [199]

On Saturday morning, for the first time in years, I overslept myself. I was frightened on coming out of the cabin to find the slaves were already in the field. They had preceded me some fifteen minutes. Leaving my dinner and water-gourd, I hurried after them as fast as I could move. It was not yet sunrise, but Epps was on the piazza as I left the hut, and cried out to me that it was a pretty time of day to be getting up. By extra exertion my row was up when he came out after breakfast. This, however, was no excuse for the offence of oversleeping. Bidding me strip and lie down, he gave me ten or fifteen lashes, at the conclusion of which he inquired if I thought, after that, I could get up sometime in the *morning*. I expressed myself quite positively that I *could*, and, with back stinging with pain, went about my work.

The following day, Sunday, my thoughts were upon Bass, and the probabilities and hopes which hung upon his action and determination. I considered the uncertainty of life; that if it should be the will of God that he should die, my prospect of deliverance, and all expectation of happiness in this world, would be wholly ended and destroyed. My sore back, perhaps, did not have a tendency to render me unusually cheerful. I felt down-hearted and unhappy all day long, and when I laid down upon the hard board at night, my heart was oppressed with such a load of grief, it seemed that it must break.

Monday morning, the third of January, 1853, we were in the field betimes. It was a raw, cold morning, such as is unusual in that region. I was in advance, Uncle Abram next to me, behind him Bob, Patsey and Wiley, with our cotton-bags about our necks. Epps happened (a rare thing, indeed) to come out that morning without his whip. He swore, in a manner that would shame a pirate, that we were doing nothing. Bob ventured to say that his fingers were so numb with cold he couldn't pick fast. Epps cursed himself for not having brought his rawhide, and declared that when he came out again he would warm us well; yes, he would make us all hotter than the fiery realm in which I am sometimes compelled to believe he will himself eventually reside.

With these fervent expressions, he left us. When out of hearing, we commenced talking to each other, saying how hard it was to be compelled to keep up our tasks with numb fingers; how unreasonable master was, and speaking of him generally in no flattering terms. Our conversation was interrupted by a carriage passing rapidly towards the house. Looking up, we saw two men approaching us through the cotton-field.

* * * * *

Having now brought down this narrative to the last hour I was to spend on Bayou Boeuf—having gotten through my last cotton picking, and about to bid Master Epps farewell—I must beg the reader to go back with me to the month of August; to follow Bass' letter on its long journey to Saratoga; to learn the effect it produced—and that, while I was repining and despairing in the slave hut of Edwin Epps, through the friendship of Bass and goodness of Providence, all things were working together for my deliverance.

CHAPTER XXI.

I am indebted to Mr. Henry B. Northup and others for many of the particulars contained in this chapter.

The letter written by Bass, directed to Parker and Perry, and which was deposited in the post-office in Marksville on the 15th day of August, 1852, arrived at Saratoga in the early part of September. Some time previous to this, Anne had removed to Glens Falls, Warren county, where she had charge of the kitchen in Carpenter's Hotel. She kept house, however, lodging with our children, and was only absent from them during such time as the discharge of her duties in the hotel required.

Messrs. Parker and Perry, on receipt of the letter, forwarded it immediately to Anne. On reading it the children were all excitement, and without delay hastened to the neighboring village of Sandy Hill, to consult Henry B. Northup, and obtain his advice and assistance in the matter.

Upon examination, that gentleman found among the statutes of the State an act providing for the recovery of free citizens from slavery. It was passed May 14, 1840, and is entitled "An act more effectually to protect the free citizens of this State from being kidnapped or reduced to slavery." It provides that it shall be the duty of the Governor, upon the receipt of satisfactory information that any free citizen or inhabitant of this State, is wrongfully held in another State or Territory of the United States, upon the allegation or pretence that such person is a slave, or by color of any usage or rule of law is deemed or taken to be a slave, to take such measures to procure the restoration of such person to liberty, as he shall deem necessary. And to that end, he is authorized to appoint and employ an agent, and directed to furnish him with such credentials and instructions as will be likely to accomplish the object of his appointment. It requires the agent so appointed to proceed to collect the proper proof to establish the right of such person to his freedom; to perform such journeys, take such measures, institute such legal proceedings, &c., as may be necessary to return such person to this State, and charge all expenses incurred in carrying the act into effect, upon moneys not otherwise appropriated in the treasury. (See Appendix A)

It was necessary to establish two facts to the satisfaction of the Governor: First, that I was a free citizen of New-York; and secondly, that I was wrongfully held in bondage. As to the first point, there was no difficulty, all the older inhabitants in the vicinity being ready to testify to it. The second point rested entirely upon the letter to Parker and Perry, written in an unknown hand, and upon the letter penned on board the brig Orleans, which, unfortunately, had been mislaid or lost.

A memorial was prepared, directed to his excellency, Governor Hunt, setting forth her marriage, my departure to Washington city; the receipt of the letters; that I was a free citizen, and such other facts as were deemed important, and was signed and verified by Anne.[200] Accompanying this memorial were several affidavits of prominent citizens of Sandy Hill and Fort Edward, corroborating fully the statements it contained, and also a request of several well known gentlemen to the Governor, that Henry B. Northup be appointed agent under the legislative act.[201]

On reading the memorial and affidavits, his excellency took a lively interest in the matter, and on the 23d day of November, 1852, under the seal of the State, "constituted, appointed, and employed Henry B. Northup, Esq., an agent, with full power to effect" my restoration, and to take such measures as would be most likely to accomplish it, and instructing him to proceed to Louisiana with all convenient dispatch. (See Appendix B)

The pressing nature of Mr. Northup's professional and political engagements delayed his departure until December.[202] On the fourteenth day of that month he left Sandy Hill, and proceeded to Washington. The Hon. Pierre Soule, Senator in Congress from Louisiana, Hon. Mr. Conrad, Secretary of War, and Judge Nelson, of the Supreme Court of the United States, upon hearing a statement of the facts, and examining his commission, and certified copies of the memorial and affidavits, furnished him with open letters to gentlemen in Louisiana, strongly urging their assistance in accomplishing the object of his appointment.

Senator Soule especially interested himself in the matter, insisting, in forcible language, that it was the duty and interest of every planter in his State to aid in restoring me to freedom, and trusted the sentiments of honor and justice in the bosom of every citizen of the commonwealth would enlist him at once in my behalf. Having obtained these valuable letters, Mr. Northup returned to Baltimore, and proceeded from thence to Pittsburgh. It was his original intention, under advice of friends at Washington, to go directly to New-Orleans, and consult the authorities of that city.[203] Providentially, however, on arriving at the mouth of Red River, he changed his mind. Had he continued on, he would not have met with Bass, in which case the search for me would probably have been fruitless.

Taking passage on the first steamer that arrived, he pursued his journey up Red River, a sluggish, winding stream, flowing through a vast region of primitive forests and impenetrable swamps, almost wholly destitute of inhabitants. About nine o'clock in the forenoon, January 1st, 1853, he left the steamboat at Marksville, and proceeded directly to Marksville Court House, a small village four miles in the interior.[204]

From the fact that the letter to Messrs. Parker and Perry was post-marked at Marksville, it was supposed by him that I was in that place or its immediate vicinity. On reaching this town, he at once laid his business before the Hon. John P. Waddill, a legal gentleman of distinction, and a man of fine genius and most noble impulses. After reading the letters and documents presented him, and listening to a representation of the circumstances under which I had been carried away into captivity, Mr. Waddill at once proffered his services, and entered into the affair with great zeal and earnestness. He, in common with others of like elevated character, looked upon the kidnapper with abhorrence. The title of his fellow parishioners and clients to the property which constituted the larger proportion of their wealth, not only depended upon the good faith in which slave sales were transacted, but he was a man in whose honorable heart emotions of indignation were aroused by such an instance of injustice.[205]

Marksville, although occupying a prominent position, and standing out in impressive italics on the map of Louisiana, is, in fact, but a small and insignificant hamlet. Aside from the tavern, kept by a jolly and generous boniface, the court house, inhabited by lawless cows and swine in the seasons of vacation, and a high gallows, with its dissevered rope dangling in the air, there is little to attract the attention of the stranger.

Solomon Northup was a name Mr. Waddill had never heard, but he was confident that if there was a slave bearing the appellation in Marksville or vicinity, his black boy Tom would know him. Tom was accordingly called, but in all his extensive circle of acquaintances there was no such personage. *Platt.*

The letter to Parker and Perry was dated at Bayou Boeuf. At this place, therefore, the conclusion was, I must be sought. But here a difficulty suggested itself, of a very grave character indeed. Bayou Boeuf, at its nearest point, was twenty-three miles distant, and was the name applied to the section of country extending between fifty and a hundred miles, on both sides of that stream. Thousands and thousands of slaves resided upon its shores, the remarkable richness and fertility of soil having attracted thither a great number of planters.[206] The information in the letter was so vague and indefinite as to render it difficult to conclude upon any specific course of proceeding. It was finally determined, however, as the only plan that presented any prospect of success, that Northup and the brother of Waddill, a student in the office of the latter, should repair to the Bayou, and traveling up one side and down the other its whole length, inquire at each plantation for me. Mr. Waddill tendered the use of his carriage, and it was definitely arranged that they should start upon the excursion early Monday morning.

It will be seen at once that this course, in all probability, would have resulted unsuccessfully. It would have been impossible for them to have gone into the fields and examine all the gangs at work. They were not aware that I was known only as Platt; and had they inquired of Epps himself, he would have stated truly that he knew nothing of Solomon Northup.

The arrangement being adopted, however, there was nothing further to be done until Sunday had elapsed. The conversation between Messrs. Northup and Waddill, in the course of the afternoon, turned upon New-York politics.

"I can scarcely comprehend the nice distinctions and shades of political parties in your State," observed Mr. Waddill. "I read of soft-shells and hard-shells, hunkers and barnburners, woolly-heads and silver-grays, and am unable to understand the precise difference between them. Pray, what is it?"

Mr. Northup, refilling his pipe, entered into quite an elaborate narrative of the origin of the various sections of parties, and concluded by saying there was another party in New-York, known as free-soilers or abolitionists. "You have seen none of those in this part of the country, I presume?" Mr. Northup remarked.

"Never, but one," answered Waddill, laughingly. "We have one here in Marksville, an eccentric creature, who preaches abolitionism as vehemently as any fanatic at the North. He is a generous, inoffensive man, but always maintaining the wrong side of an argument. It affords us a deal of amusement. He is an excellent mechanic, and almost indispensable in this community. He is a carpenter. His name is Bass."

Some further good-natured conversation was had at the expense of Bass' peculiarities, when Waddill all at once fell into a reflective mood, and asked for the mysterious letter again.

"Let me see—l-e-t m-e s-e-e!" he repeated, thoughtfully to himself, running his eyes over the letter once more. "'Bayou Boeuf, August 15.' August 15—post-marked here. 'He that is writing for me'—Where did Bass work last summer?" he inquired, turning suddenly to his brother. His brother was unable to inform him, but rising, left the office, and soon returned with the intelligence that "Bass worked last summer somewhere on Bayou Boeuf."

"He is the man," bringing down his hand emphatically on the table, "who can tell us all about Solomon Northup," exclaimed Waddill.

Bass was immediately searched for, but could not be found. After some inquiry, it was ascertained he was at the landing on Red

River. Procuring a conveyance, young Waddill and Northup were not long in traversing the few miles to the latter place. On their arrival, Bass was found, just on the point of leaving, to be absent a fortnight or more. After an introduction, Northup begged the privilege of speaking to him privately a moment. They walked together towards the river, when the following conversation ensued:

"Mr. Bass," said Northup, "allow me to ask you if you were on Bayou Boeuf last August?"

"Yes, sir, I was there in August," was the reply.

"Did you write a letter for a colored man at that place to some gentlemen in Saratoga Springs?"

"Excuse me, sir, if I say that is none of your business," answered Bass, stopping and looking his interrogator searchingly in the face.

"Perhaps I am rather hasty, Mr. Bass; I beg your pardon; but I have come from the state of New-York to accomplish the purpose the writer of a letter dated the 15th of August, post-marked at Marksville, had in view. Circumstances had led me to think that you are perhaps the man who wrote it. I am in search of Solomon Northup. If you know him, I beg you to inform me frankly where he is, and I assure you the source of any information you may give me shall not be divulged, if you desire it not to be."

A long time Bass looked his new acquaintance steadily in the eyes, without opening his lips. He seemed to be doubting in his own mind if there was not an attempt to practice some deception upon him. Finally he said, deliberately—

"I have done nothing to be ashamed of. I am the man who wrote the letter. If you have come to rescue Solomon Northup, I am glad to see you."

"When did you last see him, and where is he?" Northup inquired.

"I last saw him Christmas, a week ago to-day. He is the slave of Edwin Epps, a planter on Bayou Boeuf, near Holmesville. He is not known as Solomon Northup; he is called Platt."

The secret was out—the mystery was unraveled. Through the thick, black cloud, amid whose dark and dismal shadows I had walked twelve years, broke the star that was to light me back to liberty. All mistrust and hesitation were soon thrown aside, and the two men conversed long and freely upon the subject uppermost in their thoughts. Bass expressed the interest he had taken in my behalf—his intention of going north in the Spring, and declaring that he had resolved to accomplish my emancipation, if it were in his power. He described the commencement and progress of his acquaintance with me, and listened with eager curiosity to the account given him of my family, and the history of my early life. Before separating, he drew a map of the bayou on a strip of paper with a piece of red chalk, showing the locality of Epps' plantation, and the road leading most directly to it.

Northup and his young companion returned to Marksville, where it was determined to commence legal proceedings to test the question of my right to freedom. I was made plaintiff, Mr. Northup acting as my guardian, and Edwin Epps defendant. The process to be issued was in the nature of replevin, directed to the sheriff of the parish, commanding him to take me into custody, and detain me until the decision of the court. By the time the papers were duly drawn up, it was twelve o'clock at night—too late to obtain the necessary signature of the Judge, who resided some distance out of town. Further business was therefore suspended until Monday morning.

Everything, apparently, was moving along swimmingly, until Sunday afternoon, when Waddill called at Northup's room to express his apprehension of difficulties they had not expected to encounter. Bass had become alarmed, and had placed his affairs in the hands of a person at the landing, communicating to him his intention of leaving the State. This person had betrayed the confidence reposed in him to a certain extent, and a rumor began to float about the town, that the stranger at the hotel, who had been observed in the company of lawyer Waddill, was after one of old Epps' slaves, over on the bayou. Epps was known at Marksville, having frequent occasion to visit that place during the session of the courts, and the fear entertained by Mr. Northup's adviser was, that intelligence would be conveyed to him in the night, giving him opportunity of secreting me before the arrival of the sheriff.

This apprehension had the effect of expediting matters considerably. The sheriff, who lived in one direction from the village, was requested to hold himself in readiness immediately after midnight, while the Judge was informed he would be called upon at the same time. It is but justice to say, that the authorities at Marksville cheerfully rendered all the assistance in their power.

As soon after midnight as bail could be perfected, and the Judge's signature obtained, a carriage, containing Mr. Northup and the sheriff, driven by the landlord's son, rolled rapidly out of the village of Marksville, on the road towards Bayou Boeuf.

It was supposed that Epps would contest the issue involving my right to liberty, and it therefore suggested itself to Mr. Northup, that the testimony of the sheriff, describing my first meeting with the former, might perhaps become material on the trial. It was accordingly arranged during the ride, that, before I had an opportunity of speaking to Mr. Northup, the sheriff should propound to me certain questions agreed upon, such as the number and names of my children, the name of my wife before marriage, of places I knew at the North, and so forth. If my answers corresponded with the statements given him, the evidence must necessarily be considered conclusive.

At length, shortly after Epps had left the field, with the consoling assurance that he would soon return and *warm* us, as was stated in the conclusion of the preceding chapter, they came in sight of the plantation, and discovered us at work. Alighting from the carriage, and directing the driver to proceed to the great house, with instructions not to mention to anyone the object of their errand until they met again, Northup and the sheriff turned from the highway, and came towards us across the cotton field. We observed them, on looking up at the carriage—one several rods in advance of the other. It was a singular and unusual thing to see white men approaching us in that manner, and especially at that early hour in the morning, and Uncle Abram and Patsey made some remarks, expressive of their astonishment. Walking up to Bob, the sheriff inquired:

"Where's the boy they call Platt?"

"Thar he is, massa," answered Bob, pointing to me, and twitching off his hat.

I wondered to myself what business he could possibly have with me, and turning round, gazed at him until he had approached within a step. During my long residence on the bayou, I had become familiar with the face of every planter within many miles; but this man was an utter stranger—certainly I had never seen him before.

"Your name is Platt, is it?" he asked.

"Yes, master," I responded.

Pointing towards Northup, standing a few rods distant, he demanded—"Do you know that man?"

I looked in the direction indicated, and as my eyes rested on his countenance, a world of images thronged my brain; a multitude of well known faces—Anne's, and the dear children's, and my old dead father's; all the scenes and associations of childhood and youth; all the friends of other and happier days, appeared and disappeared, flitting and floating like dissolving shadows before the vision of my imagination, until at last the perfect memory of the man recurred to me, and throwing up my hands towards Heaven, I exclaimed in a voice louder than I could utter in a less exciting moment—

"*Henry B. Northup!* Thank God—thank God!"

In an instant I comprehended the nature of his business, and felt that the hour of my deliverance was at hand. I started towards him, but the sheriff stepped before me.

"Stop a moment," said he; "have you any other name than Platt?"

"Solomon Northup is my name, master," I replied.

"Have you a family?" he inquired.

"I *had* a wife and three children."

"What were your children's names?"

"Elizabeth, Margaret, and Alonzo."

"And your wife's name before her marriage?"

"Anne Hampton."

"Who married you?"

"Timothy Eddy, of Fort Edward."

"Where does that gentleman live?" again pointing to Northup, who remained standing in the same place where I had first recognized him.

"He lives in Sandy Hill, Washington county, New York," was the reply.

He was proceeding to ask further questions, but I pushed past him, unable longer to restrain myself. I seized my old acquaintance by both hands. I could not speak. I could not refrain from tears.

"Sol," he said at length, "I'm glad to see you."

I essayed to make some answer, but emotion choked all utterance, and I was silent. The slaves, utterly confounded, stood gazing upon the scene, their open mouths and rolling eyes indicating the utmost wonder and astonishment. For ten years I had dwelt among them, in the field and in the cabin, borne the same hardships, partaken the same fare, mingled my griefs with theirs, participated in the same scanty joys; nevertheless, not until this hour, the last I was to remain among them, had the remotest suspicion of my true name, or the slightest knowledge of my real history, been entertained by any one of them.

Not a word was spoken for several minutes, during which time I clung fast to Northup, looking up into his face, fearful I should awake and find it all a dream.

"Throw down that sack," Northup added, finally, "Your cotton-picking days are over. Come with us to the man you live with."

I obeyed him, and walking between him and the sheriff, we moved towards the great house. It was not until we had proceeded some distance that I had recovered my voice sufficiently to ask if my family were all living. He informed me he had seen Anne, Margaret and Elizabeth but a short time previously; that Alonzo was also living, and all were well. My mother, however, I could never see again. As I began to recover in some measure from the sudden and great excitement which so overwhelmed me, I grew faint and weak, insomuch it was with difficulty I could walk. The sheriff took hold of my arm and assisted me, or I think I should have fallen. As we entered the yard, Epps stood by the gate, conversing with the driver. That young man, faithful to his instructions, was entirely unable to give him the least information in answer to his repeated inquiries of what was going on. By the time we reached him he was almost as much amazed and puzzled as Bob or Uncle Abram.

Shaking hands with the sheriff, and receiving an introduction to Mr. Northup, he invited them into the house, ordering me, at the same time, to bring in some wood. It was some time before I succeeded in cutting an armful, having, somehow, unaccountably lost the power of wielding an axe with any manner of precision. When I entered with it at last, the table was strewn with papers, from one of which Northup was reading. I was probably longer than necessity required, in placing the sticks upon the fire, being particular as to the exact position of each individual one of them. I heard the words, "the said Solomon Northup" and "the deponent further says," and "free citizens of New-York," repeated frequently, and from these expressions understood that the secret I had so long retained from Master and Mistress Epps, was finally developing. I lingered as long as prudence permitted, and was about leaving the room, when Epps inquired,

"Platt, do you know this gentleman?"

"Yes, master," I replied, "I have known him as long as I can remember."

"Where does he live?"

"He lives in New-York."

"Did you ever live there?"

"Yes, master—born and bred there."

"You was free, then. Now you d—d nigger," he exclaimed, "why did you not tell me that when I bought you?"

"Master Epps," I answered, in a somewhat different tone than the one in which I had been accustomed to address him—"Master Epps, you did not take the trouble to ask me; besides, I told one of my owners—the man that kidnapped me—that I was free, and was whipped almost to death for it."

"It seems there has been a letter written for you by somebody. Now, who is it?" he demanded, authoritatively. I made no reply.

"I say, who wrote that letter?" he demanded again.

"Perhaps I wrote it myself," I said.

"You haven't been to Marksville post-office and back before light, I know."

He insisted upon my informing him, and I insisted I would not. He made many vehement threats against the man, whoever he might be, and intimated the bloody and savage vengeance he would wreak upon him, when he found out. His whole manner and language exhibited a feeling of anger towards the unknown person who had written for me, and of fretfulness at the idea of losing so much property. Addressing Mr. Northup, he swore if he had only had an hour's notice of his coming, he would have saved him the trouble of taking me back to New-York; that he would have run me into the swamp, or some other place out of the way, where all the sheriffs on earth couldn't have found me.

I walked out into the yard, and was entering the kitchen door, when something struck me in the back. Aunt Phebe, emerging from the back door of the great house with a pan of potatoes, had thrown one of them with unnecessary violence, thereby giving me to understand that she wished to speak to me a moment confidentially. Running up to me, she whispered in my ear with great earnestness,

"Lor a'mity, Platt! what d'ye think? Dem two men come after ye. Heard 'em tell massa you free—got wife and tree children back thar whar you come from. Goin' wid 'em? Fool if you don't—wish I could go," and Aunt Phebe ran on in this manner at a rapid rate.

Presently Mistress Epps made her appearance in the kitchen. She said many things to me, and wondered why I had not told her who I was. She expressed her regret, complimenting me by saying she had rather lose any other servant on the plantation. Had Patsey that day stood in my place, the measure of my mistress' joy would have overflowed. Now there was no one left who could mend a chair or a piece of furniture—no one who was of any use about the house—no one who could play for her on the violin—and Mistress Epps was actually affected to tears.

Epps had called to Bob to bring up his saddle horse. The other slaves, also, overcoming their fear of the penalty, had left their work and come to the yard. They were standing behind the cabins, out of sight of Epps. They beckoned me to come to them, and with all the eagerness of curiosity, excited to the highest pitch, conversed with and questioned me. If I could repeat the exact words they uttered, with the same emphasis—if I could paint their several attitudes, and the expression of their countenances—it would be indeed an interesting picture. In their estimation, I had suddenly arisen to an immeasurable height—had become a being of immense importance.

The legal papers having been served, and arrangements made with Epps to meet them the next day at Marksville, Northup and the sheriff entered the carriage to return to the latter place. As I was about mounting to the driver's seat, the sheriff said I ought to bid Mr. and Mrs. Epps goodbye. I ran back to the piazza where they were standing, and taking off my hat, said,

"Goodbye, missis."

"Goodbye, Platt," said Mrs. Epps, kindly.

"Goodbye, master."

"Ah! you d—d nigger," muttered Epps, in a surly, malicious tone of voice, "you needn't feel so cussed tickled—you ain't gone yet—I'll see about this business at Marksville tomorrow."

I was only a "*nigger*" and knew my place, but felt as strongly as if I had been a white man, that it would have been an inward comfort, had I dared to have given him a parting kick. On my way back to the carriage, Patsey ran from behind a cabin and threw her arms about my neck.

"Oh! Platt," she cried, tears streaming down her face, "you're goin' to be free—you're goin' way off yonder where we'll nebber see ye any more. You've saved me a good many whippins, Platt; I'm glad you're goin' to be free—but oh! de Lord, de Lord! What'll become of me?"

I disengaged myself from her, and entered the carriage. The driver cracked his whip and away we rolled. I looked back and saw Patsey, with drooping head, half reclining on the ground; Mrs. Epps was on the piazza; Uncle Abram, and Bob, and Wiley, and Aunt Phebe stood by the gate, gazing after me. I waved my hand, but the carriage turned a bend of the bayou, hiding them from my eyes forever.

We stopped a moment at Carey's sugar house, where a great number of slaves were at work, such an establishment being a curiosity to a Northern man.[207] Epps dashed by us on horseback at full speed—on the way, as we learned next day, to the "Pine Woods," to see William Ford, who had brought me into the country.

Tuesday, the fourth of January, Epps and his counsel, the Hon. H. Taylor,[208] Northup, Waddill, the Judge and sheriff of Avoyelles, and myself, met in a room in the village of Marksville. Mr. Northup stated the facts in regard to me, and presented his commission, and the affidavits accompanying it. The sheriff described the scene in the cotton field. I was also interrogated at great length. Finally, Mr. Taylor assured his client that he was satisfied, and that litigation would not only be expensive, but utterly useless. In accordance with his advice, a paper was drawn up and signed by the proper parties, wherein Epps acknowledged he was satisfied of my right to freedom, and formally surrendered me to the authorities of New-York.[209] It was also stipulated that it be entered of record in the recorder's office of Avoyelles.

Mr. Northup and myself immediately hastened to the landing, and taking passage on the first steamer that arrived, were soon floating down Red River, up which, with such desponding thoughts, I had been borne twelve years before.

Scene in the cotton field—Solomon's delivery

CHAPTER XXII.

ARRIVAL IN NEW-ORLEANS—GLIMPSE OF FREEMAN—GENOIS, THE
RECORDER—HIS DESCRIPTION OF SOLOMON—REACH CHARLESTON—
INTERRUPTED BY CUSTOM HOUSE OFFICERS—PASS THROUGH
RICHMOND—ARRIVAL IN WASHINGTON—BURCH ARRESTED—
SHEKELS AND THORN—THEIR TESTIMONY—BURCH ACQUITTED—
ARREST OF SOLOMON—BURCH WITHDRAWS THE COMPLAINT—THE
HIGHER TRIBUNAL—DEPARTURE FROM WASHINGTON—ARRIVAL AT
SANDY HILL—OLD FRIENDS AND FAMILIAR SCENES—PROCEED TO
GLEN FALLS—MEETING WITH ANNE, MARGARET AND ELIZABETH—
SOLOMON NORTHUP STAUNTON—INCIDENTS—CONCLUSION.

As the steamer glided on its way towards New-Orleans, *perhaps* I was
not happy—*perhaps* there was no difficulty in restraining myself from
dancing round the deck—perhaps I did not feel grateful to the man
who had come so many hundred miles for me—perhaps I did not
light his pipe, and wait and watch his word, and run at his slightest
bidding. If I didn't—well, no matter.

We tarried at New-Orleans two days. During that time I pointed
out the locality of Freeman's slave pen, and the room in which Ford
purchased me. We happened to meet Theophilus in the street, but I
did not think it worth while to renew acquaintance with him. From
respectable citizens we ascertained he had become a low, miserable
rowdy—a broken-down, disreputable man.

We also visited the recorder, Mr. Genois, to whom Senator Soule's
letter was directed, and found him a man well deserving the wide and
honorable reputation that he bears. He very generously furnished us
with a sort of legal pass, over his signature and seal of office, and as it
contains the recorder's description of my personal appearance, it may
not be amiss to insert it here. The following is a copy:

"State of Louisiana—City of New Orleans:
Recorder's Office, Second District.

"To all to whom these presents shall come:—

"This is to certify that Henry B. Northup, Esquire, of the county of Washington, New-York, has produced before me due evidence of the freedom of Solomon, a mulatto man, aged about forty-two years, five feet, seven inches and six lines, woolly hair, and chestnut eyes, who is a native born of the State of New-York. That the said Northup, being about bringing the said Solomon to his native place, through the southern routes, the civil authorities are requested to let the aforesaid colored man Solomon pass unmolested, he demeaning well and properly.

"Given under my hand and the seal of the city of New-Orleans this 7th of January, 1853.

[L.S.]
TH.GENOIS, Recorder."

On the 8th we came to Lake Pontchartrain, by railroad, and, in due time, following the usual route, reached Charleston. After going on board the steamboat, and paying our passage at this city, Mr. Northup was called upon by a custom-house officer to explain why he had not registered his servant. He replied that he had no servant— that, as the agent of New-York, he was accompanying a free citizen of that State from slavery to freedom, and did not desire nor intend to make any registry whatever. I conceived from his conversation and manner, though I may perhaps be entirely mistaken, that no great pains would be taken to avoid whatever difficulty the Charleston officials might deem proper to create. At length, however, we were permitted to proceed, and, passing through Richmond, where I caught a glimpse of Goodin's pen, arrived in Washington January 17, 1853.

We ascertained that both Burch and Radburn were still residing in that city. Immediately a complaint was entered with a police magistrate of Washington, against James H. Burch, for kidnapping and selling me into slavery. He was arrested upon a warrant issued by Justice Goddard, and returned before Justice Mansel, and held to bail in the sum of three thousand dollars. When first arrested, Burch was much excited, exhibiting the utmost fear and alarm, and before reaching the justice's office on Louisiana Avenue, and before knowing the precise nature of the complaint, begged the police to permit him to consult Benjamin O. Shekels, a slave trader of seventeen years' standing, and his former partner. The latter became his bail.

At ten o'clock, the 18th of January, both parties appeared before the magistrate. Senator Chase, of Ohio, Hon. Orville Clark, of Sandy Hill, and Mr. Northup acted as counsel for the prosecution, and Joseph H. Bradley for the defence.

Gen. Orville Clark was called and sworn as a witness, and testified that he had known me from childhood, and that I was a free man, as was my father before me. Mr. Northup then testified to the same, and proved the facts connected with his mission to Avoyelles.

Ebenezer Radburn was then sworn for the prosecution, and testified he was forty-eight years old; that he was a resident of Washington, and had known Burch fourteen years; that in 1841 he was keeper of Williams' slave pen; that he remembered the fact of my confinement in the pen that year. At this point it was admitted by the defendant's counsel, that I had been placed in the pen by Burch in the spring of 1841, and hereupon the prosecution rested.

Benjamin O. Shekels was then offered as a witness by the prisoner. Benjamin is a large, coarse-featured man, and the reader may perhaps get a somewhat correct conception of him by reading the exact language he used in answer to the first question of defendant's lawyer. He was asked the place of his nativity, and his reply, uttered in a sort of rowdyish way, was in these very words—"I was born in Ontario county, New-York, and *weighed fourteen pounds!*"

Benjamin was a prodigious baby! He further testified that he kept the Steamboat Hotel in Washington in 1841, and saw me there in the spring of that year. He was proceeding to state what he had heard two men say, when Senator Chase raised a legal objection, to wit, that the sayings of third persons, being hearsay, was improper evidence. The objection was overruled by the Justice, and Shekels continued, stating that two men came to his hotel and represented they had a colored man for sale; that they had an interview with Burch; that they stated they came from Georgia, but he did not remember the county; that they gave a full history of the boy, saying he was a bricklayer, and played on the violin; that Burch remarked he would purchase if they could agree; that they went out and brought the boy in, and that I was the same person. He further testified, with as much unconcern as if it was the truth, that I represented I was born and bred in Georgia; that one of the young men with me was my master; that I exhibited a great deal of regret at parting with him, and he believed "got into tears!"—nevertheless, that I insisted my master had a right to sell me; that he *ought* to sell me; and the remarkable reason I gave was, according to Shekels, because he, my master, "had been gambling and on a spree!"

He continued, in these words, copied from the minutes taken on the examination: "Burch interrogated the boy in the usual manner, told him if he purchased him he should send him south. The boy said he had no objection, that in fact he would like to go south. Burch paid $650 for him, to my knowledge. I don't know what name was given him, but think it was not Solomon. Did not know the name of either of the two men. They were in my tavern two or three hours, during which time the boy played on the violin. The bill of sale was signed in my bar-room. It was a *printed blank, filled up by Burch.* Before 1838 Burch was my partner. Our business was buying and selling slaves. After that time he was a partner of Theophilus Freeman, of New-Orleans. Burch bought here—Freeman sold there!"

Shekels, before testifying, had heard my relation of the circumstances connected with the visit to Washington with Brown and Hamilton, and therefore, it was, undoubtedly, he spoke of "two men," and of my playing on the violin. Such was his fabrication, utterly untrue, and yet there was found in Washington a man who endeavored to corroborate him. *Lies*

Benjamin A. Thorn testified he was at Shekels' in 1841, and saw a colored boy playing on a fiddle. "Shekels said he was for sale. Heard his master tell him he should sell him. The boy acknowledged to me he was a slave. I was not present when the money was paid. Will not swear positively this is the boy. The master *came near shedding tears: I think the boy did!* I have been engaged in the business of taking slaves south, off and on, for twenty years. When I can't do that I do something else."

I was then offered as a witness, but, objection being made, the court decided my evidence inadmissable. It was rejected solely on the ground that I was a colored man—the fact of my being a free citizen of New-York not being disputed. *Solomon could not testify.*

Shekels having testified there was a bill of sale executed, Burch was called upon by the prosecution to produce it, inasmuch as such a paper would corroborate the testimony of Thorn and Shekels. The prisoner's counsel saw the necessity of exhibiting it, or giving some reasonable explanation for its non-production. To effect the latter, Burch himself was offered as a witness in his own behalf. It was contended by counsel for the people, that such testimony should not be allowed—that it was in contravention of every rule of evidence, and if permitted would defeat the ends of justice. His testimony, however, was received by the court! He made oath that such a bill of sale had been drawn up and signed, *but he had lost it, and did not know what had become of it!* Thereupon the magistrate was requested to dispatch a police officer to Burch's residence, with directions to bring his books, containing his bills of sales for the year 1841. The request was granted, and before any measure could be taken to prevent it, the officer had obtained possession of the books, and brought them into court. The sales for the year 1841 were found, and carefully examined, but no sale of myself, by any name, was discovered!

Upon the testimony the court held the fact to be established, that Burch came innocently and honestly by me, and accordingly he was discharged.

An attempt was then made by Burch and his satellites, to fasten upon me the charge that I had conspired with the two white men to defraud him—with what success, appears in an extract taken from an article in the New-York Times, published a day or two subsequent to the trial: "The counsel for the defendant had drawn up, before the defendant was discharged, an affidavit, signed by Burch, and had a warrant out against the colored man for a conspiracy with the two white men before referred to, to defraud Burch out of six hundred and twenty-five dollars. The warrant was served, and the colored man arrested and brought before officer Goddard. Burch and his witnesses appeared in court, and H. B. Northup appeared as counsel for the colored man, stating he was ready to proceed as counsel on the part of the defendant, and asking no delay whatever. Burch, after consulting privately a short time with Shekels, stated to the magistrate that he wished him to dismiss the complaint, as he would not proceed farther with it. Defendant's counsel stated to the magistrate that if the complaint was withdrawn, it must be without the request or consent of the defendant. Burch then asked the magistrate to let him have the complaint and the warrant, and he took them. The counsel for the defendant objected to his receiving them, and insisted they should remain as part of the records of the court, and that the court should endorse the proceedings which had been had under the process. Burch delivered them up, and the court rendered a judgment of discontinuance by the request of the prosecutor, and filed it in his office."[210] *no record of the trial exists*

There may be those who will affect to believe the statement of the slave trader—those, in whose minds his allegations will weigh heavier than mine. I am a poor colored man—one of a down-trodden and degraded race, whose humble voice may not be heeded by the oppressor—but *knowing* the truth, and with a full sense of my accountability, I do solemnly declare before men, and before God, that any charge or assertion, that I conspired directly or indirectly with any person or persons to sell myself; that any other account of my visit to Washington, my capture and imprisonment in Williams' slave pen, than is contained in these pages, is utterly and absolutely false. I never played on the violin in Washington. I never was in the Steamboat Hotel, and never saw Thorn or Shekels, to my knowledge, in my life until last January. The story of the trio of slave-traders is a fabrication as absurd as it is base and unfounded. Were it true, I should not have turned aside on my way back to liberty for the purpose of prosecuting Burch. I should have *avoided* rather than sought him. I should have known that such a step would have resulted in rendering me infamous. Under the circumstances— longing as I did to behold my family, and elated with the prospect of returning home—it is an outrage upon probability to suppose I would have run the hazard, not only of exposure, but of a criminal prosecution and conviction, by voluntarily placing myself in the position I did, if the statements of Burch and his confederates contain a particle of truth. I took pains to seek him out, to confront him in a court of law, charging him with the crime of kidnapping; and the only motive that impelled me to this step, was a burning sense of the wrong he had inflicted upon me, and a desire to bring him to justice. He was acquitted, in the manner, and by such means as have been described. A human tribunal has permitted him to escape; but there is another and a higher tribunal, where false testimony will not prevail, and where I am willing, so far at least as these statements are concerned, to be judged at last.

We left Washington in the 20th of January, and proceeding by the way of Philadelphia, New-York, and Albany, reached Sandy Hill in the night of the 21st. My heart overflowed with happiness as I looked around upon old familiar scenes, and found myself in the midst of friends of other days. The following morning I started, in company with several acquaintances, for Glens Falls, the residence of Anne and our children.

As I entered their comfortable cottage, Margaret was the first that met me. She did not recognize me. When I left her, she was but seven years old, a little prattling girl, playing with her toys. Now she was grown to womanhood—was married, with a bright-eyed boy standing by her side. Not forgetful of his enslaved, unfortunate grand-father, she had named the child Solomon Northup Staunton. When told who I was, she was overcome with emotion, and unable to speak. Presently Elizabeth entered the room, and Anne came running from the hotel, having been informed of my arrival. They embraced me, and with tears flowing down their cheeks, hung upon my neck. But I draw a veil over a scene which can better be imagined than described.

When the violence of our emotions had subsided to a sacred joy—when the household gathered round the fire, that sent out its warm and crackling comfort through the room, we conversed of the thousand events that had occurred—the hopes and fears, the joys and sorrows, the trials and troubles we had each experienced during the long separation. Alonzo was absent in the western part of the State. The boy had written to his mother a short time previous, of the prospect of his obtaining sufficient money to purchase my freedom. From his earliest years, that had been the chief object of his thoughts and his ambition. They knew I was in bondage. The letter written on board the brig, and Clem Ray himself, had given them that information. But where I was, until the arrival of Bass' letter, was a matter of conjecture. Elizabeth and Margaret once returned from school—so Anne informed me—weeping bitterly. On inquiring the cause of the children's sorrow, it was found that, while studying geography, their attention had been attracted to the picture of slaves working in the cotton-field, and an overseer following them with his whip. It reminded them of the sufferings their father might be, and as it happened, actually *was,* enduring in the South. Numerous incidents, such as these, were related—incidents showing they still held me in constant remembrance, but not, perhaps, of sufficient interest to the reader, to be recounted.

My narrative is at an end. I have no comments to make upon the subject of Slavery. Those who read this book may form their own opinions of the "peculiar institution." What it may be in other States, I do not profess to know; what it is in the region of Red River, is truly and faithfully delineated in these pages. This is no fiction, no exaggeration. If I have failed in anything, it has been in presenting to the reader too prominently the bright side of the picture. I doubt not hundreds have been as unfortunate as myself; that hundreds of free citizens have been kidnapped and sold into slavery, and are at this moment wearing out their lives on plantations in Texas and Louisiana. But I forbear. Chastened and subdued in spirit by the sufferings I have borne, and thankful to that good Being through whose mercy I have been restored to happiness and liberty, I hope henceforward to lead an upright though lowly life, and rest at last in the church yard where my father sleeps.

Arrival home and the first meeting with his family

After Freedom: What Happened?

by Sue Eakin as edited by Sara Eakin Kuhn

After the closing of his narrative, neither Solomon Northup nor David Wilson, the ghost writer, left documents detailing the rest of Solomon's life. However, we are all curious; what happened to this man who had suffered slavery for twelve years far away from his family? What happened to the kidnappers? Were they allowed to retain their freedom, perhaps continuing to kidnap innocent free men and women and then sell them into slavery? What was life like for the Northup family before he was kidnapped? What was it like after this disruption of twelve years?

Though there is no authoritative record by one of the principals to answer these questions, many answers can be attained through the diligent work of examining public records and newspapers of the period. Indeed, David Fiske has done this work and published in 2012 *Solomon Northup: His Life Before and After Slavery,* if the reader wishes more detail after reading this chapter.

The book inflamed the passions of abolitionists and fueled the public debate over slavery, as it received extensive coverage in major Northern newspapers. Updates on Solomon and his story appeared frequently in the press. Also, Solomon Northup and his family left records in the court system. Here are information and conclusions based upon those sources. *jump to p. 715*

Life Before the Kidnapping

First, who was Solomon Northup? What kind of man was he? He was apparently a very social person who knew how to perform the fiddle in front of groups and mingle with the people. The fact that he was in most ways an average black man in Saratoga Springs makes his story all the more significant.This kidnapping could have happened to any black man in the North, as it did to Robert and to Arthur, as recorded in *Twelve Years A Slave.*

As for his education, like other upstate New Yorkers, white or black, this new country had not had the time yet to think much about it, other than the practical sort needed to create hands to help build primitive dwellings and to work farms. Education, for the most part, could wait; children were needed for tasks such as helping with the clearing of land and establishing homes on the frontier. Mintus Northup, Solomon's father, probably sent his sons to Sabbath schools, often not lasting very long, but it was the best opportunity that existed for black children.[211]

Solomon married Anne Hampton in 1828, and there were three children.[212] At home Anne was dependable and never wanted for a job, and, as for the children, when their mother had to live away from Saratoga Springs, they simply moved in with her sister, who cared for them. Solomon hunted for jobs of one kind or another, but Anne was the stable financial supporter. Probably some of the other free men of color, of whom there were twenty-eight in Saratoga Springs, had similar arrangements, and took jobs waiting tables or cooking, as Myra B. Young Armstead writes most colored men did.[213] Intelligent, curious, and creative, Solomon might not have wanted a position as a waiter or cook, especially as it meant being tied down to long hours that probably ran seven days a week during the tourist season. There would have been little time for his explorations and his music.

Solomon went from job to job. Indications of the kinds of work Solomon performed as well as a clue as to what might have caused him to go with two strangers to the South without his freeman papers in his possession at all times appear in court documents. In June of 1838, Solomon had a contract to deliver lumber by raft to Washington Allen in Waterford. Allen and Northup quarreled about the quality of Northup's work, with Allen firing Northup. The reason for Allen's complaint seems to be that Northup had been drinking to the point that he was not capable, and Allen hired someone else to complete the job. When Allen wouldn't pay Northup what was owed under the contract, Northup filed suit. The testimony of witnesses states that Northup had indeed been drinking; Prindle, the man who would later warn Solomon against leaving Saratoga Springs with the "circus promoters," stated that Northup was drinking a lot on the job, but that he could still perform his duties. He went on to indicate that Northup often drank, though not usually to excess. The jury in the suit and a subsequent appeal both ruled in Northup's favor.[214]

Perhaps this occasion reflects the point that Solomon makes in Chapter One of his narrative, when he refers to Saratoga Springs in this way:

> The society and associations at that world-renowned watering place, were not calculated to preserve the simple habits of industry and economy to which I had been accustomed, but, on the contrary, to substitute others in their stead, tending to shiftlessness and extravagance. (*Twelve Years a Slave*, 26)

Such habits would also perhaps explain the fact that he is listed in the Index of Convictions for Saratoga County as having been convicted of three incidences of assault.[215] The incidences of his drinking and misbehavior may at least partially illustrate the characteristics that led him to accompany Merrill and Russell to Washington.

Getting Home

Shortly after Solomon Northup and Henry Northup arrived in Washington, D.C., a reporter for the *New York Times* had the first interview with Solomon and generated considerable public interest in the case, especially throughout New York. *The Saratogian* and other area newspapers copied the article and stimulated still more public interest in the story of the daring rescue of a free man of color, a New York citizen, by a prominent New York politician, Henry B. Northup.

The front page article in the *New York Times* on January 20, 1853, gave much information about this powerful human story. The information that it published was from Washington, D.C., and the newspaper stated that the article was "a more complete and authentic record" than had previously been printed. It summarized Solomon's life, stating that he was a free colored citizen, born in Essex County of the United States about 1808, and that he had lived and married in Washington County. He was living with his wife and children in Saratoga Springs in the winter of 1841. With the reference to the material either summarized or quoted from this article appearing at the end of of this section, here is what the article stated about the kidnapping itself:

January 20, 1853:
THE KIDNAPPING CASE.
Narrative of the Seizure and Recovery of
Solomon Northup.

Interesting Disclosures.

. . . and while there was employed by two gentlemen to drive a team South, at the rate of a dollar a day. In fulfillment of his employment he proceeded to New-York, and having taken out free papers, to show that he was a citizen, he went on to Washington City, . . . and put up at GADSBY'S Hotel. Soon after he arrived, he felt unwell and went to bed. While suffering with severe pain some persons came in, and, seeing the condition he was in, proposed to give him some medicine and did so. That is the last thing of which he had any recollection until he found himself chained to the floor of WILLIAMS' slave pen in this City, and handcuffed. In the course of a few hours, JAMES H. BURCH, a slave-dealer, came in and the colored man asked him to take the irons off from him, and wanted to know why they were put on. BURCH told him it was none of his business. The colored man said he was free and told where he was born. Burch called in a man by the name of EBENEZER RODBURY [sic], and they two stripped the man and laid him across a bench, RODBURY holding him down by the wrists. BURCH whipped him with a paddle until he broke that, and then with a cat-o'-nine tails, giving him a hundred lashes, and he swore he would kill him if he ever stated to any one that he was a free man. From that time forward the man says that he did not communicate the fact from fear, either that he was a free man, or what his name was, until the last summer . . .

The article continues with a description of Solomon's being delivered to Williams' slave pen in Washington and being kept there for ten days, then boarding the brig *Orleans* for New Orleans. Solomon was hospitalized with small pox, recovered adequately, and was sold to Mr. Ford. The article tells of the letter that finally reached Henry Northup, the legal steps that were necessary to deliver Northup, and Henry and Solomon Northup's return to New Orleans, where the two men traced the titles of Solomon through the ownership of his masters. In short, the article gives an abbreviated summary of some of the portions of *Twelve Years a Slave* regarding the kidnapping, servitude, and rescue of Solomon Northup.

The Identification and Arrest of Burch[216]

Solomon Northup and Henry B. Northup, as stated in the *New York Times,* were in Washington, D.C., where the slave trader Burch lived. They located the man who was keeper of the slave pen at the time (1841) when Solomon Northup was placed there by Burch; he verified these facts. The two men proceeded to file a complaint against Burch for kidnapping and selling Northup into slavery with the Washington Police. Burch was arrested and held until a fellow slave trader made his bail of $3,000.

The newspaper includes this interesting comment before continuing to describe the legal machinations to bring Burch to trial:

> It is but justice to say that the authorities of Avoyelles, and indeed at New-Orleans, rendered all the assistance in their power to secure the establishment of the freedom of this unfortunate man, who had been snatched so villainously from the land of freedom, and compelled to undergo sufferings almost inconceivable in this land of heathenism, where slavery exists with features more revolting than those described in "Uncle Tom's Cabin."

On the day after Burch was arrested, both Burch and Northup appeared, each with witnesses and counsel, Henry Northup being Solomon's attorney. Burch was accompanied by two slave traders. Henry Northup tried to have Solomon Northup approved as a witness for the prosecution, but his testimony was declared inadmissible because of his status as a colored man, handicapping the plaintiffs. Though Solomon was not allowed to testify, others were:

> Mr. Shekels [a slave trader who paid Burch's bail and was serving as a witness for the defense] ... testified that some ten or twelve years ago he was keeping public house in this city; that BURCH boarded at the house and carried on the business of buying and selling slaves; that in that year, two white men came into his barroom and stated that they had a slave for sale ... The white men stated that they were from Georgia; had brought the negro with them from that State; that the negro expressed a willingness to be sold in order to return to Georgia; SHEKELS, however, was unable to state the names of either of the white men, or the name of the colored man; was unacquainted with either of them previous to that time, and had never seen either since that transaction; that he saw them execute a bill of sale to BURCH, saw BURCH pay him $625 and take the bill of sale ...

A century and a half later, these details aid in discovering exactly what happened. The inability of Solomon Northup to testify made it impossible to punish Burch, since there was no one who would identify Burch as one of the men buying the slave. Burch was not tried.

Arriving in New York

Henry Northup, returning home to New York after his long journey to rescue Solomon Northup, gave little thought to taking a rest. Instead, the dedicated New York Whig attorney felt his job had just begun. The kidnappers had to be apprehended and prosecuted for the kidnapping of Solomon Northup. At the same time, Solomon Northup began speaking at abolitionist rallies, and donations for his use were sometimes taken.

Solomon and Anne are mentioned as being together in the Census of the State of New York for 1855. Anne Northup, 48, is listed as living in Washington County for eight years with her husband

Solomon from Essex County, who had lived in the home for two years. Solomon Northup was listed as a land owner and carpenter, which trade would have allowed him the freedom to go to different places. However, it would not be a stable income.

Some indication of Solomon's financial condition after he returned to Saratoga Springs from slavery may be seen by several mentions of him in Warren County records.[217] On May 16, 1853, a document indicating the purchase of a lot of land in the Town of Queensbury began with "an indenture" [deed] secured with a payment of $140 of a total of $275 [Grantee Index, Warren County, State of New York, U297, sale between Abraham and Mary Ann Tice and Solomon Northup, May 16, 1853]. In Warren County, there was the case of John T.B. Traphagan and Charles R. Bennett against Solomon Northup. On June 10, 1854, judgment was rendered against the defendant for $43.84, plus costs of $1.03, the debt "remaining unsatisfied," to amount of $44.87 plus 25 cents for transcripts [See *John T.B. Traphagan and Charles R. Bennett vs. Solomon Northup*]. In September 1854, the Supreme Court of Warren County issued a judgment in the case of William Arlin against Solomon Northup in which a judgment was granted the plaintiff on October 23, 1854, for $150.64 plus court costs for an unpaid debt of $102.64 to be paid by January 8, 1855. In 1854, on October 9, Benjamin Carlle, Jr. received a judgment against Solomon Northup for a debt of $102.92, plus court costs of $53.80, for a total of $156.75. It's clear that soon after Solomon returned to New York, financial problems began and apparently never ended.

Soon after their return to New York, the attorney began traveling with Solomon around the state looking for a publisher for a book to tell Solomon Northup's story. An agreement was reached with Derby and Miller Publishers, who were to pay $3,000 to Solomon Northup for the copyright of his story.[218] There is no confirmation that the copyright payment of $3,000 was ever made. Also, the people of Arkansas planned to send him $5,000, according to *The Salem Press*, but, if that money was ever sent, there has been no evidence found that the money reached him.[219]

David Wilson, the writer, lived within five miles of Henry Northup's home.[220] Likely, Henry Northup had already talked over the story with him and piqued his interest for the book to be published as quickly as possible. As for the information needed for writing, Wilson had Solomon Northup and the attorney Henry Northup available for interviews as often as he needed them. He also had the benefit of the *New York Times* article published shortly after the Northups arrived in Washington, D.C. from Louisiana. Henry Northup himself played a major supporting role, furnishing considerable firsthand information to the ghost writer. With only three to four months in which to write the book and have it published, David Wilson needed all of the help he could get.[221]

The fact that the book was being written was discussed in papers of the time, including this example from an article in Warren County, with no date or additional information provided: "Another Uncle Tom. We learn that a legal gentleman in this country is engaged in writing the life of Sol. Northup, the kidnapped slave rescued through the agency of Mr. Northup. We suppose the work will be entitled, 'Uncle Sol.'"

The proliferation of articles in the New York papers during these years that dealt with the Northup case attest to the interest New York citizens had in the unfolding events. Although the newspapers created a groundswell of public information about the kidnapping, Henry Northup was relying on the book to give more detail about the kidnappers in order to reach people who could identify the criminals so they could be brought to justice. For that reason, he determined that the book should be published as soon as possible. Under such pressure, the ghost writer, with Henry Northup helping in every way he could, produced the book in three and a half months—an astounding feat! Though sales of the book did not equal the extraordinary level of *Uncle Tom's Cabin*, the narrative was highly publicized and was widely read before the beginning of the Civil War. After its publication around the middle of July, 1853, more interest in finding the kidnappers erupted than even Henry Northup could have expected.

The Arrest of Merrill and Russell

Shortly after the book was published, newspapers ran accounts of the continuing efforts to bring the kidnappers to trial. Here are accounts of the arrests of Merrill and Russell, as reported in an article titled "The Arrest of Solomon Northup's Alleged Kidnappers" by a correspondent of the *Washington County Post* on July 14, 1853:

... Merrill was arrested this morning at his mother's at Wood Hollow, and brought here [Gloversville] for examination. Henry B. Northup has spent a great deal of time and money in ferreting out the scoundrel, and they have no doubt got the man. Solomon Northup identifies him without a doubt. Merrill has long been regarded as a desperate fellow. They found him asleep, with a heavy bowie knife and brace of pistols on the floor by his side. The arrest has caused a very general excitement.

... An officer from Saratoga County, accompanied by Officer Brazier, arrested this morning a canal boat captain named J. L. Russell, of the boat J.F. Crain, of the Rochester City line, charged with being Merrill's associate in the kidnapping. He was hand-cuffed, and taken to Ballston. On his way to the cars, he admitted that he was in Washington at the Inauguration in 1841.

Other newspapers reported the arrests as well, with at least one stating that the men were identified through the descriptions and incidents recorded in Northup's book ("Trial of the Suspected Kidnappers...," *New York Times*, July 12, 1854). A year later, according to the *Saratoga Whig* as reported first in *Albany Evening Journal* in "The Northrop [sic] Kidnapping Case," on July 13, 1854, Merrill and Russell were arraigned, based on this testimony:

... Solomon Northup sworn, says he was 47 the 10th of this month; resided at Saratoga Springs in the month of March, 1841, had a family at that place consisting of wife and three children. Knows the prisoner now in court; first saw him at Saratoga Springs in 1841, latter part of March. There was another man with him, an associate, who is now sitting beside him. One now known as Merrill, called his name Merrill Brown, and the other called his Abraham Hamilton. He first saw them at Mr. Moon's Tavern at Saratoga Springs; they did not appear to have any particular business; they wished to hire witness to go to New York with them to drive their carriage and play the fiddle in a circus company to which they said they belonged; they offered him one dollar per day and expenses from the time he left until he returned. They had a carriage and span of horses there at the time; he drove their horses attached to the carriage to Albany by Cohoes, and then to New York City. After his arrival in New York he wished to leave, but prisoners wanted him to stay and go to Washington with them; he finally concluded to go with them, and accordingly went to the Custom House and obtained free papers, as he was afraid to go to Washington without them; prisoners went with him to what they called the Custom House, and got what witness supposed to be free papers . . .

Merrill, Russell, and Solomon proceeded to Baltimore through New Jersey, where they saw Thaddeus St. John. They went to Gadsby's Hotel in Washington on the evening before General Harrison's funeral. Solomon, in his testimony, said that he had spent the day with Merrill and Russell, smoking and drinking. They reminded him frequently to stay with them, but he became ill during the afternoon, progressing until he was "insensible" by evening. Then he awakened handcuffed and fettered to a ring in the floor of Williams Slave Pen, in Washington, D.C. The article originally from the *Saratoga Whig* continues:

The first white persons that came in were James Birch and Ebenezer Radburn; one asked him how he felt; [Solomon] told him he was sick, didn't know what was matter, and asked reason why he was fettered and handcuffed there; Birch said he had bought witness; told Birch he was a free man, and Birch said that he was a liar, and that he had run away from Georgia; told him never been in Georgia and could get evidence from New York that he was born free and had always been free man; Birch said he would not hear any of his lies, and if he denied having run away from Georgia would flog him . . . Birch told Radburn to get paddle and cat-o-nine-tails. Radburn held him across a bench with his feet on his handcuffs and then Birch broke the paddle on him, after which he took the cat-o-nine-tails and whipped him with that until Radburn told him to stop, as he would be too sore to go to New Orleans. . . . He was kept in slavery for nearly twelve years up to January 3, 1853. He was on that day set at liberty and returned to his family. He has never seen either of the prisoners from the time he was taken sick in Washington until last week. He first saw Merrill in Fulton co., two miles from Fonda's Bush; first saw him in bed at the house of prisoner's father . . . [See *Albany Evening Journal*].

During his cross examination, Solomon Northup stated that he had no memories of being in Albany with the prisoners, nor of places where they stayed while traveling to New York. He wasn't sure which of the prisoners asked him to continue with them past New York, but he thought it was Russell. Both men, however, offered him one dollar a day and his expenses if he would continue to Washington. One or the other of the two men poured liquor for him to drink during that last day when he became sick. He met Thaddeus St. John in Washington and believes that he joined the drinking party.

The next witness to testify was Norman Prindle, who lived in Saratoga Springs in March of 1841, where he was a stage driver. He knew Solomon Northup from 1826 or 1827; Solomon also had lived in Saratoga Springs in 1841. According to the article, Prindle identified Merrill, whom he saw in Saratoga Springs in a carriage accompanied by a man with "long hair and large whiskers." Prindle testified that he saw Solomon Northup leave in the carriage with these two men. Prindle had earlier spoken with Solomon Northup and urged him not to leave with the men to the South. Prindle indicated that others spoke to Solomon Northup with the same advice.

Merrill and Russell were held in jail without bond at the time, though soon a civil suit was filed, and bail was set at $5000 each [See *Albany Evening Journal*].

A letter to the editor of the *Washington County People's Journal* by I.M. Van Namee[222] provides vivid insights into the lives of Alexander Merrill and Joseph Russell, excerpts of which appear next. Mr. Van Namee attended the legal proceedings summarized above. We start with his description of the defendants:

...Merrill was first brought in. He is an ugly looking fellow, (one of Mrs. Stowe's 'bullet headed' gemman) and in spite of years of practice in dissimulation, could not conceal that in his position he felt "rather uneasy." Immediately after on the motion of Northup, Russel [*sic*] was also put on trial. He too, appeared to be a hardened specimen of humanity. Solomon Northup was first sworn: when he testified to all the facts related in his published life, that could have any bearing on the case at issue . . .

After Solomon Northup had testified and been cross-examined, Thaddeus St. John was called. He told of going to General Harrison's funeral by way of Baltimore, where Merrill and Russell appeared:

...Expressed some surprise on seeing the former [Russell], and asked what business called him there; whereupon M. told him in R.'s not to call them by their real names. On again inquiring their business, Merrill with a significant gesture, pointed to the negro who was with them. That negro was Solomon Northup. He was not surprised to find M. there, who was a wandering fellow and had often been South. Parted with them at Baltimore, and next saw them at Gadsby's Hotel in Washington . . . Had never seen the Negro until at Baltimore [unclear] and remarked that they had changed their appearance for some other reason than mere fancy. They made no reply, but laughed. . . . R. however, at length found me and took seat by my side. M. come and sat in the seat behind me . . . Thereupon he took off his mantle, drew out his watch, and thrust his hand into his pocket and drew forth a handful of gold . . . As the next exhibition he opened his watch, drew out a $1000 bank bill, and scratched up two more from the case of it. . . . I then took a piece of paper and with my pencil put down $3000 for the bills; what I value of the watch, the gold, the negro at $500, when M. quickly told me to add $150 to that, making $650 for the negro . . .

Norman Prindle was then sworn. He testified to the facts sworn to by Solomon in regard to the manner in which he left Saratoga Springs. Says he told him that those men would not let him come back in; to which Solomon replied he would risk their selling or leaving him.

> . . . Reports from Fulton Co. place the character of these men in no very favorable light. It is said that M. some years ago endeavored to entice a negro boy in his own neighborhood, by persuading him to let him sell him, then run away and be again sold, each time dividing the booty. He is also said to have declared at one time that he had followed kidnapping for years; and that he felt as safe in that as in other business. These and many others come from reliable sources; but perhaps the cap-leaf of all is the manner in which Russell concealed a horse thief some years ago. He had him in his own house, and when the officers were about to search it, he concealed him in a bed between his two daughters . . .

Very respectfully yours,
I.M. Van Namee [223]

Court Proceedings

After a number of delays, the trial was scheduled in Oyer and Terminer Court for February 13, as reported in *The Temperance Helper*, which listed the four charges against Merrill and Russell. Their attorneys objected to the first three:

> The first count charged the prisoners with feloniously inveigling and kidnapping one Solomon Northup, with the intent unlawfully without his consent and against his will, to cause him to be sold as a slave; and that they did feloniously and against his will sell him as a slave; . . .
>
> The second count charged the prisoners with feloniously inveigling said Northup to accompany them to the District of Columbia with intent feloniously to cause him to be sold as a slave.

The third count charged the prisoners with feloniously inveigling said Northup from this State to the District of Columbia; and that there they unlawfully and feloniously sold and transferred his services or labor without his consent.

The fourth charged them with feloniously inveigling said Northup from this State to the District of Columbia, with intent there to cause him to be sold as a slave; and that they there did sell him as a slave. [*Temperance Helper*, Feb. 15, 1855; Feb. 22, 1855]

Merrill and Russell's lawyers requested dismissal of all but the last of the charges because the charges did not state that the prisoners kidnapped Solomon with the intent to keep him confined within the State of New York secretly, or to transfer him against his will out of New York, or to cause him to be sold or forced into service against his will. In other words, since the charges did not specify New York as the area where these activities began, but focused on Washington, D.C., where Solomon was actually sold, the court did not have jurisdiction.

After listening to the arguments, the Court required that the objection be formally presented as a demurrer, so that it could be reviewed by the Court at General Term. This action deferred the trial until the General Term could decide whether New York had jurisdiction over this case [See *Temperance Helper*, Feb. 15, 1855; Feb. 22, 1855].

The required depositions from Birch and Radford were taken. Birch gave the same fabricated story of the purchase of Solomon Northup, answering thus in cross interrogatories:

I have bought and sold Slaves for several years but not since the year 1842. 2d. Had a partner in the year 1841 named Theophilus Freeman who resided in New Orleans, La. The partnership commenced in 1841 and ended in 1842. Freeman's place of business and residence, as before stated, was New Orleans, La. 3d. Have bought slaves in the City of Washington and sent them all to the South for sale. Number not recollected. Not aware that I have sold any in this place as slaves but

have Sold several to themselves to pay me when they
could and some to their friends for the same purpose.
The document is signed by Joseph C. Lewis. [See The
People vs. Alexander Merrill and Joseph Russell]

Merrill and Russell applied for release based on adequate bail set
to guarantee their attendance at the following term of the Oyer and
Terminer Court. Because the District Attorney had concerns about
whether the Statute of Limitations were applicable, Russell's bail was
nominal. Merrill's bail was $800 [See *Washington County People's
Journal*].

In order to understand the long, drawn out, legal actions
involving the kidnappers at this point, the reader should understand
that disputed legal cases could be appealed from the county court, in
this case, Oyer and Terminer of Saratoga County, to the New York
Supreme Court. If there was further disagreement with a decision, the
case could be appealed to the Court of Appeals for a final judgment.
The decision of the Oyer and Terminer Court to demur the case until
after the New York Supreme Court decided jurisdiction in the four
counts against Merrill and Russell was the first step in this process.

The *Ballston Democratic Whig Journal* reported on the results that
July 17, 1855, stating that the first count of the indictment, that of
Merrill and Russell tricking Solomon Northup into leaving Saratoga
County in order to sell him as a slave, was found good. However, the
other counts were dropped because the crimes listed were committed
in the District of Columbia, not in New York; therefore, New York
courts had no jurisdiction. The decision was appealed to the New
York Supreme Court, but it was confirmed. The District Attorney
decided at that point to appeal to the New York Court of Appeals
[See *Ballston Democratic Whig Journal*].

Throughout these years as the case wended its way through the
New York Court system, all of the press of New York actively
followed the court proceedings. The small contingent of African
American papers were, naturally, especially interested. Suspicious of
the proceedings, they still hoped for justice, as witnessed by these
two examples printed in 1855, at least one year before the trial was
scheduled:

THE NORTHRUP [*sic*] KIDNAPPERS.

What will be done with the kidnappers of SOLOMON NORTHRUP [*sic*]? This is a query we have often made, and one which has as often been propounded to us. The question could be very easily answered, and the case would have been settled long ago, had the aggrieved party been a white man. We hope the vile offenders, MERRILL and RUSSELL, will have ample justice meted out to them. We learn from the Saratogian, that the Supreme Court has sustained the demurrer to the indictment against them. The effect of this decision will be the striking out of these counts of the indictment in each of which the crime was charged to have been committed in the District of Columbia, and to leave only the count in which the inveigling of MR. NORTHRUP [*sic*] is charged to have been committed in the County of Saratoga, with intent to sell him as a slave, and that he was afterwards sold in pursuance of that intention.

The proceedings in this case have not been quite as 'summary' as they might have been or as they would have been if SOLOMON had kidnapped his kidnappers, or had he been a recaptured fugitive. This is a strange face land we live in, to say the least, abounding in kidnappers, and women whippers, and Fourth of Julys, and Stringfellows, and Atchisons with a considerable sprinkle of proslavery preachers to add a charm to the delightful and expressive picture... [See *Frederick Douglass Paper*, July 20, 1855].

And from another article of the black abolitionist press:

THE NORTHRUP [*sic*] CASE. It now looks marvelously as though the scoundrelly kidnappers of Solomon Northrup [*sic*], the free man of color who was inveigled from Washington County, N.Y., to Washington City, and there sold as a slave, would escape unwhipped of justice. Three counts of indictment against them have been swept away by the court, leaving only a single count in which they are charged with having inveigled their victim abroad for the purpose of selling him. The final decision was given on the 4th inst. The defendants are under five hundred dollars bond only, a less sum than would be required if they were under indictment for stealing a spavined horse [See *Frederick Douglass Paper*, August 24,1855].

When the case finally reached the New York Court of Appeals, it reversed the decisions of the lower courts because the indictment legally could not be split, with one count being acceptable while the other three were ruled not acceptable. Consequently, the case was returned to the county. These conclusions are explained in the New York Court of Appeals' "Report of Cases".[224]

After that ruling, *The Daily Saratogian* reported that the trial on the indictment of Russell and Merrill would likely be in September of 1856. However, in a column headed "Court Proceedings" in the *Ballston Journal* of May 26, 1857, the following terse statement appears: "The People agst Henry Merrill and Joseph Russell, under an indictment for kidnapping Solmon [*sic*] Northup. Case discharged." The case was never brought to trial.[225]

The Fate of Solomon Northup

The fate of Solomon Northup following the terse announcement by Oyer and Teminer Court that the case was cancelled has puzzled readers. Solomon had not appeared for the trial. Why? No one knew what had happened to him.

Despite all of the publicity in New York newspapers and the impact of Solomon's story, which resonated throughout the pre-war period, there was no outcry from the public as to the fate of Solomon Northup. A New York researcher, studying the accounts in the state's newspapers of the 1850s dealing with the Northup story, remarked that in a case that had fascinated New York for four years, from the rescue of Solomon by Henry Northup in 1853 to the trial scheduled for 1857, it would seem enough interest had been focused on the story to bring questions from abolitionists or humanitarians or the simply curious as to what was the final resolution to the case. Not a word of inquiry, much less a demand for investigation, has been found by this editor or other researchers trying to find what happened to Solomon Northup. Not only the editor but highly qualified New York researchers have searched for information on the subject to be included in this volume, but in vain. What follows are the bits and pieces of the story that remain to help us conjecture about what may have happened.

As to why Solomon disappeared, there are many conjectures. Some felt that Northup might have been killed by his kidnappers, or perhaps he was kidnapped a second time. Yet, in summer 1857, he was in Canada as a speaker, as is apparent from notices regarding disruptions of his speeches by angry mobs, so there is evidence he was alive after the case was dismissed. There is some evidence that Solomon was involved in the Underground Railroad, aiding escaped slaves in reaching Canada, and perhaps he felt it too dangerous to the people of the railroad and to himself to appear. Or perhaps the district attorney found the case too difficult to prosecute with Solomon Northup himself always away from the area earning speaking fees and others wondering if Solomon himself had been a party to the kidnapping (Fiske, 43-51).

There has always been some conjecture that Solomon might have been a willing accomplice to Russell and Merrill. In other words, Solomon might have planned, with the two men, to go with them and allow them to sell him into slavery, with the idea that they split the sales money with him after they arranged for him to be freed. This theory is reflected in a couple of newspaper columns of the time, including the following:

> *The Saratoga Press* [Republican] in reply to inquiries of the *Albany Evening Journal*, in regard to the *nolle prosequi* entered in the case of Merrill and Russell, the alleged kidnappers of Sol Northup, at the last Oyer and Terminer, says: "We would answer by saying that since the indictment was found, the District Attorney was placed in possession of facts that whilst proving their guilt in a measure, would prevent a conviction. To speak more plainly, it is more than suspected that Sol Northup was an accomplice in the sale, calculating to slip away and share the spoils, but that the purchaser was too

sharp for him, and instead of getting the cash, he got something else. [See *Glens Falls Free Press*, May 1, 1858]

This scenario is one that Merrill had attempted earlier in his kidnapping career, according to testimony of John S. Enos.[226] However, there is no evidence to prove that Solomon Northup's kidnapping was anything other than what he represented in *Twelve Years a Slave.*[227]

As to Solomon's whereabouts, there was never a confirmation of rumors that he had decided to travel on some mission of his own and had been kidnapped again. However, the most provocative thought on this theory came from lawyer E.R. Mann, who summarized the Northup case in the *The Bench and Bar of Saratoga County* in 1876:

> [The demurrer] narrowed the issue down to the kidnapping charge, but, before the indictment was brought to trial, Northrup [*sic*] again disappeared. What his fate was is unknown to the public, but the desperate kidnappers no doubt knew. A nolle pros. was entered in their case in May, 1857, by District Attorney John O. Mott.[228]

No grave of Solomon Northup has ever been found. Some in his family have said that the time of his death has been passed down as occurring in 1864, that he had gone to Mississippi and been killed. No evidence has been found substantiating this story, either of the trip or his death. There is some evidence that he visited a colleague in the Canadian Underground Railroad after the Emancipation on January 1, 1863, and in 1875 the New York State Census listed the marital status of his wife, Anne, as "Widowed" (Fiske, slideshow, *What happened to Solomon Northup?*).

John Henry Northup, born in Sandy Hill in 1822, a nephew of Henry Northup, was well acquainted with both Solomon and Henry Northup. He wrote his version of the story in 1909 in a letter to his cousin, Edith Carman Hay, who recounted it:

> John Henry Northup said not long after they came home, Henry B. "got a young lawyer to hear Sol's story. Soon by questions he got enough to write a book."

According to John Henry, *Solomon Northup: 12 Years in Slavery* [*Twelve Years a Slave*], written quickly and published in 1853, "created a sensation for it came out a short time after *Uncle Tom's Cabin* [*sic*] by Mrs. Stowe. The last I heard of him," said John Henry in 1909, Sol "was lecturing in Boston to help sell his book . . . All at once," said John Henry, "he disappeared . . . We believed that he was kidnapped and taken away or killed or both."[229]

The Solomon Northup story reeks of tragedy and injustice, not just in the South at the time, but across the nation. In our pride as citizens in a nation dedicated to freedom, equality, and justice, we must be reminded that these are ideals toward which we continually struggle. Throughout our history, they have not become a reality for all citizens, black, white, red, or yellow. Slavery has existed for millennia throughout the world, with all races enslaving not only other races, but also members of their own. In the United States prior to the Civil War, slavery was a national, not merely a Southern, institution. Slavery still exists in some nations, and even in the U.S. in the form of human trafficking. Residuals of racism exist among our diverse people across the United States. Facts of history must temper our pride and instill a determination to bring democracy nearer to the ideal of the Founding Fathers.

ORIGINAL APPENDICES

Original Appendix A

NEW YORK ACT.

An act more effectually to protect the free citizens of this State from being kidnapped, or reduced to Slavery.

[Passed May 14, 1840.]

The People of the State of New-York, represented in Senate and Assembly, do enact as follows:

1. Whenever the Governor of this State shall receive information satisfactory to him that any free citizen or any inhabitant of this State has been kidnapped or transported away out of this State, into any other State or Territory of the United States, for the purpose of being there held in slavery; or that such free citizen or inhabitant is wrongfully seized, imprisoned or held in slavery in any of the States or Territories of the United States, on the allegation or pretence that such a person is a slave or by color of any usuage [sic] or rule of law prevailing in such State or Territory, is deemed or taken to be a slave, or not entitled of right to the personal liberty belonging to a citizen; it shall be the duty of the said Governor to take such measures as he shall deem necessary to procure such person to be restored to his liberty, and returned to this State. The governor is hereby authorized to appoint and employ such agent or agents as he shall deem necessary to effect the restoration and return of such person; and shall furnish the said agent with such credentials and instructions as will be likely to accomplish the object of his appointment. The Governor may determine the compensation to be allowed to such agent for his services besides his necessary expenses.

2. Such agent shall proceed to collect the proper proof to establish the rights of such person to his freedom, and shall perform such journeys, take such measures, institute and procure to be prosecuted such legal proceedings, under the direction of the Governor, as shall

be necessary to procure such person to be restored to his liberty and returned to this State.

3. The accounts for all services and expenses in carrying this act into effect shall be audited by the Comptroller, and paid by the Treasurer on his warrant, out of any moneys in the Treasury of this State not otherwise appropriated. The Treasurer may advance, on the Warrant of the Comptroller, to such agent, such sum or sums as the Governor shall certify to be reasonable advances to enable him to accomplish the purposes of his appointment, for which advance such agent shall account, on the final audit of his warrant.

4. This act shall take effect immediately.

Original Appendix B

MEMORIAL OF ANNE.

To His Excellency, the Governor of the State of New York:

The memorial of Anne Northup, of the village of Glens Falls, in the county of Warren, State aforesaid, respectfully sets forth—

That your memorialist, whose maiden name was Anne Hampton, was forty-four years old on the 14th day of March last, and was married to Solomon Northup, then of Fort Edward, in the county of Washington and State aforesaid, on the 25th day of December, A. D. 1828, by Timothy Eddy, then a Justice of the Peace. That the said Solomon, after such marriage, lived and kept house with your memorialist in said town until 1830, when he removed with his said family to the town of Kingsbury in said county, and remained there about three years, and then removed to Saratoga Springs in the State aforesaid, and continued to reside in said Saratoga Springs and the adjoining town until about the year 1841, as near as the time can be recollected, when the said Solomon started to go to the city of Washington, in the District of Columbia, since which time your memorialist has never seen her said husband.

And your memorialist further states, that in the year 1841 she received information by a letter directed to Henry B. Northup, Esq., of Sandy Hill, Washington county, New-York, and post-marked at New-Orleans, that said Solomon had been kidnapped in Washington, put on a vessel, and was then in such vessel in New-Orleans, but could not tell how he came in that situation, nor what his destination was.

That your memorialist ever since the last mentioned period has been wholly unable to obtain any information of where the said Solomon was, until the month of September last, when another letter was received from the said Solomon, post-marked at Marksville, in the parish of Avoyelles, in the State of Louisiana, stating that he was held there as a slave, which statement your memorialist believes to be true.

That the said Solomon is about forty-five years of age, and never resided out of the State of New-York, in which State he was born, until the time he went to Washington city, as before stated. That the said Solomon Northup is a free citizen of the State of New-York, and is now wrongfully held in slavery, in or near Marksville, in the parish of Avoyelles, in the State of Louisiana, one of the United States of America, on the allegations or pretence that the said Solomon is a slave.

And your memorialist further states that Mintus Northup was the reputed father of said Solomon, and was a negro, and died at Ford Edward, on the 22nd day of November, 1829; that the mother of said Solomon was a mulatto, or three quarters white, and died in the county Oswego, New-York, some five or six years ago, as your memorialist was informed and believes, and never was a slave.

That your memorialist and her family are poor and wholly unable to pay or sustain any portion of the expenses of restoring the said Solomon to his freedom.

Your excellency is entreated to employ such agent or agents as shall be deemed necessary to effect the restoration and return of said Solomon Northup, in pursuance of an act of the Legislature of the State of New-York, passed May 14th, 1840, entitled "An act more effectually to protect the free citizens of this State from being kidnapped or reduced to slavery." And your memorialist will ever pray.

(Signed), ANNE NORTHUP.
Dated November 19, 1852.

STATE OF NEW-YORK:
Washington county, ss.

Anne Northup, of the village of Glens Falls, in the county of Warren, in said State, being duly sworn, doth depose and say that she signed the above memorial, and that the statements therein contained are true.

(Signed), ANNE NORTHUP.
Subscribed and sworn before me this
19th November, 1852.
CHARLES HUGHES, Justice Peace

We recommend that the Governor appoint Henry B. Northup, of the village of Sandy Hill, Washington county, New-York, as one of the agents to procure the restoration and return of Solomon Northup, named in the foregoing memorial of Anne Northup. .

Dated at Sandy Hill, Washington Co., N.Y., November 20, 1852.

(Signed)
PETER HOLBROOK, DANIEL SWEET
B. F. HOAG, ALMON CLARK,
CHARLES HUGHES, BENJAMIN FERRIS,
E.D.BAKER, JOSIAH H. BROWN
ORVILLE CLARK.

STATE OF NEW-YORK:
Washington County, ss:

Josiah Hand, of the village of Sandy Hill, in said county, being duly sworn, says, he is fifty-seven years old, and was born in said village, and has always resided there; that he has known Mintus Northup and his son Solomon, named in the annexed memorial of Anne Northup, since previous to the year 1816; that Mintus Northup then, and until the time of his death, cultivated a farm in the towns of Kingsbury and Fort Edward, from the time deponent first knew him until he died; that said Mintus and his wife, the mother of said Solomon Northup, were reported to be free citizens of New-York, and deponent believes they were so free; that said Solomon Northup was born in said county of Washington, as deponent believes , and was married Dec. 25th, 1828, in Fort Edward aforesaid, and his said wife and three children—two daughters and one son—are now living in Glens Falls, Warren county, New-York, and that the said Solomon Northup always resided in said county of Washington, and its immediate vicinity, until about 1841, since which time deponent has not seen him, but deponent has been credibly informed, and as he verily believes truly, the said Solomon is now wrongfully held as a slave in the State of Louisiana. And deponent further says that Anne Northup, named in the said memorial, is entitled to credit, and deponent believes the statements contained in her said memorial are true.

(Signed), JOSIAH HAND
Subscribed and sworn before me this
19th day of November, 1852,
Charles Hughes, Justice Peace

STATE OF NEW-YORK:
Washington county, ss:

Timothy Eddy, of Fort Edward, in said county, being duly sworn, says he is now over—years old, and has been a resident of said town more than —years last past, and that he was well acquainted with Solomon Northup, named in the annexed memorial of Anne Northup, and with his father, Mintus Northup, who was a negro, —the wife of said Mintus was a mulatto woman; that said Mintus Northup and his said wife and family, two sons, Joseph and Solomon, resided in said town of Fort Edward for several years before the year 1828, and said Mintus died in said town A.D. 1829, as deponent believes. And deponent further says that he was a Justice of the Peace in said town in the year 1828, and as such Justice of the Peace, he, on the 25th day of Dec'r, 1828, joined the said Solomon Northup in marriage with Anne Hampton, who is the same person who has subscribed the annexed memorial. And deponent expressly says, that said Solomon was a free citizen of the State of New-York, and always lived in said State, until about the year A. D. 1840, since which time deponent has not seen him, but has recently been informed, and as deponent believes truly, that said Solomon Northup is wrongfully held in slavery in or near Marksville, in the parish of Avoyelles, in the State of Louisiana. And deponent further says, that said Mintus Northup was nearly sixty years old at the time of his death, and was, for more than thirty years next prior to his death, a free citizen of the State of New-York.

And this deponent further says, that Anne Northup, the wife of said Solomon Northup, is of good character and reputation, and her statements, as contained in the memorial hereto annexed, are entitled to full credit.

(Signed), TIMOTHY EDDY.
Subscribed and sworn before me this
19th day of November, 1852,
TIM'Y STOUGHTON, Justice

STATE OF NEW-YORK:
Washington County, ss:

Henry B. Northup, of the village of Sandy Hill, in said county, being duly sworn, says, that he is forty-seven years old, and has always lived in said county; that he knew Mintus Northup, named in the annexed memorial, from deponent's earliest recollection until the time of his death, which occurred at Fort Edward, in said county, in 1829; that deponent knew the children of said Mintus, viz, Solomon and Joseph; that they were both born in the county of Washington aforesaid, as deponent believes; that deponent was well acquainted with said Solomon, who is the same person named in the annexed memorial of Anne Northup, from his childhood; and that said Solomon always resided in said county of Washington and the adjoining counties until about the year 1841; that said Solomon could read and write; that said Solomon and his mother and father were free citizens of the State of New-York; that sometime about the year 1841 this deponent received a letter from said Solomon, post-marked New-Orleans, stating that while on business at Washington city, he had been kidnapped, and his free papers taken from him, and he was then on board a vessel, in irons, and was claimed as a slave, and that he did not know his destination, which the deponent believes to be true, and he urged this deponent to assist in procuring his restoration to freedom; that deponent has lost or mislaid said letter, and cannot find it; that deponent has since endeavored to find where said Solomon was, but could get no farther trace of him until Sept. last, when this deponent ascertained by a letter purporting to have been written by the direction of said Solomon, that said Solomon was held and claimed as a slave in or near Marksville, in the parish of Avoyelles, Louisiana, and that this deponent verily believes that such information is true, and that said Solomon is now wrongfully held in slavery at Marksville aforesaid.

(Signed), HENRY B. NORTHUP.
Subscribed and sworn to before me
This 20th day of November, 1852,
CHARLES HUGHES, J. P.

STATE OF NEW-YORK:
Washington County, ss

Nicholas C. Northup, of the village of Sandy Hill, in said county, being duly sworn, doth depose and say, that he is now fifty-eight years of age, and has known Solomon Northup, mentioned in the annexed memorial of Ann Northup, ever since he was born. And this deponent saith that said Solomon is now about forty-five years old, and was born in the county of Washington aforesaid, or in the county of Essex, in said State, and always resided in the State of New-York until about the year 1841, since which time deponent has not seen him or known where he was, until a few weeks since, deponent was informed, and believes truly, that said Solomon was held in slavery in the State of Louisiana. Deponent further says, that said Solomon was married in the town of Fort Edward, in said county, about twenty-four years ago, and that his wife and two daughters and one son now reside in the village of Glens Falls, county of Warren, in said State of New-York, and was born free, and from his earliest infancy lived and resided in the counties of Washington, Essex, Warren and Saratoga, in the State of New-York, and that his said wife and children have never resided out of said counties since the time said Solomon was married; that deponent knew the father of said Solomon Northup; that said father was a negro, named Mintus Northup, and died in the town of Fort Edward, in the county of Washington, State of New-York, on the 22nd day of November, A.D. 1829, and was buried in the grave-yard in Sandy Hill aforesaid; that for more than thirty years before his death he lived in the counties of Essex, Washington and Rensselaer and State of New-York, and left a wife and two sons, Joseph and the said Solomon, him surviving; that the mother of said Solomon was a mulatto woman, and is now dead, and died, as deponent believes, in Oswego county, New-York, within five or six years past. And this deponent further states, that the mother of the said Solomon Northup was not a slave at the time of the birth of said

Solomon Northup, and has not been a slave at any time within the last fifty years.

(Signed), N.C. NORTHUP.
Subscribed and sworn before me this 19th day
of November, 1852.
CHARLES HUGHES, Justice Peace.

STATE OF NEW-YORK:
Washington County, ss.

Orville Clark, of the village of Sandy Hill, in the county of Washington, State of New-York, being duly sworn, doth depose and say—that he, this deponent, is over fifty years of age; that in the years 1810 and 1811, or most of the time of those years, this deponent resided at Sandy Hill, aforesaid, and at Glens Falls; that this deponent then knew Mintus Northup, a black or colored man; he was then a free man, as this deponent believes and always understood; that the wife of said Mintus Northup, and mother of Solomon, was a free woman; that from the year 1818 until the time of the death of said Mintus Northup, about the year 1829, this deponent was very well acquainted with the said Mintus Northup; that he was a respectable man in the community in which he resided, and was a free man, so taken and esteemed by all his acquaintances; that this deponent has also been and was acquainted with his son Solomon Northup, from the said year 1818 until he left this part of the country, about the year 1840 or 1841; that he married Anne Hampton, daughter of William Hampton, a near neighbor of this deponent; that the said Anne, wife of said Solomon, is now living and resides in this vicinity; that the said Mintus Northup and William Hampton were both reputed and esteemed in this community as respectable men. And this deponent saith that the said Mintus Northup and his family, and the said William Hampton and his family, from the earliest recollection and acquaintance of this deponent with him (as far back as 1810,) were always reputed, esteemed, and taken to be, and this deponent believes, truly so, free citizens of the State of New-York. This deponent knows the said William Hampton, under the laws of this State, was entitled to vote at our elections, and he believes the said Mintus Northup also was entitled as a free citizen with the property qualification. And this deponent further saith, that the said Solomon Northup, son of said Mintus, and husband of said Anne Hampton, when he left his State, was at the time thereof a free citizen of the State of New-York. And this deponent further saith, that said Anne Hampton, wife of Solomon Northup, is a respectable woman, of good character, and I would believe her statements, and do believe the facts set forth in her memorial to his excellency, the Governor, in relation to her said husband, are true.

(Signed), ORVILLE CLARK.
Sworn before me, November 19th, 1852.
U.G. PARIS, Justice of the Peace.

STATE OF NEW-YORK:
Washington County, ss.

Benjamin Ferris, of the village of Sandy Hill, in said county, being duly sworn, doth depose and say —that he is now fifty-seven years old, and has resided in said village forty-five years; that he was well acquainted with Mintus Northup, named in the annexed memorial of Anne Northup, from the year 1816 to the time of his death, which occurred at Fort Edward, in the fall of 1829; that he knew the children of the said Mintus, namely Joseph Northup and Solomon Northup, and that the said Solomon is the same person named in said memorial; that said Mintus resided in the said county of Washington to the time of his death, and was, during all that time, a free citizen of the said State of New-York, as deponent verily believes; that said memorialist, Anne Northup, is a woman of good character, and the statement contained in her memorial is entitled to credit.

(Signed), BENJAMIN FERRIS.
Sworn before me,
November 19th, 1852.
U. G. PARIS, Justice of the Peace.

STATE OF NEW-YORK:
Executive Chamber, Albany, Nov. 30, 1852.

I hereby certify that the foregoing is a correct copy of certain proofs filed in the Executive Department, upon which I have appointed Henry B. Northup as Agent of this State, to take proper proceedings in behalf of Solomon Northup, therein mentioned.

(Signed), WASHINGTON HUNT.

By the Governor.

J. F. R., Private Secretary.

STATE OF NEW-YORK:

Executive Department.

WASHINGTON HUNT, *Governor of the State of New-York, to whom it may concern, greeting:*

Whereas, I have received information on oath, which is satisfactory to me, that Solomon Northup, who is a free citizen of this State, is wrongfully held in slavery, in the State of Louisiana:

And whereas, it is made my duty, by the laws of this State, to take such measures as I shall deem necessary to procure any citizen so wrongfully held in slavery, to be restored to his liberty and returned to this State:

Be it known, that in pursuance of chapter 375 of the laws of this State, passed in 1840, I have constituted, appointed and employed Henry B. Northup, Esquire, of the county of Washington, in this State, an Agent, with full power to effect this restoration of said Solomon Northup, and the said Agent is hereby authorized and empowered to institute such proper and legal proceedings, to procure such evidence, retain such counsel, and finally to take such measures as will be most likely to accomplish the object of his said appointment.

He is also instructed to proceed to the State of Louisiana with all convenient dispatch, to execute the agency hereby created.

In witness whereof, I have hereunto subscribed my name, and affixed the privy seal of the State, at Albany, this 23rd day of November, in the year of our Lord 1852.

(Signed), WASHINGTON HUNT.

James F. Ruggles, Private Secretary.

Original Appendix C

RELEASE DOCUMENT.

STATE OF LOUISIANA:
Parish of Avoyelles.

Before me, Aristide Barbin, Recorder of the parish of Avoyelles, personally came and appeared Henry B. Northup, of the county of Washington, State of New-York, who hath declared that by virtue of a commission to him as agent of the State of New-York, given and granted by his excellency, Washington Hunt, Governor of the said State of New-York, bearing date the 23d day of November, 1852, authorizing and empowering him, the said Northup, to pursue and recover from slavery a free man of color, called Solomon Northup, who is a free citizen of the State of New-York, and who was kidnapped and sold into slavery, in the State of Louisiana, and now in the possession of Edwin Epps, of the State of Louisiana, of the Parish of Avoyelles; he, the said agent, hereto signing, acknowledges that the said Edwin has this day given and surrendered to him as such agent, the said Solomon Northup, free man of color, as aforesaid, in order that he be restored to his freedom, and carried back to the said State of New-York, pursuant to said commission, the said Edwin Epps being satisfied from the proofs produced by said agent, that the said Solomon Northup is entitled to his freedom. The parties consenting that a certified copy of said power of attorney be annexed to this act.

Done and signed at Marksville, parish of Avoyelles, this fourth day of January, one thousand eight hundred and fifty-three, in the presence of the undersigned, legal and competent witnesses, who have also hereto signed.

(Signed), HENRY B. NORTHUP.
EDWIN EPPS.
ADE. BARBIN, Recorder.
Witnesses:
H. TAYLOR,
JOHN P. WADDILL.

STATE OF LOUISIANA:
Parish of Avoyelles.

I do hereby certify the foregoing to be a true and correct copy of the original on file and of record in my office.

Given under my hand and seal of office as Recorder [L. S.] in and for the parish of Avoyelles, this 4th day of January, A. D. 1853.

(Signed), ADE. BARBIN, Recorder.

Original Song

ROARING RIVER.

A REFRAIN OF THE RED RIVER PLANTATION.

"Harper's creek and roarin' ribber,
Thar, my dear, we'll live forebber;
Den we'll go to de Ingin nation,
All I want in dis creation,
Is pretty little wife and big plantation.

CHORUS.

Up dat oak and down dat ribber,
Two overseers and one little nigger."

Image and Map Gallery

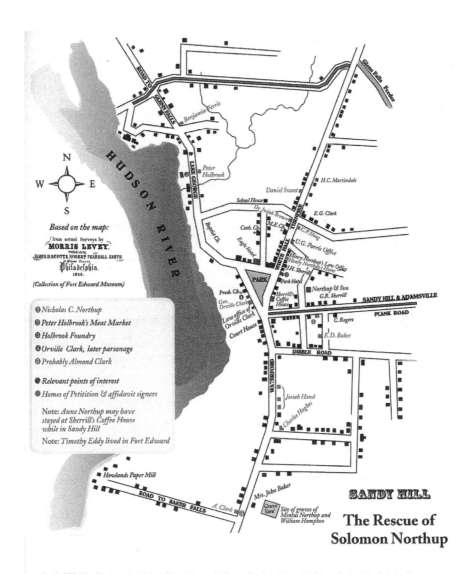

Sandy Hill, New York, on the Hudson River. Home of Solomon Northup prior to his kidnapping in 1841. Includes Henry Northup's law office location and grave site of Solomon's father.

Rawdon .Clark & Co   Alb?

UNITED STATES HOTEL,

Before his kidnapping, Northup worked at the United States Hotel in Saratoga Springs, New York.

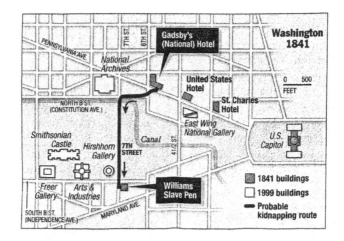

Top: map of Washington, D.C., at the time of Solomon's kidnapping in 1841, showing the location of Williams Slave Pen just blocks from the U.S. Capitol.

Bottom: drawing of Williams Slave Pen based on a narrative by a fugitive slave.

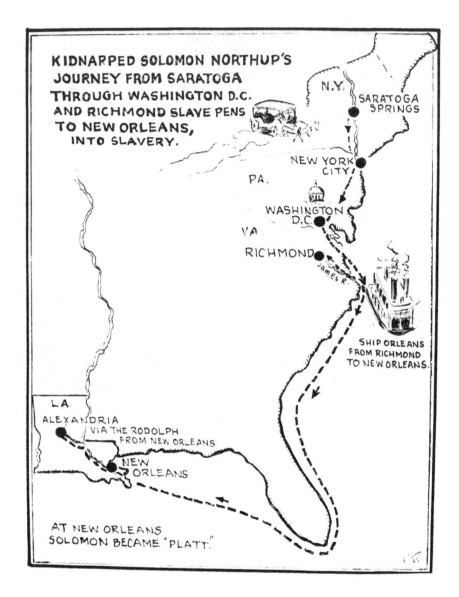

Map of the route traveled by Northup from freedom in New York to slavery in Louisiana.

Present-day photograph of the docks in New Orleans, where Northup debarked from the brig *Orleans*, adjacent to the French Quarter. The slave pen operated by Theophilus Freeman was located minutes from the docks at the corner of Baronne and Gavier Streets near the St. Charles Hotel. An image of the original manifest of the brig *Orleans* can be viewed in the Extras & More section of our website.

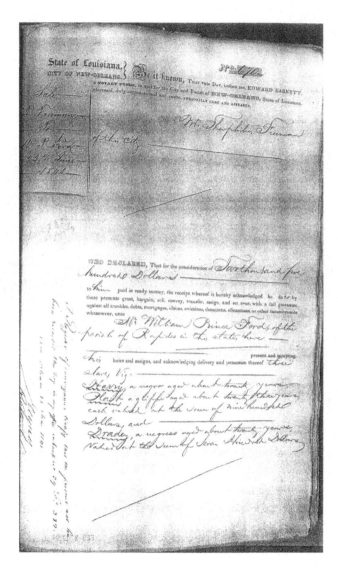

The conveyance record for the sale of Northup, aka "Platt," from Theophilus Freeman to planter William Prince Ford. See an original sketch of a New Orleans slave auction in the Extras & More section of our website.

Present-day Bayou Boeuf at the old William Prince Ford property.

Present-day cane field at the old Jabez Tanner property.

Present-day photograph of Mary McCoy's Big House near Cheneyville, Louisiana. She was described by Northup as "the beauty and the glory of Bayou Boeuf." The home was given to her as a wedding gift. See a present-day photograph of Edwin Epps' house, described by Northup, in the Extras & More section of our website.

CAMPBELLITE CHURCH

Ruins of the Campbellite Church, founded by William Prince Ford and Jabez Tanner in 1843, following a schism with their former church, Beulah Baptist in Cheneyville. The Campbellite religious movement was sweeping the frontier, and such splits caused fractures in the maze of plantation family connections.

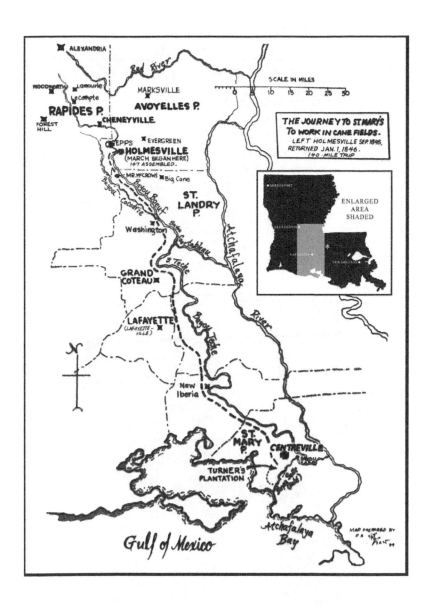

Map of Northup's trip to St. Mary's Parish to work in the cane fields.

44

Marksville Lᵃ. January 1853

1853
Jany 1ˢᵗ To day I was employed by Henry B Northup Esqr. of Sandy Hill, Washington county state of New York, to bring suit against Edwin Epps. to reclaim from slavery a free negro named Soloman Northup who had been kidnapped in the City of Washington in 1841
Jany 4 To day the slave Soloman was released. & I received fifty Dollars for my services
Paid Louis Sugouff fifty Dollars.

Diary entries of lawyer John Waddill in January, 1853, regarding Henry Northup's engagement of his services and Solomon's release.

Henry B. Northup, Solomon's rescuer, was a lawyer, powerful politician and abolitionist whose family had emancipated Solomon's father, Mintus, in 1797. See a photograph of Solomon's present-day descendants in the Extras & More section of our website.

Marksville Courthouse: John P. Waddill, the lawyer employed by Henry Northup; Judge Ralph Cushman, who issued the order granting Northup's freedom; Aristide Barbin, recorder of the court documents.

The only known signature of Solomon Northup is included in this contract signed in 1838.

Acknowledgements

Since my discovery of the original 1853 edition of *Twelve Years a Slave* as a young girl on Bayou Boeuf, a host of people have contributed in so many ways in the over seven decades of work in documenting his story. I could not have done this work without them, and without their help this project could never have been completed. I want to express my deepest appreciation.

It was my father, a fifth-generation Louisiana planter, Sam Lyles, who told me much about Boeuf plantation history, while my mother, Myrtle Guy Lyles, encouraged my writing efforts. Sonia Taub, a retired research librarian of Saratoga Springs, New York, visited the Boeuf country some years ago and returned to research the story of Northup, generously enriching my own research.

Other people, such as my sister, Betty McGowen, helped me in many small but important ways, such as providing her hospitality at her Walnut Grove Plantation by inviting visitors wanting to learn about Solomon. Kenneth Perry, who lived out his life near Indian Creek, gave me a log from the Ford sawmill and set the record straight on the exact location of the mill.

Many genealogists have enhanced my understanding of the years Solomon Northup spent in the Boeuf country. Mr. and Mrs. Charles Ford of Redding, California, assisted with the genealogies of William Prince Ford and the Prince families, while Rene Pernoud, a descendant of William C.C.C. Martin, shared her information of the Martins. Field Horne and Dr. Clifton Brown of Schenectady, New York, both sent me information on the black and white Northup families. Mr. and Mrs. Bob Epps drove from Texas on July 4, 1982, to bring me the genealogy of the Edwin Epps family. Mrs. Edith Wyckoff, of Long Island, New York, a descendant of attorney Henry Northup, mailed me, a stranger, a framed picture of her ancestor, who figures so large in the Solomon Northup story. She also sent a lengthy history of her research on her family and the writings of Henry Northup.

It was the interest of Chancellor Robert Cavanaugh who helped in my work to get the Edwin Epps house moved to the campus of LSU-Alexandria. A committee of local people, blacks and whites, at Bunkie, Louisiana, where I live, added their efforts with mine to preserve the Epps house despite undeserved harassment from our community, some of whom thought the entire story foolish. In the end it was M.D. Descant and his son, Don Pat, of M.D. Descant Contractors, Inc., who restored the old house on the LSUA campus in faithful detail. It is available for all visitors to see a typical plantation "Big House"—in this case the very one from which Edwin Epps operated his plantation.

While the South takes considerable pride in its reputation for hospitality, it could hardly be more so than that extended to me from a number of New Yorkers who graciously contributed information they gleaned over the years. Members of the Whitehall Free Library—all volunteers—shared the considerable work they completed, while David Fiske of Saratoga Lake, Dr. Edward Knoblauch of Albany, and Paul Loding of Hudson Falls, were all especially helpful.

Always helping in this effort in every way they could were my colleagues: Dr. Patsy Barber at LSU-Alexandria; Dr. John Tarver of the Louisiana Agricultural Extension; Dr. Rouse Caffey, Chancellor of the Extension; and Raymond Laborde, Lieutenant Governor. My heartfelt appreciation is extended to these individuals, as well as to President W.C. Jenkins of Louisiana State University. One of my students, Elizabeth Brazelton, allowed me to use the valuable documents of her great-grandfather, attorney John Waddill, which were vitally important in my documentation. The late Dr. Edwin Adams Davis, historian at LSU, helped me gain recognition for my research on Northup. Rufus Smith at the Rapides Parish Courthouse shared his wisdom with me over the years, while nobody could have done more than Avoyelles Clerk of Court Sammy Couvillion and his father, Gradni, who was Clerk of Court preceding him. Both went beyond the call of duty many times over the years in securing essential documents relating to Solomon Northup's experience in Avoyelles Parish.

In 1968, I published the first modern edition of *Twelve Years a Slave* and continued to build my Northup archive throughout my teaching career. After retiring as professor of History at LSU-Alexandria in 1987, with my five children grown and about their business in far away places, I literally lived and breathed the story of Solomon Northup. After years of such dedication, and in my mid-80's, I realized I had reached my breaking point and could not get the manuscript for my final definitive edition checked and polished for publication. I telephoned my daughter, Dr. Sara Kuhn, a professor of English at Chattanooga State Community Technical College, and told her, "Sara, I can't do anything more. If you can't finish what needs to be done, I guess it just won't get done." I'll never forget the cheerful voice that came back to me. "That's all right, Mom. I'll take care of it. Get it in the mail and get some rest!" There are no words for the countless hours, e-mails exchanged, and complete dedication of Sara Eakin Kuhn in editing the book and converting my documentation into the proper Chicago Style Manual essential for publication. I also appreciate the valuable assistance of my sister, Manie Culbertson, another English teacher, who performed the final proof reading.

Finally, it is complete. Solomon's story, one of the most important in American history, has been authenticated and placed in the context of the times. I have given my fullest effort. Now Solomon, and I, can rest.

Bibliography

Albany Evening Journal (NY). "From *The Union Gasette*. Northup's Kidnappers." July 12, 1854.

Albany Evening Journal (NY). "Literary News." June 6, 1856.

Albany Evening Journal (Albany, NY). "The Northrop Kidnapping Case." July 13, 1854.

Albany People's Journal (NY). "The Northup Kidnapping Case" from *Saratoga Whig*. July 13, 1854.

Allen, R. L. "Letters from the South.-No. 12." *American Agriculturist*, November 1847, 336-38.

Armstead, Myra B. Young, Field Horne, and Gretchen Sorin. *A Heritage Uncovered: The Black Experience in Upstate New York, 1800-1825*. Elmira, NY: Chemung Historical Society, 1988.

Bacon, Edward. *Among the Cotton Thieves*. Bossier City, LA: Everett Publishing, 1989.

Ballston Democratic Whig Journal (Ballston, NY). "The Kidnappers of Northup." July 17, 1855.

Ballston Journal (Ballston, NY). "Court Proceedings." May 26, 1857.

Ballston Spa v. Solomon Northup (Oyer and Terminer May 1, 1839).

Bancroft, Frederic. *Slave Trading in the Old South*. New York, NY: Ungar Publishing, 1959, quoted in Harry M. Ward, *Richmond: An Illustrated History* (Northridge, CA: Windsor Publishing, 1985), 106.

Bank of Kentucky v. Conner, et al., 4 1849 317 (Louisiana State Supreme Court 1849).

Bascom, Robert O. *The Fort Edward Book Containing Some Historical Sketches with Illustrations and Family Records*. Fort Edwards, NY: n.p., 1903.

Beecher, Harris H. *Record of the 114th Regiment, New York State Volunteers*. Norwich, NY: J.F. Hubbard, Jr., 1866.

Benjamin Carlle, Jr. v. Solomon Northup (Supreme Courts, State of New York, Wayne County Oct. 9, 1854).

Benjamin P. Burham v. Anne Northup (Supreme Court Warren County Judgments Mar. 1 to Apr. 25, 1859).

Bennett, Ezra. "Day Book of Bennett Store." Unpublished raw data, 1838. Sue Eakin Papers, LSU Alexandria Archives, Alexandria, LA.

Bennett, Charles D. Charles D. Bennett to Virginia, 1894. Ezra Bennett Papers. Louisiana State University Alexandria, Alexandria.

Bennett, Ezra. "Bennett Papers." Sue Eakin Papers. Louisiana State University Alexandria, Alexandria, LA.

————. Ezra Bennett to C. Toledano, September 8, 1840. Sue Eakin Papers. Louisiana State University Alexandria, Alexandria, LA.

————. Ezra Bennett to Dear Brother Charles, August 26, 1847. Sue Eakin Papers. Louisiana State University Alexandria, Alexandria, LA.

————. Ezra Bennett to George Turrell and Calhoun, August 1841. Ezra Bennett Papers. Louisiana State University Alexandria, Alexandria.

————. Ezra Bennett to Loflin and Stephens, March 5, 1842. Sue Eakin Papers. Lousiana State University Alexandria, Alexandria, LA.

————. Ezra Bennett to Samuel A. Belden, September 8, 1840. Sue Eakin Papers. Louisiana State University Alexandria, Alexandria, LA.

Bennett, S. P. B. Letter, "to My Dear Son," March 13, 1852.

Biographical and Historical Memoirs of Northwest Louisiana. Nashville, TN: Southern Publishing, 1890.

Boyd, Esther Wright. Interview by James Fleming. Baton Rouge, LA. 1903.

————. Interview by Walter Fleming. Baton Rouge, LA. 1904.

Brooksher, William Riley. *War Along the Bayous: The 1864 Red River Campaign in Louisiana.* Washington, DC: Brassey's, 1998.

Brown, John. *Slave Life in Georgia-A Narrative of the Life, Sufferings and Escape of John Brown, a Fugitive Slave Now in England.* Edited by L. A. Chawerovzow. London: W.M. Watts, 1855.

Bureau of the Census, U.S. Census, 1850, Rep. (1850).

Bureau of the Census, U.S. Census 1850, Rep. (1850).

Bureau of the Census, U.S. Census 1840, Rep. (1840).

"Charity Hospital Admissions Records 1841." Unpublished raw data, New Orleans Public Library, n.d.

Census Committee, U.S. Census of 1840, Doc. (1840).

Champomier, P. A. *Statement of Sugar Made in Louisiana 1849-1850*. New Orleans, LA: Cook, Young, and Co., 1800s.

Cheney, Rosa. "Diary." Unpublished manuscript, Sue Eakin Papers, Louisiana State University Alexandria, Alexandria, LA, n.d.

"Conveyance Record Q." Legal Record, Rapides Parish Courthouse, Alexandria, LA, September 18, 1892.

"Conveyance Record Q." Document 5754, John M. Tibaut to Edwin Epps, Avoyelles Parish Courthouse, Marksville, LA, May 3, 1843.

"Culture of the Sugar-Cane." *American Agriculturist*, August 1847, 241-43.

Daily Saratogian (Saratoga, NY). "The Soloman Northrop Case." July 11, 1856.

Davidson, Marshall B. *Three Centuries of American Antiques: American Heritage*. New York, NY: Bonanza, 1980.

DeBow's Review, 2 - 3 ser., nos. 2 & 3 (1847-48).

DeForest, John William. *A Volunteer's Adventures: A Union Captain's Record of the Civil War*. New Haven, CT: Yale University Press, 1946.

Dickens, Charles. *The Oxford Illustrated Dickens: American Notes*. N.p.: Oxford University Press, 1991.

Dowdy, Clifford. *The Great Plantation: A Profile of Berkley Hundred and Plantation Virginia from Jamestown to Appomattox*. New York, NY: Bonanza Books, 1957.

Dunbar v. Conner et al., No. 2496 (Fifth District Court of New Orleans 1850, 1851).

Durkee, Cornelius E. "Reminiscences of Saratoga." In *The Saratogian*, compiled by Cornelius E. Durkee, 148-48. N.p.: n.p., 1927. Previously published in *The Saratogian*, 1927-28.

Eakin, Sue, ed. *The Centennial Album, Alexandria Daily Town Talk*. Alexandria, LA: McCormick, 1983.

―――. "Ezra Bennett and the World He Lived In." Sue Eakin Papers. Louisiana State University Alexandria, Alexandria.

————. "Negro Folk Songs from Bayou Boeuf Plantations." *Louisiana Heritage Magazine*, Summer 1969.

————. "The Plantation System in the Lower Red River Valley." Speech, Louisiana State University- Shreveport, Shreveport, LA, 1983.

————. "The Plantation System in the Lower Red River Valley." *Proceedings of the 1985 Red River Symposium*, 1986.

————. *Rapides Parish: An Illustrated History*. Northridge, CA: Windsor Publications, 1987.

————. *A Source Book: Rapides Parish History*. Alexandria, LA: Central Louisiana Historical Association, 1976.

————. *Washington, Louisiana*. Shreveport, LA: Everett Press, 1988.

Eakin, Sue, and Manie Culbertson. *Louisiana: The Land and Its People*. 3rd ed. Gretna, LA: Pelican Press, 1992.

Edmonds, David C., ed. *The Conduct of Federal Troops in Louisiana During the Invasions of 1863 and 1864*. Lafayette, LA: Acadiana Press, 1988. Originally published as *Official Report Relative to the Conduct of Federal Troops in Western Louisiana During the Invasions of 1863 and 1864* (Shreveport, LA: News Printing Establishment, 1865).

Ellis, David M., James A. Frost, Harold C. Syrett, and Harry J. Carman. *A History of New York State*. Rev. ed. Ithaca, NY: Cornell University Press, 1967.

Fisher, Caldwell. Telephone interview by Sue Eakin. Evergreen and Bunkie, LA. June 2003.

Fiske, David. *Solomon Northup: His Life Before and After Slavery*. N.p.: n.p., 2012.

Fogleman, Fred. Interview by Sue Eakin. Bunkie, LA. September 25, 2003.

Ford, William Prince. William Prince Ford to Elder Jesse D. Wright, December 25, 1844.

————. William Prince Ford to William Tecumseh Sherman, September 10, 1859. David Boyd Collection. Louisiana State University Archives, Baton Rouge.

Forest. "Diary." Walter Prichard, editor. Unpublished manuscript, 1864.

Frederick Douglass Paper (Rochester, NY). "The Northrup Case." August 1855.

Frederick Douglass Paper (Rochester, NY). "The Northrup Case." August 24, 1855.

Gaeinne, Patty. "Aunt Emmie." Unpublished manuscript, 1966.

Gasquet v. Keary, No. 4154 (District Court, Avoyelles Parish Sept. 7, 1865).

Gibb, Carson. "Captain Berry's Will: Debauchery, Miscegenation & Family Strife Among 18th Century Gentry." 2000. Maryland State Archives.

Glens Falls Free Press (Glen Falls, NY), June 13, 1857.

Goins, Charles Robert, and John Michael Caldwell. *Historical Atlas of Louisiana.* Norman, OK: University of Oklahoma Press, n.d.

Goode, James. *Capital Losses.* Washington, DC: Smithsonian, 1979.

Gray, Lewis Cecil. *History of Agriculture in the Southern United States to 1860.* Vol. I. Gloucester, MA: Peter Smith, 1958.

Greenaugh, Carol. Carol Greenaugh to Sue Eakin, fax, January 1, 2000. In "Local History Sketches," unpublished manuscript. Sue Eakin Papers. Louisiana State University Alexandria, Alexandria, LA.

Greenaugh, Carol. Carol Greenaugh to Sue Eakin, "fax concerning manuscript," January 1, 2000. "Local History Sketches." Mrs. John T. Morton. Whitehall, NY.

Haskins, James. *One Nation Under a Groove: Rap Music and Its Roots.* New York, NY: Hyperion Books for Children, 2000.

Headrick, Joan D. *Harriet Beecher Stowe: A Life.* New York, NY: Oxford Univeristy Press, 1994.

Hepworth, George W. *Whip, Hoe, and Sword or, the Gulf Department in '63.* Boston, MA: Walker, Wise and Company, 1864.

Historical Sketches of the Old Fort House Museum. N.p.: New York State Division for Youth and Fort Edward Historical Association, 1988.

Holland, Alice. Alice Holland to Sue Eakin, memorandum, March 2003. Sue Eakin Papers. Louisiana State University Alexandria, Alexandria, LA.

Johnson, Jerah. "The 'Picayune:' From Colonial Coin to Current Expression." *Louisiana History* 3 (Summer 1962).

Johnson, Ludwell H. *Red River Campaign: Politics & Cotton in the Civil War.* Kent, OH: Kent State University Press, 1993.

John T. B. Traphagan and Charles R. Bennett v. Solomon Northup (Justice Courts June 10, 1854).

Jordan, Terry G. *Trails to Texas, Southern Roots of Western Cattle Ranches.* Lincoln, NE: University of Nebraska, 1981.

Judy Jacobs v. William O'Neal, No. 4142, Term 1893 (10th Judicial District Court, Rapides Parish, State of Louisiana).

"Keary Papers." Unpublished manuscript, Mississippi Department of Archives, Jackson, MS, n.d.

Knoblauch, Edward. Edward Knoblauch to Sue Eakin, February 26, 2003.

Knoll, J. L. Interview. Bunkie, LA. 1965.

Kollner, Augustus. *Views of American Cities*. New York, NY: Goupsil, Vibert, 1848.

Kramer, Ethel Elizabeth. "Slavery Legislation in Ante-Bellum Louisiana, 1803-1860." Master's thesis, Louisiana State University, 1942.

Lambeth, William. *U.S. Census of Avoyelles Parish*. N.p., 1850.

Lewis, L. R. L. R. Lewis to Librarian Doris Morton, November 8, 1961. Whitehall.

————. L. R. Lewis to Mrs. John T. Morton, March 29, 1962.

Lockett, Samuel H. *Louisiana as It Is: A Geographical and Topological Description of the State*. Edited by Lauren C. Post. Baton Rouge, LA: Louisiana State University Press, 1969.

Loding, Village Historian Paul. Telephone interview by Sue Eakin. Hudson Falls, NY. February 2003.

Lyles, Sam. Interview by Sue Eakin. Cheneyville, LA. 1970?

Mabee, Carleton. *Black Education in New York State from Colonial to Modern Times*. Syracuse, NY: Syracuse University Press, 1979.

————. Carleton Mabee to Sue Eakin, June 1, 2002. Sue Eakin Papers. Louisiana State University Alexandria, Alexandria.

Mann, E. R. *The Bench and Bar of Saratoga County*. Ballston, NY, 1876.

Marksville Weekly News (Marksville, LA), republished February 7, 1991.

Martinez, Raymond J. *The Story of Spanish Moss: What It Is and How It Grows*. New Orleans: Hope Publications, n.d.

Menn, Joseph Karl. *The Large Slaveholders of Louisiana*. Gretna, LA: Pelican Publishing, 1998.

"Minutes." Unpublished manuscript, Avoyelles Parish Police Jury Meeting, December 1842.

Morgan, LaGrande F. LaGrande F. Morgan to Sue Eakin, March 9, 1996. Containing information from Donald J. Hebert, *Southwest Louisiana Records*. Sue Eakin Papers. Louisiana State University Alexandria, Alexandria, LA.

Morrow, Mary H. "Diaries." Unpublished manuscript, Sue Eakin Papers, Louisiana State University Alexandria Archives, Alexandria, LA, n.d.

"The Narrative of Solomon Northup." In *The National Era*. Previously published in *Detroit Tribune* (Detroit, MI), August 25, 1853.

New Orleans Bee (New Orleans). "A Striking Contrast." January 22, 1853.

The New Southwest Devoted to the Great Southwest, March 1904?

New York Daily Times (New York, NY), January 1853.

The New York Daily Times (NY). "The Kidnapping Case." January 20, 1853.

New York Times. "The Kidnapping Case." January 21, 1853.

New York Times (New York, NY). "The Kidnapping Case. Narrative of the Seizure and Recovery of..." January 20, 1853.

New York Times (New York). "Trial of the Suspected Kidnappers of Solomon Northrup." July 12, 1853.

Niles Register, Volume 53, October 28, 1837, 129, as quoted in G.P. Whittington, *Rapides Parish, Louisiana* (Baton Rouge: Franklin Press, reprint from the *Louisiana Historical Quarterly*, 1932, 1933, 1934, 1935), 89-90.

Northup, Solomon. *Twelve Years A Slave*. Lafayette, LA: Center for Louisiana Studies, University of Louisiana at Lafayette, 2007.

———. *Twelve Years a Slave*. Edited by Sue Eakin and Joseph Logsden. Baton Rouge, LA: Louisiana State University Press, 1996.

Olmstead, Franklin Law. *The Cotton Kingdom*. Indianapolis, IN: Bobbs, 1971.

Omans, Donald James, and Nancy West Omans, eds. *Montgomery County Marriages, 1798-1875*. Athens, GA: Iberian Publishing, 1987.

O'Neal, William. *The Life and History of William O'Neal*. Edited by Sue Eakin. Bossier City, LA: Everett Co., 1988. Originally published as *The Man Who Sold His Wife* (St. Louis, MO: A. R. Fleming and Co., 1896).

———. *William O'Neal, The Man Who Sold His Wife*. Edited by Sue Eakin. Bossier City, LA: Everett Companies, 1988.

Pellet, Elias P. *History of the 114th Regiment, New York State Volunteers*. Norwich, NY: Telegraph and Chronicle Power Press, 1866.

The People v. Alexander Merrill and Joseph Russell, No. #3 (Oyer and Terminer Jan. 6, 1855).

People v. Alexander Merrill and Joseph Russell, XIV New York Reports 75-77 (Court of Appeals of the State of New York 1888).

The People v. Merrill and Russell, No. # 3 (Oyer and Terminer Jan. 6, 1855).

"The People vs. Alexander Merrill and Joseph Russell." In *Reports of Decisions in Criminal Cases Made at Term, in Chambers, and in the Courts of Oyer and Terminer of the State of New York*, compiled by Amasa J. Parker, 590-605. Vol. II. Albany, NY: Banks, Gould, and Co., 1856.

Pernaud, Rene B. Rene B. Pernaud to Sue Eakin, May 22, 1999. Sue Eakin Papers. Louisiana State University Alexandria, Alexandria.

Perrin, William Henry. "Southwest Louisiana: Historical and Biographical 1891." In *Southwest Louisiana: Historical and Biographical*. Baton Rouge, LA: Claitor's Publishing Division, 1971.

Prichard, Walter. "Outline of Louisiana History." Unpublished manuscript, Louisiana State University, Baton Rouge, LA, 1930.

"A Probable Kidnapper." Editorial. *The National Era* III, no. 394 (July 1854).

Robert, Carl. "Cheneyville." Sue Eakin Papers, Louisiana State University Alexandria, Alexandria, LA, 1958.

Robert, Carl. Carl Robert to Sue Eakin, March 1962. Sue Eakin Papers. Louisiana State University Alexandria, Alexandria, LA.

————. Letter, August 1963. Sue Eakin Papers. Louisiana State University Alexandria, Alexandria, LA.

Robinson, W. Stitt, Jr. *Mother Earth: Land Grants in Virginia, 1607-1699. Jamestown Booklet No. 5*. Charlottesville, VA: University of Virginia, 1980.

Root, Lewis Carroll, and William H. Root. "The Experiences of a Federal Soldier in Louisiana in 1863." *Louisiana Historical Quarterly* 19, no. 3 (July 19, 1936).

Sale Between Abraham and Mary Ann Tice and Solomon Northup. *275 Grantee Index, Warren County, State of New York*. N.p., May 16, 1853.

The Salem Press (Salem, NY). "Recovery of a Free Negro." January 25, 1853.

"Sale of Land, Document 7862, John Parkes to Edwin Epps." Unpublished manuscript, St. Landry Parish, Opelousas, LA, March 10, 1852.

Sandy Hill Herald (Sandy Hill, NY). "Uncle Sol." March 22, 1853.

Saratoga Whig (Saratoga, NY), October 22, 1852.

Schafer, Judith Kelleher. *Slavery, the Civil War, and the Supreme Court of Louisiana.* Baton Rouge, LA: Louisiana State University Press, 1994.

Smith, Pete. Interview by Sue Eakin. LA. October 1964.

Solomon Northup v. Washington Allen (Court of Common Pleas of County of Saratoga, NY 1838).

Stafford, George Mason Graham. *Three Pioneer Families of Rapides Parish: A Geneaology.* Baton Rouge, LA: Claitor's, 1946.

———. *The Wells Family of Louisiana and Allied Families.* Alexandria, LA: Wells, 1969.

Staples, Brent. "Editorial Observer: Wrestling with the Legacy of Slavery at Yale." *New York Times,* August 14, 2004. Accessed August 14, 2004. http://www.newyorktimes.com.

"Sugar and Slavery in Louisiana. From 'Hill's Monthly Visitor.'" *Southern Cultivator,* October 1847.

"The Sugar Crop of Louisiana. From the 'New Orleans Delta.'" *Southern Cultivator,* December 1847.

Sylvester, Nathaniel Bartlett. *History of Saratoga, New York.* Philadelphia: Evarts and Ensign, 1878.

Tarver, John. Interview. Baton Rouge and Bunkie, LA. 2003-2004.

———. Telephone interview by Sue Eakin. Baton Rouge and Bunkie, LA. 1992.

Taub, Sonia. Sonia Taub to Sue Eakin, April 23, 1993. Sue Eakin Papers. Louisiana State University Alexandria, Alexandria, LA.

Taylor, Joe Gray. *Negro Slavery in Louisiana.* Baton Rouge, LA: Louisiana Historical Association, 1963.

Temperance Helper (NY). "The Northup Kidnappers." February 15, 1855.

Theophilus Freeman v. His Creditors, 15 Louisiana Annual #397 829 (Louisiana 1860).

Thompson, Edgar T. Plantation Societies, Race Relations, and the South: The Regimentation of Populations to *Selected Papers of Edgar T. Thompson*. Durham, NC: Duke University Press, 1975.

Tyler-McGraw, Marie, and Gregg D. Kimball. *In Bondage and Freedom: Antebellum Black Life in Richmond, Virginia-1790-1860*. Richmond, VA: Valentine Museum, 1988.

" *Uncle Tom's Cabin* --No. 2." In *The Salem Press*. Salem, NY, 1853. Previously published in *Albany Evening Journal* (Albany, NY), July 26, 1853.

Vandereedt, John K. John K. Vandereedt to Sue Eakin, July 17, 1995.

Van Namee, I. M. "Letter to the Editor." *Washington County People's Journal* (Washington County, NY), July 1854.

Van Woert, Nathaniel. "Diary." Unpublished Civil War manuscript, n.d. Private collection of George Windes, Brea, CA.

Waddill, John Pamplin. "Diary." Sue Eakin Papers. Louisiana State University Alexandria, Alexandria, LA.

Ward, Harry M. *Richmond: An Illustrated History*. Northridge, CA: Windsor Publications, 1985.

Washington County People's Journal (Washington County, NY). "How the Sol. Northup Case was Disposed Of." March 8, 1855.

Washington County People's Journal (Ballston Spa, NY). "An Individual Identified by Solomon Northup..." July 13, 1854, 2.

Washington County People's Journal (NY). "Sol. Northup's Kidnappers." July 20, 1854.

Washington County Post (Washington Co., NY). "The Arrest of Solomon Northup's Alleged Kidnappers." July 14, 1853.

Wells, Doris. Doris Wells to Sue Eakin, July 15, 2003. Sue Eakin Papers. Louisiana State University Alexandria, Alexandria.

Wells, Gilbert. Interview by Sue Eakin. Cheneyville, LA. 1970?

Whittington, G. P. *Rapides Parish, Louisiana: A History*. Alexandria, LA: Alexandria Committee of the National Society of the Colonia Dames of Louisiana, n.d.

Wright, Esther Boyd. Interview by Walter Fleming. Sue Eakin Papers, Louisiana State University Alexandria Archives.

Wright, Porter, and Barbara Wright. *The Old Evergreen Burying Ground*. Rayne, LA: Hebert Publishing, 1990.

Writers Program of Works Progress Administration, comp. *Louisiana: A Guide to the State*. NY, NY: Hasting House, 1941.

Wyckoff, Edith. "Autobiography of a Family." Unpublished manuscript, n.d.

———. Letter, n.d. Family documents. Edith Wycliff, Locust Hill.

———. Telephone interview by Sue Eakin. Locust Hill, NY and Bunkie, LA. 1990-2000.

Wyckoff, Edith Hay. *Autobiography of a Family*. Fort Edward, NY: Washington County Historical Society, 2000.

Notes To Introduction

1. "People vs. Alexander Merrill and Joseph Russell," Oyer & Terminer, January 6, 1855, Document 3, Deposition by James H. Birch.

2. Benjamin Owen Sheekell, in an appearance before a magistrate in Washington, D.C., on January 18, 1853, concerning a complaint from Solomon Northup by his attorney, Henry Northup, testified that he and Birch had been partners prior to 1838 and "after that time he was a partner of Theophilus Freeman, of New Orleans. Burch bought here - Freeman sold there!" (Solomon Northup, *Twelve Years a Slave* [1853]), 315.

3. Joan D. Hedrick, *Harriet Beecher Stowe* (New York: Oxford University Press, 1994), 118.

4. Bibliographic assistance provided through personal correspondence from librarian David Fiske, Ballston Spa, NY, to Sue Eakin, Bunkie, LA, June 7, 2003; Solomon Northup, *A Freeman in Bondage or Twelve Years a Slave* (Philadelphia: Columbian Publishing Company, 1890); and Solomon Northup, *Twelve Years a Slave*, eds., Sue Eakin and Joseph Logsdon. (Baton Rouge: Louisiana State University Press, 1968).

5. In addition to *Twelve Years a Slave*, Wilson also penned *The Life of Jane McCrea, with an Account of Burgoyne's Expedition of 1777* (New York, 1853); *Henrietta Robinson: The Veiled Murderess* (Auburn, NY, 1855); *A Narrative of Nelson Lee, a Captive Among the Comanches* (1859); and is reputed to be the author of *Life in Whitehall: a Tale of Ship-Fever Times* (Auburn, 1850).

6. Personal correspondence from Carol Senaca, Historical Society of Whitehall, NY, to Sue Eakin, Bunkie, LA, September 11, 2003; phone conversation of Carol Senaca with Sue Eakin, March 13, 2004.

7. Clarence E. Holden, "Local History Sketches," *Whitehall Democrat*, February n.d., 1852.

8. *Ibid.*, 1870.

Chapter Notes
And
Historical Context

Composed by Sue Eakin

Chapter One

1. Though Solomon Northup was a freeman in New York, one should not assume he enjoyed all of "the blessings of liberty" in his native state. In reality, as a free man of color and citizen of New York, he lacked the rights provided whites. Documentation for this assertion includes the following: "Although the first steps toward equality had been taken more than twenty years earlier [than 1821], the Negro had, and for many decades continued to have, inferior status socially, politically, and economically" [See Ellis et al., 225].

Such policies did not change even amid the intense hostility against slavery in the 1850s or even later. According to these authors:

> [t]he Negro population suffered much inequality both within and outside the law. The Constitution of 1822 discriminated against free Negroes by requiring them to meet a property qualification higher than that required by white voters. Although the property qualification for whites was abolished in 1826, that for the free Negroes was retained. On three occasions, 1846, 1860, and 1867, the public refused to approve a constitutional amendment permitting equal suffrage for Negroes. It required the Fifteenth Amendment to eliminate the property qualification imposed on Negroes. In addition to legal inequities, the Negroes met the usual round of discrimination and lack of opportunity. The Irish immigrants in particular fought desperately for the jobs as manual laborers, waiters, and domestic servants which previously had offered Negroes their best opportunities for employment. [See Ellis et al., 281]

In the Bayou Boeuf plantation area of Louisiana where Solomon Northup lived twelve years as a slave, the population of African Americans in the total population was around eight blacks to ten whites; blacks in the New York population in 1855 comprised 1.3% [See Eakin, "The Plantation System in the Lower Red River Valley," 21]. A booklet, *A Heritage Uncovered: The Black Experience in Upstate New York, 1800-1825*, published by the Chemung County Historical

Society in 1988, provides insights into the lives of three small towns in New York, and specifically something of the lifestyle of Solomon and Anne Northup in Saratoga Springs:

> Solomon Northup, perhaps the best known of Saratoga's antebellum year-round residents, and his wife, Anne, illustrate the employment options available to early nineteenth century black Saratogians. First arriving in Saratoga Springs in 1834, Northup generally worked summers as a hack driver for Washington Hall, a local boarding house, and winters as a violinist. He supplemented his income with a brief stint as a railroad laborer for the Troy and Saratoga line while it was under construction and at various odd jobs at the United States Hotel. Anne found regular employment as a cook. [See Armstead, Horne, & Sorin, 28]

While Solomon's wife regularly left their home at the end of the season for the Saratoga Springs resort business, Solomon faced each "off season" without a job and with the uncertainty of finding work until the new resort season opened. Menial jobs of one kind or another were his only choice. As for the violin or fiddle affording means for regular employment, engagements depended upon dances or other social occasions in which the fiddler was contracted, and this was sporadic, not dependable, sustained income. Regarding the "off season," Solomon states, "Anne, as was her usual custom had gone over to Sandy Hill, a distance of some twenty miles, to take charge of the culinary department at Sherill's Coffee House, during the session of the court" [See Northup, 28]. Anne had a job as a cook, the same kind of job she held at the United States Hotel; her husband did not have that security.

2. The reference, of course, is to *Uncle Tom's Cabin* by Harriet Beecher Stowe, published on March 20, 1852, less than a year before *Twelve Years a Slave*. The contract with the publisher gave Stowe 10-percent of sales, which resulted in about $10,000 in royalties in the first three months of publication—"'the largest sum of money ever received by any author, either American or European, from the sale of a single work in so short a time,' the press noted" [See Hedrick, 223].

On April 10, 1853, about the time Solomon's ghost writer, David Wilson, began work on *Twelve Years a Slave*, Stowe sailed for England and "made her triumphant tour of Great Britain, where sales of *Uncle Tom's Cabin* were more than triple the phenomenal figures of the United States, reaching a million and a half in the first year" [See Headrick, 233].

A contemporary review of *Twelve Years A Slave* from 1853 compares the two books:

> THE NARRATIVE OF SOLOMON NORTHUP. READ WHAT THE REVIEWERS SAY. Next to 'Uncle Tom's Cabin,' the extraordinary Narrative of Solomon Northup is the most remarkable book that was ever issued from the American Press. Indeed, it is a

more extraordinary work than that because it is only a simple unvarnished tale of the experience of an American freeman of the 'blessings' of Slavery, while Ms. Stowe's Uncle Tom is only an ingenious and powerfully wrought novel . . ." [See "Narrative of Solomon . . ."]

3. The declaration by Solomon Northup that this is his truthful story of his slave experience on Bayou Boeuf is meant to establish that Solomon vouches for every observation. However, it is important to note that ghost writer David Wilson interviewed Solomon, and portions of the story may have been embellished with his own views. (There were other contributors too, including that of Attorney Henry Northup.) The basic facts of Solomon's journey to Louisiana and his movement through the Bayou Boeuf plantation country during his twelve years as a slave have been validated and provide the framework on which the story is based. Names of people and places are unquestionable. While some of the events said to have transpired are open to question, some errors noted may have resulted from the speed with which this book was written and published, and incorrect names may have been supplied to David Wilson, or he may have simply improvised.

Wilson accomplished the impossible: completing the book and seeing it published within a little over three-months' time. Attorney Henry Northup spurred him on and gave all the assistance he could. Attorney Northup's goal was to see the book published as quickly as possible while newspapers were giving wide coverage to the ordeal of Solomon and his rescue. The attorney correctly figured that information from the forthcoming book would reach readers who could and would identify the kidnappers [See all Wyckoff documents. Edith Wyckoff was a direct descendant of Henry Northup.].

4. With the indirect reference to *Uncle Tom's Cabin* by noting *"works of fiction,"* ghost writer David Wilson emphasizes his attempt to establish Northup's book as a firsthand account of slavery and to differentiate it from the famous novel.

That Northup and Wilson were successful in persuading many news editors that Northup was providing an accurate firsthand account is shown in such articles as this one:

> From the *Union Gasette*.
> Northup's Kidnappers.
>
> Solomon Northup has suffered twelve years of Slavery through the agency of these men. He was born free as they, and with a better heart. He resided in Washington county at the time he was stolen, and were it not that he left warm and influential friends behind him, his subjugation to the Slave-whip would have been lifelong.
>
> As it was he spent twelve years under the hands of Southern task-masters. How he was finally released is a familiar story and need not be repeated. And now that the men who robbed him of twelve years of a freeman's life are caught, what punishment can any one, who will for a moment imagine himself the wronged, deem too

great! Kidnapping, like Murder, 'hath miraculous organs.' So many years have elapsed since Northup was sold into Slavery that difficulty was apprehended in proving the guilt of Merrill and Russell—but these apprehensions are dispelled. Testimony of the most unimpeachable character is at hand.

In 1841, when Northup says, in his narrative, that he was beguiled to Washington by Merrill and Russell, Thaddeus St. John, Esq. of Fulton county saw them with a colored man at Baltimore and in Washington. Mr. St. John not only suspected their design, but intimated his suspicions to Russell.

On his return from Washington Mr. St. John met these men again in the car without the colored man. Mr. St. John is a gentleman of the highest intelligence and character. [See *Albany Evening Journal,* Feb. 15, 1855; Feb 22, 1855]

With the support and contribution of Henry Northup, a passionate abolitionist who had gone on a risky 5,000 mile journey to Louisiana and met with Avoyelles Parish officials, Wilson had all of the ingredients for a successful telling of a remarkable story. The time was right for *Twelve Years a Slave,* with abolitionists kindling passions in people hungry for such a book, as the North-South controversy continued to intensify.

The success of both books owed a great deal to the hostile debate over the Fugitive Slave Law of 1850 and the later increasingly furious controversy over the status of Kansas: free or slave. Stowe's biographer, Joan D. Hedrick, explains:

> Passed by Congress and signed by President Fillmore in September 1850, the Fugitive Slave Law had, as Henry Ward Beecher observed, provisions odious enough 'to render an infamous thing consistently infamous throughout.' Section Five commanded citizens 'to aid and assist in the prompt and efficient execution of the law, whenever their services may be required.' Under Section Seven, persons who gave shelter, food, or assistance to an escaping slave were liable for a fine of $1000 and six months in prison. The Fugitive Slave Law effectively abrogated individual rights such as habeas corpus and the right of trial by jury and provided what abolitionists called bribes to commissioners by awarding them $10 for every alleged fugitive they remanded to slavery, but only $5 for everyone they determined to be free. [See Hedrick, 203]

The debate over Kansas worsened the dispute. In the heat of the North-South arguments, *Twelve Years a Slave* appearing as a firsthand account served in part to confirm Stowe's narrative and added fuel to the flames between the sections.

The close association of *Twelve Years a Slave* with *Uncle Tom's Cabin* was quickly and often noted in New York newspaper accounts. In *The New York Daily Times*: "[Northup's] nine years that he was in the hands of Epps, was of a character nearly approaching that described by Mrs. Stowe, as the condition of 'Uncle Tom' while in that region" [See *New York Daily Times,* January 20, 1853]. In the *Albany Evening*

Journal: "Literary News, The success of 'Uncle Tom' was the incitement to a great many trashy novels on the same subject.

But none have equaled it in pathos and interest. The true narrative of 'Sol. Northup' came nearest to the fiction of 'Uncle Tom.' . . . [See "Literary News," June 6, 1856]. In the *Salem Press:*

'Uncle Tom's Cabin'—*No.2:* The rescue of Solomon Northup, a Free Man who was Kidnapped and sold into Slavery, of which he had TWELVE YEARS experience, has given the public another view of the practical workings of that peculiar Institution. NORTHUP'S NARRATIVE is 'UNCLE TOM'S CABIN' without its Romance . . . The book, though less exciting than that of Mrs. Stowe, is deeply interesting, and will be extensively read . . . [See *"Uncle Tom's Cabin*—No. 2," July 26, 1853]

5. Mintus Northup, father of Solomon, was emancipated not once but twice. The first came in 1797 with the will of Captain Henry Northup. Mintus Northup is the subject of an interesting paragraph dealing with his second emancipation in a book published by the Vermont Historical Society:

> On the 25th of April [1822] in the same year, Mintus Northup of the town of Fort Edward, being duly sworn, said that he had always understood and verily believed that he was born in the town of North Kingston, in the State of Rhode Island, and that he 'was borned free,' and at that time he was of the age of forty-five years and eight months, and that since he had arrived at the age of twenty years he had acted and continued as a free man. The affidavit was sworn to before Timothy N. Allen, a justice of the peace; and Timothy Eddy made oath that he had been acquainted with Mintus Northup for twenty years and upwards, and verily believes that during all that time the said Mintus was always considered a free man; and John Baker, one of the judges of the court, certifies that this proof is satisfactory to him, and that he is of the opinion that Mintus Northup is free according to the laws of the State of New York . . . [See Bascom, 162]

Mintus Northup (1791-1826) worked for various people in New York including Henry B. Northup's half-brother, Clark Northup, who lived in Granville, New York. Family genealogist Edith Wyckoff, a great-granddaughter of Henry B. Northup, who rescued Solomon from slavery, wrote:

> In 1909 John Henry wrote a letter to my grandmother [Edith Carman Hay] about Solomon and his father. 'Mintus' said John Henry 'lived a mile or two east of Fort Edward.' John Henry said that when he was a boy 'Mintus used to come to Sandy Hill and make little beds in the garden for each of us children . . .' Mintus and his son were well known to the Northups of New York, especially

Henry B. (the attorney who rescued Solomon). [See Wyckoff, *Autobiography of a Family*, 121]

6. Henry B. Northup (1805-1877), one in a long line of Henry Northups, was the seventh child of John Holmes Northup of Hebron, New York. At sixteen Henry left the farm to sail to New England where he hoped "to seek a berth on a whaling boat." After a rather tempestuous adolescence, young Henry B. Northup, supported by his father, prepared himself to become a lawyer. He graduated from Middlebury College in 1829 and studied law in the office of Henry C. Martindale. As the protégé of Martindale, he became district attorney. Later he was named as a judge in the court of common pleas. He became a congressman and a leader among Whig politicians in the state. His law office stands on Center Street, Hudson Falls, New York. Wyckoff states the history of Henry B. from that time:

> For six years from 1837-1843, Henry B. was clerk of the board of supervisors of Washington County, New York. In 1838 he received a master of arts degree from Middlebury and in 1839 became counselor of the New York State Supreme Court. Five years later, in 1844, he was made counselor of the New York Court of Chancery and in 1853 attorney and counselor of the United States Supreme Court. From 1847 to 1851 he was a district attorney and in 1856 was elected to the New York State Assembly. Henry B. and Electa had seven children. The oldest, Julia, was born in 1832 . . . the youngest, Edward, born in 1844. [See Wyckoff, *Autobiography . . .*, 57]

Whether or not Mintus was the son of a white Northup cannot be ascertained, but the relationship among the black and white Northups lasted for generations. Wyckoff said that she did not know who his father was. Solomon is described as a "griffe," defined by *Webster's 3rd New International Dictionary* (1964) as "the offspring of a negro and a mulatto: a person of 3/4 Negro and 1/4 white blood." Wyckoff used extensive family records of her family to write a book about the Northups and provide a genealogical chart. Her *Autobiography of an American Family* states that the first Northup, Stephen (ca. 1620), came to America with Roger Williams when he was returning from England where he had gone to get the first charter for the Providence plantations. Wyckoff continues:

> After Stephen had been in Rhode Island for 11 years, he was granted 25 acres at a town meeting. This probably was not his first grant, for the record says that in 1654 he had already sold 60 acres, but it is the first time his name appears in a record as a land owner . . . He built a house close by the Moshassuck River. With all the other houses in the town, it was destroyed during King Philip's War . . . In time he sold his land near Providence and moved to Kingstown, Rhode Island . . . The colony of Connecticut claimed jurisdiction over Narragansett country in which Stephen lived, ordered him to appear in court in Connecticut. Stephen said that if the government of Rhode Island ordered him to go to Connecticut

he would, but he refused to accept any orders from Connecticut.
[See Wyckoff, *Autobiography*, xvii]

7. There has been some question raised about where Solomon was born. Mabel
Jones, Town Historian, Minerva, New York, wrote a letter to the Editor of the
Washington Post-Star on May 23, 1984, p. 5:

> From reading the original book, and the comments on the second
> edition, I gathered these facts: Solomon Northup later in life
> reported that he was born in Minerva in 1808. There was no town
> by that name until 1817 when it was separated from Schroon, but a
> settlement was begun here in 1800 which was called Dominick
> Settlement because it was in Dominick Patent. Thanks to Louise
> Schroon, I have the 1810 Census of Schroon and from later records
> am able to pick out the people who lived in Dominick Settlement in
> that year, as they are all listed together. There is no Northup family
> on the list nor any Negro family. The population at the time was
> 137. It may be that the Northup family had by that time moved on
> to Granville. [See Wells to Eakin]

8. Clark Northup was the half-brother of attorney Henry Northup, as shown in the
genealogical chart in Wyckoff's *Autobiography of an American Family* [See Wyckoff,
Autobiography . . . chart].

9. The name of the town Sandy Hill, a small port on Lake Erie, was changed to
Hudson Falls in 1910. Originally the town was named Baker's Falls [See Loding
interview].

10. Pulitzer-winning New York historian Carleton Mabee, an authority on black
education in New York and author of *Black Education in New York State*, states:

> In Northup's *Twelve Years a Slave*, he appears to be literate but
> perhaps only on a moderate level. Your introduction [to 1968
> edition] calls him 'educated' (p. x) and 'literate' (p. xvi). Northup at
> various times, as I understand it, was a carpenter, fiddler, rafter,
> canal or railroad or farm laborer, or hack driver, none of which
> would necessarily require significant literacy. But this work might
> have been facilitated if he was significantly literate. Northup 'entered
> into contracts' for rafting [p. 8, 1968 edition]. To do this effectively
> might well require the ability to read and understand the contracts.
> (See image of contract signed by Solomon Northup in photo
> gallery). [See Mabee to Eakin]

11. The lowlands of the Bayou Boeuf area were unhealthy in the subtropical
summer climate when rains caught in pools became stagnant water where
mosquitoes bred. It wasn't until 1907 when it was discovered that malaria was
caused by anopheles mosquitoes, and effective treatment was developed. The 2,000

additional breeds of mosquitoes caused other fevers, sometimes deadly. Because of this, all who could afford to do so spent the warm months in shacks along the creeks running through nearby piney woods. In Cheneyville, Dr. Jesse Wright from Connecticut became a very important medical doctor for the area [See Stafford, *Three Pioneer Families*].

In the early settlement era in New York, health conditions under frontier conditions were no better:

> Life expectancy in this period [1775-1825] was a fraction of its present figures. Disease ravaged the population almost unchecked and little understood. Disorders almost unknown today were commonplace. Smallpox left its scars upon thousands, while tuberculosis filled 20 times as many graves in proportion to the population as it did in 1967. Malaria, sometimes called 'the shakes' or 'Genesee fever,' riddled the frontier population. Typhoid and many other contagious diseases struck every community, and cholera hit the seaports. Only one-half the number of children born reached their fifth birthday—a sobering statistic in the light of modern advances. Medical attention, if available, was practically worthless. [See Ellis et al., 207]

12. Solomon Northup would have been unusual among people, black or white, in upstate New York during this settlement period. The Bible and the *Farmer's Almanac* were usually the only two books, if there were any, in homes in the newly settled country with a scattered population. There were no public libraries or schools. Upper New York State was at such a stage in its development during Solomon Northup's early years. A graphic description from Cornell historians regarding New York applies equally to Louisiana, certainly to Bayou Boeuf, settled mostly after 1812:

> The amount of improved farmland rose from about 1,000,000 acres in 1784 to 5,500,000 acres in 1821. These rough and impersonal figures cannot begin to describe the backbreaking task of hewing farms from the wilderness, an accomplishment which wore out at least one generation. The pioneer's cabin, built from logs selected during the clearing process, was a temporary structure until the farmer could afford to erect a house made from boards, nails, and glass. [See Ellis et al., 163,165]

13. Fiddling, for those born talented, black or white, was a very special gift in the days before invention of radio and television; fiddling added much to everyday lives and was a valuable asset to the performer. Entertainments like dancing required music by the musically gifted, and fiddling or skill on other portable musical instruments brought distinction and, sometimes, a little money. Solomon was undoubtedly one of those who was in demand, often unpaid, but contributing grandly to enhancing the lives of himself and his peers.

Notwithstanding Northup's description of his fellow slaves as "simple beings among whom his lot was cast," many were skilled and extraordinary people, like William O'Neal and Old Hawk:

> Old Hawk, the negro slave, was generalissimo around the stables and on the training track. He was said to have been one of the most astute trainers in the country at that period. [See Stafford, *The Wells Family of Louisiana and Allied Families...*, 93]

The most famous horse he trained was Lecomte, who beat his half brother, Lexington, at the Metairie race track in New Orleans on April 8, 1854; thus, "the race crowned Lecomte champion of the American turf" [See Stafford, *Wells Family...*, 93]. Mallard, a slave in New Orleans, became one of the most famous cabinetmakers in the South. Outstanding cabinetmakers, seamstresses, cooks, inventors of farm equipment, and those with many other specialized skills were among Bayou Boeuf slaves [Davidson, *Three Centuries of American Antiques*, 263].

14. A room at the Fort Edward House is furnished as nearly as possible to replicate one of the rooms of Solomon Northup when he and his family lived there [See *Historical Sketches of the Old Forthouse Museum*, 15-16].

15. The money Solomon used for the new business came from payment after a lawsuit against his earlier employer, Washington Allen. A suit filed July 13, 1838, *Solomon Northrop [sic] vs. Washington Allen*, was sent to the Court of Appeals. Northup signed a contract with Allen "to deliver 6 lockings containing each 2 cribs of Dock Sticks from White Hall to Gleason [?] lockes in Waterford on the Champlain Canal for the sum of $7.50 each crib." Upon arrival at the designated destination, Allen discharged him "on account of intemperance and did the work himself, was compelled to hire other hands & sustained damage and paid expenses . . ." A trial was held in Saratoga County courthouse on June 25 and "a verdict rendered for the plaintiff of 50 dollars and judgment was rendered thereon for that sum and costs amounting to 55 Dollars in the whole." Interestingly enough, James L. Prindle, who would testify for him after his rescue and return to New York, testified at this time. Prindle stated:

> that the deft [defendant] said he had discharged Plff. [Plantiff] from the work when he had first undertaken it, because he the Plff, was intoxicated and had torn or would tear the cribs; that the witness saw him that day about that time he thot. [thought] Plff. had been drinking considerable, but not so much as to disqualify him for business: that Plff general character was that he was industrious and not in the habit of being intoxicated, tho [though] in the habit of drinking some. [See Solomon Northup vs. Washington Allen]

Other witnesses commented with varying perspectives on how much Solomon had been drinking:

The defendant introduced David Morehouse as a witness who testified that he saw Allen discharge Northup, and that Northup had been drinking & thought he was not competent to take charge of the rafts on account of his intemperance . . . Allen said he did not want him, but took charge of the raft at White hall . . . [See Solomon Northup vs. Washington Allen]

The verdict was rendered in Solomon Northup's favor, probably because he had delivered the lumber, and the problems causing Northup's suit against Allen occurred at the destination. The contract between Solomon Northup and Washington Allen involving rafting is filed at the Saratoga County Clerk's Office, Box A33. Ms. Sonia Taub, retired librarian, Saratoga Springs, provided copies of these documents and other information.

16. The Louisiana lumbermen were likely not formally educated, but they were professionals in their work, skilled and knowledgeable not only about the trees, but also the wildlife that lived there. Rafting was, and had been for many years prior to Solomon's arrival, a daily part of their lives. Of course, Solomon Northup may have been the first to raft the circuitous route over the shallow streams which took him to Lamourie.

Even before the Europeans' arrival, Indians lived in the Louisiana forests covering an estimated one-third of the state. They moved logs in a country laced with bayous, creeks, and big rivers. The forests allowed the colony what little commerce developed. Lumber, tar, and pine resin were manufactured [See Tarver interviews].

17. Saratoga Springs was a most extraordinary resort city:

For most of the nineteenth century and well into the twentieth, Saratoga Springs, New York, enjoyed a national reputation as a leading summer resort. The waters of its myriad springs, reputed for their medicinal value, attracted outsiders as early as 1783 when Phillip Schuyler, Revolutionary War general, established Schuylerville as his country estate and began inviting his friends to partake of High Rock Springs in what is today called Saratoga Springs. The nation's young aristocracy, eager to mimic the habits of its European counterparts, for whom regular visits to established spas were part of the regular social circuit, responded enthusiastically. [See Armstead et al., 27]

18. The United States Hotel has an interesting history. In *Views of American Cities*, Augustus Kollner writes:

By the 1840s the United States Hotel had become the most popular of the major hotels. Many distinguished people had been guests there: Joseph Bonaparte, former king of Spain and Naples, the Marquis de Lafayette, J. Fennimore Cooper, President Martin Van

Buren, Henry Clay, Daniel Webster, and Washington Irving. [See Kollner, 178]

A newspaper article in the *New York Herald* for August 21, 1847, reported:

> The elite of Saratoga—the northern millionaires, the southern planters, and the fashionables, who comprise probably about a fifth of the five or six thousand visitors at the springs,—quarter at the magnificent United States Hotel . . . These people are many of them exceedingly profuse in their expenditures. Many of the ladies lavish a mine of wealth, and tax the ingenuity of all the modistes, on the costly splendor and variety of their dresses . . . The proprietors of this hotel realize a net profit of $20,000 to $40,000 during the season of three months, the sum varying according to the general prosperity of business in the country. This United States Hotel burned on June 18th, 1865. A new United States Hotel opened on the same place in June of 1874. [See Kollner, 178]

19. According to Ellis et al.:

> Apprenticeship, indentured servitude, and slavery lost ground because New Yorkers found free [meaning freemen] labor more efficient, reliable and flexible . . . Slavery, however, was losing ground during the last half of the 18th century. People found it generally cheaper to hire free labor than to maintain slaves during periods of idleness as well as usefulness. [See Ellis et al., 86-87]

Perhaps because of these conclusions, New York provided a method for slaves to become free, as Solomon Northup was:

> In New York State, the gradual Manumission Act of 1799 stated that the children of slaves born after July 4th of that year were to be freed at the ages of twenty-eight and twenty-five, respectively, depending on whether they were male or female. The Act of 1817 freed all slaves as of July 4, 1827. [See Armstead, et al., 5]

20. Solomon Northup was twice convicted of assault and battery, once in February 1834 and on May 1, 1834. He was again convicted of assault and battery on May 1, 1839, as shown in the Court of Oyer & Terminer, Ballston Spa, New York [See Ballston Spa vs. Northup].

While Solomon was a slave on Bayou Boeuf in Louisiana, his family was growing up. Alonzo, his son, served honorably as a Union soldier:

> Private Alonzo D. Northrup [*sic*] enlisted #1028 as laborer, page 27, on February 15, 1864; Company F, U.S. Colored Infantry; described as black and 5'8" tall; saw action at Beaufort, South Carolina as a teamster on July 7, 1864, transferred to the 20th U.S. troops as per instructions from the War Department, mustered out on August 28,

1865, at Hilton Head, South Carolina. [National Archives and Records Administration, Washington, D. C.]

21. Neighbors seemed not to have been surprised about his sudden absence because he was known to leave home without explanation and return when he chose [See Lewis to Morton, March 29, 1962].

Chapter Two

22. Northup, in testimony given at the hearing of the case, described his meeting with the strangers in Moon's Tavern, who later turned out to be his kidnappers:

> 'Northup testified that he first saw Merrill and Russell at Mr. Moon's Tavern at Saratoga Springs; they did not appear to have any particular business; they wished to hire witness to go to New York with them to drive their carriage and play the fiddle in a circus company to which they said they belonged.' This testimony was given by Solomon Northup at an examination held before Abel Meeker and David W. Maxwell, Esquires, Justices of the Peace, at Ballston Spa, on Tuesday, July 11, 1854. [See "The Northup Kidnapping Case"]

A man named Prindle, a friend of Solomon since 1826 or 1827, added significant details regarding the kidnappers. His testimony was at the same hearing held at Ballston Spa on Tuesday, July 11, 1854, and reported in the *Saratoga Whig*:

> Identifies Merrill, and says he saw him on Montgomery Hall stoop at Saratoga Springs, and a day or two after saw him in a carriage there; another man in carriage who had long hair and large whiskers. Saw Solomon Northup drive away; the carriage containing the two men. Had some conversation with Solomon before he started, told him that he had not better go off with those men as they would not know him when they got away south; others told Solomon the same story.
> On cross examination, Prindle says, he remembers having prisoners pointed out to him as [being] from the south and about to buy Mr. Seaman's horse. Solomon told witness that he would risk the prisoners selling him; told him again he had better not go south with them, meant to the slave states. [See "The Northup Kidnapping Case"]

23. Merrill Brown was the alias of Alexander Merrill, and Abram Hamilton was the alias of Joseph Russell [See "Sol. Northup's Kidnappers," 2].

24. The fact that the neighbors did not consider Solomon's disappearance in 1841 unusual may have related to the circumstances in which he lived, with irregular employment at different jobs over the years:

The brevity of this summer season left year-round black workers/residents of Saratoga scrambling to make ends meet during the long months of winter unemployment. Several strategies helped them survive these lean times, but chief among them were reliance on summer savings and the use of credit... Very few Afro-Americans escaped the economic marginality and financial insecurity brought on by their seasonal and/or low-paying positions at work [See Armstead et al., 29-30].

25. As recorded by James Goode:

Charles Dickens, who visited Washington in 1842, a year after Northup was abducted, describes his stay at a Washington hotel which almost certainly was Gadsby's. Created in 1826 out of a row of houses, the hotel was sold and remodeled extensively in 1844 after Gadsby's death. At that time it was renamed the National Hotel. Dickens describes it as "a long row of small houses fronting on the street and opening at the back upon a common yard..." It would therefore have been easy to conduct Northup unseen out into the yard and thence into an alley alongside of the hotel. Dickens also describes buildings across the street from the hotel. One of these may have been the source of the light seen by Northup as he emerged from the alley onto Pennsylvania Avenue [See Goode, 168-169]. (Editor's note: There are inaccuracies in the Goode piece cited, including an error in the hotel's location and the year Dickens stayed there.) [See Dickens, 115-116]

26. The drug slipped into Solomon's drinks could have been belladonna or laudanum, or a combination of both drugs [Northup, 1968 edition, 19].

Chapter Three

27. Both names, Burch and Birch, are listed in the U.S. Census 1840 as living in Washington, D.C. Wilson spelled the name as Burch, but the spelling given by the commander of the Auxiliary Guard to Joseph C. Lewis during the trial of the kidnappers was Birch. Thus, the editor is spelling the name with an "i," believing this to be the spelling used by the trader, James H. Birch. The thirty-nine-year old resident of Washington, D. C., was a major slave trader at the head of what the editor calls a Reverse Underground Railroad. The full extent of the criminal operation is not known, but it involved a number of professional criminals in the business of kidnapping people of dark complexion and selling them in the southern slave market, where there was a need for labor on the plantations. Slave traders at Richmond, Virginia, and New Orleans, with close ties with Birch, are cited in the Northup story, and there may have been others. There is still the question of the connection of the brig, *Orleans*, with the ring. Other men kidnapped en route to New Orleans and placed on the *Orleans* experienced captures closely resembling

that of Solomon Northup. Birch owned considerable property in the capital and evidently enjoyed important contacts with powerful political figures. In 1852 he was appointed commander of the Auxiliary Guard, a volunteer group working with the police force in the City of Washington and the District of Columbia [See People vs. Merrill and Russell]. When a deposition from Birch was taken by Joseph C. Lewis in Washington, D.C., during the trial of The People vs. Alexander Merrill and Joseph Russell, the document read:

> By virtue of the annexed commission I proceeded to open the Same in the City of Washington and District of Columbia on the 6th day of January, 1855, when James H. Birch, one of the witnesses named in the Said Commission, personally appeared and, after being duly Sworn made the following answer to interrogatories in Said Commission:

> I state that my name is James H. Birch—that I was fifty years old in October last—that I was appointed by the Mayor of Washington, D.C. to the Command of the Auxiliary Guard in June, 1853, which said Guard is part of the Police force of the City and District aforesaid and which office I still hold—that I reside in the City of Washington, D.C. [See People vs. Merrill and Russell]

28. Theophilus Freeman, former partner of James H. Birch, managed Freeman's Slave Pen in New Orleans and continued a business relationship with Birch. This is clear with the nine slaves belonging to Birch being shipped on the brig *Orleans*, documented by the ship manifest, to Theophilus Freeman at New Orleans. An advantage to selling kidnapped slaves in New Orleans, the way Solomon Northup was sold, was less risk of exposure of the crime, since slaves were sold into remote west central Louisiana. Rural Louisiana was at the edge of the western frontier with sparse population and difficult communication with the urban North. Historian Judith Kelleher Schafer describes Freeman:

> A series of cases involving New Orleans slave dealer Theophilus Freeman dealt with simulated sales and donations intended to defraud creditors. Freeman was an unscrupulous businessman who falsified slave ages, sold young children away from their parents, and whipped and kicked bondsmen in the slave pen ... Freeman lived with his ex-slave and mistress, a mulatto laundress named Sarah Conner, who had purchased her freedom from him in 1841 for $700. Just after her emancipation Freeman's finances became shaky, and he transferred most of his assets to her to avoid having them seized by creditors. He was arrested several times in 1845 because authorities feared he would flee the state. Litigation concerning Freeman's fraudulent sales, secret donations, and transactions to Conner's name continued until 1861, when it was interrupted by the Civil War, during which time Freeman left New Orleans. [See Schafer, 175]

The civil cases against the property of Theophilus Freeman include one, at least, for the value of his mistress, Sarah Conner, which found that Sarah Conner was entitled to her freedom on May 6, 1846 [See Dunbar vs. Conner et al.].

However, the Bank of Kentucky and its president and directors, as creditors of Theophilus Freeman, sued both Sarah Conner and Theophilus Freeman on November 9, 1846. The suit was to cancel the ruling allowing Sarah Conner her freedom and return her to status as property of Theophilus Freeman; her value then could be used to offset his debt. The judgment was made by default and then confirmed. Sarah Conner appealed to the Louisiana Supreme Court, but the judgment was sustained [See Bank of Kentucky vs. Conner et al.].

In another civil suit against Freeman in 1860, John Valentine, executor for the estate of Whiting Valentine, filed to be paid from assets held by the sheriff as the result of other creditors' suits [See Theophilus Freeman vs. His Creditors].

Court cases against Theophilus Freeman include: Civil Code, Art. 190, p. 29; Union Bank of Maryland vs. Freeman, #4938, 3 Rob. 485 (1843); Mielkie vs. Freeman, #5238, 5 Rob. 524 (1843); Lambeth and Thompson vs. Freeman (Unreported) Commercial Court of New Orleans #6492 (1845); Freeman vs. Profilet, (Unreported) Parish Court of New Orleans (1845); Romer vs. Woods, #1846, 6 Louisiana Annual 29 (1851), 25; Freeman vs. his creditors, #948, 3 Louisiana Annual 669 (1848); Bank of Kentucky vs. Conner, #1315, 4 Louisiana Annual 365 (1849); Dunbar vs. Conner, Ann. 669 (1848); Dunbar vs. Conner, Unreported Louisiana Supreme Court Case #1700 (1850, 1851); Freeman vs. His Creditors, #6473, 15 Louisiana Annual 397 (1860).

29. Ebenezer Radburn testified on January 18, 1854, before the magistrate after the arrest in Washington, D.C., of James H. Birch, Benjamin O. Shekels, Benjamin A. Thorn, and Ebenezer Radburn. Radburn testified that he was forty eight years old and the keeper of Williams Slave Pen. He said that he had known Birch for fourteen years. [See a sketch of Williams Slave Pen and a photo of Birch's slave trading business in the Extras & More section of our website at www.TwelveYearsASlave.org].

30. A description of Freeman's slave pen was left by Georgia slave John Brown in his memoirs. The layout of the slave pen suggests something of what a slave's life might have been like in such a place. In a chapter of his book entitled "The Slave-Pen in New Orleans," Brown recalled:

> I have stated that the slave-pen to which I was taken, stood facing the St. Charles Hotel. It had formerly been an old Bank. It consisted of a block of houses forming a square, and covering perhaps an acre of ground. The centre of this square had been filled up with rubbish and stones, as high as the back of the first floor of the houses, so as to form a solid foundation for the yard of the pen, which, it will be understood, was level with the first floor, and nicely graveled for the slaves to take exercise in. The houses themselves were built upon brick pillars or piers, the spaces between which had been converted into stores. Of these there were a great number, one of them being

used as the negro auction-room. The accommodation for the negroes consisted of three tiers of rooms, one above the other, the yard I have spoken of being common to all. There were two entrances to the pen, one for the 'niggers,' the other for visiters [sic] and buyers. The windows in front, which overlooked the street, were heavily barred, as were those which overlooked the yard. It was an awfully gloomy place, notwithstanding the bustle that was always going on in it.

I may as well describe here the order of the daily proceedings, as during the whole time I remained in the pen, they were, one day with the other, pretty much the same. A mulatto named Bob Freeman, and who was called the Steward, had charge of the arrangements that concerned the slaves. He had a great deal of power of a particular kind, and did very nearly what he liked in the way of making them comfortable or otherwise; shutting them up if he disliked them, or they displeased him: according as they favourites [sic] with him or not. The pen would contain about five hundred, and was usually full. The men were separated from the women, and the children from both; but the youngest and handsomest females were set apart as the concubines of the masters, who generally changed mistresses every week. I could relate, in connection with this part of my subject, some terrible things I know of, that happened. [See Brown, 110-111]

31. In the case of Radburn, his cruelty was apparently not tempered by the financial interests of the slave trading enterprise. Ward states in his book on Richmond that "scars upon a slave's back were considered evidence of rebelliousness or unruly spirit and hurt his sale" [See Ward, 55].

32. Clemens Ray may be the man listed as Clem Woodard, #36, a nineteen year-old male, 5'7" tall, and of black complexion, one of the slaves of James H. Burch [sic] listed as sailing on the *Orleans*, March, 1841 [See *Orleans* manifest available in our Extras & More section of our website www.TwelveYearsASlave.org].

33. John Williams is not listed among slaves in the *Orleans* manifest.

34. Randall appears to be listed on the manifest as #35, Rudal Ames, 4'7" tall. The size is consistent with a child [See *Orleans* manifest].

35. Emily Cooper #39, female, age 7, 3'7" tall, black complexion, is listed on the *Orleans* ship manifest as one of the slaves of James H. Burch [sic] [See *Orleans* manifest].

36. Eliza Cooper, renamed "Dradey" as a slave, is listed as #38 in the *Orleans* ship manifest, as a female twenty-seven years old, 5'5" tall, black complexion, on May 24, 1841 [See *Orleans* manifest].

37. In 1850 Elisha Berry, sixty-three, lived in Prince Edward County, Maryland, in a household headed by Deborah Burgess, owner of five slaves. Deborah Burgess's real property is listed as $3,500. According to the U.S. Census of 1850, Elisha Berry had no occupation. Three other males lived in the household: Richard Berry, thirty, whose occupation is listed as farmer; Dorsey Berry, twenty-seven, carpenter; and Walter Berry, twenty-five, millwright. A woman, Sarah R., is also listed as a member of the household [See Bureau of Census, 1850].

38. In 1850 Jacob Brooks, a sixty-seven year old mulatto and free man of color, lived in the household with Jane, whom Wilson identifies as the daughter of Elisha Berry. Jane is described as black in color, along with Jane Ridgly, ten years old, and Sarah Ridgly, twelve years old, both black. All were free. No occupation is listed for Jacob Brooks [See Bureau of the Census, 1840; 1850].

39. A pioneer Louisiana geographer, Samuel H. Lockett, a professor at Louisiana State Seminary at Pineville (later to become Louisiana State University and moved to Baton Rouge) wrote:

> Red River: the next most important river in Louisiana [to the Mississippi] is Red River, the only tributary of the Mississippi flowing in from the west within the limits of the state. Red River flows diagonally across Louisiana, from northwest to southeast, and thus occupies a position of the utmost possible importance. In many respects it is very similar to the Mississippi. Its waters are excessively turbid, and of a deep red color; its current is swift; its banks are constantly washing away at one point and building up at another; cut-offs are frequent; islands, old rivers, and abandoned channels are numerous; bayous are sent off from the parent stream; overflows and crevasses occur; in fact, all the phenomena of the greater stream may be observed in the lesser. [See Lockett, 122]

In 1869 Lockett surveyed Louisiana traveling across the state on horse or mule, by buggy, sulky, train, and even boat. His work was not published by the impoverished state until 1969 [See Lockett, 122].

Chapter Four

40. Jacob Brooks, a mulatto and free man of color, according to the U.S. Census, 1840, is described in endnote 38 [See Bureau of the Census, 1840].

41. According to the U.S. Census, Elisha Berry lived in a household with individuals, one of whom may have been his wife. He is listed as having no business. There is no evidence that he had a plantation [See Bureau of the Census, 1840]. For more information, see note 37.

42. Goodin at the Richmond slave pen, like Theophilus Freeman, is described as being greeted as a friend of Birch, the circumstances appearing to connect him with

Birch as a business associate or, perhaps, a partner. Richmond had a significant slave market:

> Richmond was the center of the Southern slave trade and in the late antebellum era thousands of slaves were sold yearly from Virginia to feed the cotton boom in the lower South. Most of these slaves left Virginia through Richmond. The purchase and resale of slaves was a highly profitable and highly visible business as public slave auctions became increasingly common in Richmond . . . The auctions linked the city with the countryside and with the larger regional economy. Slaves were vital in Richmond, not only for their labor but for their marketability. [See Tyler-McGraw and Kimball, 2]

In the Richmond directory for 1840 there were fifteen slave traders listed [See Tyler-McGraw and Kimball, 27-28]. Research in Richmond was performed by attorney Jonathan Blank.

43. Robert is likely Robert Jones, the last slave listed of those slaves traveling on the *Orleans*. He is described as being thirty-five years old, 5'7" tall, yellow complexion, from Dayton, Ohio [See the *Orleans* manifest in the Extras & More section of our website at www.TwelveYearsASlave.org]. He was captured through exactly the same technique as that used in Solomon Northup's kidnapping. The editor is indebted to David Fiske, Saratoga Springs, New York, who provided the manifest of the *Orleans*, which he located at the National Archives. According to the manifest the Master of the brig *Orleans* was William Wickham, who sailed with crew and passengers from Richmond, Virginia, on April 27, 1841, and from Norfolk, Virginia, on May 1, 1841, for the Port of New Orleans [See *Orleans* manifest].

44. David (listed is a "Davy Singleton, 22, 5'3" tall) and Caroline Parnell, age 20, 5'2" tall, are listed on the manifest of the *Orleans* as being shipped by George M. Barnes to Theo. Freeman.

45. A slave named Mary McCoy, 16, 5'1" from Norfolk, was shipped by Barnes to Freeman in New Orleans, according to the manifest of the *Orleans*. Mary McCoy was also the name of a plantation owner referenced by Northup in Chapter 20.

46. Lethe Shelton, 25, 5' tall, listed as brown, was one of the forty-one slaves on the *Orleans*.

47. William Wickham was master of the brig, sailing with forty slaves from Richmond to New Orleans on May 21, 1841. A group of nine of the slaves were shipped by James H. Burch [*sic*] to New Orleans, arriving May 24, 1841. F. Jacobs signed the information written on the manifest as inspector.

Chapter Five

48. "Platt Hamilton" is #33 on the manifest of the brig *Orleans* (note the surname is that of Abram Hamilton, the pseudonym of one of the kidnappers), twenty-six, 5'7" tall, yellow complexion. [See the *Orleans* manifest in the Extras & More section of our website at www.TwelveYearsASlave.org].

49. No Frederick is listed. Henry Wallace, fifty, 5'7" tall, with brown complexion, is listed as #4 on the *Orleans* manifest. Another Henry, Henry Williams, twenty-five, is listed as #29, 5'5" tall and having a black complexion, but there is a seventeen-year-old boy, Joe Singleton, 5'3" tall, black, who is #8.

50. Maria, #31 on the *Orleans* manifest, might have been Birch's slave, Mehala Irvin, 23, 5'6" tall and black. The names of slaves were often changed by masters, and the age is about right.

51. Arthur Curtis, unnumbered on the manifest, kidnapped in Norfolk, Virginia, is the second slave listed on page 2 of the manifest with his description as a twenty-two year-old male, 5'10" tall and black. The fact that the man was kidnapped and then held in a Norfolk slave pen until the *Orleans* arrived may also link him as a victim of the Reverse Underground Railroad based in Washington, D.C. He is listed as one of Birch's slaves [See *Orleans* manifest].

52. Number 1 on the *Orleans* manifest was Cuff Singleton, 40, a male 5'6" tall with black complexion; #28 was Jim Whiteus, 27, 6' tall, black. There were eight young women in their twenties on the *Orleans* manifest list of slaves, one of whom may have answered to the name "Jenny" [See *Orleans* manifest].

53. A note regarding Robert Jones, who was one of Birch's nine slaves shipped on the brig *Orleans* to Freeman's slave pen in New Orleans, was included in the report of Master Wickam inscribed across page 2: "Examined and found correct with the exception of Robert Jones, who Captain Wickham states, died on the voyage. New Orleans, 24 May 1841. Signed by T. Jacobs, Imp rt" [See *Orleans* manifest].

54. Manning did as he had promised in mailing the letter, but a copy was never found. Confirmation that it was mailed came from Henry B. Northup. He acknowledged in an affidavit that he had received the letter, but since Solomon was in chains aboard a ship and did not know his destination, he could do nothing more than guess Solomon's destination.

55. Eliza is listed by her slave name as #38 Dradey Cooper. Her children are #39 Emily Cooper, age 7, 3'7" tall, and #35 Rudal Ames, age 11, 4'7" tall, who is the boy Randall mentioned in the narrative [See *Orleans* manifest].

56. Henry Hyman, who is #3 on the manifest, was 40, 5'8" and black complexion, and #30 is Lethe Shelton, 25, 5' tall with brown complexion; they are listed among

the forty-one slaves aboard the *Orleans*. Henry and Harry could be the same person [See *Orleans* manifest].

Chapter Six

57. Theophilus Freeman and James H. Birch had been partners at an earlier date and maintained "a relationship"; Birch shipped slaves to Freeman's slave pen.

58. During the early nineteenth century, life on the western frontier with Louisiana at its fringe revolved around land. Bayou Boeuf planters of central Louisiana, all with small plantations, had their investments mostly in their slaves, and many of the slaves were mortgaged. To complete the essential work to support a plantation on Bayou Boeuf, the planter and slaves were interdependent, and the planter's goal was to maintain the plantation in order to earn a profit. Thus, while there were cruel slave owners who whipped their slaves regardless of the economic consequences, there were others who did not inflict damage on their property out of self-interest or who were genuinely non-violent.

59. The U.S. Census for Louisiana, 1810-1890, lists thirteen males named Carr as living in New Orleans [See Bureau of U.S. Census, 1810-1890].

60. The Hospital of St. John, or the Charity Hospital, was established in 1740 during the French colonial period. The poor were taken care of there. Ursuline nuns cared for patients after 1770. The hospital was destroyed by a hurricane and rebuilt in 1779 by Andres Almonester y Rojas during the Spanish period. Under Almonester the name of the hospital was changed to St. Carlos. It was destroyed, this time by fire, but was again rebuilt by Almonester [See Prichard. LSUA now has the editor's copy, given to her by the widow of Dr. Prichard].

61. Microfilm of the Charity Hospital admissions records for this period is on file at the New Orleans Public Library and confirms Northup's statement regarding his stay there [See Charity Hospital Admission Records].

62. [See Charity Hospital Admission Records].

63. The sale of Solomon Northup (as Platt), Eliza (as Dradey), and Harry to William Prince Ford can be viewed in the sale papers recorded in Notarial Acts of New Orleans. Platt, then thirty-three years of age, was listed as twenty-three years old, and Dradey was probably older than twenty. Since youthful age with years of service ahead brought higher prices, the ages of slaves were routinely lowered at a sale. For the men, $900 each and $700 for Dradey were prices in keeping with slave prices of 1841.

The signatures of Freeman and William Prince Ford appear on the front and back of the sale papers. Included also are witnesses F.N. Newton and Alphonse Barnett with Schraw Barnett, officer of the court [Notarial Acts of New Orleans, June 23, 1841, XVII, 670. See image of actual conveyance record of Solomon/Platt to Ford in the Extras & More section of our website at www.TwelveYearsASlave.org].

64. Emily is listed as a seven-year-old black female. Freeman may not have known the rules for inclusion in the famous quadroon balls; qualifications included skin of light color, as implied by the word "quadroon," and years of preparation. It is unlikely Emily would have qualified as one of the elite, although Freeman may have had in mind a sale to an individual not among the privileged group for whom the quadroon balls were staged.

65. "Her infant voice grew faint and still more faint"—describing seven-year-old Emily—is an example of Wilson's dramatic writing style.

Chapter Seven

66. The *Rodoph* was a regular carrier in the commerce between New Orleans and the inland port of Alexandria [See Bennett to Turrell and Calhoun].

67. Voluminous documents of George W. Kelso [spelled Kelsow in text] are located in the archives at Louisiana State University, Alexandria, Louisiana. Judge John Clement, who presided over a lengthy case related to Kelso's estate, wrote September 19, 1892, that George W. Kelso was seventy-two years old and resided at his plantation on Bayou Robert on the northwest side of the road along the bayou, about ten miles south of Alexandria. He had been at this location since 1840. In the U.S. Census report of slaves in 1850, George W. Kelso owned 330 slaves, 162 of which were employed in agriculture. He died in 1854 and left a will that brought strong dissent from descendants from the time of his death until this court case years later [See Conveyance Record Q, 379-380].

68. William Prince Ford (1804-1861) was one of the first pioneers to establish a plantation in the picturesque country bordering Hurricane Creek, near present-day Forest Hill. A native of Tennessee, he was brought to Louisiana as a boy of thirteen by his parents, who settled near Cheneyville. He married Martha Tanner (1808-1849), eleventh child of Robert Tanner, founder of Cheneyville. Although he operated a 200-acre plantation south of Cheneyville that Martha inherited, he and Martha made their home at the place on Hurricane Creek. There he operated a variety of small businesses, including a mattress manufacturing shop, a brick manufacturing facility, and a "pony" sawmill in partnership with William Ramsay. The sawmill was built January 3, 1840, in "the Great Pinewoods" about ten miles north of Ford's home on Hurricane Creek. His partnership purchased 79.87 acres at $99.84 per acre. Copies of the sale documents are in the United States Land Office, District of Opelousas, Rapides Courthouse.

Ford was a minister at Spring Hill Baptist ·Church, which he and a small group of Cheneyville summer residents established on Hurricane Creek. He was also headmaster at Spring Creek Planters Private Academy. Children of Cheneyville planters comprised the largest number of the students, but a few students from Bayou Rapides planters also attended [See Stafford, 280].

A letter from W.P. Ford from "Wallfield," apparently the name he gave his place on Hurricane Creek, was written on September 10,1859, to President William

T. Sherman at the Louisiana State Seminary, scheduled to open in 1860. The letter provides an insight to Ford's variety of small business enterprises:

> Dear Sir:
>   I was in Alexandria several days ago for the purpose of seeing the Committee appointed to have the State Institution of learning prepared for the reception of students. I saw only Mr. Henarie, who told me you were absent from the Parish. He recommended that I should see you on your return, or write to you. I wish to furnish the Institution with mattresses; and my object is to get you to recommend that the person who makes the purchases in that line for you, come and see my factory before he makes engagements elsewhere. I know that I can make it the permanent interest of the Institution to buy from me. If necessary, I will meet you in Alexandria any day that you will name. [signed] W.P. Ford [See Ford to Sherman]

Ford was a highly respected leader among the white planters in this area of Bayou Boeuf. His strategy regarding the treatment of slaves was not unusual; it was the modus operandi of many slave owners in the area. Later in Northup's narrative, Ford is quoted in an admonition to Tibeats, who mistreated Solomon:

> This is no way of dealing with them, when first brought into the country. It will have a pernicious influence and set them all running away. The swamps will be full of them. A little kindness would be far more effectual in restraining them, and rendering them obedient, than the use of such deadly weapons. Every planter on the bayou should frown upon such inhumanity. It is for the interest of all to do so [Northup, 150].

Since plantations formed the base of the Southern economy, policies related to master-slave relationships had been developed over the centuries of plantation operations from the time the first plantations were settled by the Virginia Company in 1616-1617. Plantations were originally considered "small colonies." To expand the population of the Virginia colony, Sir Edwin Sandys proposed societies of adventurers to send at their own expense with tenants, servants, and supplies; the associates were given certain governmental powers over the settlement that allowed them to effectively create an independent colony. These were "the hundreds of particular plantations" which saved the colony [See Robinson, 17-18, and Dowdy, 3-10].

69. "The Great Piney Woods" was a sixty-mile stretch of virgin long leaf pine forest extending west from the end of the alluvial soil from Indian Creek to the Sabine River, forming the borderline between Louisiana and Texas.

70. Alexandria, established in 1805, was named for its founder (or his daughter), Alexander Fulton. Fulton, migrating from Pennsylvania in the early 1790s, became

an Indian trader with a monopoly ceded to him and his partner, William Miller. Both acquired huge tracts of land. Their trading post was located at the present site of Alexandria on Red River. Miller married Mary Henrietta Wells, daughter of Samuel Levi Wells, whom the traders employed as surveyor of their lands. Alexandria grew slowly, having fewer than 2,500 residents in 1860. In 1812, when Louisiana became the eighteenth state in the Union, Major Amos Stoddard wrote that "Most of the settlers have planted themselves some miles back, and the whole population may be computed at about 640 whites and 200 slaves" [See Eakin, *A Source Book: Rapides Parish History*, 11, 13].

71. A small settlement called Lamourie developed on a small bayou of the same name that flowed into Bayou Boeuf. This settlement of pioneers included a large mill that produced shingles from logs supplied from the nearby woods to send to the Oklahoma Territory. A boarding house, a small general store, and a few primitive dwellings were located at the settlement. The entrepreneur, Ralph Smith, worked to secure construction of a gate which would help control the water flow. In the 1850s, after years of lobbying the state legislature, funds were made available to provide a brick gate in Bayou Lamourie with the purpose of regulating the water level of Bayou Boeuf into which the smaller bayou flows. The locks can still be seen about twelve miles south of Alexandria, Louisiana, from LA Highway 71 [See Eakin, *Washington, Louisiana*, 50-52; Eakin, *Rapides Parish: An Illustrated History*, 25; and Eakin, *The Centennial Album, Alexandria Daily Town Talk*, 158-160].

72. The first railroad built west of the Mississippi River was the Red River Railroad (later renamed for its founder, Ralph Smith Smith) in 1837. Smith had been employed in the Baltimore and Ohio Railroad project, one of the early railroads built in the United States. The Connecticut engineer, who had laid a mile of railroad in New Orleans, apparently was contacted by planters on the remote northern end of Bayou Boeuf with serious problems getting their produce to the New Orleans market. Smith, envisioning a transportation empire, purchased one of the first newspapers published in Alexandria, *The Planter Intelligencer*, and the *Rapides, Avoyelles, and Catahoula Advertiser*, to promote shares of stock to build the first railroad. With the first sale he built twelve miles of railroad from Alexandria to Lamourie [See Eakin, *Ezra Bennett and the World He Lived In*].

A planter's daughter living before the Civil War near Cheneyville left memoirs providing some insight into the situation of the little railroad; her recollections referred to the railroad after six more miles were added in 1842 to provide a terminal in Lecompte:

> When I was a child in the 1850's there was one (possibly more than one) railroad in Louisiana running into New Orleans and another one about 15 miles long between Alexandria and Lecompte. Lecompte was about 8 miles from Cheneyville, and we went there by carriage and took the car for Alexandria. We had coffee and a light breakfast very early, and left Lecompte at 8 or 9 A. M. and got back before dark. The "train" consisted of a locomotive, baggage car, and passenger car. When the Yankees destroyed the road they

"laughed until they cried" over the "loco" which was so antique that they had never seen the like. But the road was built and operated by a Yankee—Mr. Ralph Smith of the Northeast, who lived and died in Alexandria and whose descendants are still living there and in the parish. The stage was running all through my childhood and youth, and the war probably ended its day. [Boyd interview. A transcript of the interview is available in the Jesse Wright Collection, LSU Archives. Esther Wright Boyd was the wife of LSU president David French Boyd.]

73. "The Texas Road" actually referred to a number of trails beat out across the forests leading to and from Texas, both coming through Louisiana, one in the south and another in the northern part of the state. There were added trails alongside each of them, probably cut in the wilderness when heavy rains or obstacles in the trail caused travelers to go around the beaten path. These trails at some points were called the El Camino Real. Trails running from the little inland port of Washington to the Sabine River also were called the Texas Road, chiefly referring to a ridge of slightly higher ground than the surrounding woodlands, reaching through virgin pines to the Sabine River separating Louisiana and Texas. These trails were followed by Texas cowboys driving herds of cattle to the inland port of Washington for shipment by steamboat to the New Orleans market. Blacksmith shops available for shoeing horses and boarding places grew up along the Texas Road [See Eakin, *Washington, Louisiana*, 6-22; Eakin, *Rapides Parish . . .,*19-20; and Eakin, *Centennial Album . . .,*149].

74. Reuben Carnal and Timothy Flint owned plantations which Ford and his slaves walked across after leaving the Red River Railroad car. The turning rows through the Carnal and Flint plantations led to the Boeuf where a crude bridge was crossed to get into the Great Pine Woods.

Reuben Carnal in 1819 migrated from Martin County, North Carolina, to the Bayou Boeuf area and became one of the first planters in his section of the bayou. His home was in the pine woods, as were several planter homes, and he was buried there. He developed two large plantations—Quantico and Sugar Bend. One of his plantations became the settlement which developed into Lecompte. A native of Massachusetts, Timothy Flint was born in 1770 and studied for the ministry; he was ordained after graduating from Harvard College. He became pastor of a church in Massachusetts at Lunenburg, a name he bestowed on a Bayou Boeuf plantation given to his son. He became a Presbyterian missionary, traveling with his family through New York, Pennsylvania, Ohio, Indiana, Kentucky, and Illinois. He moved to Missouri, remained there briefly, and left for Arkansas before taking a church in New Orleans. A committee from Rapides Parish searching for a headmaster of a proposed new school to be founded contacted Reverend Flint, who with his wife and five children moved to Alexandria in 1823. The Rapides Academy opened that same year, with Reverend Flint and William Gunning in charge. The minister left the Academy in 1826 and moved to Cincinnati, where he opened a book business. He returned to his birthplace in Salem, Massachussetts, where he died in 1840. All of his children are buried in Alexandria [See Whittington, 92-95; and Gaeinne].

75. Concerning the characteristics of the land around Red River:

> Red River runs through the [Rapides] Parish, from the northwest to
> the southwest corner . . . Although I [Lockett] have classed it
> [Rapides Parish] among the Pine Hill parishes because the larger part
> of its surface is covered with the longleaf pine, it has a great deal of
> fertile land within its borders and is a wealthy, populous parish . . .
> On the northern side the base of the hills is not very far from the
> river. At Pineville, opposite Alexandria, the hills strike the river
> bank. From this point northward they bear off from the river . . .
> South of Pineville the hills are never more than a mile from the
> river's banks and form bluffs at numerous points down to Grimes'
> Bluff in Avoyelles just beyond the limits of Rapides. On the south
> side of Red River, there is a bluff just south of Colfax, called
> DeRoches' Bluff, then another above the mouth of Bayou Jean de
> Jean, and from this point, the base of the hills follows the course of
> Bayou Rapides and Bayou Boeuf to Cocodrie Lake . . . The space
> included between the lines thus traced is all Alluvial Land. It is
> between ten and fifteen miles wide and nearly forty miles long. The
> banks of Red River are generally arable land, settled and under
> cultivation . . . [See Lockett, 77-78]

76. Wild cattle, small, dark animals thought to be of Spanish origin, roamed the
woods. They were of no use for milk or meat, but first settlers killed and skinned
them for their hides, which they sold, and their horns, which sold on the New
Orleans market for manufacturers of buttons. Tallow made from the hides was also
a valuable commodity for the first settlers to market. Under the topic, "Wild Stock
in the Woods," Lewis Cecil Gray writes, "There were numerous wild cattle, horses,
and swine in Florida, and during the early years of British occupation hunting wild
stock was an important source of food" [See Gray, 139]. The wild cattle mentioned
as roaming Louisiana woods during the early colonial period, usually attributed to
Spanish herds, were more like those Gray notes existed in Maryland in 1661: ". . .
the governor was authorized to appoint a number of persons in each precinct to
hunt wild cattle, allowing two shares to the chief hunter, and one share to each of
the others, but reserving the tallow and hides to the Lord Proprietor" [See Gray,
139]. Perry G. Jordan focused on cattle in Texas, but the same situation with wild
cattle existed in Louisiana. Jordan notes that "wild cattle . . . sought refuge" and
that "sale impregnations appear in most part of the country, and are of benefit to
the large herds of wild and tame cattle which roam over the immense prairies and
woods" [See Jordan, 86].

77. William "3 C's" Martin was named for William Charles Cole Claiborne, the
governor of the Mississippi Territory, where Martin was born in 1802. By 1850 he
owned 25,000 acres of land and eighty-two slaves, making him one of the largest
slaveholders in the state; also, he was a member of the Rapides Parish Police Jury.
Like other planters, he maintained a home in the pine woods, where he lived much
of the year while operating his plantations in the lowlands. The site of the Martin

home where Reverend Ford and the three slaves stopped is still marked by a country road titled "Martin Springs Road." Martin Springs still gushes ice cold water that pours into the crystal clear creek that flowed at the rear of the Martin home. The Martins' private cemetery contains the graves of William C.C.C. Martin and members of his family. His wife was the former Sophia LaMothe, daughter of Polycarpe LaMothe, one of the early settlers of the area. LaMothe was married to Editha Wells, sister of Samuel Levi Wells, the surveyor who owned thousands of acres along Bayou Boeuf [See Pernaud; Stafford, 194; and U.S. Census, 1850].

78. During these years Ford was not wealthy. The lumber mill on forty acres of land in the pine woods was the smallest of lumber mills—called a "grasshopper mill" because of its small size and the fact that it was so light it could be moved. The mill was jointly owned with William Ramsay. With the creeks running through the Great Pine Woods no more than five or six feet deep, there was no way to generate power for any but the small mills such as Ford's, along with grist, syrup, and sugar mills, as well as small cotton gins. A cypress log preserved in Indian Creek for over a century was a part of Ford's sawmill and is now displayed at the library of Louisiana State University at Alexandria. It contains the imprint and incision of the water wheel. The 200-acre plantation on Bayou Boeuf was inherited by his wife. Ford owned eighteen slaves, according to the U.S. Slave Census, 1850. This number of slaves included men, women, and children. The hill farm he patented was not valuable at that time.

79. Sam is not on the list of slaves belonging to Beulah Baptist Church in Cheneyville, but he was very likely a member of the church. It was said that there were more black members of the church than whites, which would have been likely, since in plantation country, as in Cheneyville on Bayou Boeuf, there were seven or eight blacks to one white. Walton, Ford's slave, was one of a number of slaves listed as members of Beulah Baptist Church in Cheneyville [Beulah Baptist Church Membership List].

80. The name Taydem was not found in the 1850 United States Census for Louisiana. As scattered as settlers were during the settlement period, there were likely many missed by the census taker.

81. Rafting was nothing new to Louisiana, with nearly a third of its surface covered with trees, according to Dr. John Tarver, retired professor of history, Louisiana State University Agricultural Center [Tarver, 1992]. Northup may have been the first to raft logs over this particular route, which necessitated the narrow cribs and required rafting down Indian Creek to Bayou Clair and then to Bayou Lamourie. However, Louisiana forests are laced with streams, and the Indians would have developed rafting skills centuries before the Europeans came. Pioneers then settled these flat lands, learning from the Indians how to traverse and use the bayous and then adding their own improvements.

82. An unknown author described the Indians of the time:

> The tribe of Indians that was spoken of as living on Indian Creek
> were Choctaw Indians and there were few Indians of any other tribe.
> Banks, his wife, Maria, and Maria's mother, Aunt Betsy, were Biloxi
> Indians and of a much higher type than the Choctaws. Aunt Betsy
> was very old when I remember her living at Lecompte (in about
> 1887) and she made the most beautiful baskets. The Indians
> congregated at Lecompte, La., on a given date to be taken to the
> Indian Territory. Through miscarriage of plans, they were not sent
> for but for the kindness and generosity of James P. Moore, they
> would have suffered greatly. They were given camping grounds at
> the back of Mr. Moore's farm at Lecompte and they picked cotton
> and made baskets to pay for a few provisions to add to the wild
> game which they killed.
>   Mr. Moore gave them potatoes and corn. They pounded the
> corn and made a thick mush of it. The women hung their papooses
> up in the trees when they went to work, and the babies never cried.
> Mr. Moore knew Mr. Cascalla and his son-in-law, John Baltise. Ole
> Blue Eyes, son of the last chief of the Choctaw tribe, gave Mr.
> Moore his father's silver crown and some ornaments in the shape of
> crescents and a beaded belt that belonged to his father, the chief.
> [Author unknown, document dated 1827, sent to Sue Eakin by
> Agatha Brewer]

83. The Indians lived in the "Great Pine Woods" in Avoyelles Parish, neighboring parish to Rapides.

84. John M. Tibaut, an itinerant living in Rapides Parish, gave his occupation as manufacturing and trade in U.S. Census 1840. He owned one slave. He lists no one in his household but himself (Tibaut is referred to as Tibeats or Tibbets in *Twelve Years a Slave* as well as some other documents).

Chapter Eight

85. Franklin Ford was the sixth son of Jesse and Dully Barry Prince Ford of Kentucky. While William Prince Ford, his brother, was a Baptist minister, Franklin became a distinguished Presbyterian minister in Shreveport, Louisiana. He opened a private boarding school for girls in Minden, Louisiana. William Prince Ford co-signed a note with him to finance the school. When Franklin could no longer pay an increasing indebtedness on the school, William Prince Ford had to make the payment, for which he had no funds. This forced him to sell some slaves, including Solomon Northup, to meet his obligation [See Stafford, *Three Rapides Families*, 279].

The three major yellow fever epidemics during the decade of the 1850s and the increasing conflict between the South and North with threat of war undoubtedly affected the enrollment at the Minden Female Boarding School. The school did not close during those years, however. A Cheneyville native, Esther G.

Wright Boyd, attended Franklin Ford's boarding school until shortly after the war began. She related in an interview:

> Went in fall to Minden, La. [after graduating from Mansfield Boarding School] because Miss Brainard was teaching there. I was there three years, going home every vacation and graduating in July, 1861. Minden Female College was undenominational & our Pres. was the Rev. Jesse Franklin Ford [Presbyterian]. Miss Brainard's health failed & she returned to Brooklyn before I left Minden. I always roomed in the building called "Miss Brainard's house" and roomed next door to her.
>
> She was a fine woman, yet I did not become especially attached to her. As I look back on the five years I was off at school I understand perfectly why Mr. Boyd was so sure boarding schools were bad places for girls. I had a fine time, but with a mob of girls whose rudeness was hardly neutralized by the refinement of the teachers. It must have been during the John Brown episode that for several nights we were much alarmed by talk of negro insurrections. A dozen or more girls were gathered in my room one night with the door locked talking over the reports of such insurrections when there was a knock at the door & the voice of a mulatto woman who waited in the dining room was asking for me. We thought the tragedy was at hand! My recollection is that it was only an ordinary message.
>
> My sisters and brother at school in New Haven [sic] [CT] heard of some of the agitation over 'bleeding Kansas,' and Miss Dutton, the Principal at Grove Hall, presented a flag to someone & made the presentation remarks. I do not remember that there was any sectional feeling aroused among the Southern pupils.
>
> On my graduation day there were few young men in the audience for they had gone to the war. Their drills before leaving were of great interest to us but we had no idea of the seriousness of the situation. After examinations were over, my roommate, Annie Conway, and I were notified one day that we were wanted in Mr. Ford's study. We went down & he informed us that I had received the Valedictory address & she the salutatory. The other girls of the class came over to congratulate us. We wrote our compos—every word, & therefore they were honest at least. And so my school days ended. I was anxious to go to school, but was prevented. Sally Stafford went back to Minden the following session, but as the war grew more serious she was sent for & returned before the close of the session. Before we came home in 1861 her father (my bro.-in-law) and brother (17-years-old) had joined the Army of Virginia. From Minden we went by carriage to Mr. McFarland's plantation, which was on Red River. The river was very low and we stayed there several days waiting for a boat. Mrs. McFarland was Bro. Leroy's half sister & was a handsome woman with black eyes & black hair. She had been married before & had two pretty brunette children—

Ruffie (Ruffin, I suppose) & Nina. On the Sunday we spent there, July 21, the Battle of Bull Run was fought, but we knew nothing of it then. [Boyd interview. Esther Wright Boyd was the wife of LSU President David French Boyd. A transcript of the interview is available in the Jesse Wright Collection, LSU Archives.]

86. Peter Baillio Compton was born April 17, 1818, the son of John Compton and Amelia Baillio. He married Esther Eliza Tanner, daughter of Lodowick and Ann Martha Tanner, who owned Tiger Bend Plantation in the same area where Edwin Epps would buy land later. Although Peter Baillio Compton was born on his father's estate at Meeker, three miles south of Lecompte, his own plantation was located on Red River thirty miles away. Unless the property was a part of his father's vast estate of 6,200 unimproved acres and 2,300 improved acres, no slaves are listed for Peter Baillio. He could not have operated a plantation without slaves. The John Compton Estate (his father's property) included 377 slaves, so probably there were some living on his son's plantation [See Stafford, *Three Rapides Families . . .*, 153; and Menn, 377].

87. Tibeats owed William Prince Ford $400, and Northup himself was the collateral for that money. Later in the narrative, as Northup implies, the existence of the mortgage of $400 literally saved Northup's life as Tibeats became enraged and planned to hang him.

88. Bayou Boeuf and the land surrounding it are accurately described here:

Bayou Boeuf rises in a cypress lake near McNutt's Hill, and, after receiving several clear streams from the pine woods, becomes a bold, broad bayou some six or eight miles below Alexandria, and so continues throughout its course. Its total length to the junction with Bayou Cocodrie is not much less than eighty miles. It receives, as a distributary from Red River, Bayou Robert, which debouches from the river . . . and enters Bayou Boeuf twelve miles from that place. Three miles farther it sends off Bayou Lamourir [*sic*] through an extensive swamp back to Red River . . . The Boeuf has at all seasons a steady current of pure water and is one of the prettiest bayous of Louisiana. On either side of the Boeuf and Bayou Robert throughout their length are, or rather were [before the four years of the Civil War] some of the finest plantations in the state. The front lands of Bayou Boeuf are fertile in the highest degree—light, sandy, reddish colored, and easily worked . . . The Boeuf and the Cocodrie by their junction form Courtableau, . . . [See Lockett, 78] and,

The northern section of the Bayou Boeuf to which Northup was brought as a slave was not settled until around 1812 because of its remoteness to New Orleans when Louisiana became a state. Supplies had to be obtained and farm products shipped on the Boeuf. After the inland port of Washington developed on Courtableau Bayou, large warehouses were constructed in which cotton, sugar cane, molasses, and other products from the Boeuf plantations were stored to wait for a steamboat coming from New Orleans to transport crops to market and secure farm and family supplies. The Bayou Boeuf region developed a busy commerce, serving as the lifeline of the pioneer families migrating to establish plantations there. [See Eakin, *Washington* . . .,3-9. See a present-day photo of Bayou Boeuf taken at the old William Prince Ford property in the Extras & More section of our website at www.TwelveYearsASlave.org]

89. Peter Tanner, who was the son of Robert Tanner, one of the founders of Cheneyville, with his wife Providence, became an influential planter, first owning a plantation south of Cheneyville adjoining that of his brother, Jabez. The Ford children crossed a small bridge across the bayou to attend private school at the Peter Tanner plantation "Big House" [See Bennett, S.P.B.; see a present-day photo of the Big House owned by Jabez Tanner and a sugar cane field on the property in the Extras & More section of our website at www.TwelveYearsASlave.org].

Porter and Barbra Wright's detailed account of people buried in the cemetery of Bayou Rouge Baptist Church, Evergreen, Louisiana, in their *The Old Burying Ground*, provides insights into the person who was Peter Tanner:

> Wheeler dealer Tanner was a big man even among the Grandees on the Rio Boeuf. 3,400 acres it is said, his home and all, he sold because he and his next door neighbor, brother Jabez, in 1859 had this violent disagreement over who was the rightful owner of a $5 gin pole. That was the cause, as handed down to Great Grandson Dan Brunson, for the sale and the move to Tanner Hill in Evergreen. The Tanners were known to have these outbursts among themselves. But for an outside intruder, caveat! We have no reason to believe the two brothers were not reconciled. Both were extremely religious. Jabez was the founding father of the Christian Church in Cheneyville and Peter was a deacon at Beulah Baptist Church there. They often preached at their respective meeting houses. The church book at Bayou Rouge Baptist does make mention of an 1846 resolution requesting Peter Tanner 'to preach here as often as convenient . . .' Peter Tanner served in the Louisiana Legislature from Rapides Parish. [See Wright, 74-75]

90. Anderson Leonard Chafin [spelled "Chapin" in text] married Sarah Ann Providence Rutledge and lived at the edge of the Great Pine Woods about a dozen miles from the settlement later called Lecompte. He was in the tanning business [See Stafford, *Three Rapides Families* . . ., 33).

91. The term "Great House" reflects a misunderstanding of what was meant by "the Big House" originally and then elaborated upon by people without knowledge of plantation country. The "Big House" was probably first applied by slaves on plantations, and it was adopted by people mostly outside the South in its literal

meaning. In reality, the expression meant to slave workers the designation of the site of the home of the planter, or master. Some of these houses were modest log buildings when Northup arrived on Bayou Boeuf. The inference of wealth comes from use of the term by outsiders, but planters often had little or no wealth. Thousands of acres of land were awarded to some men by the Spanish government for surveying land, but it took years of work to convert the land into cultivation. Land appreciated from a nominal value of fifty cents to several dollars in the first decade, beginning in 1812 when Louisiana became a state, to $40 or $50 an acre by the 1850s. When unsettled lands lay from the Mississippi River to the Pacific Ocean, land was either there for the taking or bought for a pittance [See Eakin and Culbertson, 194].

A plantation was a place employing a kind of farming involving a relatively large work force on a relatively large area of land. It was also a lifestyle. There were many plantations of 200-1,000 acres of land in the Lower Red River Valley. When Solomon Northup was in the area, land was still being cleared of woodlands and made ready for cultivation, which meant that even large landholdings ordinarily did not indicate the size of the area cultivated.

For the pioneers among whom Northup lived, land was of relatively little value at a time when thousands and thousands of acres to the Pacific were open for settlers. Land on the Boeuf sold by speculators to settlers ranged from about $1.25 an acre to $5.00. As late as the early 1900s, the railroad companies issued large numbers of booklets to promote settlement along their lines. The available land not yet settled included some in the Bayou Boeuf area. One of the monthly brochures, *The New Southwest Devoted to the Great Southwest*—actually a tabloid-sized, slick-paper publication of about twenty-eight pages—was published by the Missouri Pacific-Iron Mountain System in Saint Louis, Missouri, and advertised such things as "Special One-Way Colonist Excursions" and "Winter Tourist Rates for Colorado, Texas, Louisiana, and Mexico," emphasizing the vast amount of unsettled land that was available. In the March brochure, the Missouri Pacific Railway and Iron Mountain Route also advertised "Homeseeker's Excursions" through Arkansas, Texas, Louisiana, Kansas, Missouri, Indian and Oklahoma Territory." [See *The New Southwest Devoted to the Great Southwest*, published by Missouri Pacific Immigation Bureau]

92. "Piazza" is not a word used by people in Bayou Boeuf country. "Porch" or "gallery" would have been the words used by people in this area. Wilson may have substituted "piazza" for one of the local words.

93. The editor has found no account of the details of this incident.

94. Cook and Ramsay, as overseers, probably were overstepping their authority to make a decision to hang the rebellious Solomon, but they were acting under the mandate that a slave must not be allowed to strike a white man. There was the belief that this could incite more violence between blacks and whites within the tightly controlled plantation society. Since plantations formed the base of all Southern society, this control was critical. In such an encounter of a slave with a white man, the danger to the black slave was overwhelming. A Louisiana law

passed in 1806 provided the death penalty for striking a master, mistress, or one of their children so as to cause contusion or effusion of blood. A similar act in 1814 included striking an overseer with similar effect [See Gray, 517].

Dr. Edgar Thompson, premiere plantation scholar of Duke University, called the unwritten code that ruled plantation country, "The Plantation Survival Code." This code was required in the caste society where maintaining the status quo had much to do with securing the base of the economy: the plantation and slavery. The code included rules developed to maintain plantations with a dependable slave work force, and breaking them was not permitted—whether by a white or black dissenter.

Gray confirms the role of neighbors and the community regarding the control of slaves:

> The actual well-being of slaves, however, was dependent not so much on laws as to the humane instincts and economic interest of the master, and the power of neighborhood opinion. The latter was undoubtedly an important source of protection.
>
> Sir Charles Lyell declared, "The condition of negroes is the least enviable in such out-of-the-way and half-civilized adventurers and uneducated settlers, who have little control of their passions, and, who, when they oppress their slaves, are not checked by public opinion as in more advanced communities." [See Gray, 517]

James Cook, one of the overseers mentioned in this chapter, was married to Mary Eliza Robert, daughter of Alonzo and Tuzette Eliza Pearce Robert. He managed his father-in-law's plantation south of Cheneyville [See O'Neal, 95-97]. Ramsey, the other overseer mentioned, was a partner in Ford's sawmill venture, as previously noted.

95. Tibeats, an itinerant carpenter, would have had low status in the plantation community partly because he had not learned to live by the rules such as the one enunciated by William Prince Ford and overheard by Solomon Northup. Such a person was almost as unwelcome as an abolitionist in planter society.

Chapter Nine

96. John David Cheney married twice: Elizabeth Martha Fendon, by whom he had two children, and Henrietta Polhill Audebert, by whom he had two other children. His progenitor, according to Stafford, was John Cheney, who was a resident of Newton, Massachusetts in 1637 [Stafford, *Three Pioneer Families . . .*, 406].

97. "John Gilpin" is a reference to William Cowper's popular comic ballad, "The Diverting History of John Gilpin," published first in 1792 in England. It is reflective of the period in which David Wilson, the ghost writer, lived.

98. Louisiana was not alone in denying a black man the right to testify in court. Solomon Northup was not allowed to testify in the case filed by him and attorney

Henry Northup in the court in Washington, D.C., against the men associated with the slave pen; he was offered as a witness but rejected "solely on the ground that I was a colored man" [*Twelve Years a Slave*, 216]. Though Northup celebrated the arraignment of his kidnappers in New York on July 11, 1854, the trial never materialized, so we don't know whether his testimony would have figured in the trial or not ["An Individual Identified by Solomon Northup ...", 2].

99. Francis Myers was among the migrants to Cheneyville from South Carolina. He was married to Alma Coe "about 1840." He is listed in the U.S. Census, 1840. He was a frequent customer at the Ezra Bennett store and evidently had a plantation in the same area as that of William Prince Ford's place. Francis Myers went with Thaddeus Sobieski Robert to pursue the 1849 Gold Rush and never returned to Louisiana [Stafford, *Three Rapides Families*, 74, 95, 121. See photo of Bennett's store in the Extras & More section of our website at www.TwelveYearsASlave.org].

100. Peter Tanner, age thirty-eight in 1850, and his brother, Jabez, forty, probably represented the best and worst of traits associated with leading planters along the Boeuf [U.S. Census, 1850]. This is especially true of Peter. He saw himself as the cocksure leader of the area, and he was certainly highly influential. He was on the board of the Planters Private Academy about fifteen miles from Bayou Boeuf at Cheneyville. The goal of the leading planters, which was passionately pursued, was not only preventing slaves from learning how to read and write, but also did not support the education of the white masses. Private academies were set up for exclusive use by the planters, using state funds for the construction of buildings under a policy of "beneficiarism." A select few "indigents" could attend these private academies, which existed across the state.

Peter Tanner, owning a large acreage of land, which appreciated in value decade after decade, is listed in the U.S. Census as having real property valued at $17,000 in 1850, [U.S. Census, 1850] with his brother Jabez listed as having a value of $30,000 in real property. Peter owned nineteen slaves, eight of these being between the ages of four to eight years. In this period when families, black or white, included a dozen or more children, nineteen slaves may have meant there were only two families on his plantation, and therefore a small farming operation despite the large acreage of land. However, Peter did operate a sugar plantation in Cuba and owned slaves there; other planters of the area also operated sugar plantations in Cuba, as evidenced by correspondence in the Ezra Bennett Collection.

Peter became a representative to the state legislature and was appointed to various positions of importance in Rapides Parish. He was known for being "hot-headed" and for his frequent outbursts in hearty laughs [Stafford, *Three Pioneer Families . . .*, 306].

Neither Peter nor Jabez were listed among large slaveowners (those with over fifty slaves). It was Jabez who was known among their neighbors for reading the Bible to his slaves on Sundays. Whether David Wilson transferred the story to Peter or whether Peter adopted the habit is not known.

101. The editor found no surviving stocks left on Bayou Boeuf, but did locate a set at Magnolia Plantation, Cane River, now included in a national park.

102. Providence Tanner, wife of one of Cheneyville's founders, Robert, was instrumental in the founding of Beulah Baptist Church at Cheneyville in 1816. Both Tanner sons, Peter and Jabez, considered themselves religious, but it was Jabez who headed the historic break of many members of Beulah Baptist Church. More slaves, who sat in a balcony of the church, belonged to Beulah Baptist than white people. In the early 1840s a division developed from an intense argument over predestination, a concept rejected by Jabez. The split impacted the Boeuf community so much that a saying repeated by residents from that decade was: "The Up the Bayou Tanners didn't speak to the Down the Bayou Tanners." Peter did not leave Beulah Baptist, but Jabez led the dissidents and published a booklet, *A Concise History of the Rise and Fall of the State of Affairs in the Religious World at this Place.* Jabez led in the founding of the Campbellite Church in 1842.

Reverend William Prince Ford presided at the installation of the board of the Campbellite Church. Because of this act and the act of serving communion to a Methodist at Spring Hills Baptist Church near his home on Hurricane Creek in the pine woods, William Prince Ford was expelled as a member of Beulah Baptist and from his position as pastor of the Hurricane Creek Baptist Church. The founder of the Campbellite Movement, Alexander Campbell from Kentucky, spoke at the new Campbellite Church in Cheneyville [See Ford letter to Wright; Eakin, *A Source Book: Rapides Parish History*, 33].

Charles David Bennett, brother of Ezra, in 1894 wrote from Cayuga, New York, to his niece: "From a region almost destitute of religious meetings, it has become used to many of them—the whites and the blacks. Besides preaching and social meetings in Cheneyville, meetings were commonly held in the Ford and Eldred neighborhood or in the Tanner and Roberts on the other . . ." [See Bennett to Virginia].

103. Peter Tanner became one of the deacons at Big Cane Baptist Church in St. Landry Parish after he moved to Evergreen in Avoyelles Parish [See Fisher].

Chapter Ten

104. The plantation "Big Houses" were usually built several decades after the plantations were in operation. They were usually built of lumber from woodlands in the back of the plantations—ordinarily with high ceilings to offer better circulation during the hot semi-tropical summers, usually one story but sometimes more. They were often made from cypress and were mostly "dog trot" houses with a central opening, later closed in to become a hall, with rooms on either side.

105. There was no law against slaves swimming in the waters of many bayous, creeks, lakes, and rivers, though some slave owners may have forbidden it.

106. Cocodrie (Pacoudrie in *Twelve Years a Slave*) Bayou marks the boundary of the alluvial soil in the area where Solomon Northup lived as a slave in the pine woods.

On Bayou Boeuf, the term "across Cocodrie" became an epithet conveying the idea of a mysterious and fearsome place. There were areas of swamp in the forests "across Cocodrie," but there were larger stretches of pine trees growing on low hills. There were tales of how folks protected the area from outsiders and made their own rules by which they lived, no matter what the outside world with its laws tried to force upon them. In the twentieth century, Prohibition bootlegging was said to be flourishing "across Cocodrie," and the inhabitants did not allow blacks to go there.

107. There were bears, wildcats, and reptiles, but the presence of tigers may have been a local rumor or myth.

108. The Ford plantation faced a ridge known as the Texas Road that wound through the pine woods from Washington, Louisiana, to the northwest. The road was called "Texas Road" because it reached the Sabine River, the boundary between Louisiana and Texas. [For more information, see endnote 73].

Chapter Eleven

109. Oranges do not grow along the Boeuf, so it's possible that Solomon was referring to tangerines.

110. John David Cheney, descendent of one of the founders of Cheneyville, William Fendon Cheney, owned eighteen slaves in 1855 [See *Biographical and Historical Memoirs of Northwest Louisiana*, 607; see endnote 96].

111. John Dunwoody ("Dunwoodie" in *Twelve Years a Slave*) (1782-1862) owned a plantation in the pine woods southwest of Lecompte. He married Delia Pearce in 1807, and they had three children, including Mary L. Dunwoody, the mother of Mary Dunwoody McCoy mentioned later in the narrative. John Dunwoody was born in Georgia. The Dunwoody cemetery, restored by the town of Lecompte, lies at the site of his plantation in the pine woods near Lecompte [See Stafford, *Three Pioneer Families . . .*, 403].

112. The strategy of William Prince Ford relating to the treatment of slaves by owners was not unique to the Reverend Ford. An unwritten Plantation Survival Code included rules that planters respected even above the law. Planters were the final authority in "the small colonies," as the first plantations laid in Virginia in the seventeenth century were called. They were macho individualists accustomed to obedience from everybody residing on the plantation, including their wives and children. As patriarchs concerned with every aspect of the lives of the people on their plantations, they simultaneously bore the responsibility for all residents— food, shelter, health and medical care, and burials.

Planters sometimes risked action against themselves by fellow planters in cases of extraordinary violence or cruelty against a slave or slaves. The Plantation Survival Code included combined planter action against a planter whose behavior toward his slaves threatened the working relationship between planters and their slaves. The reason for the Plantation Survival Code was practical. Without slaves working under the direction of a planter, no crops could be raised, which meant no income to pay off the borrowed money the planter owed. To protect their interests, planters attempted to tightly control every aspect of plantation life possible, especially since they worked under the sure knowledge that nothing could be done to protect the crops they were cultivating against other substantial risks, such as acts of nature—too much rain in the tropical climate, too much drought, winds, early freezes that made the sugar cane worthless—or the devastation caused by pests such as caterpillars and boll weevils. Crop failures happened often. In addition to the unwritten code, a Louisiana law passed in 1830 allowed courts to take control of slaves abused by a planter, sell them, and reimburse the owner from the proceeds of the sale [See Robert to Eakin].

113. The Big Cane Brake consisted of a thick grove of what must have been exceptionally large, tall switch canes through which ran Little Bayou Rouge. Pioneer settlers reported that thick forests of switch canes grew densely along the bayous of the area. In these lowlands with a network of rivers and bayous switch canes seemed to cover the land. Reportedly, an early settler on horseback riding through the canes found them taller than his height on horseback [See Goins and Caldwell].

114. Randal Eldred, Jr.("Eldret" in the narrative) was born June 1, 1780, in Beaufort District, Carolina. He married Esther Susannah Robert in February, 1801. Shortly after their marriage, they moved to Woodville, Mississippi, and a few years later moved to a bend on Bayou Boeuf about six miles south of Cheneyville. This spot at the bend of the bayou became known as Eldred's Bend. After the first wife of Randal Eldred, Jr. died in 1847, he married her sister, Mary. He died January 10, 1850 [See Stafford, *Three Pioneer Families . . .*, 208].

115. Hugh M. Keary, William V. Keary, and Patrick F. Keary (referred to as Carey in the narrative) were three brothers migrating into the Cheneyville area around 1858 from Wilkinson County, Mississippi. Because of overwhelming indebtedness, they left Mississippi to establish themselves as planters of cotton and cane in Louisiana. The Keary brothers were sued in 1865 for $14,625 plus interest and court costs by William A. Gasquet of New Orleans in relation to the purchase of a plantation south of Cheneyville in November, 1858. The property is described in the legal papers:

> A certain tract of land belonging to the said Hugh M. Keary and known by the name of the North Bend Plantation in the Parish of Rapides . . . bordered above by lands of P. Tanner and below by those of John Dunwoody and containing 1600 acres more or less together with the buildings thereon, horses, mules, cattle, and implements of husbandry belonging to the said Keary brothers and attached to said plantation. [Gasquet vs. Keary]

Hugh Keary was forty-nine years old and William V. Keary, forty-one. Patrick F. Keary was the youngest brother. They owned 140 slaves living in thirty-five dwellings. The value of their property is listed as $450,000. One thousand acres of their land was listed as improved and 3,375 as unimproved. The cash value of the farm was listed as $180,000 in 1860 [Menn, 134-135].

Mostly young men and few white women lived in this frontier country. Both older Keary brothers lived with black women in lifelong relationships. On file in Avoyelles Parish courthouse is a document placed there by Hugh M. Keary declaring his first four of fourteen children by Mary Thompson, a mulatto, as his legitimate children. He sent his children to Philadelphia to obtain an education. He left all of his property to his children [See Keary Papers; Menn, 134; Conveyance records and other documents filed at the Office of the Clerk of Court, Avoyelles Parish]. Patrick Keary, the youngest brother, married the niece of Jefferson Davis, who Davis had taken as his own when her father died.

116. There were no tigers in the Big Cane Brake, so this could have been a local rumor or myth. There were bears and alligators, however.

117. Jim Burns was not an example of a planter who used only women in his labor force. According to the list provided by the 1850 United States Census, James Burns owned two mulatto females, ages fifteen and forty-five; two black females, ages fifty and seventeen; three black males, ages forty-five, twenty-seven, and two years, and one mulatto male, age sixteen. The planter was an early settler with his small plantation located at Holmesville, a small port on Bayou Boeuf about twenty miles south of Cheneyville. The name Holmesville changed over the century to Eola, named for a local merchant. Burns' plantation lay across the Boeuf from that of Edwin Epps and is still standing and occupied by a descendant [See Morgan to Eakin].

118. John Fogleman (Fogaman in the narrative), born in 1795, was the son of George and Sarah Hoozers Fogleman. He married Polly Sandefur, daughter of another pioneer family from Holmesville, on January 1, 1819, in the Opelousas courthouse. All of the plantations around Holmesville were small plantations of 200 or 300 acres [See Morgan to Eakin].

119. Peter Baillio Compton was the son of John Compton and Amelia Baillio. His father was a pioneer planter with a big plantation located about three miles south of Lecompte. His mother was the daughter of a large planter whose plantation was located near Alexandria [See endnote 86; Stafford, *Three Pioneer Families...*, 153].

120. Madam Tanner was Ann Martha Tanner, widow of Lodowick Tanner. Peter Baillio Compton was her son-in-law. Ann Martha Tanner was an extraordinary woman who took over the Tiger Bend plantation that had originally been owned by her husband, Lodowick, and his two brothers. The three brothers went bankrupt and would have lost the property but for Peter Baillio Compton, who had married Esther Eliza Tanner and redeemed the property of the Tanners. Ezra Bennett, a New York migrant who married Ann Martha Eldred's sister, kept books for Ann

Martha when she first operated the plantation. Information about the Tanners can be found in the Bennett Papers and the Sue Eakin Papers, both housed at the LSU Alexandria Library Archives [See Stafford, *Three Pioneer Families . . .*, 153].

121. Bayou Huffpower ("Huff Power" in the narrative) is a small bayou that flows east about nine miles south of Cheneyville. The bayou flows through the town of Bunkie today.

122. Edwin Epps was an overseer from Oakland Plantation, patented by Archibald P. Williams and located about ten miles south of Alexandria. Epps received eight slaves (1850 census) as settlement from Williams after his default on payment of salary to his overseer. Epps moved south to Avoyelles Parish and after a few years bought 300 acres at Holmesville.

    Thus, the slaves who were fellow workers with Solomon Northup also lived on Oakland Plantation. The sale of Northup (Platt) to Epps occurred on April 9, 1843, for $1,500. Epps paid cash for the slave ["Conveyance Record Q." Document 5754, John M. Tibaut to Edwin Epps, Avoyelles Parish Courthouse, Marksville, Louisiana, May 3, 1843, 261-262].

Chapter Twelve

123. Joseph B. Robert was the son of Joseph Robert, one in a group of Hugenot descendants migrating to the Boeuf area around 1817. Joseph B. Robert started a small store on a bend of the Bayou Boeuf called Eldred's Bend, which belonged to his uncle and aunt, Randal and Susannah Robert Eldred. Young Joseph B. chose a highly desirable place where keelboats and flatboats in the Bayou Boeuf commerce could anchor alongside the store. At that time a lively commerce on Bayou Boeuf was critical to the settlement of the rich land alongside the bayou. Communication with New Orleans was essential to bring necessary farm and home supplies from New Orleans and to ship crops to "the city's" markets. Funds to produce crops had to be borrowed through financial agents called factors in New Orleans, usually representing financiers in New York and Boston [See Eakin, *Centennial Album . . .*,154].

    The bayou was too narrow and not consistently deep enough for even small steamboats. Each boat in the Boeuf commerce rang a bell distinctive from all others so that the crews of other boats became aware of its location [See Lyles interview; Wells interview]. So narrow and shallow was Bayou Boeuf that often derricks were built over the flatboats so that teams of heavy oxen or horses could be harnessed on both sides to pull the boat along the bayou. Olmstead noted that, instead of slaves, Irishmen navigated the bayou under an experienced captain [See Olmstead, 273]. This bayou commerce operated between the northernmost port at Cheneyville and the destination about seventy miles southeast at the small inland port of Washington on Bayou Courtableau. Small landings along the numerous plantations on both sides of the bayou were stops for the boats. Bayou Boeuf and Cocodrie Bayou, which ran roughly parallel the same distance and direction as the Boeuf, flowed together a mile and a half below Washington to form a deep enough bayou to bring steamboats through a hazardous maze of streams from New Orleans.

Joseph B. Robert moved to the Bayou Clear/Huffpower location after selling his store to Ezra Bennett, son-in-law of the Eldreds, in 1832. Robert's small cottage on Bayou Huffpower where he moved after leaving Eldred Bend is preserved today as a core within the handsome frame house belonging to Mrs. Catherine Luke near Bunkie [Abstract of the Luke Place courtesy of J.B. Luke, Jr. and Mrs. Catherine Luke, Bunkie, LA].

124. Solomon Northup/Platt was an intelligent observer of farming on Bayou Boeuf, and the ghost writer may have also used other sources of information about farming.

The journal *American Agriculturist* "absorbed more than thirty agricultural journals, including *Genesee Farmer, Alabama Farmer, American Farmer's Magazine, Connecticut Homestead, Farm Journal and Progressive Farmer* and others" [WorldCat database, August 13, 2004]. Regular contributions from R.L. Allen, of New Orleans, to *American Agriculturist*, shed some light on the status of agriculture and farm migrants in the newly settled country:

> No country of equal extent on the face of the globe seems to possess such a prodigal affluence, such an unstinted measure of agricultural wealth as the alluvial portions of Louisiana . . . every acre of this State seems teeming with the elements of vegetation, the foundation of future wealth, and the sustenance of future millions. And every section of it is accessible within a convenient distance, by navigable waters, or admits of the easy construction of roads. Even the waters which pervade and border the State, would furnish sufficient food for a population larger than the population than now inhabits it . . . Actual want or suffering under such circumstances cannot exist, but that absence of individual prosperity is often to be found, that creates a morbid restlessness under present exigencies, and induces efforts for its alleviation in the removal to some fancied El Dorado in the yet unexplored wilderness . . . (Editor's comment: This statement was probably registering dismay at the record number of migrants from the eastern states who traveled through Louisiana, perhaps stayed a year or two, and moved on to Texas. "GTT" was a popular slogan of those days: GONE TO TEXAS! Land to the west was offered free of charge).
>
> Cotton may be ranked next [to sugar cane] in the order of the staples of this state. But a few years since this was the leading product; but while it has been reclaiming new territory and advancing in quantity, in much of the old, the profit afforded by the cane has enabled the latter to usurp many of the plantations hitherto

exclusively devoted to the former. In the cultivation of this leading export of America, much improvement has been witnessed within the few past years; and although excessive rain or drought, the army worm or caterpillar, blight, mildew, or rust, occasionally disappoints the hopes of the planter, yet a closer study of the habits and diseases of the plant, a careful selection of seed, the introduction of new and improved varieties, and a nicer and more careful cultivation, are all aiding to swell the aggregate of the cotton-fields. [See Allen, 336-338]

Allen's comments at the close of the article carry additional insight into cultivation in the Bayou Boeuf region:

The false ambition for large plantations, and operations and achievements beyond the legitimate means of the owner, has been and still continues to be, the bane of citizens of our new States. This policy may result in giving to the few, large landed estates, yet really less pecuniary income, than would result to the shrewd manager where a denser population existed, and more aggregate and active wealth circulated among the mass, the necessary result of a greater and more intense production. In looking over some of the plantations of this region, where large bodies of land are either wholly or partially unsubdued, and the remainder admits of much higher cultivation, one cannot but be forcibly impressed with the consideration, that the old maxim, divide and conquer, if applied to southern plantations generally, would have a much more pregnant and salutary bearing on the welfare of the human race, than was ever assigned to it by the ambitious Roman. A little land well tilled, while vastly more beneficial to the State and the middle property-classes, is, perhaps, of equal or even greater advantage to the opulent, than the present system of over-grown and over-cultivated estates . . . [See Allen, 338]

125. Wilson writes of the whipping of slaves from morning until night; this reported continual whipping raises questions about how such violence against the bodies of slaves might have affected their work and value. While there may have been countless acts of individual cruelty and even a single whipping would be abhorrent, Wilson's claim of around-the-clock whippings may have been a dramatic embellishment to appeal to the book's audience. This continuous violence would have run counter to the unwritten Plantation Survival Code designed to restrain the slaves and maintain the status quo under the strategy described by William Prince Ford in the narrative [See endnote 112]. The slave owner's investment in slaves represented the extent of his negotiable property [See endnote 58].

Available are written records for five people who lived on these same Boeuf plantations, and they provide no description of daily atrocities in Boeuf plantation country. One of the five people, William O'Neal, was a slave himself during the same period as Northup who dealt with the same people; he also employed a ghost writer for his own book. O'Neal made enough money on his free time to buy his freedom. In dealing with his white master and son in his purchase, O'Neal told of their dishonesty, causing him to pay twice the price for himself, much higher than the price upon which the slave had agreed [See O'Neal, chapter 6].

126. While there is a lack of evidence in Bayou Boeuf antebellum records suggesting a general, frequent use of extraordinary violence against slaves, there was at least one instance of an extrajudicial execution of nine slaves, who were hanged for an aborted insurrection headed by another slave named Lew Cheney, as described in a later chapter of *Twelve Years a Slave*, Chapter 17 [See Eakin, *Rapides Parish: An Illustrated History*, 26]. There were also cases of violence against abolitionists. A letter from Ralph Smith Smith of Waverly Plantation alludes to the murder of an abolitionist who came into the area to encourage slaves to organize against the planters.

127. Cotton picking did not change very much from Northup's years on Bayou Boeuf to the editor's years growing up on Compromise Plantation on the same bayou in the 1920s and 30s. Skill and speed at cotton picking were highly admired during both periods. Patsey's skill at cotton picking evoked the deepest admiration, for rare cotton pickers in her day achieved local stardom for what seemed to them the magic number of pounds: 300. However, it is doubtful that she possessed the skill to pick 500 pounds. In the editor's day, she watched the high respect shown to the best cotton pickers when the cotton was weighed at the end of the day. However, those numbers caused anxious looks on some faces of pickers if they might not have picked as much that day as they had hoped and therefore might lose status among their peers. There were looks of triumph and looks of disappointment, but everybody admired the picker who could pull the soft, fluffy cotton from the burr that held it tightly. Residents of the Boeuf region always looked forward to cotton season. The white sea of cotton was beautiful, the hottest weather was over, and the competition among people laughing while their fingers were flying to pick the largest quantity lifted everyone's spirit.

128. The work hours in the field were long. According to Gray:

> In the south as a whole hours of labor were about the same as for farm work in other parts of the United States; that is, from 15 to 16 hours a day in the busy season, including meal time and intervals allowed for rest . . . Breakfast was sent to the field, and a half hour allowed for eating. Two hours of rest were given at noon. Work stopped at sundown, but in rush seasons might be prolonged until dark . . . In the winter season and in 'lay-by' periods labor requirements were likely to be lighter. . . . It was the usual custom to allow Sundays to be free except in rush periods. [See Gray, 557]

Planters did work their slaves on Sundays; by Louisiana law, slaves were to be paid for Sunday work. Cotton pickers did not work in the moonlight in the fields of this area because the unwritten code by which planters operated would not allow it, if for no other reason. An effort was made by a large planter on Red River named Levi Wilson to work his seventy-five slaves at night, at least twenty miles from Cheneyville. His slaves were to pick at night by building large bonfires on the turning rows to provide light. Area planters called on him and had his slaves picked up and sold, returning the money to him. [See Robert to Eakin, August 1963]. Planters in these situations operated to protect their livelihood and lifestyle, and joined forces with other planters to enforce the unwritten rules for slave owners. The deviating planter had no choice but to comply with demands [See Gray, 511].

129. What the slave had for food was largely decided by the effort made by the slave and his family members. People helped themselves to the plentiful resources of fields, streams, and woodlands of this frontier period. As one black woman explained, "We took what we had and made it into what we needed." Some slaves raised hogs in their back yards to kill for winter meat and had chickens as well. Nobody lived on small portions of corn and pork. The fatty meat needed for cooking vegetables was probably issued to the slaves. A few planters had food cooked to serve all slaves during times when work required every hand available to complete jobs such as picking cotton "before bad weather set in." One common food, "cush-cush," no doubt introduced by the Louisiana French, is made of cornmeal dampened and fried in a small amount of grease. This is still a favorite for many Louisianians. Small animals were also popular with slaves. As Solomon Northup recounts: "The flesh of the coon is palatable, but there is nothing in all butcherdom so delicious as roasted possom." In the rich soil ditch banks along the fields grew pumpkins and cushaw, and ordinarily planters reserved many rows in the fields for vegetables, ready for the picking to everybody on the plantation. Wild turkey, deer, squirrels, quail, doves, and rabbits populated the woodlands in the back of the plantations in the frontier days. Wild pecans and walnuts, berries and mayhaws came with the spring. The many waterways held a plentiful supply of fish for catching or seining even as late as the 1950s.

130. The claim that slaves were expected to sleep on foot-wide boards and use pieces of wood for pillows seems to stretch credulity, so it's possible that the ghost writer was extending Solomon's comments regarding a type of punishment to his daily experience. One would expect the slave to sleep on the ground rather than on a board too narrow for his body. Slave owners generally wanted their workers to receive a reasonable amount of rest simply because their livelihood depended on the slave's productivity.

After the cotton crop was picked, there was always "scrap cotton" in the fields to be used to fill mattresses, pillows, and quilts. In the settlement period, moss hung in great swabs from limbs of the trees, and winds left some of it on the ground. Even shucks were washed and dried, then used for some mattresses. Everything needed for building a simple bed was readily available at little or no cost.

Moss was picked and sold to gins in Louisiana until the modern era, when the industry disappeared due to the development of synthetic material. Martinez writes of the benefits of moss as a stuffing: *contradicts*

> No known insect will attack moss fibre, eat, destroy or live within it. Moss ranks next to curled hair in resiliency. That is why it is desirable for use in upholstery. Owing to the large amount of waste matter and the resultant loss of weight with each handling, moss is, contrary to current opinion, not a cheap filler for furniture. It is used only in the finest and most expensive furniture or cushions. [See Martinez, 7]

131. Log houses were built when the settler had chosen a site where he and his family expected to live. Trees had to be cleared from the land for a house site as well as to begin to farm, a process that took considerable time, from the cutting down of the trees to picking up debris to plowing. Dirt floors were commonplace and became surprisingly hard and usable. In the antebellum period most chimneys were made of mud mixed with moss, and the fireplaces served both for warmth and for cooking. Some houses and cabins for slaves were built of brick made from clay in the area. These adobe bricks were sun-dried and sun-baked; they were soft but durable, since many slave quarters with brick cabins survived until mid-twentieth century [See Pete Smith interview].

132. Sweet potatoes were a staple along the Boeuf in the antebellum period.

133. There were no cellars due to Louisiana's low land. Louisiana's elevation ranges from five feet below sea level in parts of New Orleans to 535 feet above sea level at the top of Mt. Driskill, the highest point in Louisiana, located in Bienville Parish.

134. Meat with maggots in it would probably not have intentionally been distributed to valuable slaves whose productivity was a primary concern of the planter.

135. In 1699, when the first European settlers were sent by France's King Louis XIV to Louisiana to occupy the land before England or Holland did, they found a small animal which was good for neither milk nor their meat. "Boeuf," meaning ox or bull animal in French, was thus associated with the streams where wild cattle clustered along the banks at a watering hole. There are several Bayou Boeufs and a River Boeuf in the state. The French called the streams "the Boeuf" because of the many wild cattle watering at the streams [See Prichard, 35].

136. Vegetables are grown in spring, summer, and fall. Flowers bloom throughout the year.

Chapter Thirteen

137. Solomon Northup would have heard of "thinning cotton" on Bayou Boeuf, the name applied to this procedure. It had probably been passed down by generations of planters. After the planting when seeds were sown in a row, the plants were thinned by scraping clear a prescribed distance between each plant.

138. Edwin Epps owned a 300-acre plantation.

139. Dr. Robert Dumville Windes [referred to as Wines; see Bennett, Daybook, December 12, 1838] owned twenty-nine slaves in 1855. His grave is marked and visible in the Ferguson graveyard, only a few miles from Epps's plantation. George Windes of Brea, California, descendant of Dr. Windes, shared the small Civil War diary of 1863 kept by Nathaniel Van Woert, Windes' ancestor and a member of Boone's Battery, which was comprised of residents of Avoyelles and Rapides parishes. The excerpt relates to the experience of Van Woert at Port Hudson in 1863. Port Hudson is located on the east bank of the Mississippi River about thirty miles south of Baton Rouge, Louisiana:

> January 23, 1863 - There were [?] rows of white cotton tucking tents facing toward each other with the officer tents facing the avenue formed by the company's tents ... Was then assigned to Sergeant Griffin's Gun Squad and became a member of mess number one, thanks to the courtesy of Mr. Robert Dumville Windes of Avoyelles Parish, who was already a member of it. He was my wife's cousin and only son of Dr. Windes, a planter and practicing physician living near Holmesville in Bayou Boeuf. Young Windes was a typical southerner, a graduate of a Kentucky college, was thoroughly educated especially in the classics and also took a post-graduate course in law. He had his own body-servant with him, a faithful negroman named Rice ... [See Van Woert, January 23, 1863 to July 13, 1863]

140. In Chapter 12, "When a new hand ... is sent for the first time into the field, he is whipped up smartly" [See *Twelve Years a Slave*, 165]. In this chapter, "Epps threatened the severest flogging, but in consideration of my being a 'raw hand,' concluded to pardon me on that occasion." It is therefore difficult to determine the circumstances under which this custom applied.

141. See endnote 125.

142. It took Edwin Epps six years, beginning in 1845, to pay $2,500 for "that certain tract or parcel of land, situated lying and being the Parish of Avoyelles, on the East side of Bayou-Boeuf, & bounded above by lands of John A. Glaze and below by lands of Fuselier and in the rear by those of Carey (Keary) & brother, containing the quantity of three hundred acres, more or less ..." Witnesses

included neighbors Mathew Vernon, James Burns, and Francis Collum [See Sale of Land, 90].

143. The U.S. Slave Census for 1850 confirms the list of Epps slaves: Abram—male, forty years old, black (actual age: sixty); Wiley—male, thirty-four years old, black (actual age: forty-eight); Phebe—female, thirty-seven years old, black; Bob—male, twenty years old, black; Henry—male, seventeen years old, black; Edward—male, eleven years old, black; Patsey—female, nineteen years old, black (actual age: twenty-three); Susan—female, died; Platt—male, thirty-four years old, black (actual age: forty-two).

144. Both William Tassle and James Burford ("Buford" in the narrative) are listed in the 1840 U.S. Census for Williamsburg County, South Carolina. The financial situation of Burford reflects the circumstances of many planters whose yearly profits were as undependable as the weather. Substantial wealth existed mostly among landowners with political clout who were recipients of huge acreages of lands across the South, land that appreciated considerably in value with every passing decade.

145. Chain gangs were not a common method of transporting slaves. More often, slaves walked, rode in wagons, or rode on mules or occasionally horses, as described in manuscripts from that period, such as the Rosa Cheney diary of her family's long trek to Texas to avoid the Union troops invading the Lower Red River Valley [See Cheney].

Chapter Fourteen

146. Caterpillars ate large portions of the cotton crops on Bayou Boeuf plantations in the Cheneyville area during the 1840s and 1850s [See Bennett to Belden]: "My business has been as good as I could expect for this season of the year, better than it will be for the remainder of the year. The Cotton Crop of this Parish will fall short more than one half from last year's crop. The catapillars [sic] are literally eating up the cotton through this section of the country . . ." [See Bennett to Belden]. On the same day, Ezra Bennett wrote to Mr. C. Toledano: "The caterpillars are doing immense damage to the present crop of cotton. [T]hey have eaten the laves [sic] clean from the stalk and are now eating the green bowls...[See Bennett to C. Toledano]. On March 5, 1842, Bennett wrote to his factor: "Times are cruel tight in the country & can't be got on any terms . . ." [See Bennett to Loflin and Stephens]. *DeBow's Review*, which began publication in New Orleans in 1846, ran articles about the increased numbers of caterpillars infesting the fields during the period [See *DeBow's Review*, 2: 277, 354; 3: 535-43]. Ezra Bennett wrote to his brother in 1847: "My cotton is about as good as my neighbors which is generally poor. I do not think there will be over half or two thirds crop provided the worms do not come to eat it up" [See Bennett to Dear Brother Charles].

The plight of cotton planters had reached a critical low during the prior decade, with the Andrew Jackson-Biddle Bank War bringing depression and hitting the bayou country hard in the mid-1830s.

147. Sending slaves to work in St. Mary's Parish cane fields often took place, and there was a similar sending of slaves when help was needed by cotton planters of Cheneyville during cotton picking in the fall. Some area cotton planters also operated sugar cane plantations in St. Mary's Parish. There were kinship ties between the populations of the two parishes. Mrs. Esther Wright stated that Baynard Robert, an uncle of Edwin Epps' wife, owned a sugar plantation there. When as a young man Ezra Bennett arrived around 1830 from Nunda, New York, he came to visit his uncle, Joel Coe, in St. Mary's Parish. From there he went to Cheneyville to visit relatives of Joel Coe [See Wright interview with Walter Fleming].

148. Bayou Teche is one of the most beautiful of Louisiana bayous. It flows into the Atchafalaya River in South Louisiana, made famous by Henry Wadsworth Longfellow in his epic poem "Evangeline."

149. Alanson Green Pearce ("Alonson Pierce" in the narrative), son of William, Sr. (1816-1863) and Frances Tanner Pearce, owned a plantation, Lone Pine, only a few miles from Oakwold, the home of his parents in Evergreen, Louisiana. Both plantation houses, built before the Civil War, still stand. Patrick Henry Toler was a neighbor of Alanson Pearce on his plantation in Evergreen. Grimball Addison Robert, a half-brother of Mrs. Epps' father, was born near Cheneyville in 1812 [Stafford, *Three Pioneer Families . . .*, 76, 345].

150. Lafayette, established as Vermilionville in 1823, has become over the years an unofficial capital of French Louisiana in the lower southern part of the state [See Writers Program of Works Progress Administration, 273].

151. At Grand Coteau, St. Landry Parish, the Sisters of the Sacred Heart established a Sacred Heart Academy for Girls in 1821. A Jesuit St. Charles College was established at Grand Coteau in 1838 [See Writers Program, 120-122].

152. Judge William Turner and Mrs. C. Ferguson are among those listed in Champomier's book stating the sugar production of Louisiana cane planters for 1849-1850: "Mrs. C. Ferguson, thirty-nine, William Turner, nineteen, 58 hhds of sugar, Bayou Salle, St. Mary Parish." Turner is similarly listed with Mrs. Ferguson in Champomier's publications of 1850-1851 and 1851-1852 [See Champomier]. These statements were issued annually.

153. These unwritten expected customs related to Sunday prevailed on all plantations in Louisiana and probably throughout the South. Planters who did not abide by this code of behavior would have been dealt with by their fellow planters. The pay undoubtedly varied from plantation to plantation.

154. The name Yarney is not listed in the 1840 U.S. Census.

155. Joseph Jedediah Robert, father of Mrs. Edwin Epps, was an exception among those who taught private lessons in Louisiana before the Civil War. Most teachers came from the North where formal education, both public and private, was available. To control plantation country, an elite group of influential planters throughout the South used private education as the major tool to establish and maintain a caste society.

156. Many trusted slaves were allowed to use firearms. Some hunted game not only for themselves but for their owners: "Despite strict laws regarding the possession of firearms by slaves, many Negroes had guns and many did hunt . . . The black man added squirrel, turkey, duck, rabbit, and perhaps venison to his diet and also contributed to the master's table . . . Some animals were caught with simple snares, and the raccoon and opossum were hunted at night with dogs" [See Taylor, 126].

157. There is documentation that Indians used fish traps of various kinds as well as cane poles cut from the banks of the streams with a cord holding a baited hook, seines, and other means to secure fish. With "water, water everywhere," Indians in Louisiana found streams a primary source of food. The French, Spanish, and English settlers also lived off what the land and the streams offered. They adopted the ways of the Indians and added new ideas about securing food.

158. Douglas Marshall, an aristocrat in the caste society of antebellum Louisiana who seemed to perpetuate the stratification of the Old World, was a descendant of the brother of Supreme Court Justice John Marshall of Virginia. The elite had the money and power to obtain a formal education, which was inaccessible to the vast majority of the population. However, there were small numbers of whites and blacks who individually managed to educate themselves surprisingly well, and some of the moneyed elite did not choose to seek a formal education.

159. The home of Dr. Jewel, the murdered victim, was in Opelousas, Louisiana, according to Dr. W.D. Haas' note in 1930 in the flyleaves of his copy of the first edition of *Twelve Years a Slave*. Dr. Haas (1867-1940), a grandson of Douglas Marshall, was a descendant of an immigrant named Sam Haas, who came from Alsace Lorraine before the Civil War. Sam Haas became a captain in the Civil War, returning to open a country store in central Louisiana at Chicot. He was an astute businessman and loaned money from his own resources that he stored in a safe inside his home, thus beginning a sort of banking operation on the Louisiana frontier. Dr. Haas' mother was Maccie Marshall, descendant of William Marshall of Virginia, a brother of United States Chief Justice John Marshall [See Holland. Alice Holland is a descendant of Dr. Haas.]

Chapter Fifteen

160. Cutting cane on the lead row required the highest skill; all of the cane cutters competed for the honor. Not only was a lead cane cutter setting the pace as the one who could strip the stalk of flags, cut the stalk with one swift strike, and stack the

stalk across the rows faster than anybody else, he was recognized as a leader in encouraging the team. Often songs or chants lifted spirits in what was typically forbidding weather.

161. In addition to Solomon's recollections of sugarcane production, ghost writer David Wilson also had access to numerous agricultural publications of the period. There were many articles about the sugar industry, growing sugar cane and making sugar. One example of facts about sugar is included in "Culture of the Sugar-Cane," an article in *American Agriculturist*:

> There are three varieties of the sugar-cane cultivated in the U.S. The Creole was first raised in Louisiana by the immigrants from the West India Islands. It is the smallest, but yields the richest and most valuable juice. The Otaheite was introduced into Georgia early during the present century, from the Sandwich Islands, and within a few years after, was carried from that state into Louisiana. It produces a large, luxuriant stalk, yielding profusely in juice, which is, however, much inferior in quality to that from the Creole. The blue-ribbon, brought to this country from Jamaica, subsequent to both others, is beautifully variegated with regular longitudinal stripes of blue and yellow, alternating in direction between each joint. It yields a juice of medium quantity and quality; but being by far the hardiest, it has usurped almost the entire sugar plantations of this State. Each of these varieties has undoubtedly originated in the East Indies, where the cane has been cultivated from time immemorial.
>
> It was formerly the practice to plant the cane in rows, from 2 1/2 to 4 feet apart, and it is perhaps owing to this, and the careless system of culture, that the Creole may have degenerated and become the pigmy plant we now see it. A more rational system has been adopted for many years, by the most intelligent planters, and by them the rows are seldom permitted to be nearer than 8 feet. This is attended with many advantages. The rows contain three, and in some instances four parallel lines of plants, which furnish a greater number of stalks per acre than the more closely planted. They afford room for burying the trash (the worthless tops cut from the cane in the fall and destitute of saccharine matter), and the bagasse (the residuum of the cane after expressing the juice), between the rows, where it can lie undisturbed in the soil till decomposed. The sun and air have free access through the field, both of which are of vital importance in giving the fullest development to the plants; and finally, they allow of the use of the two-horse plow, by which a deeper furrow is made, the grass and weeds are more effectually turned under and destroyed, and a more thorough pulverization of the soil is effected, all of which is accomplished with the same expenditure of the animal, and with half that of the human labor employed with the single horse. Where deep plowing is not required to be repeated, but the destruction of weeds and grass is the only

object sought, the greater width of the rows permits the use of the three-share plow, or a large steel-tooth or other cultivator,* by which one laborer will get over six acres in a day instead of two only with the plow. In fields suited to it, this practice has been adopted, the present season, with some of the New York implements, and has been attended with the most satisfactory results.

In preparing the land for cultivation, after providing a sufficient number of deep ditches as before described the surface is deeply turned over with four-horse plows. Sometimes this is done by a huge plow, called the giraffe, requiring six good animals to move it. The intended bed for the cane is then excavated to a depth of 4 to 6 inches, with a wide fluke, or a double-mould-board plow, leaving a furrow eight to twelve inches wide. The more careful planters clean out this by hand, and place three or four rows of the best plant in parallel lines four inches apart, lapping each and arranging them so that the eyes which occupy opposite sides may germinate horizontally, and shoot upward at the same time, thus giving evenness of growth to each stalk.

The planting may be commenced in December, and should be completed early in March. If done during the winter, protection from frosts requires that they be covered to a depth of four or five inches. On the approach of warm weather, this earth is removed within an inch or two of the cane, at which depth it is covered if the planting is deferred till this time. This is done to promote early germination, which is of great importance to secure a satisfactory maturity of the cane in this climate.

After the young shoots appear, the fine earth is gradually brought around and over it, and the plow is used for turning the furrow towards the rows. This operation is repeated as often as is necessary to keep the land sufficiently light and clear of weeds, and gradually lead the soil to the roots. When the cane has acquired sufficient growth to shade the ground, the final operation of ridging up, or laying by the crop, is performed with the plow and the hoe. The cane ought to be so forward as to admit of this by the middle of June.

*The steel-tooth cultivator is a new and very superior article, admirably adapted for cane as well as all other kinds of culture. It can be had at our agricultural warehouse, (187 Water Street. Price-- $7.50 . . . [See "Culture of the Sugar-Cane," 241-243]

Another such article providing information about sugarcane cultivation is "Sugar and Slavery in Louisiana" in 1847:

The report of the Commissioner of Patents contains a list of all the sugar planters in the State of Louisiana with the product of each plantation for the year 1844. The corrected aggregate of the sugar raised in that year is put at 215,000,000 pounds. . . At the beginning of the year there were in operation seven hundred and sixty-two sugar mills, of which four hundred and eight were worked by steam power and three hundred and fifty-four by horse power—the number of planters being about nine hundred. At the end of the year the number of mills had increased to eleven hundred and four, and the number of planters to one thousand eight hundred and fifty . . .

The sugar plantations of Louisiana lie along the shores of the rivers and bayous . . .

The way that much of the new States of Louisiana, Alabama, Mississippi, & c., have grown into their great production and prosperity has been by the removal of planters with their slave families from the old to the new States . . . [See "Sugar and Slavery in Louisiana," 55]

Still another article on sugar is "The Sugar Crop of Louisiana":

It is estimated by competent judges that the crop of sugar in this State will exceed the crop of last year by at least one hundred thousand hogsheads . . . Two hundred and forty thousand hogsheads is an estimate which no one regards as extravagant. At the rate of $50 per hhd., (lower, we believe than a fair average,) this will give the splendid sum of twelve millions of dollars as the value of one single agricultural product of twenty-three parishes of the State . . . there are but fourteen in which sugar is the leading or principal product. In St. Landry, Calcasieu, Lafayette, Vermillion, Avoyelles, Rapides, West Feliciana, and Pointe Coupee, sugar is cultivated to a limited extent, cotton and corn being the chief products, and grazing an extensive employment of the people. [See "The Sugar Crop of Louisiana," 179]

162. Winrowing was a familiar scene on Bayou Boeuf during cane cutting time.

163. Hawkins Mill, located about three miles south of Cheneyville on Waverly Plantation, was the largest sugar mill for many miles. Remains of the mill survived for years, and were said to have come from a terrible explosion. Another Cheneyville slave, William O'Neal, born in 1827, worked building a sugar-house at the same mill in 1848. O'Neal's description of the work at the sugar mill has a different tone than in David Wilson's writing:

By October the tenth the sugar-house is ready for grinding; the fires blaze in the great furnaces, the wheels began to revolve, and it has become a thing of life. William has been inducted into the mysteries of engineering, and as we glance into the sugar-house we see him managing the great engine with deliberation characteristic of his nature.

The grinding season is a merry time on the sugar plantation, every-thing grows sleek and fat. All are full of life, buoyant and happy. In the fields may be heard many voices blending softly those sweet old plantation songs, once heard never to be forgotten.

Ah! There is romance indeed lingering about the old sugar plantation, distinctively characteristic of Louisiana. The broad acres of waving cane, where the keen knives glisten in the morning sunlight, wielded by a hundred sturdy hands.

The heavy two-wheeled carts roll by, laden with juicy cane, its purple stalks like the bloom on the ripened grapes of Italy. Long trains of these immense vehicles are coming and going, in the vain attempt to satiate the maw of that great colossus which is continually belching forth smoke and flame.

No time for idling now; for day and night all through the grinding season, which lasts until the last stalk of cane has passed through the crushers and emerged from the immense evaporators in the form of commercial sugar, all hands are kept busy. Thus ended the first season at the new sugar-house of Dr. Hawkins. [See O'Neal, *The Man Who Sold His Wife*, 90-91]

164. Before the Civil War there were sugar mills, which varied in size, an estimated every mile and a half apart along the bayou from Washington to Cheneyville. Almost all were destroyed during the invasion of Bayou Boeuf in 1863 and 1864.

P.A. Champomier does not list a Hawkins Mill in his publication, known as the authority on Louisiana sugar mills, 1849-1850. A large Rapides sugar mill is listed as Lambeth and Maddox. In Avoyelles, Lambeth is listed with sugar production at Leinster Plantation (Lambeth and Wells); on Bayou Huffpower at Meredith Plantation (Lambeth and H.P. Robert) and with another on Bayou Clair, and Lambeth and Cullum on Lucky Hit Plantation [See Champomier; and William Lambeth, U.S. Census of Avoyelles Parish, 1850]. Champomier also published such statements for 1840-49; 1850-51; and 1851-1852].

165. The amount of free time available to slaves varied from plantation to plantation according to the owner. The regulation on a given plantation had a great deal to do with how much of their food the slave or the master was expected to furnish. Gray writes:

> Slaves were never expected, however, to provide all of their food from their gardens, as in some of the West India Islands. Probably the nearest approach to this in the South was in Louisiana, under the French regime, where masters sometimes gave slaves all of Saturday and Sunday to work on slave crops, but suspended their rations in those days. [See Gray, 564]

Louisiana has many rainy days, and these would have had some effect on free time as well. Field work was not possible, and the limited amount of work that could be accomplished under shelters would have given some free time to the slave. Still, of course, as Gray states: "The actual wellbeing of slaves, however, was dependent not so much on laws as on the humane instincts and economic interest of the master, and the power of neighborhood opinion. The latter was undoubtedly an important source of protection" [See Gray, 517].

166. Christmas celebrations were not the only entertainment slaves enjoyed. Most forms of entertainment depended upon the slave himself or herself and their ability to make the most of any time afforded them from work. The African tradition of oral expression and movement in interpreting emotions proved a priceless legacy in surviving the restraints imposed by slavery.

According to other sources, Christmas was by no means the only time for celebrating. The diary of a soldier of the Seventy-Fifth New York Regiment of Infantry, edited by historian Walter Prichard, had this entry:

—Tuesday 19th (1864)—
Staid in camp all day. We are in the district that formed the theatre of Solomon Northup's bondage. Old Epps' plantation is a few miles down the Bayou and Epps himself is on his plantation, a noted man made famous by the circumstances of his owning Solomon Northup. Plenty of Negroes are found about here who say that they knew Platt well and have danced to the music of his fiddle often. [See Prichard, "Forest Diary of the 75th New York Regiment"]

The houses of the slaves formed villages. Blacks congregated on their front galleries during the evenings to relax and talk among themselves.

167. There was a wealth of food available in the streams and in the woods. "No objections are made to hunting," [See *Twelve Years a Slave*, 200] and fishing in the Boeuf and other streams nearby was a part of life.

168. Solomon/Platt's remembrance of the Christmas music provides a record of the rap music of that day. Modern rap traces its roots back through such early African-American music and then further to Africa:

The beginnings of rap music are to be found hundreds of years ago and an ocean away from the black urban neighborhoods of the United States. In many West African countries, music-making was the province of the griots, male and female professional singers and storytellers who performed using a variety of techniques against a background of drums and other musical instruments. Among the techniques used by a griot was call and response, in which a solo verse line is alternated [answered] by a choral response of a short phrase or word.

Griots were entertainers, keepers of history, and commentators on events of the present. "A griot is required to sing on demand the history of a tribe or family for seven generations," Paul Oliver writes, "and, in particular areas, to be totally familiar with the songs of ritual necessary to summon spirits and gain the sympathy of ancestors. . . He also must have the ability to extemporize on current events, chance incidents, and the passing scene. [Griots'] wit can be devastating and their knowledge of local history formidable." The griot's position in society was that of keeper of records and more. Griots were highly esteemed, and as Wolfgang Bender observes, "The Griots are highly referred to as the archives and libraries of this part of Africa. Thus the famous proverb, 'whenever a griot dies, a library dies.'" They were interpreters of current politics, transmitting messages and orders from the governing power to the people. As musicians with contacts with other musicians outside the court, they were able to learn the opinion of common people and could convey sentiments of the populace to the ruler.

In an oral culture, a culture without written records, a griot held a place of great importance. [See Haskins, 13-15]

Evidently Solomon Northup did not describe the singing and dancing among the black people that was omnipresent. Perhaps its very omnipresence is why he didn't bring that to the ghost writer's attention. Those gifts of oral expression came as a priceless part of their cultural inheritance from generations of ancestors. It was spontaneous. It was universal among them. I wrote about it in the 1930s on Bayou Boeuf:

> . . . the sound of those Negro voices singing still echoes over the years. Many a summer night when the windows were flung open everywhere to catch what breezes might stray through the bayou country, I have sat, enthralled, and heard the clear sweet voices ring out from St. Philip Baptist Church at Loyd Bridge in what to me is unrivaled beauty. They sang for me too, and I knew the tragedy and beauty and joy and misery of plantation life. So I felt with the surge and flow of life's ecstasy and pain, so exquisitely blended, the music they poured into the warm air of the old country church. The words didn't matter so much; you got the whole story from the sound of it! One memorable day my grandmother walked with me across the bayou to the home of a mother and daughters acting out a little drama on their own gallery.
>
> The vivid portrayals of Bible stories, told in the bayou lingo, were superb. If there were names to those songs, nobody knew them; but I remember especially the brilliant spectacle drawn by five women singing in a manner so convincing that you walked right through the pearly gates with them.
>
> The five—if you are under the spell of the old folk song— have just been admitted through the gates of heaven. Gabriel has blown his horn, and St. Peter has checked them off his list. They are standing, dazzled at the splendor and beauty that surrounds them.

The youngest of the five is the first to speak. "Sit down," she suggests to the other four. Perhaps she is tired from the journey all the way from earth to heaven.

"No, Chile ... No, Chile ... No, Chile ... No. Can't sit down," the four answer musically.

The younger cannot understand. "Sit down," she urges.

"No, Chile, No, I can't sit down—Just got to heaven; Want to walk around . . ."

It is the oldest of the five who sings the response, all the time swinging her arms rhythmically and clicking her fingers until you can fairly see her beginning her eager inspection of heaven's wonders.

Poignantly beautiful is the moving Negro chant which must undoubtedly have been revived by slaves in the cotton fields from memories of African life and passed down through the ages. No one can easily imitate this strange chant—though it is not really a chant at all, for there are no words. Neither is it mere humming, for the crescendo in its loudest cry is an intense lament which always ends in the same note of abysmal despair and utter futility. Perhaps the Negro first wordlessly expressed in this strange new land his unhappiness, but in those plaintive tones lie the expression of the elemental grief and misery of us all . . .

Life as represented in the folk songs and sermons I remember, was almost always depicted as a long travel ending in the sky. Perhaps these were but bayou adaptations of written songs someone had heard and brought back to the bayou country, but it always sounded to me like one group of songs was composed when the railroad first went through the bayou side in the 1880s.

Negroes sang at work or at play, in kitchens, in the fields, walking along bayou roads, frolicking under the moonlight on warm evenings. Whatever the song and wherever the singer, the songs contained the enduring charm of being vibrant with the attitude, the life philosophy, and passions of an expression of hungry people . . .

Although there were, perhaps, folk songs identifiable with all the plantation-south, it seems much more likely that each pocket of plantation culture, varying widely from one to another, held within it its own unique repertoire of Negro folk songs. These from the Bayou Boeuf country probably had their counterparts wherever there were plantation communities, and undoubtedly some songs took hold and spread over wider areas to other communities. But wherever they are sung, they are a priceless part of our great American heritage, and the contribution of the plantation Negroes, which, we hope, is being preserved. [See Eakin, 24]

169. Recognition of marriages by slave masters often took place. In the Avoyelles Parish records (those in Rapides Parish were burned during the burning of Alexandria by Union forces in 1864) there are many records of slave marriages that

lasted a lifetime. The law forbade blacks and whites to legally marry, but that did not preclude alliances that also produced stable marriages.

An example of a plantation wedding is given in records that include the testimony of William O'Neal in a civil suit over inheritance among members of his family:

> My brother and Lucinda were married in 1851. I was at the marriage and witnessed the ceremony. Mr. Charles Johnson performed the marriage ceremony on his plantation where Mr. Peter Butler now lives in Rapides Parish, La. Mr. Johnson was the master of Lucinda and Mr. Alonzo Roberts the master of my brother. Charles was also present and witnessed the ceremony. He was then overseeing for Mr. Johnson. These owners gave Charles and Lucinda a big wedding and supper, as stated in William O'Neal's testimony. [See Jacobs vs. O'Neal]

During the same trial, Lucinda Anderson testified:

> Charles Smith, the son of Laura Smith and the father of Lauretta, and myself were married in the parlor of my mistress Mrs. Martha Johnson wife of Mr. Charles Johnson in 1851 in Rapides Parish. We had a big wedding and supper. At the same time my sister-in-law Harriet Brooks married Martin Williams. Mr. Charles Johnson married us. He was my master. My master always performed the marriage ceremony when his servants got married. There was a big crowd present and my master and mistress gave us a fine supper. [Lucinda Anderson testimony, Judy Jacobs versus William O'Neal, Judicial Case Number 4142, Term 1893, 10th Judicial District Court, State of Louisiana, Rapides Parish]

Chapter Sixteen

170. William Ford, Edwin Epps, and Eldred had plantations of 200-300 acres.

171. There were laws to protect slaves from cruelty and there is evidence they were enforced in Louisiana. For instance, in 1854 Attorney John Waddill in Marksville was employed by a man to defend him against the charge of being cruel to a slave: "March 26 Today Jean Baptiste Ducote, employed me to defend him in the case of the *State vs. Jean Bapt. Ducote*, for cruel treatment to a slave. Paul St. Romain acted as his interpreter. my fee at $50" [See Waddill, 145].

172. Healthy cane cutters were vital to the harvesting of the crop, which was always threatened with a freeze that might render it an entire loss, and the planters generally would have made certain that their slaves were fed and rested enough to maintain productivity.

173. It is likely there was precious little note paper in most Bayou Boeuf homes except the amount used to write infrequent letters. The exception would have been the homes of large planters, doctors, lawyers and other professionals.

174. Though Solomon refers to Shaw's slave wife as Charlotte here, in Chapter 18 her name is given as Harriet.

175. Miasma is a thick vapor that was thought to be poisonous, "harmful to health or morals," according to the *American Heritage Dictionary of the English Language*.

Chapter Seventeen

176. From the Avoyelles Parish Police Jury Meeting, 1842:

> Sec. 2. . . . the same [captain of the patrol] shall and is hereby authorized to keep a strict Police order over the slaves apprehended in his district, and therefore shall and is hereby authorized to examine Negro huts if they shall deem necessary, take up and punish Slaves that they may find away from their Master's premises without a permit, provided however that slaves driving wagons, carts, etc. having about them evidence to justify a belief that they are on their Masters' Service with their owner's permission, shall not come under the provision. Edwin Epps was appointed a road overseer—a patroller—in 1843. [See Minutes]

177. Dogs were plentiful on Bayou Boeuf, mostly used for hunting.

178. Solomon is referring to the property of three prominent brothers named Keary [See endnote 115].

179. Stocks [See endnote 101] stood on the ground. Some of the panels were made with holes for the individuals to place their legs, while others included holes spaced for both arms and legs.

180. There were stories among slaves that if one could escape into Texas, considered to be Mexican territory long after it belonged to the United States, the Mexican government would emancipate them. As a fifteen year-old slave, William O'Neal decided to try to escape on a pony. He found an older man named Russ, a slave of Hadley Roberts, who might be interested in going with him. O'Neal describes this scene in his book:

> Sunday, May 31st might have been seen a boy and Man sitting under a large live-oak tree situated on the Keary plantation, engaged in earnest conversation. The boy seems to be doing most of the talking, and as he talks he is drawing or sketching something like a map on the ground. As we draw near to them we discover the boy to be William O'Neal and the man his friend Russ.

William is saying: "Do you see this ring? Well, that is Cheneyville; now right up this line running northwest is Lecompte. Here we will make another little ring. Now follow this line and it takes us a little to the west. Thirty miles from Lecompte we cross the bayou on this line and then following this road, which runs directly west, we come to Leesville in Vernon Parish. We will then be forty-five miles from Sabine river. A road runs from Leesville to Devil's Ferry; here we can cross the Sabine in Mexico, where we are no longer slaves but free men," and his eyes kindled at the sound of those magic words. [See O'Neal, *Life and History of William O'Neal*, 80-81]

181. Lew Cheney, belonging to David Cheney, reported plans for an uprising in the area. Fellow slaves later claimed that Cheney was one of the leaders in these plans and became frightened at the consequences and reported it to save himself. A story appeared in the *Niles Register*, October 28, 1837:

On the 18th instant intelligence was received at New Orleans that the negroes in a portion of the Parish of Rapides near Alexandria, had projected an insurrection.

One account says it was divulged and frustrated as follows:

A slave of a planter, Mr. Compton, informed his master that the negroes were forming plans to kill all the white males and spare the females and children, and that if he would go to a certain meeting house, where his negroes assembled for the purpose of preaching, he would discover all their plans. Mr. Compton did go in company with four others but learned very little more of the matter. His informer then told him that the ringleader of the gang was one of his own slaves and that he had sworn revenge against his master for taking him out of the house and sending him to the field. The plan of this fellow, it appears, was to raise an insurrection at Alexandria, next at Natchitoches, and then to turn steps to New Orleans and kill all the whites. The negroes, however, could not agree, which frustrated all their plans. One party was for sparing the women and children; the other for an indiscriminate massacre. Mr. Compton, upon learning these facts, arrested his house servant, the chief, and he confessed on the gallows that it had been his intention to kill his master.

On the 10th and 12th [August] instant, nine were hung and thirty others were taken and imprisoned. It is hoped that all their plans will be discovered. A strong patrol and guard is constantly kept up by day and night and confidence is continued.

Besides the slaves, three free negroes have been hung, and it was intended to drive away all free persons of color. Two companies of United States troops had been stationed throughout the disaffected district. Everything was quiet and the negroes completely subdued. [See *Niles Register*]

Because there were slaves executed, the planters who owned them were given recompense, and also money was paid for the freedom of Lew Cheney as well as money for the slave to leave the state:

> According to the acts of the Legislature that authorized paying for the slaves legally executed, Samuel Cakford owned two, John Pettway owned one, Carter Beaman owned two, John Compton owned one and Vincent Page one. The same act authorized "that the sum of $1,500.00 be paid David Cheney on his warrant as the value of the man Lewis, who discovered the conspiracy among the slaves in the parish of Rapides in the year 1837, on his emancipating the said slave. That on the emancipating of said negro Lewis that shall be paid him out of the money in the treasury the sum of $500.00 to enable him to leave the state and provide for his security." [See *Niles Register*]

182. Two incursions into the Boeuf country occurred during the Civil War, both led by General Banks. The first, in 1863, resulted in massive numbers of freed slaves following the Union army. For many slaves the joy of freedom soon turned to horror, as tragedy awaited them due to a lack of preparations.

Nathaniel P. Banks was appointed as general early in the war by President Abraham Lincoln, not because he had any military experience but because of his political connections. Banks was an elegant and even charismatic character who, himself, had presidential ambitions, though Lincoln may not have known that. Banks wanted military victories to improve his own political opportunities. However, Banks did not find military victory easy to achieve, suffering several defeats [See Brooksher, 1-3], and he therefore was assigned to Louisiana as commander of the Department of the Gulf in late 1862, arriving in New Orleans in December of 1862 [See Brooksher, 3].

When Banks took command in Louisiana, Union leaders needed to bring the remainder of Louisiana under control and create an opening to Texas. The object was to reach the Texas Unionists and to provide cotton to mills in New England, England, and France. Also, the hope was this action would dissuade the European countries from either recognizing the Confederacy or joining the war against the Union [See Brooksher, 3].

In March and April of 1863, Banks and his army made the first incursion into the Boeuf country. Banks moved from Brashear City, now called Morgan City, and took Opelousas and Alexandria. During this time, General in Chief of the Army Halleck wrote to Banks several times, urging him to help Grant lay siege to Vicksburg. Grant's success would split the Confederacy and give the Union complete control of the Mississippi River, just as General Winnfield Scott had suggested in his "Anaconda Plan." Halleck was annoyed that Banks, rather than help with this overall plan, was marching up into the Bayou Bouef country. Dr. Harris Beecher, a Union soldier, described the regiment's march:

May 10, 1863.

The road they traveled that day followed the windings of Bayou Boeuf, which is the most singular stream in the state. For over sixty miles it pursues its winding course, without any considerable tributary . . . It is derived from Red River, and flows with a still and rapid current. It is a narrow stream, but a few rods wide, yet it is navigable by a species of canal boat, propelled by horses upon the bank. [See Beecher, 175-176]

After a tiresome march of 30,000 troops, heavy artillery, and supplies for the troops—all pulled by numerous mules and horses—starting at Brashear City, the troops moved up the Bayou Teche and finally to the inland port of Washington where Banks established his headquarters. From there the massive columns moved northward along roads that were actually narrow lanes beaten out on both sides of the narrow Bayou Boeuf. When the troops heading the march reached Cheneyville about thirty miles south of Alexandria, Banks hurried into the Red River port town in a frantic effort to reach there before naval troops sailing up Red River could claim that distinction.

Halleck called these operations of Banks "eccentric," and told him to stop. Instead, he wanted Banks to unite with Grant as quickly as possible and assured him that he would watch his movements with the "greatest Anxiety . . . I assure you the government is exceedingly disappointed" [See Brooksher, 10-11]. This response from Halleck must have bitterly disappointed Banks. Halleck ordered Banks to command his troops, still arriving in Alexandria, to turn around and retrace their steps to the coast. With some of the soldiers already as far north as Alexandria, Banks sent out an order for them to turn back towards the coast. To the Union soldiers strung out from Bayou Boeuf where it mingles its waters with the Courtableau Bayou, these latest orders to reverse their march made no sense at all. Brevet-Major Elias P. Pellet tells of the ensuing events:

Here we were met by an officer of General Banks' Staff, with orders to turn back and collect all able-bodied Negroes and take them to Brashear. Swearing availed nothing, and we were soon measuring back the road over which we had passed.

As one looks at the Map of Louisiana, and places one finger at Brashear City and another on Cheneyville, it seems but a step from the one place to the other; he can hardly comprehend the dusty roads, the burning sun, the scarcity of water." [See Pellet, 78]

Beecher, also of the 114th, wrote:

A weary road of one hundred and fifty miles had again to be traversed. No wonder that our men were discouraged, when it was known that they were short of rations, that their shoes were nearly worn, and that rebel bands were concentrating in their rear. With sad hearts the Regiment countermarched, and passed again through Cheneyville. [See Beecher, 178]

Banks gave orders to his troops to send emissaries into every plantation quarters along the way to the coast and tell them they were to follow the army in the march south. Banks himself, with some of his men, would march west to Port Hudson on the Mississippi River. A letter written July 29, 1863, and signed by General Banks, in combination with text from the Official Report, confirms the reason for his orders to have the slaves from all of the plantations en route ordered to go with the army to the Gulf Coast:

> Upon moving our small column across the Mississippi, for the reduction of Port Hudson, he [Colonel Chickering] was charged with the safe conduct of the train—of nearly a thousand wagons, embracing our whole transportation—which it was impossible to move across the river to New Orleans. I regarded the safety of our train as the guage [sic] of our success in the campaign. [Edmonds, 126]

The Official Report continues after the copy of the letter to say:

> There is a material discrepancy, it will be perceived, between the statement of General Banks that the train consisted "of a thousand wagons," and that of Colonel Chickering in his diary, who fixed his transportation at fifty army wagons. The former doubtless intended to include what the latter denominated "emigrant wagons," and which formed the largest part of this transportation for the "caravan."
>
> It was therefore not the battles he had fought, and the armies he had conquered, that Gen. Banks regarded as "the guage [sic] of his success," but the safe arrival of the vehicles laden with the Negroes and the rich plunder "collected" in Opelousas and Attakapas. [See Edmonds, 126]

Most of the soldiers wearily began returning south. At the plantation quarters, following Banks' orders, they told the slaves that they were free now, and they were going to be given the plantations and all that went with them:

> The social condition was to be inverted; the slave was to be served by his master, and to occupy his place and condition; he was to enjoy an uninterrupted exemption from labor; fine equipages were to await his bidding, and he was to enjoy his case in the quiet mansion of the planter, or in the confiscated dwellings of the City, with their rich furniture and their splendid decoration. [See Edmonds, 100]

The report then gives details of how these slaves joined the wagon train of Chickering:

Vehicles of every description were hastily packed with household goods and human beings. With the aged, the infirm, and the children thus provided for, the more robust mounted in the greatest disorder on horses and mules and precipitately joined the Federal ranks. [See Edmonds, 106]

Comments from the diaries of various soldiers estimate the parade as ranging from about five to nine miles. Similarly, estimates of the number of soldiers ran from 8,000 to 12,000. The actual number was evidently around 4,000. This migration of all able-bodied freed slaves from the Beouf country occurred in late May of 1863. By the hundreds they left with the Union Army, filling the narrow, winding bayou road, going towards the coast.

A correspondent writing from the scene recorded:

At New Iberia I halted and let the train pass. It consisted of four hundred and six carts, each cart averaging not less than six negroes. Every day added to our number. In addition to these, the able-bodied male portion either marched or rode captured horses as we proceeded down. It was a sight perhaps never witnessed before, and may never be again. The carts were those used to transport cane and cotton from the field, and would hold as much as a small canal boat. They were covered with awnings made of all kinds of material. Carpetings, clothing, reed mattings, dried cow hides, boards and everything else which would serve to protect from the sun were used . . . Some of the carts were drawn by oxen, some by horses, some by mules, an ox and a mule drawing at the same cart were not infrequent, and in one case a cow and a mule were harnessed together. The cooking utensils, clothing, bedding, and in fact all the traps of a negro cabin were loaded on, and the aged and the young were piled in promiscuously together . . .

The train was over five miles in length, and when we reached Brashear our crop of negroes was not less than twelve thousand heads. [See Pellet, 82-83]

At the end of the march, the freed slaves, never having known what lay at the end of this journey, found no plans had been made for them. There is no evidence that Banks' orders to bring the former slaves to the Gulf was proceeded by any planning for their welfare once they reached the coast. George W. Hepworth wrote:

Six thousand came from the plantations between the bay and Alexandria; and are living in such a way, that the mortality during the summer will be most terrible. The able-bodied men have enlisted. The old, the young, and the women are living in little huts, with nothing to do, with no comforts when they are ill, and with more than a fair prospect for a speedy death before them. They are free; but alas! freedom only means the power to die. [See Hepworth, 30]

A large sugar house was taken over for a shelter by a number of the slaves traveling to the coast while others found space at any vacant outbuildings they could or camped at the batture to wait for help. Able-bodied men were sent to join the Union Army, and a number of strong men and women were sent to confiscated plantations to work in the production of sugar cane for the Union Army. A free labor system devised by Banks was used [See Edmonds, 119-144].

Some of the preceding as well as other testimony of the long trip of the former slaves following the Union army is found in *The Conduct of Federal Troops in Louisiana During the Invasions of 1863 and 1864*, the official report prepared by a commission in 1865 as requested by Louisiana Gov. Henry W. Allen. The material presented in the report, though prepared by a commission under the direction of a Confederate general and written by others in service to the state of Louisiana under the Confederacy, is, according to the edition edited by David C. Edmonds, "nonetheless a credible addition to the literature of the period," as it was compiled from sworn testimony as well as supported by countless other legal documents and papers of Louisianians of the time. Moreover, the diaries and letters of Northern soldiers support these accounts [See Edmonds, vii-viii]. In his charge to the commission, Governor Allen insisted that the publication that resulted should contain "intrinsic evidence of its own credibility." Governor Allen also particularly asked that any "special acts of kindness that may have been done to our citizens by Federal officers or soldiers" be reported. [See Edmonds, xi-xii]

One of those interviewed by Governor Allen's Commission was Dr. George Hill. Dr. Hill had been in medical and surgical practice in Opelousas for forty years at the time, and therefore had his professional background to guide him in his official statement, given under oath. The portions that became part of the Commission's report follow:

> In the summer of 1863, Berwick's Bay and a portion of the Lafourche country were taken possession of by the Confederate army. I, with many others who had lost property by the raid which the Federal army made between the 20th of April and the 20th of May of this year, visited the Bay for the purpose of recovering our property. I was among the first to cross the bay; and having been informed on the night of my arrival by a gentleman named March that several of my lost Negroes were at the sugar house of Dr. Sanders, and that others were there in a dying condition, I, in the morning as soon as sugar house of Dr. S [*sic*] and entered it by a door in the west end.
>
> The scene which then and there presented itself can never be effaced from my memory. On the right hand female corpses in a state of nudity, and also in a far advanced stage of decomposition. Many others were lying all over the floor; many speechless and in a dying condition.
>
> All appeared to have died of the same disease: bloody flux. The floor was slippery with blood, mucus, and feces. The dying, and all those unable to help themselves, were lying with their scanty garments rolled around their heads and breasts—the lower part of

the body naked—and every time an involuntary discharge of blood and feces, combined with air, would pass, making a slight noise, clouds of flies, such as I never saw before, would immediately rise and settle down again on all the exposed parts of the dying. In passing through the house a cold chill shook my frame, from which I did not recover for several months, and, indeed, it came near causing my life. [See Edmonds, 117-118]

During this period of time, while this exodus south was in progress, Banks looked for other options for his own troops. The Red River was low, making naval support impossible for any further movement into Louisiana north of Alexandria. In May through July of 1863, Banks laid siege to Port Hudson, south of Vicksburg, where Grant was laying siege. Halleck was annoyed with this move, chastising Banks and suggesting he should give up the attack, but Banks would not. Shortly after Vicksburg fell, so did Port Hudson, and Banks was recognized for making his contribution [See Brooksher, 10-11].

Pressure to make inroads into Texas increased after this, especially from Halleck. Banks would have preferred to attack Mobile, but Halleck insisted that army and navy movements through the Red River up to Shreveport would provide an opening to northern Texas. Banks agreed to go to Texas, but his plan was to attack Galveston from the sea. The sea invasion of Texas in early September of 1863 failed [See Brooksher, 15-20].

Banks tried again in October and established a presence in Texas. However, Halleck had not been informed of Banks' plans for hitting Texas; Banks responded to Halleck's inquiries that he felt this choice was better than Halleck's preferred method of going up the Red River to invade Texas, because water levels were too low to do that. The gains in Texas did not grow and activities in Louisiana were halted [Brooksher, 23-24].

In January of 1864, Halleck again pushed an excursion up the Red River on Banks [See Brooksher, 29]. In March of 1864, the second incursion into the Boeuf country began, continuing through May, when Banks retreated to New Orleans [See Edmonds; Pellet; DeForest; Bacon; Johnson; Root and Root].

Chapter Eighteen

183. Warren O'Niel, a widower, married Emma, the daughter of Leonard Anderson and Sarah Ann Providence Chafin. Chafin was the overseer for William Prince Ford [See Stafford, *Three Rapides Families*, 31].

184. There has been speculation that "Uncle Abram" was selected by David Wilson to be analogous to Uncle Tom in *Uncle Tom's Cabin*. There was indeed a slave named Abram on the Epps plantation, and he was about 60 [See Endnote 143]. As to whether his portrait as presented by Wilson was designed to recall Uncle Tom, no one can know.

185. As noted in Endnote 174, Chapter 16, Solomon Northup and/or David Wilson confused the first name of this slave wife, calling her Charlotte in one chapter and Harriet in this one.

186. Solomon Northup gave an interview after his return home recounting this story. According to the story on page one of the *New York Times*, January 20, 1853, the reporter wrote the following: "Blood flowed from her neck to her feet, and in this condition she was compelled the next day to go into the field to work as a field hand" [See *New York Times* "The Kidnapping Case . . ."].

187. Many Southern whites at the time believed that slaves were a different species of humanity, without intelligence or normal reaction to injustice.

188. Plantations notoriously operated on credit, and in Louisiana that money was borrowed from factors whose funds came from the Wall Street and Boston firms they ordinarily represented. Money was loaned to Louisiana planters with liens taken on the crops, the crops being shipped to the factor, who then sold the crop and settled with the planter. The factor shipped supplies to the planters throughout the year and loaned the money with interest, sometimes compounded, to be paid back when the crop was gathered and sold. Most planters made an annual visit to settle business with his or her factor and to make arrangements for the upcoming year.

New York was a major port for shipment of cotton to Europe, and the South bought most manufactured goods from the North. It was, of course, Boston that launched the Triangular Trade with three-way journeys to Africa to secure slaves to sell, then to the planters in the Caribbean where the slaves were exchanged for sugar to be made into rum, then back to the United States. There were other arrangements for the Triangular Trade that included England.

According to Brent Staples of the *New York Times*, Americans tend to believe that slavery was peculiar to the South and that the North, particularly the New England region, had always been "free." This erroneous belief stems in part from mistaken ideas about the Civil War—the central metaphor of American popular history—and partly from the sterling reputations left by Northeastern abolitionists like Horace Greeley, William Lloyd Garrison and Harriet Beecher Stowe. The truth is that slavery existed to some degree across the early United States. It lingered in Greeley's New York until 1827, and in Stowe's Connecticut until the late date of 1848 [See Staples].

Following the abolition of slavery in New York in 1827, being a free person of color did not provide the freedom of choice of education, earning a livelihood, and status in the general society.

Chapter Nineteen

189. The carpenter, Henry Avery, is listed in the U.S. Census of 1850 as a twenty-seven year-old farmer born in Louisiana. He was married to Mary, twenty-one, and they had two children, Amos, five, and Sidna, a three-month-old baby. The Epps' house he built in 1852 survived minus only the detached kitchen, which was

connected to the main house by a short covered walk. Such kitchens were a customary feature of houses in that period as protection against fire. The Epps kitchen-dining room burned in the 1880s. [See a photo of Epps' house in the Extras & More section of our website at www.TwelveYearsASlave.org.]

Dr. J.L. Knoll, born in 1888 in Bunkie, Louisiana, lived from birth through childhood in the old house and described it as follows:

> This house was an old house when I was born in 1888, wasn't fancy on the colonial style. It was a simple built house with wooden shutters, a story and a half facing west on Bayou Boeuf. There was a long gallery along the front of it with white rectangular columns. It didn't have a hall running through it although there was a breezeway between the kitchen and the rest of the house. It was built out of such lumber as they had at the time, cyprus, and built in the days before the steam sawmill of handsawed lumber. [See Knoll]

Due to its historic significance, the house was preserved and moved to Louisiana State University at Alexandria in 2001, where it stands today.

190. Information about the identity of Samuel Bass was discovered by the editor in the diary of the Marksville lawyer, John Pamplin Waddill, who would figure later in the trial in which Northup was freed. The diary was furnished to the editor by her former student, the great-granddaughter of Waddill, Elizabeth Brazelton. Waddill recorded these entries:

> July 29, 1853 – Today I wrote the last will and testament of Samuel Bass, about 11 o'clock at night.

> August 11, 1853—Today I wrote out a form of an olographic will for Samuel Bass to copy as his own. My fee $10.

> August 12, 1853 - Today I called to see S. Bass to learn whether he had copied said will. He informed me that he had not, & that he was so ill he would sick up.

> August 30, 1853 - Today about twelve o'clock Samuel Bass died in Marksville, at the home of Justine Tounier, f.w.c. His disease was pneumonia. He was 48 years of age and was born in upper Canada where he has a wife and four children. He had been separated from his wife for 12 or 15 years. His only complaint against her was that she had such a temper as to preclude any man from living with her. Her name was Lydia Catlin Lane before she married him. She is living near Prescott upper Canada or Ogsdenburg. His two daughters Catherine and Martha Bass are in Manchester, New Hampshire at work in a cotton factory. He had a brother-in-law residing in Ogle County, Illinois near Daysville. Annis Martin in that vicinity has his land titles & many other valuable papers in her possession. He says

that his above mentioned Brother-in-law Freeman Woodcock knows where Annis Martin resides. He appointed William Sloat of this Parish as his executor. [See Waddill, 99]

191. Settlement along the river in Louisiana began around 1715 with Spain and France claiming much of the same land along its borders. Bayou Boeuf is not connected with Red River. The Bayou flows about thirty miles south of the Red River. Thousands of years before, the Boeuf may have been a tributary of the Red River. A fast-growing population, despite the stringent business of settling new country, suggests early settlers did not find the Red River country any less healthy than other frontier regions. Like other frontiers, there was a dearth of doctors. According to Cornell professors Ellis, Frost, Syrett, and Carman, describing the years 1775-1825 during a comparable period of increased settlement, New York also had its problems, as did the entire nation:

> Life expectancy in this period was a fraction of its present figure. Disease ravaged the population almost unchecked and little understood. Disorders almost unknown were commonplace. Smallpox left its scars upon thousands, while tuberculosis filled 20 times as many graves in proportion to the population as it did in 1967. Malaria, sometimes called "the shakes," or "Genesee fever," riddled the frontier population. Typhoid and many other contagious diseases struck every community, and cholera hit the seaports. Only one half the number of children reached their fifth birthday—a sobering statistic in the light of modern advances. Medical attention, if available, was practically worthless. [Ellis et al., 207]

192. Northup/Platt was assigned by Edwin Epps to assist the carpenter; Samuel Bass was a carpenter, perhaps an assistant to Avery.

193. William Perry, fifty-two, a young merchant in Saratoga Springs, had in his household: Elizabeth Perry, forty-nine; Sally Perry, forty; Harriet Perry, thirty-eight; a laborer from Vermont named George, age fifty; another laborer, age fifteen, from New York. They lived in Saratoga Springs, New York [See U.S. Census of 1840, Schedule 2, page 25]. Cephas Parker was also a merchant in Saratoga Springs [See Durkee, 148]. Judge James Madison Marvin was born in the Town of Ballston, Saratoga County, New York, February 27, 1809. An Englishman, he moved to this country in 1835 [See Sylvester].

194. James Guillot was the Marksville postmaster in 1849 [See Marksville, LA list, U.S. Post Office Records, National Archives].

Chapter Twenty

195. Although an outsider from the North and a recent immigrant to Avoyelles Parish, Bass understood very well the fine line that existed between order and chaos in the plantation community—indeed, across Louisiana and the rest of the

South. Any hint of an interference that broke the unwritten code of labor relations between slaves and their owners could cause an instant crisis. Bass correctly reasoned that the Marksville postmaster, James Guillot, might become suspicious of some plot that would cause serious trouble in the community [See *Marksville Weekly News*].

196. Mary Dunwoody McCoy (1834-1913), an orphan, was reared by her uncle and aunt, Mr. and Mrs. Silas Talbert, a justice of the peace and large landowner. Young Mary was the daughter of Mary L. Dunwoody, member of a prominent plantation family whose plantation was located south of Lecompte, and James Dickson McCoy, who was apparently some kind of salesman. Nineteenth century records, including personal letters from antebellum residents of the Cheneyville area, frequently mention the winsome Mary McCoy. She was not only known by a wide circle of people who invariably mentioned her affectionately, but she also became a person of considerable influence. She married Dr. Dewitt Clinton Rhodes (1853); Austin Willis Burgess (1860); and minister Silas H. Cooper (1876). Her son by husband Austin Willis Burgess became a doctor and practiced in Cheneyville until he died in 1896 [See Stafford, *Three Pioneer Families . . .*, 403-407].

197. Lodowick and Ann Martha Eldred Tanner owned Tiger Bend Plantation. It lay in the same vicinity as Douglas Marshall's plantation, across the Bayou Boeuf from the Epps plantation. A leading Rapides Parish planter, Ezra Bennett, living on Bayou Boeuf, left an extensive collection of documents and copies of letters that provide much information regarding Tiger Bend plantation, which was owned by his sister-in-law, widowed Ann Martha Eldred Tanner [See Bennett Papers]. Douglas Marshall was the son of Roger Banks Marshall, an immigrant to Holmesville from Virginia and brother of United States Attorney General John Marshall. Roger Banks Marshall owned the plantation across Bayou Boeuf from the Epps' plantation, where his son lived. Douglas Marshall is not mentioned in any Avoyelles Parish conveyance records. He is buried in the now abandoned Marshall cemetery, Evergreen, Louisiana.

198. An H.A. Varnell is listed in the U.S. Census for 1850, but no William Varnell. Nor is William Pierce listed. "Pierce" is probably the wrong spelling of the name Pearce, the surname of a large Pearce family living in the Evergreen area, where Alanson Pearce's home still stands. There is no William Pearce or William Pierce listed in the 1850 U.S. Census of Avoyelles or Rapides parishes. However, other male Pearce members of the family lived in the area.

199. "Bits and picayunes" were a part of the Spanish monetary system widely used in Louisiana; the names are sometimes used in Louisiana to this day. A "bit" is half of a quarter in U.S. money, and the term "picayune" is frequently used as a derogatory term, a holdover from the time a picayune represented 1/16 of a dollar [See Johnson, 245-58].

Chapter Twenty-One

200. There is no mention of a letter mailed to Anne Northup, but to William Perry, Cephas Parker, and Judge Marvin. Attorney Henry Northup, abolitionist and political figure that he was, wrote the letter signed by the wife of Solomon to appeal for the designation of an agent to rescue the free citizen of New York. [See a photo of Henry Northup in the Extras & More section of our website at www.TwelveYearsASlave.org].

Anne Northup was not literate, as shown by the fact that in a judgment from the Supreme Court, Warren County, rendered against Anne Northup on March 25, 1859, Anne Northup's acknowledgement of her indebtedness is signified by a mark. In part the document reads:

> I, Ann Northup, defendant hereby confess myself indebted to the Glens Falls Bank in the Sum of forty-nine dollars and seventy-five cents with interest from the 26th of September 1857 and authorize said Bank or its attorney or assigns to enter judgment against me for that amount . . . And I hereby state that above sum by one [word unclear] is justly due to the said Bank.
>
> Dated March 21, 1859
> Ann Northup X [her mark]

[See Benjamin P. Burham vs. Ann Northup]

201. Henry Northup, an attorney and leading Whig political figure in New York, was a passionate abolitionist who had championed another beleaguered black in a hard-fought lawsuit. In another book also published in 1853, Wilson wrote about that event. L.R. Lewis, respected attorney and also a leading New York Methodist, wrote concerning the other case:

> Henry B. Northup represented Joseph S. Brown, a negro preacher and missionary to Liberia in a New York civil case demanding that Brown's superior official in the African church admit the inaccuracy of slanderous remarks made by the official against Brown. I think he had to do with "Brown's Journal" which is the story of the negro preacher's experiences leading up to his efforts in Liberia and concluding with the conclusion of the civil action. [See Lewis to Morton]

202. The letter Samuel Bass wrote for Solomon Northup arrived at a most opportune time. Henry Northup was able to secure the appointment to rescue Solomon while a fellow Whig, Washington Hunt, was still governor of New York. That same fall, Hunt had lost his bid for reelection to a Democrat, Horatio Seymour, who might not have been receptive to a Whig request to be named the agent to rescue the f.m.c. (free man of color) who was a citizen of New York. Henry Northup's timely appointment while he could secure it from a Whig governor was only one of a series of events critical to Solomon Northup's rescue.

Without Henry Northup's gaining free time to pursue the project, there would probably have been no rescue attempt at that time [See *New York Times*, January 20, 1853].

203. The Northup rescue was taking place in an atmosphere of growing acrimony between North and South. By the 1850s the conflict had become more and more bitter. The Compromise of 1850 with the Fugitive Slave Act did nothing to allay the anger of either section. In Avoyelles Parish, Louisiana, as all through the South, hostility over what citizens considered an invasion of their states' rights rose to fever pitch. At stake was the plantation system, the base of the economy on which the entire population, including that of New Orleans, depended. Tempers flared quickly on what to Southerners seemed the destruction of their only means of a livelihood. Had politically powerful figures, including Soulé, attempted to dictate a course of action to Avoyelles Parish officials, Solomon Northup would likely have lived out his life as a slave on a Bayou Boeuf plantation.

204. Had attorney Northup gone on to New Orleans rather than take passage up Red River to Marksville 3.5 miles away, he would have missed Bass, and finding Northup among the thousands of slaves on Bayou Boeuf would have been like looking for a needle in a haystack. His timing—later than he had originally planned for the trip—happened to be equally fortunate. Northup had pressing business of his own in his bid to become a New York Congressman representing the Whig party in Washington. With his own party selecting him to run for the office, he was in the midst of a campaign for the election, which he lost to a Democrat who had once belonged to the Free Soilers. The election was so close Whigs challenged the outcome, and the final decision in favor of the Democrat was not made until November [See *Saratoga Whig*, October 22; November 12, 26, 1852, as cited in footnotes 1 and 2, *Twelve Years a Slave* (1968), 227].

205. The most critical action marking the success of the venture came with the meeting between New York attorney Henry Northup and the Marksville attorney Waddill, himself a planter and owner of over 200 slaves. The backlash in Marksville against the fervor of the North to free the slaves involved more than profound respect for the law by Waddill and that of other Avoyelles Parish officials. The dignity and respect with which Henry Northup stated his mission to Waddill and the instantly positive response of the Avoyelles attorney contributed the *sine qua non* to the success of Northup's rescue effort. With the business-like approach of these men, they were able to get the job done. Waddill followed the law and Henry Northup obtained the freedom of a New York citizen.

Waddill, although an Avoyelles courthouse authority, could not have prevailed without the New Yorker's mannerly request for help in freeing the free man of color. Clearly, this was no simple situation with a slave to be located bearing a name unheard of in Bayou Boeuf country.

As it happened, the two men enjoyed moments of conversation about politics in their respective states during the interval in which Waddill developed his plan. Waddill searched for answers as to how to locate Platt, lost among the thousands of slaves on plantations along both sides of Bayou Boeuf about twenty-three miles south of Marksville. After the puzzle of Northup's identity was solved when Waddill determined that Bass had written the letter, Waddill knew that speed was of the essence in reaching Bayou Boeuf. The rescuers reached the Epps place in a buggy or carriage traveling over new land where there were no roads; some areas may well have been covered with water from sub-tropical rains.

206. Louisiana was one of the five "Cotton States" bordering the Gulf of Mexico. Settled by the French beginning in 1699 and owned by the Spanish for most of the last half of the eighteenth century, it was after Louisiana became a state in 1812 that English-speaking pioneers migrated into the state by the thousands, often bringing slaves. The rich lands along the Mississippi River were settled, and New Orleans was becoming a city, but much of inland Louisiana remained unsettled. After a short staple cotton crop was developed that would grow on almost any soil, farmers from the mostly North Louisiana hills and would-be planters alike migrated to the rich lands along the rivers, bayous, and some creeks to develop cotton plantations. The boom had come after 1793 when Eli Whitney developed a small cotton gin that separated cottonseed from the lint. Bayou Boeuf had a five-mile stretch of some of the richest land in the world. The "Great Pine Woods" stretched from its fringe to the Sabine River, which forms the border between Louisiana and Texas.

Cheap, unsettled land that had to be cleared of trees before being developed into plantations sold for as little as $1.25 an acre. A few wealthy entrepreneurs with political clout received grants of thousands of acres, most of which was slowly developed into plantations.

With all of the work converting the frontier into livable, workable plantations, slaves became nearly one-half the plantation country population, while few lived in the hill country.

207. Sugar mills such as the Northup party viewed that day were located on many plantations along Bayou Boeuf all the way to the port of Washington. They consisted of a small machine near the mill to which was attached a long pole. To the pole was harnessed a mule, horse, or probably, in some cases, an ox, that walked endlessly in circles to grind several stalks of cane stoked by the man running this operation. Cane juice, dark in color, poured into a large barrel placed under the machine. When the barrel was full, workmen carried the juice to the small mill. The mill consisted of a series of at least three iron kettles over a brick furnace fueled with wood, often pine knots. Into the largest kettle, located toward the opening to the mill, the juice from the barrel was poured. A skilled workman watched the progress of the juice until it became thicker and was poured into the second largest kettle. The quantity from first to second and then from the second kettle to the third was smaller. The boiling continued until a raw brown sugar was produced. Barrels were filled with moist brown sugar to be shipped to market in New Orleans as quickly as possible.

Before the Civil War these mills were located about a mile and a half apart on the lines of plantations on either side of Bayou Boeuf. These were almost all destroyed during the Union invasions of Red River in 1863 and 1864. The sugar industry in this region was destroyed during the war, including its small sugar mills that were built on almost all of the sugar plantations which lined the bayou. It was decades before the industry was restored.

208. Henderson Taylor, the lawyer for Epps, is noted as the syndic [civil magistrate] for the District on June 9, 1853 [See Waddill, 86]. Henderson Taylor, forty-five, a lawyer, is listed in the United States Census of 1850 as having been born in South Carolina and owning real estate valued at $19,000. He had a wife, Louisa, a male slave named Josh Lewis, and four children: Clara, seventeen; John, fourteen; Simon, eleven; and Ellen, twelve. Aristide Barbin was the recorder for Avoyelles Parish court documents.

209. Waddill, with an economy of words, noted on January 1, 1853:

> To-day I was employed by Henry B. Northup Esqr. of Sandy Hill, Washington County, State of New York, to bring suit against Edwin Epps, to reclaim from slavery a free Negro named Solomon Northup, who had been kidnapped in the City of Washington in 1841.

On January 4, 1853, he noted:

> Today the slave Solomon was released & I received fifty dollars for my services. [See Waddill, 47; see an image of Waddill's note in the Extras & More section of our website www.TwelveYearsASlave.org]

The Villager, the weekly newspaper in Marksville, commented on the treatment of attorney Henry Northup in the village to obtain the freedom of Solomon Northup, as preserved in the New Orleans Bee on January 22, 1853:

> The Villager, published in Marksville, Avoyelles parish, in this State, in its edition of the 13th inst., notices the arrival in that parish of H.B. Northup, Esq., of New York, and gives the following account of the occasion of his visit and his reception by the citizens of Avoyelles parish. The striking contrast between the treatment he received, and that accorded to Southern gentlemen who visit the North for the purpose of recovering their property, is well set forth in the concluding paragraph:
>
> A free negro of New York having some twelve years ago, gone to Washington, D.C., in pursuance of his calling as a musician, was, while there, kidnapped by some villains, sent South and sold as a slave. After passing through the hands of several masters, he eventually came into the possession of a planter of our parish. As he knew how to read and write, he either personally or by others made his friends at the North acquainted with his condition and his residence. His friends at once communicated the intelligence of Mr. N., to whose ancestors the negro's ancestors formerly belonged,

who had himself appointed as agent of the State of New York and came South in that capacity.

Mr. Northup, on his arrival here, after taking legal advice, commenced suit by having the negro sequestered. Mr. Epps, in whose possession the negro was, as being served with the writ, declared that he would offer no opposition, although he loses the amount he paid for him. On the next day Mr. Northup, accompanied by the negro, left for his home, Sandy Hill, New York.

This gentleman remained in the midst of a slaveholding population for four days, without being, although his object was known, subjected to the slightest affronts and inconvenience; on the contrary received every facility and attention that he required. What a contrast this presents to the treatment the Southerners receive at the hands of the people of the North, when in pursuit of their fugitive slaves. How different it is from the Gorauch, Kennedy, Lensnob, and other cases, which are so common in Pennsylvania, New York, Massachusetts, and other free states. Well may the south boast of its justice and loyalty. [See *New Orleans Bee*, January 22, 1853]

Chapter Twenty-Two

210. The two Northups, Henry and Solomon, arrived in Washington, D.C., before January 18, 1853, the day an arrest was made of James H. Birch. The Northups participated in the trial of Birch and left for New York shortly after the trial was over [See *New York Daily Times*, January 19, 1853]. No records have been found and none probably exists of the Washington, D.C. trial of James H. Birch. From the National Archives, Washington, D.C. to Sue Eakin, July 17, 1995:

This is in response to your May 3, 1995, letter, referral from our military record section, regarding the lawsuit against James H. Burch [*sic*].

We have searched dockets of the U.S. Circuit Court as well as the criminal dockets of the U.S. Criminal Court for the District of Columbia Records of the U.S. District Court for the District of Columbia (Record Group 21), but did not locate a reference to the above lawsuit.

Signed by John K. Vandereedt, Archives 1 Reference Branch, Textual Reverence Division.[See Vandereedt to Eakin]

Notes To After Freedom: What Happened Next?

211. Mabee records from contemporary records: "Blacks are 'growing up in ignorance of . . . everything that belongs to civilization,' said the *Long Island Farmer* of December 5, 1822. They 'have nowhere to look for instruction but to the Sabbath schools'." Mabee continues, ". . . beginning about 1815, Sunday Schools sprang up in New York State." While some whites helped found and teach in Sunday Schools for blacks, others organizing Sunday Schools for blacks "ran into continuous difficulty in finding adequate places for their Sunday school to meet . . . The reason for the difficulty, reported the Albany Sunday School society, which sponsored the school, was 'the prejudice excited against the enlightening of these people.'" Mabee further continues, "In New York City in the 1860s Quakers discovered that when they tried to run a Sunday School for blacks, they often had to shift location, for 'teaching them niggers' was . . . very unpopular. Hoodlums sometimes pelted the teachers with stones" [See Mabee, 35-42].

212. Fiske, David. *Solomon Northup: His Life Before and After Slavery*, 11.

213. Most colored men in Saratoga Springs did domestic work. The United States and Grand Union hotels, for instance, employed all-black kitchen and waiting staffs. Joseph Smith wrote in 1897, "The waiters employed at the Spa are usually colored men, the States never having had any other." Similarly Joseph Jackson, chief steward at the Help's Dining Room of the Grand Union Hotel, recalled his boyhood years in early twentieth century Saratoga, "Most of the colored men in Saratoga did hotel work. They were waiters and cooks" [See Armstead et al., *A Heritage . . .*, 219]. Solomon was one of twenty-eight free men of color living in Saratoga Springs in 1840 [See Federal Census of Saratoga County, 1840, 495-537. See a map of 1840s Saratoga (with story points) and a sketch of the United States Hotel in the Extras & More section of our website at www.TwelveYearsASlave.org].

214. *Ibid.*, 11-12.

215. *Ibid.*, 12-13.

216. The story of the legal proceedings following the arrest and identification of the kidnappers is told through testimony given in the hearing and through coverage by many New York newspapers.

217. Documents for these three court cases are in the files of the Warren County Justice Court records; the Supreme Court of Warren County records; and the Wayne County Clerk's office. [See Sale Between Abraham and Mary Ann Tice and Solomon Northup; John T.B. Traphagan and Charles R. Bennett vs. Solomon Northup; and Benjamin Carlle, Jr vs. Solomon Northup.]

218. *The Sandy Hill Herald*, March 22, 1853, in its note beginning with "Uncle Sol," had this statement: "We are informed that an extensive publishing house in this

state has offered Northup, the kidnapped slave, recently returned to this village, $3000 for the copyright of his book."

219. Under the title "Recovery of a Free Negro," a writer in the *The Salem Press* of January 25, 1853, gave this information:

> We congratulate Mr. NORTHUP on the successful termination of his benevolent mission; and full of confidence in the comity of our sister States, hope, at an early day, to lay before our readers the intelligence that the merchants, shipowners, stock-jobbers and other influential citizens of Arkansas have contributed a generous purse of—say $5200—to "indemnify" this colored man in part for his twelve years of unpaid servitude, and to enable him to retire comfortably to a farm in Washington county or Texas, if he should prefer.

220. See a map of Sandy Hill in the Extras & More section of our website at www.TwelveYearsASlave.org. The map includes the locations of Henry Northup's home and residence, and the grave site of Solomon's father, Mintus Northup. The website also includes a present-day photo of Solomon's descendants.

221. It is difficult to figure exactly how much time was spent in writing the book. Evidently the book was published prior to the summer of 1854, as the *Washington County Post* of July 14, 1852, published an account of the arrests and stated in the final paragraph that, "(t)he accused were discovered from the descriptions and incidents given in Northrup [*sic*] book."

The two Northups, Henry and Solomon, arrived in Washington, D.C., before January 18, 1853, the day an arrest was made of James H. Birch. The Northups participated in the trial of Birch and left for New York shortly after the trial was over [See *New York Daily Times*, January 19, 1853].

The Salem Press carried this note on August 16, 1853:

> We purchased a few days since, of the veritable "Uncle Sol," a volume of his work entitled *Solomon Northup Twelve Years a Slave*; and perused its pages with great Interest—gathering from them much valuable information relative to the Institution of Slavery at the South, interwoven with a thrilling account of "Uncle Sol's" hardships and privations during his twelve years of servitude. The work is chastely and elegantly written, reflecting great credit upon the editor, Hon. D. WILSON, and affords another evidence of his superior talent as a popular writer. For the sake of humanity and truth, we bespeak for the work an extensive sale. We hope Mr. Wilson may continue his labors as an author.

222. New York historian Edward Knoblauch wrote: "In the Ballston Spa Village Cemetery there is the grave of an Isaac M. Van Namee, died 22 January 1900 at the

age of 67 years, which would have made him about 21 years old in July of 1854"
[See Knoblauch].

223. *Washington County People's Journal*, July 20, 1854.

224. "The People vs. Alexander Merrill and Joseph Russell." In *Reports of Decisions in
Criminal Cases Made at Term, in Chambers, and in the Courts of Oyer and Terminer of the
State of New York*, compiled by Amasa J. Parker, 590-605. Vol. II. Albany, NY:
Banks, Gould, and Co., 1856.

225. Sonia Taub letter to Sue Eakin, April 23, 1993.

226. Enos is recorded as saying "It is said that M[errill] some years ago endeavored
to entice away a negro boy in his neighborhood, by persuading him to let him sell
him, then run away and be again sold, each time dividing the booty . . . He is also
said to have declared at one time that he followed kidnapping for years; and that he
felt as safe in that business as that in any other business." [See "Sol Northup's
Kidnappers," *Washington County People's Journal*]

227. Fiske, 17-18.

228. Mann,153.

229. See Wyckoff, 136.